ASOKA

Radhakumud Mookerji

MOTILAL BANARSIDASS PUBLISHERS
PRIVATE LIMITED • DELHI

First Edition: London, 1928
Third Revised Edition: Delhi, 1962
Reprint: Delhi, 1972, 1989, 1995

ISBN: 81-208-0086-9 (Cloth)
ISBN: 81-208-0582-8 (Paper)

Also available at:

MOTILAL BANARSIDASS

41 U.A. Bungalow Road, Jawahar Nagar, Delhi 110 007
120 Royapettah High Road, Mylapore, Madras 600 004
16 St. Mark's Road, Bangalore 560 001
Ashok Rajpath, Patna 800 004
Chowk, Varanasi 221 001

PRINTED IN INDIA

BY JAINENDRA PRAKASH JAIN AT SHRI JAINENDRA PRESS,
A-45 NARAINA, PHASE I, NEW DELHI 110 028
AND PUBLISHED BY NARENDRA PRAKASH JAIN FOR
MOTILAL BANARSIDASS PUBLISHERS PRIVATE LIMITED,
BUNGALOW ROAD, DELHI 110 007

ASOKA

TO
THE SACRED MEMORY
OF
MY MOTHER
JAGANMOHINĪ DEVĪ
1848-1920

या देवी सर्वभूतेषु मातृरूपेण संस्थिता

PREFATORY NOTE

The present work has grown out of my lectures at the Lucknow University. This mainly explains the addition of another work to the many already existing on the subject. But they are not too many for the subject. In spite of a large literature, old and new, in different languages, Pali, Sanskrit, English, French, and German, seeking from a variety of standpoints to interpret the unique personality and achievements of Asoka, the interpretation is not yet adequate or final. The very basis of the interpretation is something that is shifting, growing, and improving. The words of Asoka, telling best his own tale, and inscribed by him in imperishable characters on some of the permanent fixtures of Nature, have not themselves come to light all at once, but were discovered piecemeal, and at different places and times. The search for them in out-of-the-way places, the centres of population in Asoka's days, but now remote from the haunts of men, and hidden away in jungles, is a story of considerable physical daring and adventure in its early stages. But the discovery of the inscriptions did not mean the end of the chase. There was the difficulty of their decipherment, of finding the key to a knowledge that was lost and forgotten. The knowledge of the script in which Asoka had his words written on many a rock or pillar had remained lost to India for ages. The Chinese travellers, Fa-hien and Yuan Chwang, for instance, who had visited India in two different periods, the fourth and the seventh century A. D. respectively, and who were themselves no mean linguists, could not find local experts to help them to a right reading of the Asokan inscriptions they had come across on their itineraries. The have recorded wrong readings of those inscriptions, the results of mere guess-work or hearsay information of local people not confessing to their own ignorance of the scripts. Indeed, the recovery of this long-lost knowledge of Asokan script is a romance of modern scholarship. Even when the script was deciphered, and the words of Asoka were read, there was the further problem of their correct interpretation.

Thus Asokan scholarship has now to record more than a century of progress in its three directions of the discovery, decipherment, and interpretation of the inscriptions. The progress is marked by the following principal events :

It was about 1750 that an Asokan inscription was first discovered when Padre Tieffenthaler saw at Delhi fragments of the Delhi-Mirath Pillar.

In 1785, J. H. Harington first visited the Barabar and Nagarjuni Hill Caves. A few years earlier, Hodges on his way to the caves was assassinated "by the followers of one of the allies of Chyt Singh."

About the same time, the Delhi-Topra Pillar Inscription was found by Captain Polier, who presented some drawings of same to Sir William Jones.

In 1801 were published in the *Asiatic Researches* copies of the Delhi-Topra Pillar Inscription, and of portions of the Allahabad-Kosam Pillar Inscription from copies made by Captain James Hoare.

In 1822 the Girnar Rock Inscription was found by Major James Tod.

In 1834 was published in the third volume of the Bengal Asiatic Society's *Journal* the copy of the Allahabad Pillar Inscription made by Lieutenant T.S. Burt, together with a classified table of the Asokan letters prepared by James Prinsep. At that time Prinsep was not able to read the entire Asokan alphabet, but could only guess the value of post-consonantal *ā*, *e*, and *Anusvāra*. After six months' study, he improved his knowledge by recognising the consonants *y*, *v*, and *s*.

In 1836, the Shahbazgarhi Rock Edict was discovered by M. A. Court, a French officer of Maharaja Ranjit Singh.

The year 1837 is memorable in the history of Asokan scholarship. It witnessed the first successful reading of an

Asokan inscription, the Delhi-Topra Pillar Edict, by Prinsep, who published his reading and translation of the inscription in *JASB*, Vol. vi. He had then already had before him copies of the inscriptions on the two pillars at Lauriya Araraj and Lauriya Nandangarh. The same year he also published a lithograph of the Delhi-Mirath Pillar Inscription from impressions taken by Major P. L. Pew, as also the Queen's Edict. The last event of the year was the discovery in another remote part of India of the Dhauli Rock Edict by Lieutenant Kittoe.

In 1838, further progress in Asokan studies was achieved by Prinsep who made the first comparative study of the two Asokan inscriptions at Girnar and Dhauli, discovered their identity in script, language, and contents, and deciphered and published them with translations in *JASB*, Vol. vii. Tracings on cloth of the Girnar Inscription were made by Captain Lang in 1835 for the Rev. Dr. J. Wilson of Bombay, who then sent them on to Prinsep for decipherment. Kittoe's copies of the Dhauli Inscription were also before Prinsep in 1838. These were his revised copies which he obtained at risk to his life. As stated by him, he arrived at Dhauli "before day-break and had to wait till it was light ; for the two bear cubs which escaped me there last year, when I killed the old bear, were now full grown and disputed the ground" (*JASB*, Vol. vii. 219).

In 1839, a copy of the Sahasram Rock Edict was secured by E. L. Ravenshaw from Shah Kabiruddin.

In 1840, copies of the Shahbazgarhi Rock Edict were made by C. Masson by going to the spot through a perilous region at considerable personal risk. The copies were examined in Europe by Norris, who first read in them the word *Devānaṁpiyasa* written in Kharoṣṭhī script.

In 1840 was also discovered on the rock at Bairat the so-called Bhabru Edict by Captain Burt whose copy of it was transcribed and translated by Captain Kittoe "with the aid of the learned Pandit Kamalā Kānta" [*JASB*, Vol. ix. 617].

In 1850, the Jaugada Rock Inscription was copied by Sir Walter Elliot who could recognise it to be another version of Asoka's Edicts which had been already found at Shahbazgarhi, Girnar, and Dhauli.

In 1860, the Kalsi Rock Inscription was discovered by Forrest who found its whole surface "encrusted with the dark moss of ages."

In 1872, Carlleyle discovered the Bairat Minor Rock Edict. To him we also owe the discovery of the Rampurwa Pillar Edict about the same time.

During these seventies was also discovered the Rupnath Minor Rock Edict which was originally found and very imperfectly copied some time ago by a servant of Colonel Ellis for the Bengal Asiatic Society.

Then followed in 1879 the epoch-making publication of Cunningham on the inscriptions of Asoka, being Vol. i, of the *Corpus Inscriptionum Indicarum*. This work may be taken to mark the second stage in the history of Asokan scholarship, the first stage being represented in the work of Prinsep, Burnouf, and Wilson (1850). It will appear that of the Rock Edicts, Prinsep and Burnouf knew only of *three*, viz., those at Shahbazgarhi, Girnar, and Dhauli, and Burnouf and Wilson, of the Bhabru Edict as well ; of the Cave-inscriptions, Prinsep knew only of Nagarjuni, and Burnouf, of both Nagarjuni and Barabar ; and of the Pillar Edicts, Prinsep knew of all the versions except those at Kauśāmbī and Sanchi. By the time of Cunningham's *Corpus*, several additional Asokan Edicts were known, viz., the Minor Rock Edicts at Sahasram, Rupnath, and Bairat., and the Minor Pillar Edicts at Sanchi and Kauśāmbī.

There was still a crop of Asokan discoveries to follow.

In 1882, a fragment of R.E. VIII was discovered on a broken block at Sopara by Dr. Bhagwan Lal Indraji. Recently a boulder has been found bearing the first half of R. E. IX (*EI*, XXXII). Its language shows Sanskrit *l* changed into Prakṛita *r*.

The Mansehra Rock Edicts were discovered in parts by Captain Leigh, and by an Indian subordinate of the Panjab Archaeological Survey in 1889.

The three Mysore Minor Rock Edicts were discovered by Lewis Rice in 1891.

The Nigali Sagar Pillar Edict was discovered in 1895 and the Rummindei in 1896 by Führer.

In 1905 was discovered the Sarnath Pillar Edict by Oertel.

Lastly followed the discovery in 1915 of the Maski Rock Inscription by C. Beadon, a gold-mining engineer of the Nizam's Government.

In the meanwhile, considerable advance in Asokan studies was achieved in several publications, among which may be mentioned Senart's *Les Inscriptiones de Piyadasi* (1881), and Bühler's editions of the Asoka edicts in *ZDMG*, and *Epigraphia Indica*, Vols. i. and ii. Along with these may also be mentioned the important contributions to Asokan scholarship made from time to time by scholars like O. Franke, V. A. Smith, Fleet, Michelson, Lüders, F. W. Thomas, Hultzsch, D.R. Bhandarkar, K. P. Jayaswal, B. M. Barua, and A. C. Woolner.

The last stage in Asokan scholarship for some time to come has been reached in the new edition of the *Corpus* published in 1925 by Hultzsch whose recent death is a deplorable loss to the study of Indian history in general and to Asokan study in particular.

Now that the Asokan Text and Interpretation have practically reached a final form and stage, a convenient text book on the subject seems to be called for in the interests mainly of the growing number of students who have to offer *Asoka* as a subject of study at the University examinations. The present compilation has no pretensions to originality, except in the matter of some points in Asokan chronology and of certain passages in the Edicts, notorious for the controversy regarding their meanings, on which new interpretations have been suggested. The general interpretation of Asoka's career does not also follow always the usual or accepted lines. The annotation of the incriptions has been made fuller and comprehensive so as to include the different views and interpretations suggested, as well as parallel passages from Sanskrit and Pali works throwing light on the points at issue. The correspondence between the Asokan Edicts and Kauṭilya's *Arthaśāstra* has been specially worked out. The best preserved text of each Edict has been adopted as the standard for its study, and important variations shown in other texts have been pointed out in the footnotes. A further element of interest has been introduced in bringing together in the work illustrations of important Asokan monuments available. Most of these illustrations are based on photoprints supplied by the Archaeological Department, but a few on photographs taken by me on the spot, viz., those of Dhauli, the Kalsi elephant, and the Pillars at Bakhra, Lauriya Araraj, and Rummindei. The Dhauli photograph I owe to Mr. Nirmal Bose, M.Sc. (now Director General of Anthropological Survey, Government of India) and the Rummindei to the arrangements kindly made by my pupil, Mr. P. P. Panday, M. A., of Narharia, Basti. A plate showing the Asokan Alphabet (based on drawings kindly prepared by Principal A. K. Haldar of the Government School of Art and Crafts, Lucknow) has been added as an aid to the study of the inscriptions in the original. I owe special acknowledgments to Mr. Charan Das Chatterji, M.A., Lecturer (and since Professor) in Indian History, Lucknow University), for many valuable references and suggestions.

The system of transliteration adopted here may be understood from the following examples : *Lichchhavi, Kṛiṣṇa, Mahāvaṁśa.* Both Sanskrit and Prakrit forms have been used for certain words according to convenience.

My grateful acknowledgments are due to His Highness Sir Sayaji Rao Gaekwad, of Baroda, and his Government for their award to me of the *Sayaji Rao Gaekwad Prize* with which this work is associated, and to Benares Hindu University for *Sir Manindra Chandra Nandy Lectures* (1927), based on portions of this work.

RADHAKUMUD MOOKERJI.

THE UNIVERSITY LUCKNOW,
April, 1927.

PREFACE TO SECOND EDITION

The first edition of this work was published in London in 1928 by Messrs Macmillan and Co. Ltd. For some time it has remained out of print. There has been, however, a steady demand for it, calling for a second edition. It is now issued with several *Addenda* based on new material discovered since the first edition.

The enormous mass of transliteration of Sanskrit and Prākṛit names and words involved a good deal of difficult printing, with various diacritical marks and accented types, leaving mistakes which could not be helped. The system of transliteration adopted in the work may be understood from the following examples : *chikīchhā*, *rāño*, *Choḍā*, *Taṁvapaṁṇī*, *aṭavasha-abhisitasa*, *Priyadraśisa*.

My thanks are due to Messrs Macmillan and Co. Ltd. for their kind permission to issue this edition by waiving their copyright in my favour.

39, Ekdalia Road,
Calcutta, 19.
July, 1954.

RADHAKUMUD MOOKERJI
Member of Parliament

PREFACE TO THE THIRD EDITION

The progress of Asokan scholarship and of the growing popularity of the study of Asokan history at the Universities has called for a new edition of the work incorporating in it some of the inscriptions of Asoka discovered since the second edition and figuring in this edition as Addenda for convenience of printing. The most important of these inscriptions is that found at Shar-i-kuna off Kandahar of which the most singular feature is its two versions given in Greek and Aramaic for the benefit of the particular subjects of Asoka's empire speaking the two different languages. Other important points of the new inscriptions are brought out in their proper places in the Addenda.

I owe my grateful acknowledgements to the kind help given to me by Dr. D. C. Sircar, Carmichael Professor of the Culcutta University and by Adhir Chakravarti M. A. of Government Sanskrit College, Calcutta, for correcting the proofs and helping me materially in other ways. The design of the jacket I owe to the renowned artist Sri Asit Kumar Haldar, showing the original form of the Asokan Pillar at Sarnath.

39, Ekdalia Road
Calcutta 19,
March 1962.

RADHA KUMUD MOOKERJI

CONTENTS

C APTER PAGE

I.	Early Life and Family	I
II.	History	II
	Appendix A: On Asokan Chronology from the Legends	44
III.	Administration	47
IV.	Religion	60
V.	Monuments	79
VI.	Social Conditions	101
VII.	Translation and Annotation of the Inscriptions :	
	A. Minor Rock Edicts	107
	B. Bhabru (Bairat No. 2) Rock Edict	117
	C. Kalinga Rock Edicts (Separate)	120
	D. Fourteen Rock Edicts	128
	E. Seven Pillar Edicts	172
	F. Four Minor Pillar Edicts	193
	G. Two Commemorative Pillar Inscriptions	201
	H. Three Cave Inscriptions	205
	Appendix B : On the Chronology of the Asokan Edicts	208
VIII.	Texts of the Inscriptions	215
	Appendix C : On the Script, Dialect, and Grammar of the Inscriptions	246
	Index	255
	Addenda	275

ILLUSTRATIONS

PLATE

I. Capital of Asokan Pillar at Sarnath *Frontispiece*

II. Lauriya Araraj Pillar . . . *To face page* 14

III. Lumbini Pillar . . . . „ 37

IV. Figure of Elephant carved on Stone at Kālsi . . . . „ 61

V. Rampurwa Bull-Capital . . . . . „ 62

VI. Saṅkāśya Pillar with its Elephant Capital „ 84

VII. Bakhra Pillar with its Lion-Capital . „ 86

VIII. Rampurwa Lion-Capital . . . . . „ 90

IX. Lauriya Nandangarh Pillar . . . „ 92

X. Bharhut Sculpture showing the Bodh-Gayā Temple and an Imitation Asokan Pillar with Elephant-Capital . . „ 152

XI. Rock-cut Elephant at Dhauli . . . „ 170

XII. Lumbini Pillar Inscription . . . „ 201

XIII. Nativity in Sculpture in the Rummindei Temple . . . . „ 204

XIV. Brahmagiri Minor Rock Edict . . „ 215

XV. Asokan Alphabet . . . . . . „ 246

Map of Asoka's Empire . . . . . *At end*

CHAPTER I

EARLY LIFE AND FAMILY

In the annals of kingship there is scarcely any record comparable to that of Asoka, both as a man and as a ruler. To bring out the chief features of his greatness, historians have instituted comparisons between him and other distinguished monarchs in history, eastern and western, ancient and modern, pagan, Moslem, and Christian. In his efforts to establish a kingdom of righteousness after the highest ideals of a theocracy, he has been likened to David and Solomon of Israel in the days of its greatest glory ; in his patronage of Buddhism, which helped to transform a local into a world religion, he has been compared to Constantine [1] in relation to Christianity ; in his philosophy and piety he recalls Marcus Aurelius ; he was a Charlemagne in the extent of his empire and, to some extent, in the methods of his administration, too,[2] while his Edicts, "rugged, uncouth, involved, full of repetitions," read like the speeches of Oliver Cromwell in their mannerisms [Rhys Davids]. Lastly, he has been compared to Khalif Omar and Emperor Akbar, whom also he resembles in certain respects.

As in the case of great characters like King Arthur and his

[1] It must be noted that opinions differ on the appositeness of the comparison. Rhys Davids holds that the conversion of Asoka was the first great step on the downward path of Buddhism, the first step to its expulsion from India. Another critic holds that while "Constantine espoused a winning cause, Asoka put himself at the head of an unpopular religious reform."

[2] Compare the *missi dominici* of Charlemagne akin to the *puruṣas* of Asokan edicts, and the *Markgrafen* to the Anta-Mahāmātras.

Knights of the Round Table, the good King Alfred, or King St. Louis of France, a mass of tradition has gathered round the name of Asoka. Myths and legends have freely and luxuriantly grown round it, especially in the tropical climate of Ceylon, and it would have been very difficult to recover his true history, were it not for the fact that he has himself left us a sort of autobiography in his messages to his people, written on rocky surfaces or exquisitely finished and polished pillars of stone. In these sermons on stone we find his true self revealed and expressed, his philosophy of life, his conception of an emperor's duties and responsibilities, and the extent to which he lived to realise the high ideals and principles he professed and preached. This kind of evidence, which is not only a contemporary but a personal record, too, is unique in Indian history, and, whether suggested by indigenous or foreign precedents, it is fortunate we have it for one of our greatest men. "O that my words were written! That they were graven with an iron pen and lead in the rock for ever!" This pious wish of Job was more than realised in the case of Asoka in a series of thirty-five inscriptions published on rock or pillar, of which some are located at the extremities of his empire.

Of the two sources of his history, the legends (whether Ceylonese or Indian) rather hover over his early life and tend to retreat before the light of the edicts thrown upon his later life, his career as emperor. The two sources are, again, sometimes in agreement, but oftener in conflict, in which case the inscriptions, as personal and contemporary documents, will have to be preferred. Moreover, the legends are themselves at conflict with one another in many places, and thus betray themselves all the more.

Ceylon tradition (as narrated in the *Dīpavaṁsa* and the *Mahāvaṁsa*) makes Bindusāra the husband of sixteen wives and father of 101 sons, of whom only three are named, viz., Sumana (Susīma according to the northern legends), the eldest, Asoka, and Tiṣya (uterine brother of Asoka), the youngest son. The mother of Asoka in the northern tradition is Subhadrāṅgī,[1] the beautiful daughter of a Brahman

[1] Mentioned in the *Asokāvadānamālā*, but not in the *Divyāvadāna*.

of Champā, who bore Bindusāra another son named Vigatāsoka (Vītāśoka), and not Tiṣya of the Ceylon books. In the southern tradition she is called Dharmā, the principal queen (*aggamahesī*) [*Mahāvaṁsatīkā*, ch. iv. p. 125],[1] the preceptor of whose family was an Ājīvika saint named Janasāna—a fact which may explain Asoka's patronage of the Ājīvika Sect. Dharmā came of the Ksatriya clan of the Moriyas.[2]

According to established constitutional usage, Asoka as Prince served as Viceroy in one of the remoter provinces of the Empire. This was the province of Western India called Avantiraṭṭham[3] [*Mahābodhivaṁsa*, p. 98] with headquarters (Rājadhānī) at Ujjain in the Ceylon tradition, but in the Indian legends it is the kingdom of the Svaśas[4] in Uttarāpatha (*Div.*) with headquarters at Taxila, where Asoka was temporarily sent to supersede Prince Susīma and quell the revolt against his maladministration. There was a second rebellion at Taxila which Prince Susīma failed to quell, when the throne at Pāṭaliputra fell vacant and was promptly seized by Asoka with the aid of the minister, Rādhagupta, and subsequently held deliberately against the eldest brother who was killed in the attempt to dethrone the usurper [see *Divyāvadāna*,[5] ch. xxvi.]. But the story of the accession is

[1] I owe this passage to Mr. Charan Das Chatterji, M.A., Lecturer in Ancient Indian History at the Lucknow University.

[2] *Moriyavaṁsajā* [*Mahāvaṁsatīkā*, *ib.*; also *Mahābodhivaṁsa*, p. 98].

[3] I.e., the *rāṣṭra* or province of Avanti.

[4] Probably mistaken for *Khaśas* mentioned by Manu, x. 22, and also in an inscription [*Ep. Ind.* i. 132].

[5] While the *Divyāvadāna* represents the war of succession as between the two brothers, the *Mahābodhivaṁsa* represents it as between Asoka on one side, and a coalition of all his 98 brothers who made a common cause with their eldest brother Sumana, the *yuvarāja*, and hence the *lawful heir* to the throne. The *Div.* supports Asoka's claims by stating that even under Bindusāra, the Ājīvika saint, Piṅgalavatsa, summoned by the king, judged Asoka as the fittest of his sons for the throne. It also states that Asoka was further backed by the powerful support of the entire ministry of Bindusāra, of Khallāṭaka (Prime Minister) and 500 other ministers in his contest for the throne. We may also note here the tradition recorded by the

somewhat differently told in the Ceylonese legends, which make Asoka seize the throne from Ujjain, where he had been throughout serving as viceroy, by making a short work of all his brothers except Tiṣya.

The northern and southern legends, however, agree as regards the disputed succession, which may therefore be taken as a fact. The southern legends are far wide of the truth in making Asoka a fratricide, the murderer of 99 brothers for the sake of the throne, for which he is dubbed Chaṇḍāsoka [*Mahāv.* v. 189]. Senart [*Inscriptions*, etc. ii. 101] has well shown how the legends themselves are not at one in their account of Asoka's career of cruelty. Tāranāth makes Asoka kill only six brothers. Other authorities do not attribute to him any murder at all, but other forms of cruelty. The *Asoka-avadāna* represents him as killing his officers and wives, and setting up a hell [1] where some innocent people are subjected to the most refined tortures. The *Mahāvaṁsa* also relates how his minister under his instructions decapitates some false monks till he is stopped by his brother. In the *Asoka-avadāna*, he sets a price upon the heads of Brahman ascetics who insulted the statue of the Buddha till he is checked by his brother, Vītāśoka. Yuan Chwang records the tradition of "Asoka and his queen, in succession, making determined efforts to destroy the Bodhi

Chinese traveller, I-tsing, according to which Asoka's sovereignty was prophesied by the Buddha himself. The tradition relates that King Bimbisāra once saw in a dream that a piece of cloth and a gold stick were both divided up into eighteen fragments which, as explained by the Buddha, symbolised the eighteen schools into which his teaching would be split "more than a hundred years after his nirvāṇa, when there will arise a king named Asoka, who will rule over the whole of Jambudvīpa" [Takakusu's *I-tsing*, p. 14]. The Buddha's prophecy about Asoka as a righteous king who will enshrine his bodily relics in 84,000 "dharmarājikas" occurs in the *Divyāvadāna* (xxvi. p. 368).

[1] Yuan Chwang saw a high pillar which marked the site of Asoka's "Hell," or Prison, equipped with all imaginable instruments of torture, and relates the tradition that the sight of an imprisoned arhat, whom no tortures could destroy, made Asoka realise his sin, demolish the prison, and make his penal code liberal [Watters, ii. 89]. The story of Asoka's hell is given in greater detail by Fa-hien (pp. 56-58 in translation of Giles).

tree," and when each attempt failed and the tree grew up each time, "Asoka surrounded it with a stone wall" [Watters, ii. 115]. According to Fa-hien [Giles, p. 59], the queen tried to destroy the Bo-tree out of jealousy when Asoka, already a zealous Buddhist, was always to be found under that tree for worship. The fact is that these legends were out to emphasise the contrast between the criminal career of Asoka prior to his conversion and his virtuous conduct that followed it. They were interested in blackening his character to glorify the religion which could transmute base metal into gold, convert Chaṇḍāsoka into Dharmāsoka [*ibid.*], and make of a monster of cruelty the simplest of men ! [1]

Their testimony also contradicts that of his own words in Rock Edict V, in which his brothers (with sisters and other relatives) are specifically mentioned,[2] and also in Minor Rock Edict II, Rock Edicts III, IV, VI, XI, XII, Pillar Edict VII, and the Queen's Edict, in all of which is feelingly expressed the emperor's solicitude for the welfare of even distant relatives. We gather from these edicts that Asoka had a large family with " brothers and sisters, and other relatives settled at Pāṭaliputra and other provincial towns,"

[1] The epithet Chaṇḍāsoka suggested by Asoka's earlier cruelties does not, however, seem to be justified, if we limit his cruelties only to the murder of a single brother in the contest for the throne, while it may be that the brothers referred to as being alive well on in his reign (R.E. V and XIII) might be only his uterine brothers, of whom the legends give the name of one, viz., Tiṣya. The number of brothers slain according to the legends may be an exaggeration which marks legends, and even the edicts of Asoka. It may be well assumed, too, that the brothers slain might have been his step-brothers. According to the *Mahābodhivaṁsa* (p. 99), as already stated, these 98 brothers with their leader, Yuvarāja Sumana, were slain in the course of the war of succession they had forced on Asoka, whom they regarded as the usurper. Thus Asoka could not be held responsible for their death under such circumstances.

[2] Strictly speaking, we cannot positively state from this passage which refers only to the existence of " the harems of his brothers and sisters " that the brothers were *living* at this time. But the fact of Asoka's affection for his brothers and sisters and their families, which alone is pertinent to the point discussed here, can be positively asserted from this passage.

" sons and grandsons " (R.E. XIII and V), who were all maintained at royal expense. Pillar Edict VII contains the expression : " In all my female establishments, both here (at the capital) and in the outlying towns " (cf. also R.E. V). Besides the evidence showing the existence of the harems of his brothers at different provincial towns, we have also the evidence of such brothers (called *kumāras* and *ārya-putras*) serving as his Viceroys at headquarters named, viz., Taxila, Tosali Ujjayinī [K.R.E.] and Suvarṇagiri [M.R.E. I Brah.]. As has been shown below, these Viceroys could not be his sons. Lastly, his affection for his children, too, expresses itself in the Kalinga Edict I : " I desire for my children that they may enjoy every kind of prosperity and happiness both in this world and in the next." A man with such tender solicitude for the welfare of all his relations could not be a monster of cruelty, as the legends represent him to be.

The relations between Asoka and his younger brother appear to be quite friendly and natural in the legends, but they give different accounts of these relations. Yuan Chwang, calling him Mahendra, relates that he used his high birth to violate the laws, lead a dissolute life, and oppress the people, till the matter was reported to Asoka by his high ministers and old statesmen. Then Asoka in tears explained to his brother how awkward was his position due to his conduct. Mahendra, confessing guilt, asked for a reprieve of seven days, during which, by the practice of contemplation in a dark chamber, he became an arhat and was granted cave-dwellings at Pāṭaliputra for his residence. According to Fa-hien, Asoka's brother, whose name he does not mention, had retired to the solitude on a hill which he was loath to leave, though " the king sincerely reverenced him and wished and begged him to come and live in his family where he could supply all his wants." In the end, the king constructed for him a hill inside the city of Pāṭaliputra to live closer to him. A different story is, however, given in other works. The Pali works call him *Tiṣya*, the *Divyāvadāna* *Vītāsoka*, and some Chinese works *Sudatta* and *Sugātra*. These works also specify his offence to be that, as a Tīrthika, he had slandered the professed Buddhists as living in luxury and subject to passions. To convince him of his error, Asoka conspired with his chief minister to place him on the throne, and then appeared suddenly to accuse him as a usurper, whom he condemned to die after seven days. During this time he was treated to all pleasures and luxuries for which, however, he had no taste, with death facing him. By this example, Asoka wanted to show that no Buddhist with his dread of death and birth could ever give himself to pleasures. He then set free Vītāsoka, who, however, went away to a frontier land, became an arhat, saw Asoka at Pāṭaliputra, but soon left for another district where he was beheaded, being taken for one of the Nirgranthas upon whose heads the local king set a price. In the *Mahāvaṁsa* [v. 33], Asoka appoints his brother Tiṣya as *uparāja*, his Vice-regent, but he retired as a religious devotee under the influence of the Yonaka preacher, Mahādharmarakṣita, and was known by the name of 'Ekavihārika,' a vihāra being excavated for him at enormous expense in the rock called Bhojakagiri by Asoka, according to the story given in Dhammapāla's comment on the verses composed by Ekavihārika in the *Thera-gāthā Commentary*.[1] The same work refers to the youngest brother of Asoka, called Vītāsoka, whom it treats evidently as not the same brother as Tissa Ekavihārika. It relates [2] how he grew up, mastering all the *vidyās* and *śilpas*, arts and sciences, prescribed for the study of Kṣatriyakumāras ; then he became a householder, and, under his teacher, Giridatta Thera, mastered the Sutta Piṭaka and Abhidhamma Piṭaka, until one day, while at shaving (*massu-kamma*), he noticed in his mirror his grey hairs, which set him a-thinking of the decay of life, and he at once embraced monkhood under Giridatta and soon became an arhat. This particular text thus distinguishes between the two brothers of Asoka by their different teachers, and attributes to them different *gāthās*.

Some of the Edicts mention the names of his closer

[1] *Thera-gāthā Commentary*, Sinhalese ed., Colombo, 1918, p. 603 f. This reference I owe to Mr. C. D. Chatterji.

[2] *Ib.* p. 295 f.

relations. Thus the second Queen Kāruvākī is mentioned, together with her son, Prince Tīvara. A later inscription mentions Asoka's grandson Daśaratha. Both legends and inscriptions are at one in making Asoka a polygamist. The chronicles make his first wife the daughter of a merchant of Vedisagiri, Devī by name, whom Asoka had married when he was Viceroy at Ujjain. The *Mahābodhivaṁsa* calls her Vedisa-mahādevī (p. 116) and a Śākyānī (*ibid.*) or a Śākya-kumārī (p. 98), as being the daughter of a clan of the Śākyas who had immigrated to "*Vedisaṁ nagaraṁ*" out of fear of Viḍūdabha menacing their mother-country (*Viḍūdabhabhayāgatānaṁ Sākiyānam āvāsam Vedisam*). Thus the first wife of Asoka was related to the Buddha's family or clan. She is also described as having caused the construction of the Great Vihāra of Vedisagiri, probably the first of the monuments of Sanchi and Bhilsa (*tāya kārāpitaṁ Vedisagirimahāvihāraṁ*). This explains why Asoka selected Sanchi and its beautiful neighbourhood for his architectural activities. Vedisa also figures as an important Buddhist place in earlier literature (see *Sutta Nipāta*). Of Devī were born the son, Mahendra, and the daughter, Saṅghamitrā, who was married to Asoka's nephew, Agnibrahmā, and gave birth to a son named Sumana. According to *Mahāvaṁsa*, Devī did not follow Asoka as sovereign to Pāṭaliputra, for there his Chief Queen (*agramahiṣī*) then was Asandhimitrā [v. 85 and xx]. The *Divyāvadāna* [1] knows of a third wife of Asoka, Padmāvatī by name, the mother of Dharmavivardhana, who was afterwards called Kuṇāla. Both *Mahāvaṁsa* and *Divyāvadāna* agree in mentioning Tissarakkhā or Tiṣyarakṣitā as the last Chief Queen of Asoka. The *Divyāvadāna* mentions Samprati as Kuṇāla's son. The Kashmir Chronicle mentions Jalauka as another son of Asoka. Fa-hien [Legge's tr., p. 31] mentions Dharmavivardhana as a son of Asoka, whom he appointed as the Viceroy of Gandhāra.

[1] Ch. xxvii. The *Divyāvadāna* states that Asoka first gave to his new-born babe by his queen Padmāvatī the name of Dharmavivardhana, but on seeing the beauty of his eyes which, as his *amātyas*, or ministers in attendance, pointed out, were like those of the Himalayan bird, Kuṇāla, Asoka nicknamed him as Kuṇāla.

Thus, taking the legends and Edicts together, we find the following relations of Asoka :

Father—Bindusāra, who had many wives.

Mother—Subhadrāṅgī, as named in the northern tradition ; also called Dharmā in the southern tradition.

Brothers—(1) Sumana or Susīma, eldest, but stepbrother ; (2) Tiṣya, uterine and youngest brother ; also called Vītāsoka or Vigatāsoka in the northern legends, Mahendra by Yuan Chwang, and Sudatta and Sugātra in some Chinese works ; (3) Vītāsoka, according to *Thera-gāthā Commentary* cited above.

Wives—(1) Devī, with her full name, " Vedisa-Mahādevī Śākyakumārī " ; (2) Kāruvākī, called "*Dvitīyā devī Tīvalamātā*," " second Queen, mother of Tīvara " in the Edict ; (3) Asandhimitrā, designated as *agramahisī*, Chief Queen ; (4) Padmāvatī ; (5) Tiṣyarakṣitā.

Sons—(1) Mahendra, son of Devī ; (2) Tīvara, son of Kāruvākī ; (3) Kuṇāla, son of Padmāvatī, also known by the name of Dharmavivardhana, as mentioned in *Divyāvadāna*, and by Fa-hien ; (4) Jalauka, mentioned in the Kashmir Chronicle. The Edicts tell of four princes serving as Viceroys in four different, and remote, provinces, and designated as *Kumāras* or *Āryaputras*, as distinguished from the sons of a lower status called *dālakas* from the status of their mothers [see P.E. VII].

Daughters—(1) Saṅghamitrā, whose mother was Devī ; (2) Chārumatī.

Sons-in-law—(1) Agnibrahmā, husband of Saṅghamitrā ; (2) Devapāla Kṣatriya, married to Chārumatī.

Grandsons—(1) Daśaratha, who became king ; (2) Samprati, son of Kuṇāla ; (3) Sumana, son of Saṅghamitrā.

On the basis of the texts to which we owe most of these names, it is also possible to ascertain some dates in the domestic life of Asoka. For instance, we are told in the *Mahāvaṁsa* that Asoka's eldest son and daughter, Mahendra and Saṅghamitrā, were both ordained in the sixth year of his coronation when they were respectively twenty and eighteen years old. Taking the date of Asoka's coronation to be 270 B.C., as explained below, we get 284 B.C. and

282 B.C. as the dates of the birth of Mahendra and his sister respectively. If we take the father's age at the birth of his eldest child as twenty years, then Asoka must have been born in 304 B.C., and was thus seen by his august grandfather, Chandragupta Maurya, who died in 299 B.C. It is also stated that Asoka's son-in-law, Agnibrahmā, was ordained in the fourth year of his coronation, i.e., in 266 B.C., before which a son was born to him. Thus Saṅghamitrā must have been married in 268 B.C. at the latest, i.e., at the age of fourteen.

CHAPTER II

HISTORY

FROM his early life we now pass on to the details of his career as king.

There was an interval of about four years between his accession to the throne and formal coronation, if we may believe in the Ceylon chronicles. The hypothesis about a contested succession might perhaps explain this. A more probable explanation suggested is that the coronation of a king must await his twenty-fifth year, as pointed out in the inscription of the Kalinga king, Khāravela [*JBORS*, Vol. iii. p. 461], so that Asoka must have ascended the throne when he was about twenty-one years of age. But this suggestion, as already explained, seems to be contradicted by tradition, if we may believe in it. According to it, Asoka must have ascended the throne at thirty, and been consecrated at thirty-four The fact of an interval existing between his accession and coronation seems to be indicated in a way in the Edicts which the king is always careful to date from his *abhiṣeka,* coronation, as if to ensure that it should not be confused with accession. The Edicts also date from the coronation the events of his reign.

He assumed the two titles, *Devānaṁpiya* and *Piyadasi*, signifying respectively "the favoured of the gods"[1] and "of pleasing countenance," or, more properly, "one who

[1] Literally, "one dear to the gods" by his good deeds. The same sentiment is expressed differently in some of the legends on the coins of the later Gupta emperors: "the lord of the earth wins heaven (*divaṁ jayati*) by his virtuous actions (*sucharitaiḥ*)."

looks with kindness upon everything." The former title was used by his predecessors, as shown in the Kalsi, Shahbazgarhi and Mansehra texts of Rock Edict VIII, and also taken in the *Dīpavaṁsa* by Tissa, the contemporary king of Ceylon,[1] as well as by Asoka's grandson, Daśaratha, in the Nagarjuni Hill Cave Inscriptions; and the latter, under the name *Piadaṁsana*, seems to have been used by Asoka's grandfather, Chandragupta Maurya, as we learn from the *Mudrā-rākṣasa* (Act VI.). This title is also given to Asoka by the *Dīpavaṁsa*. All the Edicts refer to the king by his titles,[2] and omit the *name* Asoka, and scholars were at pains to prove the identity with Asoka of the person signified by the titles until the anonymity of the Edicts was removed by the discovery of a new Edict at Maski (the earliest of the Edicts), which uses the phrase—"*Devānaṁpiyasa Asokasa*," "of His Gracious Majesty, Asoka."[3]

Asoka had the singular good fortune of being spared the difficult task of founding and organising an empire. That task was effectively executed by his grandfather, Chandragupta Maurya, who bequeathed to his successors an empire extending approximately from Afghanistan to Mysore. Territories which are even now outside the Government of India were parts of the Indian empire under Chandragupta; the four satrapies of Aria, Arochosia, Gedrosia, and the

[1] And also by the Ceylon kings named Vaṅkanāsika Tissa, Gajabāhukagāminī and Mahallaka Nāga in some inscriptions [*Ep. Zeylanica*, i. 60 f.].

[2] The full form of his title, in Sanskrit, *Devānāṁpriyaḥ Priyadarśī Rājā*, is not always used in the Edicts. In some it is shortened into only *Devānāṁpriyaḥ* [*e.g.* R.E. XII and XIII]. In the Bairat M.R.E., it is only *Priyadarśī Rājā*, and in the three Cave Inscriptions *Rājā Priyadarśī*, while in Maski it is *Devānāṁpriya Asoka*. The full form occurs in the Rummindei and Nigliva Pillar Inscriptions, as also in Girnar (R.E. VIII).

[3] The other points furnished by the Edicts in favour of this identification are (1) the mention of Priyadarśī as a Māgadha king in the Bhabru Edict, (2) the reference to Pāṭaliputra as his capital in Girnar R.E. V, and (3) the reference to his contemporary Yona or Greek kings in R.E. II and XIII. It may be noted in this connexion that the *Divyāvadāna* in one passage [ch. xxvi] calls Asoka as a *Maurya*, and thus helps further the identification.

Paropanisadai, which Chandragupta wrested in about 304 B.C. from the empire of Selukos as the penalty for his ill-advised aggression. It is not known who conquered the south, whether Chandragupta or Bindusāra. Perhaps it was the former, in spite of his preoccupations with his wars in the north subverting the Nandan empire. For a definite and long-continued tradition describes Chandragupta abdicating and retiring as a Jain saint at Śravaṇa Belgola in Southern Mysore, up to which, therefore, his dominion must have extended.[1]

The extent of his empire may be, indeed, inferred from the geographical distribution of his Rock and Pillar Edicts. The former are at the following places : (1) Shāhbāzgarhi, near Peshwar ; (2) Mansehra, in the same locality ; (3) Kālsī, near Dehra Dun, at the confluence of the Tons and Jumna rivers, then a populous centre ; (4) Sopārā, in Thānā district, Bombay Presidency ; (5) Girnar, near Junāgarh, in Kathiawar, where the Edicts are inscribed on a rock on a lake, the Sudarśana lake of the Mauryan emperors ; (6) Dhauli, in Puri district, near Bhuvanesvara ; (7) Jaugada, on the Ṛiṣikulya river, in Ganjam district, where (as also at Dhauli) the two Kalinga Edicts are substituted for R.E. XI, XII, and XIII, as being locally more appropriate, though it is not clear why R.E. XIII treating of the Kalinga Conquest and its effects on the king's mind was considered unsuitable for publication in Kalinga ; (8) Chitaldroog, in Mysore, where the Minor Rock Edicts appear on hills on the Chinna Haggari river at three different localities, viz., Siddapura (supposed to be the *Isila* of M.R.E. I), Jatinga-Rāmeśvara and Brahmagiri ; (9) Rupnath, a place of pilgrimage, near Jubbulpur, where appears only M.R.E. I ; (10) Sahasram, in Bihar, with M.R.E. I only ; (11) Bairat, near Jaipur, in

[1] The conquest of the south by Chandragupta Maurya may also perhaps be inferred from the following statement of Plutarch [*Life of Alexander*, ch. lxii.] : "Not long afterwards Androkottos, who had by that time mounted the throne, presented Selukos with 500 elephants, and overran and subdued the whole of India with an army of 600,000." "The throne" in the context is the Magadhan throne, the occupation of which by Chandragupta is thus followed by two other events, viz., the defeat of Selukos, and the conquest of the remaining part of India not included in the Magadhan empire of the Nandas.

Rajputana, showing only M.R.E. I ; (12) Bhabru, with its special Edict which originally appeared on a second hill at Bairat ;[1] and (13) Maski (showing the M.R.E. I only), in the Nizam's dominions.[2] The Pillars bearing the Edicts stood at (1) Topra near Ambala, (2) Meerut, both of which were removed to Delhi by Sultan Firoz Taghlak ; (3) Kauśāmbī (removed to Allahabad probably by Akbar), where appear P.E. I-VI, the Queen's Edict, and Kauśāmbī Edict ; (4) Lauriya Ararāj (Rādhia in Champaran district) ; (5) Lauriya Nandangarh (Mathia), in the same district ; (6) Rampurwa in the same district ; (7) Sanchi, near Bhopal, bearing M.P.E ; (8) Sarnath, near Benares, giving M.P.E ; (9) Rummindei, in Nepal ; and (10) Nigliva, in Nepalese Tarai. Thus Asoka was justified in stating that " great is his dominion " [R.E. XIV], and calling his dominion as the whole earth, *pṛithivī* [R.E. V (Dhauli Text)].

Apart from the inscriptions,[3] his buildings, as will be ex-

[1] Whence it is called by Hultzsch the " Calcutta-Bairat Rock-Inscription," the block on which it appeared being now in Calcutta at the Asiatic Society.

[2] Dr. Bhandarkar [*Asoka*, pp. 36, 37] points out that, while the fourteen Rock Edicts were engraved in the capitals of the outlying provinces of Asoka's empire, the Minor Rock Edicts mark out places which separate his dominion from that of his independent or semi-independent neighbours. Thus Dhauli and Jaugada were the cities of the Kalinga province ; Girnar was capital of Surāṣṭra ; Sopārā was the city of Aparānta ; Shāhbāzgarhī might be taken to be the chief town of the Yona province, and Mansehra of the Kambojas. The locations of the Minor Rock Edicts are mostly on the borders of the empire, and these are also stated to have been meant for the *Antas* or the independent neighbouring states.

[3] Besides these inscriptions on rock and pillar discovered and deciphered up to now at the different places mentioned, there are certain inscriptions noticed by the Chinese pilgrim, Yuan Chwang, which still remain to be discovered. Thus one of these was found by him on an Asokan Tope at Rāmagrāma [Watters, ii. 20] ; two were found by him on pillars at Kuśinagara ; a fourth was found by him on a pillar at Pāṭaliputra ; and a fifth on a pillar at Rājagṛiha. The pillars, together with their inscriptions, have not yet been found out. It should be noted, however, that neither of the Chinese pilgrims, Fa-hien and Yuan Chwang, has described the inscriptions they had noticed as the inscriptions of Asoka. They generally describe them as belonging to, and recording the events of, earlier times.

PLATE II.

Lauriya Araraj Pillar.

plained below, also testify to the extent of his empire. Those in Kashmir and Nepal show that these countries were parts of his empire. Yuan Chwang saw Asokan topes in Kapis (Kafiristan), Nagar (Jelalabad), and Udyāna in the north-west. In Bengal, the authority of Asoka is proved by his stūpa at Tāmralipti, the capital of Suhma, and the famous port of embarkation for voyages towards the south. According to Yuan Chwang, there was also a stūpa of Asoka in the capital of Samataṭa or the Brahmaputra Delta, and others in different parts of Bengal and Bihar, viz., Puṇyavardhana (northern Bengal) and Karṇasuvarṇa (modern Burdwan, Birbhum and Murshidabad districts) [Watters, ii. 184 f.]. Yuan Chwang refers to Asokan topes being erected at various places in the south, in Chola and Dravida, of which the capital, Kāñchipura, has been sought to be identified with the Satiyaputra country of the Edict. Indeed, the distribution of the Asokan topes as mentioned by Yuan Chwang is almost co-terminous with that of the inscriptions, and is equally significant of the vastness of his empire.

Lastly, the extent of his empire is also indicated by his own mention in the Edicts [R.E. II, V, and XIII] of the peoples on its borders. In the south, these are mentioned as the Cholas, Pāṇḍyas, the Satiyaputra and Keralaputra, who were all within his sphere of influence. Towards the north-west, his empire marched with that of the Syrian monarch, Antiochos [R.E. II], and hence extended up to Persia and Syria which were held by Antiochos, while it is also known how Asoka's grandfather, Chandragupta, had wrested from Selukos the provinces of Aria, Arachosia, Paropanisadai and Gedrosia, which descended to Asoka as his inheritance. The peoples on the north-west frontiers who came within his sphere of influence are called Gandhāras, Kambojas and Yavanas (or Yonas), all in the modern north-western Frontier Province and the upper Kabul valley. We may also note how the empire is further marked out by several geographical names occurring in the Edicts. We have mention of the capital of the empire at Pāṭaliputra [R.E. V, Girnar], and of "outlying towns" [*ib.*], such as Bodh-Gayā [R.E. VIII], Kosāmbī [Allahabad Pillar E.], Ujjenī, Takkhasilā [K.R.E.],

Suvarṇagiri, Isila [M.R.E.], and Tosalī and Samāpā in the province of Kalinga [K.R.E.]. Thus we have a fairly definite idea of the limits of Asoka's empire in different directions. We may even hazard the conjecture that the empire was so large that Asoka did not live to visit all its parts, and inspect the execution of his inscriptions in different localities. This is apparent from the somewhat apologetic tone in which he refers to the imperfections of the Edicts, as written on the rocks, from the mere probabilities of the case, and not from direct personal knowledge. As a matter of fact, the actual imperfections are too insignificant to deserve any notice of the emperor in a special Edict [R.E. XIV]. That he could not thus travel through his empire seems all the more surprising when we remember how indefatigable was the emperor in the discharge of his administrative duties [R.E. VI], and how among such duties he included as his own innovation those of constant tours of inspection of the conditions of his people in different parts [R.E. VIII].

As Asoka himself says in his Rock Edict XIII, his only conquest was that of Kalinga. This was " when he had been consecrated eight years," i.e., in about 262 B.C. In this war with the Kalingas, " one hundred and fifty thousand persons were deported, one hundred thousand were slain, and many times that number died." The losses of the vanquished indicate the strength of their defence. We know from the earlier account of Megasthenes that the king of the Kalingas was protected by a standing army, numbering 60,000 infantry, 1000 cavalry, and 700 war elephants. This army must have been considerably expanded by the time of Asoka, when the number of casualties alone is stated to be at least 4 lacs (taking the number of those who ultimately succumbed to the wounds of war to be, say, 3 lacs). But the losses of the war to the defeated people of Kalinga were not confined only to the casualties. Asoka takes the more correct basis of the computation : he feelingly counts the suffering caused to the civilian population by " violence or slaughter or separation from their loved ones " (upaghāto vā vadho vā abhiratānām viniskramanam). The losses of the war in this ancient document are indeed computed on most modern principles under three heads: (1) the losses inflicted on the combatants by death, wounds or capture; (2) the losses suffered by the families of the combatants thus affected; and (3) the suffering caused to the friends of the bereaved or afflicted families [ll. 3-5 of the inscription]. Lastly comes the mental anguish of the sovereign, who has singly to bear the whole weight of his people's sorrows As Shakespeare says, "Never did the king sigh but with a general groan!" Thus Asoka is most modern in his estimate of the cruelties of war as equally affecting the combatants and non-combatants, or the civilian element, in a society based upon the joint family as the unit. Such a society, as truly described by Asoka, comprises religious and secular classes—Brahmans and Śramaṇas, various other dissenters, and the regular householders living in the happy harmony of domestic and social life with the cultivation of proper relations towards elders and seniors, father and mother, preceptor, friends, comrades, supporters and relations, servants and dependents. This is typical Hindu Society to the present day. In a society so closely knit together, in a system of intimate relations, it is no wonder that a war affects the civilian population almost as much as those sent to the front—the bereaved relations of the dead, and the friends of their survivors.

This deep and delicate sensitiveness to the cruel consequences of war worked a revolution in the character of Asoka.[1] He became a changed man, both in his personal and public life. Says the Edict: "Directly after the conquest of the Kalingas, the Beloved of the gods became keen in the pursuit of Dharma, love of Dharma, and inculcation of Dharma. . . . The chiefest conquest is not that by arms but by Dharma (*dharma-vijaya*)." The violence of war seen in all its nakedness makes Asoka turn completely towards Non-Violence (*Ahiṁsā*) as the creed of his life. Thus he came to change his personal religion and definitely adopt

[1] Senart [*Inscriptions*, etc., p. 101] makes the interesting suggestion that the cruelties of this war which led to Asoka's real conversion to Buddhism might have supplied the material for the legendary descriptions of the atrocities of Chaṇḍāsoka.

Buddhism, which, of all the then prevailing religions of India, stood up most for the principle of non-violence. This fact about his religious history has to be studied along with what he says in his Minor Rock Edict I: "I was a lay-disciple (*upāsaka*) without, however, exerting myself strenuously. But a year—in fact more than a year ago—I approached the Order, and since then have exerted myself strenuously." Taking this passage along with that cited from Rock Edict XIII, we arrive at the following findings, viz., that (*a*) the suffering caused by his conquest of Kalinga made Asoka's zeal for Buddhism (*dharma-kāmatā*) very keen (*tīvra*); (*b*) that before the said conquest he had been a follower, though but an ordinary or indifferent, and not a zealous, follower of Buddhism; (*c*) that before the said conquest he had been a mere lay-disciple or upāsaka of the Buddhist church for more than two years and a half, i.e., during 265-262 B.C. becoming a convert to Buddhism in 265 B.C.;[1] and (*d*) that the conquest of Kalinga (262 B.C.) was immediately followed by his closer association with the Order and strenuous exertions on its behalf. He exerted himself strenuously for more than a year, i.e., from 262-260 B.C., when he issued the Minor Rock Edict I The same year, 260 B.C., was associated not merely with his first Rock Edict, but also with the first of his "pious tours," probably that to Bodh Gayā, which took place "after he had been consecrated ten years," as stated in the Rock Edict VIII.

Next followed the publication of his main series of fourteen religious proclamations or messages to his people, which, according to Rock Edicts III, IV, and V, and also the Pillar Edict VI, took place twelve or thirteen years after his consecration, i.e., during 258-257 B.C.

The idea of issuing religious edicts is thus stated in the Pillar Edict VI:

"When I had been consecrated twelve years, I caused a

[1] This date is curiously confirmed by a passage in the *Mahāvaṁsa* [v. 37-48], which states that Nigrodha, born in the year of the death of his father, Prince Sumana, and of Asoka's accession to the throne converted Asoka when he was above seven years old, and after the seventh year of Asoka's accession, i.e., about 266 B.C.

scripture of the Dharma to be written for the welfare and happiness of mankind with the intent that they, giving up old courses, might attain growth in dharma, one way or the other."

Next, it struck him that he must so publish his Edicts that they may be read permanently. And so he declared his decision in the Minor Rock Edict I, the first of his Edicts, thus :

" And this very message is to be written on the rocks, and also, where there are pillars of stone, on such pillars also is it to be inscribed."

Thus we have his Edicts inscribed on rock and pillar, on enduring material, which enables us to hear to this day the moving voice of Asoka across the centuries. " For that purpose have I caused this scripture of the Law to be written in order that it may endure," says Asoka himself in his Rock Edicts V and VI.

The Pillar Edicts were preceded by the Rock Edicts of which the fourteenth and the last one is a sort of Epilogue explaining how they are written in a language " sometimes abridged, sometimes of medium length, and sometimes expanded. . . . There is also here something said again and again for the sweetness of the topics concerned that the people might thus follow it. There sometimes might also be writing left unfinished, taking into account the locality, or fully considering the reasons, or by the lapses of the scribe." The emperor also states : " Great is my dominion, and much has been written, and much shall I get written." The last phrase refers to the Pillar Edicts, which were yet to be issued. It may also be noted that in spite of the emperor's apologies for the imperfections of the inscriptions, there are very few imperfections left in their actual execution.

Thirdly, the emperor's religious change made itself amply felt in the domain of his personal life and habits. Most of the time-honoured customs and institutions of the royal household were abolished as being contradictory to the spirit of his new faith, and others more in consonance therewith were substituted in their place. Indeed, one of his Edicts

[Pillar Edict VI] frankly expects that "men should give up their old ways." The royal tours of pleasure, accompanied by "hunting and other similar amusements," in which Asoka had indulged for nine years in his reign, now yielded their place to "tours of religion" accompanied by "visiting ascetics and Brahmans with liberality to them; visiting elders with largess of gold; visiting the people of the country (*janapadasya*) with instruction in Dharma and discussion of that Dharma" [Rock Edict VIII]. Next, he ordered that in the capital "no animal should be slaughtered for sacrifice, nor shall any merry-making be held, because in merry-makings is seen much that is objectionable." Further, in the kitchens of the royal household where "each day many hundred thousands[1] of living creatures were slaughtered to make curries," he ordered that only three creatures were to be slaughtered for the purpose, viz., two peacocks and one antelope, and later on, even the slaughter of these creatures was prohibited so as to render the diet of the palace exclusively vegetarian. It may be noted in this connection that the Ceylon tradition [*Mahāvaṁsa*, v. 34] represents Asoka as daily feeding 60,000 Brahmans for three years—a fact in keeping with what this inscription (Rock Edict I) says about the daily requirements of the royal table.

Fourthly, the emperor's religious change impressed itself upon his public policy and administration, too. The Kalinga war was the last political event of his reign, so to speak. The intensity of its violence produced a reaction in his mind towards the principle of non-violence, the principle of observing and enforcing peace not only between man and man, but also between man and every sentient creature. Thus, while the recent bloodiest war of history has only ended in a talk about preventing future wars, the Kalinga war was, for Asoka, the end of all war, although he was not free from the provocations to war from the many unsubdued peoples of India. His deliberate policy was now thus enunciated: "Even if any one does positive harm to him, he would be considered worthy of forgiveness by His Sacred

[1] Probably an instance of the exaggeration of which the Edicts are sometimes as guilty as the legends!

Majesty so far as he can possibly be forgiven " [R.E. XIII]. And his message in respect of the unsubdued borderers was " that the king desires that they should have no fear of me, that they should trust me, and should receive from me happiness, not sorrow " [Kalinga Edict II]. This is, in effect, the doctrine of the equality of all states, great and small, in sovereignty and liberty which the modern world is striving so hard to establish. But Asoka conceived it, and gave effect to it. Elsewhere he declares in self-satisfaction that " instead of the reverberation of the war-drum (*bherī-ghoṣa*) is now to be heard the reverberation of religious proclamations, *dharmaghoṣa* " [Rock Edict IV]. This is why so many states and peoples of India were left unconquered when they could be easily conquered by a sovereign of Asoka's paramount power and position : the Cholas, the Pāṇḍyas, the Satiyaputras, the Keralaputras [Rock Edict II], the Yavanas (Greeks), the Kambojas, the Nābhapantis of Nābhaka, the Bhojas and Pitinikas, the Andhras and Pulindas. All these are mentioned as lying outside his " conquered country " (*vijita*) or direct dominion [Rock Edict XIII]. He is anxious to ensure that " his sons and grandsons may not think it their duty to make any new conquests," and takes his firm stand upon the doctrine that " the chiefest conquest is that achieved by Dharma and not by brute force " (*ib.*). He evidently believed in the brotherhood of free peoples, but " they must turn from their evil ways that they may not be chastised " (Rock Edict XIII). He believed in the brotherhood in morality.

Thus forswearing, and forbidding by his sovereign injunctions, all wars in his empire, he extended the principle of Ahiṁsā or non-violence from the world of man to that of the lower dumb animals and birds. The full extension of the principle took place later in his reign, in about 242 B.C., when an ordinance or decree was issued, prohibiting the slaughter of numerous birds and beasts specified, besides " all four-footed animals which are neither utilised nor eaten," such as the cow, for example, which was never used as a pack-animal or for food in India. On certain specified days and on the Buddhist fast days were stopped the killing even of fish, the branding of horses and oxen, and "the castration of bulls, he-goats, rams, boars or other animals."

Connected with these measures may also be mentioned his humane arrangements for the relief of suffering of both man and beast, under which the state established botanical gardens for the cultivation of the medicinal plants, herbs, roots and fruits, procured, when necessary, even by importation and then acclimatised [Rock Edict II], besides maintaining hospitals or other arrangements for the supply of medicines and medical men for the treatment of diseases. Considering the emphasis laid upon the healing arrangements for beasts, we must infer that there was no lack in Asoka's time of veterinary surgeons and hospitals.

The same humanitarian instinct was in operation on a larger scale and in a wider sphere. Says the emperor in his Pillar Edict VII :

" On the roads, too, banyan trees have been planted by me to give shade to man and beast ; mango-gardens have been planted and wells dug at every half-kos ; rest-houses, too, have been erected ; and numerous watering-places were made here and there for the comfort of man and beast."

These comprehensive measures for the comforts of outdoor life were called for as much by the heat of Indian summer as by the fact that the Indians, the classes and the masses alike, the old as well as the young, are very much given to travelling, as much in the interests of business or trade as for religion which inculcates the duty of visiting on pilgrimage the holy places of India, covering by their number and geographical distribution the entire area of this vast country.

We have thus seen what unheard-of and unexpected effects were produced by his triumph in the Kalinga war upon a nature like Asoka's : that single conquest crushed out of him the lust for further conquests which makes empires to this day. The event bore a different message to him : " Thus far shalt thou go and no farther ! " He now differently understood the mission of an emperor, which should be to establish an empire on the basis of Universal Peace, an empire resting on Right rather than Might. The war put an end to his political career properly so called. Henceforth he pursues religious ends, which explains the further events of his reign.

Before the Kalinga war, in about 265 B.C., he became a Buddhist, as we have already seen, beginning as an *upāsaka*. He remains such from 265-262 B.C., when his belief in the new faith becomes stronger as a consequence of his remorse, which came naturally to him as a Buddhist for the cruelties caused by the Kalinga war, and leads him on to a more intimate relationship with the Saṁgha. This, however, should not signify that he became a full-fledged Bhikkhu, as most historians have assumed. If that were so, the fact would have been more directly stated than by the indirect expression—*saṁgham upagate*, which refers to a condition intermediate between the *upāsaka* on the one hand and the fully-ordained Bhikkhu on the other, i.e., the Bhikkhu passing through the two stages of ordination known as *Pabbajjā* and *Upasampadā*. Asoka did not qualify even for the first stage of the monkhood by not going out of home into homelessness (*pravrajyā*). He did not renounce the world or his throne, but remained to rule, though in a spirit of being in the world and yet not of it. But that could not get over the technical requirements of the law on the subject. What, then, should be the meaning of the expression—" approaching the Saṁgha " ? The meaning is perhaps explained by a passage in the *Vinaya* [iii. 7, 8, *SBE*.] which refers to the condition of a *Bhikkhugatika* as the intermediate one between an Upāsaka and the Bhikkhu. Buddhaghosa explains *Bhikkhugatika* to mean " a person that dwells in the same Vihāra with the Bhikkhus " without being a fully-ordained Bhikkhu, though he is on the way towards the full Bhikkhuhood.[1] A careful analysis of the tradition on the

[1] I owe this suggestion to Mr. Charan Das Chatterji. I-tsing [Takakusu, tr. pp. 105 and 155 n.] refers to people residing in a monastery without being monks, " those upāsakas who come to the abode of a Bhikṣu chiefly in order to learn the Sacred Books and intending to shave their hair and wear a black robe " [*ib*. p. 155 n.]. I-tsing [*ib*. p. 73] also refers to an image of Asoka dressed in the robes of a monk, and this shows that he might have chosen to don the robes of a monk during his temporary visits to the Saṁgha. But

subject will, however, show that the expression "*saṁghaṁ upagate*" points to the stage when Asoka publicly declared himself to be a follower of the Saṁgha in the fourth year of his reign, and entered upon a career of direct service to the Saṁgha. In his previous stage, he had been only privately cultivating the company and receiving the instruction of an individual Buddhist teacher.[1]

On coming into a closer connection with the Saṁgha, Asoka devoted himself strenuously to the new faith, and initiated several lines of activity on its behalf, the supreme objective of his endeavours being the moral uplift of the community. A year's strenuous exertion produced satisfactory results. As stated in M.R.E. I, the gods were popularised, so that the people in Jambudvīpa who knew nothing of them, i.e., the wild tribes, now became associated with them (taking the word *misā* [2] to be Sanskrit *misra*, to be mixed up with), and adopted them as objects of their worship.[3] A further appeal to the religious instincts of the people was made by the emperor's organisation of shows and

the supposed representations of Asoka in the Sanchi sculptures show him dressed like a king and surrounded with all the paraphernalia of a king [see below].

[1] This point is fully explained in the annotations of the Edict.

[2] The word may also stand for Sanskrit *mṛiṣā*, false, in which case the sense of the passage will be that the popular faith of the times was purified by Asoka's propagandist work aiming at the replacement of the false gods (probably Brahminical gods) by the true ones (the Buddhist gods). Or, without committing Asoka to such a sweeping condemnation of Brahminism which is flagrantly inconsistent with his repeated inculcation of respect for Brahmins in the Edicts, we may as well interpret the false gods of the people in the Baconian sense of *idolas*, so that Asoka's reform would mean a reform in the ideals of the people in respect of such vital subjects as True Conquest, True Charity, True Ceremonial and the like, as explained in the Edicts. The word *misibhūtā* occurring in Maski Edict supports the rendering of *misa* by *misra*, though the correct Prākrit form for *misra* should be *misso*, on which see Childers. Generally, we must reject the interpretation which represents Asoka as a Buddhist iconoclast, as contrary to the lofty spirit of toleration the Edicts breathe.

[3] This is the interpretation of Thomas in *Cambridge History*. But see *note* on it under the inscription.

processions exhibiting images of the gods in their celestial cars, which were accompanied by elephants, bonfires or illuminations and other heavenly sights [Rock Edict IV]. Thus for military pageants and secular shows were substituted more edifying spectacles representing things divine. The images of the gods carried in procession need not refer to Brahminical gods only. They might be of Buddhist gods as well. The institution of Buddhist processions continued at Pāṭaliputra down to Fa-hien's time (fourth century A.D.). It is thus described by the Chinese pilgrim :

" Every year, on the eighth day of the second month, they celebrate a procession of images. They make a four-wheeled car and on it erect a structure of five stories by means of bamboos tied together. . . . They make figures of *devas* with gold, silver and lapis lazuli grandly blended. . . . On the four sides are niches, with a Buddha seated in each, and a Bodhisattva standing in attendance on him. There may be twenty cars, all grand and imposing, but each one different from the others " [Legge's tr., p. 79].

Thus Asoka seems to have been the originator of this institution, but it is extremely doubtful if he had included figures of the Buddha and Bodhisattvas in the processions, considering that in his time Buddhism was yet to develop image-worship or an elaborate pantheon, the gift of the much later form of Buddhism known as Mahāyāna. The procession of the images of gods points to the progress achieved in iconography in Asoka's time. We know from the famous Maurya passage in Patañjali's *Mahābhāṣya* [commenting on Pāṇini's Sūtra, v. iii. 99] how the Mauryan emperors traded upon the popular superstitions of the times by manufacturing portable images of the gods (*archāḥ prakalpitāḥ Mauryaiḥ hiranyārthiviḥ*) and selling them to profit. But perhaps we may exonerate Asoka from this popular charge of greed of gold, considering that he made use of the images not for his own material advantage, but for the spiritual advantage of his people by bringing their gods before their eyes.

A second line of his activities in connection with the spiritual uplift of his people has been already referred to, viz., the issue of his Edicts in a permanent and popular form, whereby the emperor's lofty ideals of thought and conduct were constantly kept before the eyes of the people, so that they might become a national possession. In reviewing his own actions in this regard, he himself states [Pillar Edict VII] : " This thought came to me : In the past the kings had this wish—How may the people grow with a proper growth in piety ? The people, however, did not have that growth. Whereby then can the people be made to grow in piety ? Whereby can I elevate any of them by a growth in piety ? . . . This thought came to me : 'I will publish precepts of piety, will inculcate instructions in piety : hearing these, the people will conform, will be elevated, and will grow strongly with the growth of piety.' For this purpose precepts of piety were published, manifold instructions in piety were enjoined. . . . "

But the emperor was not content with merely sending out these mute messages to his people. He thought of personally moving among them, preaching to them, and holding religious conferences and discussions with them. Such movements through the country among his people he calls " pious tours," which was Asoka's own innovation. For his predecessors knew only of pleasure trips and other objectionable amusements like hunting [Rock Edict VIII]. The first " pious tour " of Asoka, however, " whence arose the institution " (*tenātra dharmayātrā*), took place earlier than the issue of his Edicts, in the tenth year of his coronation (i.e., 260 B.C.), when he " went to Sambodhi " (*ayāya Sambodhim*). This might mean that he went to Bodh Gayā,[1] the place of the Buddha's *sambodhi* or enlightenment, on pilgrimage. We may recall that Asoka undertook this pilgrimage as a result of his increased devotion to Buddhism following the Kalinga war of 262 B.C., when he ceased to be an *upāsaka* and became a *Bhikkhugatika*, as already explained. The fact of his visit to Bodh Gayā and of his devotion to the Bodhi tree is also corroborated by a sculpture on the eastern gate at Sānchī, which, as interpreted by Foucher, represents the emperor's visit to the sacred tree.

Thus Asoka went on his first " pious tour " or pilgrimage

[1] Suggested by Dr. D. R. Bhandarkar [*IA*, 1913, p. 159].

after "the increase of his faith in Buddhism" in 260 B.C. It was followed by many other pilgrimages, on which both legends and inscriptions throw some light. According to northern tradition confirmed by Yuan Chwang, Asoka's preceptor in Buddhism was Upagupta of Mathurā, the son of the perfumer Gupta of Benares, who took his imperial pupil, escorted by a mighty army, on an extensive pilgrimage to the principal holy places of Buddhism, viz., Lumbini Garden where the Venerable One was born, Kapilavastu where He renounced the world, Bodhi-tree at Gayā where He attained enlightenment, Isipatana (Sarnath) where He first preached, Kuśinagara where He died, Śrāvastī where He mostly lived and taught, and where were the stūpas of some of His chief disciples like Sāriputta, Maudgalāyana and Ānanda. At each of these places, true to his own words in his Rock Edict VIII, the emperor gave largesses of gold and built also a *chaitya*. The birthplace of the Buddha is identified with Rummindei, four miles inside the Nepal frontier, by the discovery of an Asokan pillar bearing an inscription which states that it was set up to commemorate the Buddha's birthplace. The inscription indicates that it was drafted and incised by the local authorities in commemoration of the emperor's visit and gifts to the place, and not directly by the emperor, like most other Edicts.

Thus both legends and inscriptions confirm one another as regards Asoka's pilgrimage to two places, Bodh Gayā and Lumbini.

An additional place not included in the traditional list of pilgrimages is mentioned by another inscription discovered on a pillar at Nigliva, also in the Nepalese Tarai, which runs in the following words:

"By His Sacred and Gracious Majesty the King, consecrated 14 years, was enlarged to double its original size the stūpa of Buddha Koṇākamana; and by him, consecrated (twenty years), coming in person, and reverence being made, was set up (a stone pillar)."

Thus from these pillar inscriptions we gather that Asoka started on an extensive pilgrimage in 250 B.C. Considering the locations of Asokan pillars at Lauriya-Ararāj, Lauriya-

Nandangarh, Rampurwā, Rummindei and Nigliva, we are tempted to infer that they only mark the stages in the pilgrim's progress along the royal road from his capital, Pāṭaliputra, to Nepal.

These " pious tours " through the country, which Asoka first inaugurated, he did not confine to himself. He imposed them upon his higher officials—the great ministers (*mahāmātras*) and city magistrates (*nagaravyāvahārakas*) as well —as part of their official duties. This was done by about 258 B.C., the date of Rock Edict III, and is adumbrated in the two separate Edicts at Dhauli and Jaugada in Kalinga which first refer to the king's intentions in this regard. Rock Edict III states :

" When I had been consecrated twelve years this com mand was issued by me : Everywhere in my dominions, my officers, the Yuktas, Rājūkas (provincial governors ' set over many hundreds of thousands of people,' as defined in Pillar Edict IV), and Prādeśikas (district officers)—must go out on tours (*anusaṁyāna*) by turns, every five years, as well for their other business as for this special purpose, the inculcation of Dharma."

This imperial decree served upon his officers is foreshadowed in the first Kalinga Edict, which is, therefore, slightly prior in time to Rock Edict III definitely embodying the decree, and thus prior to the entire series of fourteen Rock Edicts. The passage presaging the decree runs thus :

" And for this purpose, in accordance with the Dharma, I shall send out in rotation every five years officers known for their freedom from harshness, violence of temper, and for sweetness in action (*slākṣṇārambha*, which may also mean ' considerate towards animal life ')."

In the case of some of the remoter provinces, such as those governed from Ujjain and Taxila under the Princes as Viceroys, the emperor wanted the periodical tours of the selected officers to be more frequent, once every three years. Perhaps the greater frequency of the tours was necessary in those provinces as being more populous than the newly-annexed province of Kalinga with its strong element of

" forest folks " in its population, and hence less civilised and more sparsely peopled [Rock Edict XIII].

Next year, when " he had been consecrated thirteen years," i.e., in 257 B.C., this scheme of religious tours by his officials was further expanded and systematised by the institution of a special body of officers charged with the duty of attending to the moral and spiritual welfare of all his subjects, officials and non-officials, Buddhists and non-Buddhists, and even the royal relations at Pāṭaliputra and provincial towns (*vāhyeṣu cha nagareṣu*). These officers called by the new and very appropriate title of the *Dharma-Mahāmātras* constituted a separate department of government service which did not exist before (*na bhūtapurvāḥ*) and was entirely Asoka's innovation. The activities of this department extended over a wide field, even beyond the limits of his direct jurisdiction or administration,[1] " to the Yavanas, Kambojas and Gandhāras, and other nations on the western frontier," and also to the " Rāṣṭrikas, Pitinikas " [Rock Edict V], with Nābhapantis, Bhojas, Andhras and Pulindas in other parts of India [Rock Edict XIII], and, as such, the department must have been adequately manned with an army of officers. The department had also to send out some officers as *Dūtas*, envoys or ambassadors, carrying Asoka's religious message to foreign countries both in the north and the south—to the neighbouring and distant states of Antiochos Theos of Syria, and of the four kings, Ptolemy Philadelphos of Egypt, Antigonos Gonatas of Macedonia, Magas of Cyrene, Alexander of Epirus ; and lower down (*nīcha*), in the south, to the Cholas and Pāṇḍyas as far as Tāmraparṇī or Ceylon. In a word, the imperial officers worked both " in the dominions of His Majesty the Emperor as well as among his frontagers (pratyanteṣu)," as neatly and briefly put in Rock Edict II.

As regards their functions, they are indicated in the Rock Edicts II, V, and XIII. The organisation of measures for

[1] As Sir R. G. Bhandarkar first pointed out (in his *Early History of the Deccan*), the peoples that are mentioned by name in the Edicts are to be regarded as independent or semi-independent peoples. They would not have been named, had they been Asoka's subjects.

the relief of suffering of both man and beast, as mentioned in Rock Edict II, must have been the work of this department. They seem to have been responsible for the various works of public utility—hospitals, supply of medical men, medicines, drinking water and rest-houses for travellers, etc. —as indicated in Rock Edict II and detailed in Pillar Edict VII. The reason for this assumption is that in Rock Edict XIII is mentioned how the conquests of the Law have been won in countries outside his empire through the work of his *dūtas*, while the nature and details of the conquests are given in Rock Edict II. Their other functions are detailed in Rock Edict V. They are to be employed (*a*) among all sectaries to establish them in the new faith, (*b*) among those already religious (*dharma-yuktasya*) for increase of their piety (*dharma-vṛiddhi*) and for their welfare and happiness, (*c*) among servants and dependents, Brahmins, the rich and the destitute, and the old and infirm, for their welfare and happiness; and for a similar purpose among the peoples on his frontiers such as the Yavanas, Kambojas, Gandhāras and other nations in the north-west and Rāṣṭrikas and Pitinikas (in the interior); (*d*) to secure the pious people (*dharma-yukta*) from worry; (*e*) to avert (unjust) imprisonment or execution, or other molestation, and procure release or relief in justifiable cases;[1] (*f*) in the capital and in the provincial towns, in all the female establishments of the emperor's brothers, sisters, and other relatives.

[1] The Kalinga Edict I which is earlier than this Edict, as shown below, thus contemplates cases calling for interference in the administration of justice: "Again, it happens that some individual incurs imprisonment or torture, and when the result is his imprisonment without due cause, many other people are deeply grieved. In such a case you (the Prefects of the town) must desire to do justice. . . . For this purpose has this scripture been here inscribed in order that the administrators of the town may strive without ceasing that the restraint or torture of the townsmen (*paribodha* and *parikleśa*) may not take place without due cause." The same Edict also announces the remedial measures which Asoka contemplates for miscarriage of justice: "And for this purpose, in accordance with the Moral Law, I shall send forth in rotation every five years such persons as are not harsh, not violent, but are of sweet behaviour." Those measures first adumbrated here are given effect to in Rock Edict V.

" Thus these *Dharma-mahāmātras* are employed everywhere in his dominions among the pious, whether zealous for Dharma (*dharma-niśrita*), or established in Dharma *dharmādhiṣṭhita*) or duly devoted to charity (*dānasaṁyukta*)."

The supervision of the female establishments of the members of the royal family in the metropolis and the mufussil towns, as mentioned under (*f*), was later on entrusted to a separate body of officials called the *Strī-adhyaksa-mahāmātras*, as stated in Rock Edict XII.

Pillar Edict VII gives further information on the functions of the *Dharma-Mahāmātras* as indicated in the other Edicts :

" Dignitaries of piety were appointed by me in charge of manifold indulgences (*anugrahikeṣu*), these both for ascetics and for householders ; also over all sects were they appointed —over the Saṅgha, Brahmans, Ājīvikas and Nirgranthas."

" These and various other classes were appointed in charge of the distribution of charity (*dānavisarge*), both my own and that of the queens. And in my whole harem they carry out in manifold fashions such and such measures of satisfaction, both here and in all quarters. The same has been done as regards the distribution of charity on the part of my sons and the other princes (sons of the *devis* or queens)." [F. W. Thomas in the *Cambridge History*.]

There is a short edict following the Sarnath Pillar Edict, which indicates how the charities of the royal family took the form of " a mango-garden or pleasure-grove or almshouse."

To sum up : these *Dharma-mahāmātras* were appointed to spread the dharma, mitigate the wrongs or rigours of justice, administer the charities of the king and the royal family, supervise the morals of their harems, and superintend the affairs conducted by the committees or councils (*pariṣad*) governing different sects, Buddhist, Jain, Ājīvika and others.

Thus the promotion of the moral welfare of his peoples was considered by Asoka as one of the first cares of the state, and a special department of administration was created for the purpose. He is also one of the very few monarchs in history who thought of extending this work of moral propagandism to the peoples of foreign countries. Rock Edict XIII makes express mention of the many independent, and quasi-independent, states, both on the borders of the empire, and beyond, in which the missionaries deputed by him achieved success in their work. The date of the Edict being about 258 B.C., Asoka's missionary activity in the foreign countries mentioned in that Edict must date from an earlier time, and more so because it is described in the Edict as having been already successful and borne fruit. One of the results achieved was the extension to these foreign countries of the emperor's arrangements for providing medical aid for men and animals as stated in Rock Edict II. Thus we must allow adequate time for the development of these results before 258 B.C. The earlier date of the mission is also pointed to by the reference in Rock Edict XIII to the five Hellenistic kings as being Asoka's contemporaries, but they could not all be counted as his contemporaries later than 258 B.C., the last date when they were jointly alive. Thus this date marks the latest chronological limit for Asoka's missions in foreign countries. That this work was in full swing and even extended in about 253 B.C. is evident from the *Mahāvaṁsa* which gives additional interesting information on the whole subject.

The *Mahāvaṁsa* (v. 280) relates that in the seventeenth year of Asoka's coronation was held at Pāṭaliputra, under the presidency of the monk Moggaliputta Tissa (in the northern texts, Upagupta), the third Buddhist Council, and when he brought the Council to an end, " he sent forth *theras*, one here and one there," whose names are thus given, together with the countries they were sent to [*Ib.* xii. 1-8] :

Missionary	*Country*
1. Majjhantika	Kashmir and Gandhāra [1]
2. Mahārakṣita	Yavana [2] or Greek Country

[1] Mentioned in R.E. V.

[2] Mentioned with the Kambojas in R.E. V and XIII. It is interesting to note that the Græco-Bactrian kingdom was founded about this time, in 246 B.C., by Diodotus.

Missionary	Country
3. Majjhima	Himalaya [1] Country
4. Dharmarakṣita (a Yavana)	Aparāntaka [2]
5. Mahādharmarakṣita	Mahārāṣṭra [3]
6. Mahādeva	Mahiṣamaṇḍala [4] (Mysore or Māndhātā)
7. Rakṣita	Vanavāsi [5] (North Kanara)
8. Soṇa and Uttara	Suvarṇabhūmi [6] (Pegu and Moulmein)
9. Mahendra with Riṣṭriya, Utriya, Sambala and Bhadrasāra	Laṅkā (Ceylon)

This list is also repeated in the *Samantapāsādikā*, which, however, adds some interesting details. It appears that Majjhima went to Himavantapradeśa, then divided into five districts or rāṣṭras, not alone, but with four other associates, viz., Kassapagotta, Alakadeva, Dundubhissara and Mahādeva (but the *Dīpavaṁsa* names Kāsapagota Kotiputa as the chief, and Majjhima, Duḍubhisara, Sahadeva, and Mūlakadeva as his assistants), and the evangelisers adopted as the text of their discourses the Dhammachakkappavattana Suttanta, and converted eight million souls. Similarly,

[1] The Nābhapaṁtis of Nābhaka, mentioned along with the Yonas in Rock Edict XIII, might perhaps be a Himalayan people. See note under the Edict.

[2] The Pitinikas are described as an Aparānta people in R.E. V. Literally, *Aparānta* means "the other or western ends."

[3] The Andhras and Pulindas (located about the Vindhyas in the *Aitareya Brāhmaṇa*), as well as the Rāṣṭrikas, may be taken to be peoples of Mahārāṣṭra (R.E. V and XIII).

[4] The Satiyaputras (R.E. II) would belong to this part. According to Rice [*JRAS*, 1916, p. 839] Mahiṣa-maṇḍala was South Mysore.

[5] The Edicts mention more definitely the South Indian peoples among whom the imperial missionaries worked, viz., the Cholas, Pāṇḍyas, Keralaputras.

[6] According to Fleet [*JRAS*, 1910, p. 428], this should be the region in Bengal called Karṇasuvarṇa by Yuan Chwang, or the country along the Son river known as Hiraṇyavāha, "the gold-bearer."

Yonaka Dhammarakkhita discoursed on Aggikkhandopamā Sutta,[1] converting 37,000 in Aparānta, Majjhantika on Āsīvisūpamāsutta,[2] converting 80,000 in Kashmir and Gandhāra; Mahādeva on Devadūtasuttanta[3] in Mahiṁsakamaṇḍala, converting 40,000; Rakkhita on Mahānāradakassapajātaka,[4] converting 84,000 in Vanavāsi; Mahārakkhita on Kālakārāmasuttanta[5] in Yonaraṭṭham; and Soṇa and Uttara on Brahmajālasuttanta,[6] converting 60,000 in Suvaṇṇabhūmi.

These lists show that, apart from the legends being in general agreement with the inscriptions as regards the countries that came within the purview of Asoka's missions,[7] there was an important extension of the operations of these missions to some new regions not mentioned in the inscriptions, as a result of the enthusiasm for the faith roused by the nine months' session of the third Buddhist Council. As regards the names of the individual missionaries, the truth of the legends has been unexpectedly confirmed in some inscriptions found on the Stūpas of Sanchi of the second or first century B.C. In Stūpa No. 2 at Sanchi was found a relic-box of white sandstone, on the side of which runs the following inscription in early Brāhmī characters: "(the relics) of all teachers beginning with the Arhat (?) Kāsapagota and the Arhat (?) Vāchhi Suvijayata"; while inside

[1] I.e., "The Discourse on the Parable of the Flames of Fire," found in *Aṅguttara,* IV. pp. 128-135.

[2] "The Simile of the Serpent," in *Aṅg.* II. pp. 110-111.

[3] I.e., "Discourse on the Messengers of God," which treats of Old Age, Disease, and Death as messengers of Yama, the god of death. It is found in *Majjhima,* III. pp. 178-187, and *Aṅg.* I. pp. 138-142.

[4] Fausboll, *Jāt.* vi. pp. 219-255.

[5] Geiger [*Mahāv.* tr. p. 85] takes it to "be the Suttanta 24 of the Chatukkanipāta in *Aṅg.* II. pp. 24-26," and the Kālakārāma as the place where the Buddha is supposed to have delivered this discourse.

[6] I.e., "The Net of the Religious" in *Dīgha,* I. p. 1 ff.

[7] It must be noted that the credit of these foreign missions, which belongs to the king according to the Edicts [R.E. XIII, expressly mentioning his despatch of *dūtas* to foreign countries, and R.E. II mentioning the work of these foreign missions as regards supply of medical aid], is appropriated by the clergy in the *Mahāvaṁsa.*

the relic-box were found four caskets of steatite containing fragments of human bone, the relics of the following teachers named in inscriptions on the lids of those caskets, viz.,

1. Kāsapagota, " the teacher of all the Hemavatas."
2. Majjhima.
3. Hāritīputa.
4. Vachhi Suvijayata (Vātsi-Suvijayat ?).
5. Mahavanāya.
6. Āpagīva.
7. Kodiṇiputa (Kauṇḍinīputra).
8. Kosikiputa.
9. Gotiputa (Gauptīputra).
10. Mogaliputa (Maudgalīputra).

Of these teachers, Nos. 1 and 2 were the missionaries for the Himalayan region, while the rest were the teachers who took part in the third Buddhist Council under Asoka under No. 10, i.e., Mogaliputa (Moggaliputta Tissa), as President. No. 2, Majjhima, is also mentioned in the superscription of a relic-casket found in Stūpa No. 2 at Sonāri, and No. 1 in another from the same stūpa under the name Kotiputta, while in a third urn-inscription, No. 9, Gotiputta, is mentioned along with Dadabhisāra. Thus the inscriptions corroborate the names of the following missionaries of the legends, viz., Kāsapagota, Majjhima, and Dundubhissara.[1]

While the Edicts are silent about Mahendra's mission to Ceylon, the legends are full of details describing the event. The first intercourse of Ceylon with Asoka's empire was due to the initiative of King Devānampiya Tissa of Ceylon, who sent a mission which reached Tāmralipti by a week's voyage and Pāṭaliputra from there in another week's time. Then followed Asoka's mission to Ceylon under his son Mahendra and his grandson Sumana (son of his daughter Saṅghamitrā). A second mission then came from Ceylon to Asoka, asking for the services of his daughter Saṅghamitrā and for a branch

[1] See Sir John Marshall's *Guide to Sanchi*, ch. x. The reference from the *Samantapāsādikā* I owe to Mr. C. D. Chatterji.

of the sacred Bo-tree, which was duly despatched to Tāmralipti harbour under the escort of an army led by the emperor in person. The Tree was then embarked in a vessel and carried to Ceylon. This event, according to the legends, took place in the eighteenth year of Asoka's reign, i.e., in 252 B.C. A yet third mission, under his grandson, Sumana, came to Asoka from Ceylon for the purpose of taking some relics which were enshrined in a stūpa in the island.

The truth of this legend about Asoka's mission to Ceylon seems to be confirmed by a piece of archaeological evidence. A fresco on a wall in one of the caves at Ajanta is supposed to depict the event. So far as the Edicts are concerned, Ceylon is mentioned as Tāmraparṇī in R.E. II and XIII, and as the country already included by Asoka in the list of countries to which he despatched his *Dūtas* or Messengers to prosecute his scheme of *Dharma-Vijaya* or Moral Conquest. Thus by the time of these Edicts (258-257 B.C.), Ceylon was already a sphere of Asoka's missionary activities which, according to R.E. II, included welfare work and positive social service such as measures for the relief of suffering of beast and man. As the date of Mahendra's work in Ceylon was much later (252 B.C.), a reference to it was not possible in Asoka's Edicts, which, however, tell of his relations with Ceylon that must have prepared the ground for Mahendra's work.

Considering the frequency of intercourse between Ceylon and Magadha, we may reasonably infer that the means of such intercourse were found in the development of an Indian shipping. Vincent Smith holds the same view: "When we remember Asoka's relations with Ceylon and even more distant powers, we may credit him with a sea-going fleet" [*The Edicts of Asoka*, p. viii].

The last datable event of Asoka's reign was the publication of his seven Pillar Edicts in the twenty-seventh [P.E. I, IV, V and VI] and twenty-eighth year [P.E. VII] of his reign, i.e., 243-242 B.C. The length of his reign being thirty-six to thirty-seven years, according to the concurrent testimony of the Brahman and Buddhist historians, it must

PLATE III.

Lumbini Pillar.

have closed about 232 B.C.[1] The chronological scheme of his reign thus works itself out as follows :

274 B.C.—Accession.

270 B.C.—Coronation.

265 B.C.—Conversion to Buddhism as a lay disciple or upāsaka.

265-262 B.C.—Two and a half years of indifferent devotion to Buddhism.

262 B.C.—Conquest of Kalinga, followed by his closer connection with the Saṁgha and strenuous exertion for his progress in his new faith.

260 B.C.—Issue of Minor Rock Edict I, and first " pious tour," probably to Bodh Gayā (R.E. VIII) ; addressing the Bhabru Edict to his Church ; popularising the gods (Minor R.E. I, as interpreted by some scholars).

259 B.C.—Issue of the two Kalinga (separate) Edicts.

258-57 B.C.—Issue of the fourteen Rock Edicts in one corpus ; grant of cave-dwellings in the Barabar Hills to the Ājīvikas.

257 B.C.—Institution of the officers called Dharma-Mahāmātras [R.E. V].

256 B.C.—Double enlargement of the Stūpa of Buddha Koṇākamana.

250 B.C.—Pilgrimage to Lumbini Garden, the birthplace of the Buddha ; visit to the Stūpa of Buddha Koṇākamana, and erection of commemorative pillars at both places.

243-2 B.C.—Issue of Pillar Edicts.

232 B.C.—Death of Asoka.

[1] The *Divyāvadānā* (p. 430) gives an account of Asoka's last days. In his old age Asoka nominated as his successor his grandson, Samprati, the son of Kuṇāla ; but this prince, under the influence of the high officials who had usurped all power, stopped the benefactions to the Buddhist Church of Asoka who had been now a nominal sovereign, and even reduced the services and allowances for the king until at last he sent him half an āmalaka fruit on an earthern plate. On receiving this, Asoka remarked in sadness to his courtiers that from the lordship of the entire Jambudvīpa he had now sunk to that of a half-fruit ! This tradition is also alluded to by Yuan Chwang [Watters, ii. 99]. It would thus appear that the last days of the great emperor were far from being happy with his disloyal officers and his hardly less disloyal grandson conspiring against him.

The fourteen Rock Edicts show that the following measures were passed before the date of the Edicts, and were therefore passed between 260-258 B.C.:

(1) Abolition of

(*a*) Sacrificial slaughter of animals in the capital.

(*b*) *Samājas* (merry-making of a kind, accompanied by animal fights, feasting with consumption of meat, etc.).

(*c*) Slaughter of animals for the royal table, except two peacocks and one antelope (more rarely used for food) [R.E. I].

(*d*) "Tours of pleasure" accompanied by "hunting and other similar amusements" [R.E. VIII].

(*e*) War [R.E. IV] [1] and conquest [R.E. XIII].

(2) Provision of public works of utility, viz.:

(*a*) Hospitals for man and beast.

(*b*) Botanical gardens for the culture of medicinal plants, indigenous and foreign (obtained by import)—including "herbs, roots and fruits."

(*c*) Wells and trees on the roads for the comforts of travellers and animals [R.E. II].

(3) Supply of medical aid and facilities for both man and beast in foreign countries (those of Antiochos and even of his neighbours) and in countries on the borders [R.E. II]; which implies

(4) Organisation of missionary work in foreign countries, which were objects not of his political or military but religious conquests (*dharma-vijaya*), achieved by his missionaries (*dūtas*) [R.E. XIII].

(5) Institution of Quinquennial Circuits of Officers for missionary, as well as administrative, work [R.E. III]; which afterwards leads to the

(6) Creation of a new and separate Department of Missionary Service under officers styled Dharma-Mahāmātras,

[1] In the declaration that the call to arms by sound of drum (*bherīghoṣa*) is replaced by a call to duty by its proclamations (*dharmaghoṣa*).

Ministers of Religion or Morals, for propagation of piety among his subjects (including royal relations, male and female), as also among foreign peoples [R.E. V].

(7) Institution of a new and separate set of officers called Strī-adhyakṣa-mahāmātras (ministers in charge of the superintendents of women) [R.E. XII], for the purpose of supervising female morals. This edict, engraved as it is on a separate boulder at Shahbazgarhi, must have been so engraved for its special applicability to the people of that locality whose attention was independently drawn to it.

(8) Institution of the king's own pious tours among his people, accompanied by royal gifts to ascetics, Brahmans, men disabled by age, and by holding religious conferences for preaching and discussing the Moral Law.

(9) Organisation of religious shows and processions replacing secular ones [R.E. IV].

From the Pillar Edicts (243-42 B.C.) we gather that the following further measures were taken before their dates:

(1) Regulations restricting slaughter and mutilation of animals and birds specified [P.E. V]. Cf. "On two-footed and four-footed beings, on birds and denizens of the waters, I have conferred various favours, even unto the boon of life" [P.E. II].

(2) Grant to Governors independent jurisdiction as regards Law and Justice [P.E. IV].

(3) The judicial reform granting reprieve of three days to convicts sentenced to death [P.E. IV].

(4) Institution of jail-deliveries on the anniversaries of the emperor's coronation [P.E. V].

(5) Completion of the full programme of public works which comprised:

(*a*) Planting of shade-giving banyan-trees and groves of mango-trees on the roads.

(*b*) Providing wells at every half-kos of the roads.

(*c*) Construction of rest-houses.

(*d*) Providing watering-places for use of man and beast [P.E. VII].

Regarding now the initial date of Asoka's accession or

coronation, we arrive at same by different ways. Firstly, he himself indicates a point of chronological contact between his own history and that of no less than five Western kings, mentioned as his contemporaries in R.E. XIII, whose dates are known beyond doubt. Thus we deduce the unknown from the known. All these kings, as we know from their history, continued to be Asoka's contemporaries down to the year 258 B.C., when one of them, viz., Magas of Cyrene, died, if not another, viz., Alexander of Epirus [*Cambridge History of India*, vol. i. p. 502]. Granting that the news about such distant kings might take about a year in those days to travel to Pāṭaliputra and reach the ears of Asoka, his reference to all these contemporaries as being jointly alive could not have been very much later than 257 B.C., considering that another Western contemporary of his deserved a mention about 250 B.C., when an independent Greek kingdom was founded by Diodotus in Bactria [*ib.*] Thus 257 B.C. may very well be taken as the year of Asoka's reference to his Western royal contemporaries in R.E. XIII, and, therefore, may be taken as the date of this Edict itself. Now R.E. III refers to a certain decree of the king (*ājñāpitam*) promulgated in the twelfth year of his coronation; R.E. IV refers to the matter of this Edict being inscribed (*lekhāpitam*) in the same twelfth year; while R.E. V refers to an important administrative measure of Asoka (the creation of Dharma-Mahāmātras) being introduced in the thirteenth year after his coronation. Lastly, in P.E. VI we have the definite statement of the king that his body of Dharma-lipis was inscribed (*dharma-lipi lekhāpitā*) in the twelfth year of his coronation. On the basis of all these references, it is reasonable to infer that all his Rock Edicts (along with the measures referred to therein) must have been issued during the twelfth and thirteenth year of his coronation, and that they could not have been issued earlier than the dates of the incidents they record. Thus if 257 B.C. was the date of R.E. XIII, it was, at the latest, the thirteenth year of Asoka's coronation which thus took place in 270 B.C. Accepting now the truth of the tradition recorded in *Mahāvaṁsa*, v. 22, that there was an interval of four years between his accession and coronation, we obtain 274 B.C. as the date of his accession. It is again to be noted that we arrive at the same date for Asoka's accession through a very different source. The Purāṇas assign a reign of twenty-four years to his grandfather, Chandragupta Maurya, i.e., a reign up to 299 B.C. from 323 B.C., the probable date of his achievement of sovereignty, and to his father Bindusāra, a reign of twenty-five years, i.e., up to 274 B.C., the date we obtain from the other sources for Asoka's accession to the throne. The date 274 B.C. for Asoka's accession is again confirmed by a curious piece of evidence furnished by a passage in the *Mahāvaṁsa* [v. 45], which states that Nigrodha, then only seven years old, converted Asoka to Buddhism in the seventh year of his reign, and was also born in the year when his father, Prince Sumana, was killed and Asoka ascended the throne. When different lines of inquiry lead to the same conclusion, all the assumptions and hypotheses taken for granted in the course of the inquiry stand confirmed.

Quite recently, however, a radically different view is taken[1] about these dates of Asoka, and about the inner chronology of his Edicts. It has been argued that the Pillar Edicts are prior to the Rock Edicts, because P.E. VII, issued in the twenty-seventh year of his reign as a résumé of the various measures undertaken by him on behalf of his Dharma, is silent about the most important of such measures recorded in R.E. II, V, and XIII, viz., the welfare work and moral propagandism organised by Asoka in the foreign countries under the Greek rulers. Arguments from silence are always unreliable, and in the present case seem to be specially so. What is stated about the scope or intention of P.E. VII is not stated in the Edict itself, but is a mere assumption. It is inferred from the contents of the Edict. The contents would rather lead one to infer that the Edict was meant to be a résumé of the various domestic measures introduced by Asoka for the moral uplift of his *own* people, and not of what he had done for foreign peoples. All these, which are also mentioned in the R.E., are mentioned in this

[1] By Harit Krishna Deb, M.A., in his paper on *Asoka's Dhammalipis* and by Dr. D. R. Bhandarkar in his *Asoka*.

Edict with a degree of elaboration and generalisation that is almost a sure indication that it was issued later than the R.E. The chief officers mentioned in the R.E., viz., the Rājūkas and the Dharma-Mahāmātras, are also mentioned in P.E. VII; the functions of these newly-created Dharma-Mahāmātras, which are fully described in R.E. V, are summarised in P.E. VII; the information about the public works of utility consisting of "wells and trees planted along the roads for the needs of both man and beast," as given in R.E. II, is elaborated and supplemented in P.E. VII in a manner that undoubtedly points to the latter being later than the former; lastly, as instances of generalisation and reference in the P.E. VII to the R.E., may be mentioned the statement that for the spread of the Dharma, Asoka has had religious messages (*dhaṁma-sāvanāni*) proclaimed (*sāvāpitāni*) and religious injunctions (*dhaṁmānusathini vividhāni*) ordained (*ānapitāni*), along with his Pillars of Piety (*dhaṁmathaṁbhāni*) and the special officers to preach and expound (*paliyovadisaṁti pavithalisaṁti*) the Dharma. There is also the other generalised statement in the same Edict that the growth in Dharma of the people may be accomplished in two ways, by *Dhaṁma-niyama*, by regulation, and by *Nijhati*, reflection. Thus the contents of P.E. VII, viewed as a whole, show without doubt that it is meant to sum up Asoka's moral measures for his people, and, as such, it was the last of his Edicts. Above all, arguments from the inclusion or omission of certain matters in the two classes of Edicts cannot be conclusive. Does not Asoka himself warn us on the point—"*Nacha sarvaṁ sarvatra ghaṭitam*," "nor is all *suitable* in all places"?

It is also possible to find in the other Pillar Edicts indications of the priority to them of the Rock Edicts. They refer to the term *Puruṣa* as a general name, not used in the Rock Edicts, for all government servants of high, low, or middle rank [P.E. I, IV, and VII]. Though the *Antas* are referred to in the M.R.E. I and Rock Edicts II and XIII, the officers created to work among them, and called *Anta-Mahāmātras*, are first mentioned in P.E. I. Again, P.E. IV gives to the *Rājūkas* more powers than are mentioned under

R.E. III, and also some of the powers in regard to Law and Justice which are given to the Dharma-Mahāmātras in R.E. V. Further, while the Rock Edicts in a general way insist on non-violence towards living beings [R.E. I, III, IV, IX, and XI], it is left to one of the Pillar Edicts [P.E. V] to specify those to be specially protected.

The Rock Edicts also give indications of a chronological order among themselves. The Minor Rock Edicts are taken to be prior to the Rock Edicts, as both in the Rupnath and Sahasram versions, there is a reference to the king's order that the Edicts should be incised on rock and pillar, thus presaging both the Rock and Pillar Edicts. Next comes the Bhabru Edict, which is addressed to the Saṁgha directly and not through its Mahāmātras, who are put in charge of the Saṁgha under R.E. V, and mentioned as such in M.P.E. at Sanchi and Sarnath. Then come the two special Kalinga Rock Edicts with their anticipation of the appointment, for checking abuses of justice, of special officers who are afterwards called Dharma-Mahāmātras in R.E. V, and are also indicated in R.E. III. Thus among the Rock Edicts themselves, as has been shown above, R.E. III is prior to R.E. V. Thus the Rock Edicts must have been issued between 258 and 257 B.C. in two stages or chronological orders. Again, R.E. XII seems to be later than R.E. V; while the latter assigns the supervision of women to the Dharma-Mahāmātras, the former mentions a special class of officers for the work, viz., the Strī-adhyakṣa-mahāmātras.[1]

[1] Quite recently, a novel view of the chronology of the Edicts has been propounded in his *Asoka Edicts in New Light* by Dr. B. M. Barua, who considers (*a*) the Rock Edicts to be earlier than the Pillar Edicts, (*b*) the Kalinga Rock Edicts later than the Pillar Edicts, and (*c*) the Minor Rock Edicts as the latest. This view has been dealt with in the annotations of the Edicts.

APPENDIX A.

ON ASOKAN CHRONOLOGY FROM THE LEGENDS

THE chronology of Asoka's life and reign as presented in his inscriptions may be usefully compared with that revealed in tradition, both southern and northern, as preserved in texts like the *Mahāvaṁsa* and the *Divyāvadāna*. The two systems of chronology, though derived from different sources, will be seen to present many points of contact or agreement. Starting from the established chronological point of 270 B.C. as the date of Asoka's anointment as emperor, we can work out the dates of the following events, arranged in their chronological order, in his life and history :

304 B.C.—Birth of Asoka (inferred from the date of birth of his eldest son given below).

286 B.C.—Asoka sent out by his father, Bindusāra, from Pāṭaliputra, as his Viceroy, to Ujjayinī [*Mahāv.* xiii. 8-11] (at the age of eighteen).

286 B.C.—Asoka's marriage with Devī of Vedisa (Besnagar, Bhilsa) [*Ib.*].

284 B.C.—Birth of Asoka's eldest son, Mahendra [*Ib.* v. 204].

282 B.C.—Birth of Asoka's eldest daughter, Saṅghamitrā [*Ib.*].

274 B.C.

(1) War of Succession.

(2) Death of the Crown Prince Sumana.

(3) Asoka's accession to the throne.

(4) Birth of Prince Sumana's posthumous son, Nigrodha [*Ib.* 40-50].

270 B.C.—Asoka's Coronation [*Ib.* 22].

270-266 B.C.—Asoka's younger brother, Tissa, as his Vice-regent (*uparāja*) [*Ib.* 33].

270–240 B.C.—Asandhimitrā as Asoka's *agramahiṣī*, Chief Queen [*Ib.* 85 ; xx. 2].

268 B.C.—Saṅghamitrā married to Agnibrahmā.

267 B.C.—Birth of Asoka's grandson Sumana, son of Saṅghamitrā [*Ib.* v. 170].

266 B.C.

(1) Conversion of Asoka to Buddhism by Nigrodha, then only seven years old [*Ib.* v. 45].

This date is important (*a*) as demonstrating that the years mentioned in the *Mahāvaṁsa* are to be counted from Asoka's coronation (as done by V. A. Smith), and not from his accession (as taken in the *Cambridge History*, p. 503) ; (*b*) as furnishing another proof of the date of Asoka's accession being correct ; and (*c*) as confirming the date derivable from M.R.E. I. of Asoka bceoming a Buddhist *upāsaka*.

(2) Asoka converts his brother, Tissa, his Vice-regent, to Buddhism [*Ib.* 160].

(3) Tissa ordained by Mahādhammarakkhita [*Ib.* 168].

(4) Agnibrahmā, nephew and son-in-law of Asoka, ordained [*Ib.* 170].

(5) Appointment of Prince Mahendra as Vice-regent in place of Tiṣsa [*Ib.* 202] (at the age of eighteen).

266–263 B.C.—Building of vihāras and chaityas by Asoka [*Ib.* 173 ; *Div.* xxvii].

264 B.C.

(1) Ordination of Mahendra by the thera Mahādeva, with Majjhantika as president of the chapter performing the *Kammavācham* ; second ordination of Mahendra by Moggaliputta Tissa as his *upādhyāyā*.

(2) Ordination of Saṅghamitrā by her *ācharyā* Ayupālā and *upādhyāyā* Dhammapālā [*Mahāv.* v. 204-209].

(3) Promotion of Asoka from the status of a *pachchayadāyaka* to that of a *sāsanadāyāda* [*Ib.* 197].

263 B.C.—Birth of Kuṇāla, son of Asoka's wife, Padmāvatī [*Div.* xxvii.].

262 B.C.—Death of the monks, Tissa and Sumitta, followed by increase in the number of undesirable members in the Saṅgha and the consequent retirement of Moggaliputta Tissa [*Mahav.* v. 227-30].

262–254 B.C.—The Saṅgha under the headship of Mahendra ;

recall by Asoka of Moggaliputta Tissa, who taught him the doctrine of the Saṁbuddha; meeting of the Saṅgha under him and expulsion of heretical monks by Asoka [*Ib.* 231-274; cf. Sanchi and Sarnath Pillar Edicts].

260–250 B.C.—Possible period of Asoka's pilgrimage to Buddhist holy places which followed his completion of the *dharmarājikas* according to *Div.* xxvii., which states that Asoka was taken by his preceptor Upagupta first to *Lumbini Vana* and afterwards to *Bodhimūla*. R.E. VIII refers to Asoka's visit to *Sambodhi* in 260 B.C., and the Rummindei Pillar Edict to his visit to Lumbini in 250 B.C.

253 B.C.—Meeting of the Third Buddhist Council under Moggaliputta Tissa, and despatch by him of missionaries to different countries [*Mahāv.* xii. 1-8].

252 B.C.—Mahendra on way to Ceylon visits his mother Devī at Vedisa [*Ib.* xiii. 1. 8-11], when already twelve years a monk.

240 B.C.—Death of Asandhimitrā, "the dear consort of Asoka and faithful believer in the Saṁbuddha" [*Ib.* xx. 2].

236 B.C.—Tiṣyarakṣitā raised to the rank of Chief Queen [*Ib.* 3; also *Div.* xxvii., where she is mentioned as Asoka's *agramahiṣī*].

235 B.C.—Kuṇāla sent out as Viceroy to Taxila, then in revolt [*Div.* p. 407].

233 B.C.—Tiṣyarakṣitā's jealousy against the Bodhi-tree, which she tries to destroy [*Mahav.* xx. 4-6; also referred to in the *Div.* without the date (p. 397, Cowell's ed.)].

232 B.C.—Death of Asoka in the thirty-eighth year of his reign [*Mahāv.* xx. 1-6].

CHAPTER III

ADMINISTRATION

We have now given an account of the principal events and measures in Asoka's life and reign. We shall now describe his work as an administrator, religious reformer, and builder.

The government of India under Asoka was an absolute monarchy in the legal and political sense of the term. Nevertheless, autocracy in India was much more limited in many directions than the autocracies of the West. "The Indian king is no sultan with the sole obligation of satisfying his personal caprice. The origin of royalty is the growth of wickedness and the necessity of chastisement, the virtue of which the Indian writers celebrate with a real enthusiasm. It is as guardian of the social (including domestic and religious) order and defence against anarchial oppression that the king is entitled to his revenue; failing to perform this duty, he takes upon himself a corresponding share of the national sin. Educated in these precepts among a moralising people, he would have been more than human had he escaped the obsession of this conception of his duties. Hence we not seldom hear on royal, as well as on priestly, lips the expression that the king should be the father of his people" [*Cambridge History of India*, vol. i. p. 491]. But apart from this living sense of his moral responsibility to his people, there was an important limitation upon his autocracy from the fact that he was not the source of Law, but rather its support. Sacred law, according to Manu and other legal authorities, is derived from four sources, viz., (1) the Vedas, (2) the Smṛitis, (3) the practices of the pious (*śiṣṭāchāra*), and (4) the opinions of the pious on doubtful points, while the sources of secular law were the manifold groups and communities which legislated for themselves, so that " Whatever may have been practised by the virtuous, and by such twice-born men as are devoted to the law, that only he shall establish as law if it be not opposed to the laws of castes, communities (*jānapada*), guilds, and families [Manu, viii. 41, 46]. As I have explained elsewhere [*Nationalism in Hindu Culture,* London, 1920, p. 99], " it is the quasi-instinctive postulates and conventions of group-life which come to be formulated as *law*, and not the mandate, command, or decree, of a single, central authority in the state. Law, under these conditions, is not an *arte-fact*, but a natural growth of consensus and communal life." The fact of the matter was that the defects of personal rule were very largely remedied by the king's own submission to the laws which he had no hand in making or annulling, so that the impersonal rules were the real rulers in the country. In Asoka's case, the sovereign was theoretically only an autocrat, for he proceeded much farther than the law-books to prescribe limitations upon his own authority by adding to his own duties and responsibilities, and emphasising the supremacy of moral laws even in the secular spheres of life. A great emphasis is laid upon the paternal principle of government in his Edicts: " All men are my children; and, just as I desire for my children that they may enjoy every kind of prosperity and happiness both in this world and in the next, so also do I desire the same for all men " [Kalinga Edict II]. He wants the newly-subdued Kalingas " to grasp the truth that 'the king is to us as a father; he loves us even as he loves himself; we are to the king even as his children' " [*ibid.*]. But this abiding sense of parental responsibility for his people was not confined to the king alone. It belonged to his agents, too, to whom he committed the care of his people " as a man would make over his child to a skilful nurse and, feeling confident, says to himself: 'The skilful nurse is eager to care for the happiness of my child'; even so my Governors have been created for the welfare and happiness of the country "

[Pillar Edict IV]. A king with these ideas of his position and responsibility is practically more representative of his people than the so-called representative assembly or legislature in a regular democracy. Here " the Head of the State represents the people directly and primarily in his person, whether, as in the case of the Mikado or of a Hindu Sovereign, as the symbol of the Shinto, the Dharma or the Law, in hereditary succession and transmission,—or, as in the case of the President of the United States, as the elected representative of the people's sovereignty, standing in an even more direct and vital relationship to the people than the members of the Representative Assemblies and Legislatures." [1] His relationship to the people is more natural and primary, more direct and intimate, than the legal, factitious, and consensual relationship of the electorate and the elected in modern democracies. Indeed, the Head of the State and his people are but integral parts of one corporate and constitutional unity. A democracy only seeks to embody the unitary, undivided sovereignty in a body politic and its various limbs and organs, the various political assemblies and organisations, but in practice it has realised its ideals only partially, in different degrees, in even the most democratically advanced countries of the west. The defects of democracy show that the problem of government cannot be solved by representative or electoral methods alone, but by the processes of organic growth which it can stimulate by encouraging all vital modes of association prevailing among the people concerned. Thus, " one of the characteristics of the present-day political *theory* is its reaction against the state, and a salient political *fact* to-day is the increasing amount and power of group-life—trade unions, professional societies, citizens' leagues, neighbourhood associations, etc." [M. P. Follet's *New State*]. Ancient Hindu monarchy did not aim at centralisation or over-government, but gave full scope to the varieties of group-life to which the people have been used from time immemorial, even prior to the emergence of a centralised government among them. Thus it was an

[1] *Report on Mysore Constitutional Reform* by Sir. B. N. Seal, Vice-Chancellor, Mysore University.

autocracy limited from below by a vast subterranean democracy, so to speak, a complete system of local self-government embodied in various types of institutions.

Asoka did not spare himself in trying to realise his high conception of imperial duties and responsibilities. He was an ideal public servant, the most hard working of all his officials. He gave himself to public business at all hours and places. Says he in Rock Edict VI: "A long period has elapsed during which in the past administrative business or information was not attended to at all hours. So by me the arrangement has been made that at all times, when I am eating, or in the harem, or in the bedroom, or in my ranches, or even in the place of religious instruction, or in my pleasure-grounds, everywhere the reporting officials should make known to me the people's affairs. In all places I shall attend to public business." He says further [*ibid.*]: "I never feel satisfaction in my exertions and dispatch of business. For work I must for the welfare of all the folk; and of that, again, the root is energy and the dispatch of business; for nothing is more essential than the welfare of all the folk." Hardly has a king emphasised more his obligations to his own subjects! The Brahminical sacred texts insist on three debts which every man is born to and which he must discharge, the debts to his religion (*devariṇa*), to the Ṛiṣis (i.e., to learning) and to his ancestors (whose race is to be perpetuated), but Asoka says that a king has a fourth debt to pay: "And whatsoever efforts I make, they are made that I may obtain release from my debt to my fellow-human beings" [*ibid.*]. The sovereign of a large empire, Asoka also recognised his duty of touring the country—touring not for sport or pleasure as his predecessors did, but for "the inspection of the country and the people" (*jānapadasya janasya darśanaṁ*) [R.E. VIII]. But his empire was so extensive that he could not visit all its parts, as is apparent from a passage in the Rock Edict XIV, where he assumes that in some of his Edicts "something has been written incompletely by blunders of the writer." These blunders in his published Edicts are merely supposed by him: he could not have referred to them if he had actually examined them on the spot, for there are hardly any such glaring blunders in so many of his separately executed and located Edicts.

The empire was divided for administrative purposes into a number of provinces, of which the more remote ones were placed under Viceroys. The Viceroyalties were generally reserved for the Princes called Kumāras or Āryaputras in the Edicts. The Edicts refer to four princely Viceroys, viz., those governing the provinces with headquarters at Taxila, Ujjain, Tosali and Suvarṇagiri [Kalinga Edict I; Kalinga Edict II, Dhauli version; Minor Rock Edict I, Brahmagiri version]. Gandhāra is mentioned by Fa-hien as another viceroyalty under Prince Dharmavivardhana. Since Dharmavivardhana, according to *Divyāvadāna*, was another name for Kuṇāla, who was sent out by Asoka towards the end of his reign as his Viceroy to Taxila for subduing its hostility, we may take it that the province of Gandhāra had its headquarters at Taxila. Sometimes, instead of the Princes, we find local chiefs appointed as Viceroys. Thus Puṣyagupta, the Vaiśya, was Chandragupta's Viceroy (*Rāṣṭrīya*) of the western provinces with Girnar as headquarters, which, under Asoka, came under another Viceroy named Raja Tusāspha, the Persian [Rudradāman's inscription in *Ep. Ind.*, viii. pp. 46-7]. The more centrally situated provinces were placed under Governors directly appointed from the capital by the king, and are perhaps marked out by the Pillar Inscriptions, while the Rock Inscriptions are to be found in the outlying regions of the empire.

While the Edicts do not name any Viceroy, the legends name some. When Bindusāra was emperor, he appointed his two sons, Susīma (or Sumana) and Asoka, as his Viceroys at Taxila and Ujjayinī respectively. When later, Taxila was in revolt which could not be suppressed by Susīma, Asoka was transferred there as more competent for the purpose. Prince Kuṇāla, as we have already seen, is mentioned as Asoka's Viceroy at Taxila. The emperor on his consecration is also said to have appointed as his deputy or Viceregent (*Uparāja*) his younger brother, Tiṣya, who, on his retirement as a religious devotee, was succeeded by Prince Mahendra, though he remained in office only for a short time prior to his ordination [*Mahāv.* v. 33]. Probably the Viceregent (*Uparāja*) was something like the Prime Minister and different from *Yuvarāja*, heir-apparent. Bindusāra, Asoka's father, had, as his Prime Minister, *Agrāmātya*, Khallāṭaka, who is said to have supported Asoka in his contest for the throne. Tradition gives to Asoka himself a trusted minister named Rādhagupta, who also helped him in gaining the throne and in his administration, and was his *Agrāmātya* (the term used in the *Divyāvadāna*).

The Viceroys, too, had their own ministers. The northern books tell us how the people of Taxila during the reign of Bindusāra revolted against the oppressive ministers, and not against the princely Viceroy. In the legend of Kuṇāla, the Viceroy of Taxila, it was the ministers who received the spurious dispatch from headquarters, directing that he be blinded. The Kalinga Edict II shows how the Viceroys, like the king, were empowered to appoint their own officers of the status of Mahāmātras for periodical inspection and supervision of judicial administration.

That Viceroys were associated with Mahāmātras or Ministers is also shown by the Minor Rock Edict I, Brahmagiri text, and the Kalinga Edict I, Dhauli text. In the former the Prince (*Āryaputra*), acting with his Mahāmātras, addresses the king's message to the Mahāmātras of Isila; in the latter, the king addresses the Prince and the Mahāmātras together. Again, the Jaugada text of the Kalinga Rock Edict II mentions a class of Mahāmātras who are described as *Lājavachanikas*, i.e., those who were entitled to receive the king's messages directly, and not through the royal Viceroys. Thus these *Mahāmātras* might be regarded as Provincial Governors, as they are given independent charge of their province. Samāpā (Jaugada) or Isila [M.R.E. I, Brahm.] was the seat of such a governorship, as Tosalī was of a viceroyalty. In the same way, the Kauśāmbī Edict is addressed by the king directly to the Mahāmātras of Kauśāmbī, which must have been, therefore, the headquarters of another province. Perhaps these Mahāmātras were distinguished from the other classes of Mahāmātras by the designation, *Prādeśika Mahāmātras*. The term *Prādeśika* (Provincial Governor) is used in R.E. III for a class of officers who were expected to tour through their charges completely every five years, just as the Mahāmātras are required to do in K.R.E. I. And so these *Prādeśikas* had really the status of a Mahāmātra. Strictly speaking, the charge of a Prādeśika-Mahāmātra was like the Commissionership of a Division, as P.E. IV makes the *Rājūka* the Provincial Governor proper.

The ordinary Provincial Governors were called *Rājūkas* who were " set over hundreds of thousands of souls " [P.E. IV, R.E. III]. The office of the Rājūkas had been in existence before Asoka, but Asoka invested them with greater authority. They are granted independence in their administration of Law and Justice in order that they may perform their duties confidently and fearlessly, bestow welfare and happiness upon the people of the country, and confer favours upon them. They will also know of their joys and sorrows. As the child is committed confidently to a skilful nurse, the people are committed to the care of these Governors who are created for their welfare and happiness with intent that fearlessly, unselfishly, and cheerfully, they may discharge their duties [P.E. IV].

Sometimes, however, these lofty ideals of duty set before the Governors were not realised. Cases of their neglect of duty or indifference to his injunctions called forth vigorous but dignified protests from the emperor, like the following : " With certain natural dispositions success (in administration) is impossible, to wit, envy, lack of sustained efforts, harshness, haste, want of application, indolence, and lassitude. You must desire that such dispositions be not yours. At the root of the whole matter lie steadiness, and patience. He who is tired in administration will not rise up, but one must needs move, advance, go on. There will be special officers to remind you of your obligations to the king and of his instructions. Fulfilment of these bears great fruit, non-fulfilment brings great calamity. By those who fail, neither heaven nor royal favour can be won. By fulfilling my instructions you will gain heaven and also pay your debt to me " [Kalinga Edict I]. In these we probably hear the very words of Asoka, still bringing home to us his impassioned exhortations across the centuries. Lest his words be forgotten by those for whom they are meant, the emperor, besides having them indelibly engraved on the rocks, ordered that they be recited publicly " at the beginning of each season of four months, (i.e., each of the three seasons, hot, rainy and cold) on the Tiṣya day, (i.e., when the moon is in that constellation) " [K.E. II), nay, even once a month on the Tiṣya day, and in the intervals between the Tiṣya days, and on fit occasions even to a single person [K.E. II].

Thus Asoka's government was from the very nature of the case partly imperial, i.e., directly under the emperor, and partly local, i.e., under the Viceroys and Governors. The charge of a Viceroy was more extensive than that of a Governor. Details are wanting as regards the extent of the administration which the emperor took upon himself as his own work. From the Edicts we may infer that the emperor's first duty was to settle the fundamental principles on which he wanted his government to be based, the policy to be pursued by his administrators, and to issue his notifications for them from time to time as occasion arose. In Asoka's case, the Imperial Edicts announcing his policy, principles, and the measures to be taken for their realisation remain permanently gazetted on " tables or pillars of stone." Thus the subject of legislation seems also in certain matters to have been imperialised. The laws of the realm passed by Asoka on his own initiative have been already indicated from the Edicts. Thirdly, the subject of the public works of utility seems also to have been an imperial concern from the account of the same already given. Fourthly, the Department of Dharma was also under the imperial government. The Ministers of Morals (*Dharma-Mahāmātras*) do not appear to be provincial officers, as their work embraced the entire area of the empire, and even areas outside of it. Fifthly, the Buddhist Church came to be one of the concerns of Asoka who practically assumed its temporal leadership, as will appear from the several Edicts bearing on the subject [the Bhabru Edict, and the Pillar Edicts of Sārnāth, Kauśāmbī and Sānchī]. These Edicts announce the imperial decree fixing the penalty for those who promote schism in the church and the means of its publication and enforcement. Lastly, Asoka made periodical touring through his empire as one of his duties, as he insisted it upon all his local officers.

It is apparent that the emperor could not depend upon himself alone for the satisfactory discharge of these manifold and heavy duties and responsibilities which he had fixed for himself. His general supervision of the work of government was exercised with the aid of a special set of officers—his private secretaries, who were to report to him on the affairs of the people at all hours and places, and were thus called *Paṭivedakas* [R.E. VI]. Next, the emperor was also assisted in his administrative work by his Privy Council or *Pariṣad*, referred to in his Rock Edicts III and VI. The number of the Cabinet is not known. Kauṭilya makes it depend on the requirements of administration. According to tradition, Bindusāra had a Privy Council of 500 members.

The inscriptions indicate how the king's administrative orders were issued. They are called *śāsanam* (*hevāṁiyaṁ sāsane* in Sarnath P.E.) and *anusāsanam* or *anuśiṣṭam* (*hevaṁcha Devānaṁpiyasa anusathi* in K.R.E. I). They were written down (*likhita*) by the *Lipikara* [cf. *lipikarāparādhena* in R.E. XIV; and *Chapaḍena likhitaṁ lipikareṇa* in M.R.E. II] in accordance with the king's words [*Devānaṁpiyasa vachanena* in K.R.E. II (Dhauli)] in documents called *lipi* [cf. *ikaṁcha lipiṁ* (Sarnath M.P.E.) and *ayaṁ dhaṁmalipi lekhāpita* of the R.E. and P.E.]. When the king's order was proclaimed, it was called *śrāvaṇam* [cf. *iyaṁ cha sāvaṇe sāvāpite* in M.R.E. I, Brahm.]. The preamble to the king's orders was of the form, "Thus saith the king" (*evamāha*, as in many R.E. and P.E.) or "thus ordains the king" (*mayā idaṁ āñapitam*, R.E. III; or *Devānaṁ piye āṇapayati*, M.R.E. I). The first form, according to Kauṭilya (II. 10), applies to *prajñāpana-lekha*, and the second to *ājñā-lekha*, i.e., writs of information and command respectively.

As regards the Provincial Governments, some sort of a general scheme is indicated in the Edicts. The head of the administration, the highest local officer, was the *Rājūka*, while a smaller jurisdiction was placed under the *Prādeśika*,[1] the divisional commissioner. There were also the Heads of Departments, called *Mukhas* in Pillar Edict VII, and also known by the general title of Mahāmātras,[2] while the department assigned to them was indicated by its name being prefixed to that title. The Edicts tell us of the *Dharma-Mahāmātras* in charge of the Department of Morals, the *Strī-adhyakṣa-Mahāmātras* in charge of the affairs of women, and the *Anta-Mahāmātras* in charge of the frontiers [P.E. I]. The Mahāmātras in charge of cities were called *Mahāmātra-nāgarakas* or *Mahāmātra-Nagaravyavahārakas* [the Kalinga Edicts]. Where the name Mahāmātra is used by itself without any prefix, it denotes the Ministers (as in Kalinga Edict II, Dhauli text, or Minor R.E. I]. This sense is also borne out in a passage in Rock Edict VI, where the king is said to entrust matters of urgency to the Mahāmātras for discussion by the Council of Ministers, *Pariṣat*, of which the Mahāmātras are also members. Lastly, the Mahāmātras were also deputed abroad to work as the king's *dūtas* or ambassadors, not merely in the frontier states among the *Antas*, but also in foreign states, viz., those of the five Greek kings, the Choḍas and Pāṇḍyas, and the island of Ceylon, as mentioned in R.E. V and XIII.

Thus there was organised a regular Civil Service assisting the Viceroys and Provincial Chiefs. The Civil Servants were called by the general name of *Puruṣas* [P.E. I, IV and

[1] Rock Edict III mentions the "Yuktas, Rājūkas and Prādeśikas," probably in an ascending order of rank, as is evidently done in P.E. VII in mentioning the Rājūkas *after* the Puruṣas. In that case, the *Prādeśikas* might be provincial officers administering some specified interests of the whole province. F. W. Thomas takes the Prādeśika to be the same as the *Pradeṣṭri*, "head of the executive revenue and judicial service" [*JRAS*, 1914, pp. 383-6], and the Rājūkas to be officers in charge of such subjects as "survey, land settlement, and irrigation," as suggested by the title itself [*rajjugrāhakas*=land-measurers, as used in Pāli works; see *Cambridge History*, pp. 487, 508]. See the notes on these terms below.

[2] Mahāmātras as Heads of Departments had their offices or secretariats in buildings called *Mahāmātrīya* by Kauṭilya [II. 5].

VII] and are distinguished as being of high, low, or middle rank [P.E. I]. In Pillar Edict IV, the *Puruṣas* are differentiated from the *Rājūkas* as a separate body of officers who were acquainted with the wishes of the king, and whose duty was to exhort the Rājūkas into loyal service of the king, while in Edict VII they are spoken of as being "set over the multitude" (*vahune janasi āyatā*) contrasted with "the many hundred thousands of souls" under the charge of the Rājūkas. Thus the Puruṣas might have been like the secret agents, the *gūḍha-puruṣas* of Kauṭilya, or the inspectorate of the government. The Civil Servants of subordinate ranks are called *Yuktas* [R.E. III]. The *Yuktas* were like the Secretaries whose duty, as indicated in R.E. III, was to codify royal orders in the office of the Mahāmātras or Ministers under the instructions of the Pariṣad or Council to which they were attached. They had also to accompany their official superiors on tour. The scribe, *lipikara*, is also mentioned [Minor R.E. II, Brahmagiri version].

There seems to have prevailed the system of tours by government servants, high and low. In the case of the Viceroyalties of Ujjain and Taxila, the rules of service provided for such tours every three years for the Mahāmātras (K.R.E. I], while the usual rule in other provinces was to have them every five years [*Ib.* and R.E. III]. The officers sent out on such tours included the Yuktas, the Rājūkas, and the Prādeśikas [R.E. III].

Frontier administration, too, was successfully tackled by the employment of methods suggested by its special circumstances and problems. In general, the paternal principle of government was specially emphasised in dealing with the subdued and "unsubdued borderers" alike, and also with the backward communities, the forest folks [the Kalinga Edicts]. The frontiers were in charge of the *Anta-Mahāmātras* already mentioned, whose exact duties are not indicated in the Edicts. But they are mentioned by Kauṭilya, who calls them *Antapālas*. Their duty was to impose the transit dues (*vartanī*) on imported goods, and after examining their quality to stamp them with their seals [II. 21] and pass them on to the Superintendent of Tolls. They had also to make good losses to merchants by thefts committed within their jurisdiction.

Lastly, there must have been some officers to look after the public works of utility about which Asoka was so keen, though but few of them are mentioned in his Edicts. The *Vraja* [R.E. VI] must have been the charge of the *Vraja-bhūmika* [R.E. XII], who might also have within his purview the public parks, *udyāna* [R.E. VI], mango-groves, *āmravātikā* [P.E. VII], wells, *kūpa* [R.E. II] or *udapāna* [P.E. VII] and travellers' rest-houses, *niṣadyā* [P.E. VII and Cave Insc. III.], along the public roads, *patha* or *mārga* [R.E. II]. There must have been horticulturists, too, to look after the botanical gardens for the growth of medicinal plants, and medical officers to arrange for the *chikitsā* or treatment of the diseases of both man and beast, *manuṣya-chikitsā* and *paśu-chikitsā* [R.E. II]. The king's *nāga-vana*, elephant forest [P.E. V], must have been under an officer like the *Hastyadhyakṣa* of Kauṭilya [II. 31], for elephants were "the special property of the king," as noted by Megasthenes.

As regards the policy of the empire, it may be summed up in Asoka's message : "The chiefest conquest is the conquest of Right and not of Might" [R.E. XIII]. First, war was abolished within the empire by one stroke. The sovereignty of the smaller states and weaker peoples was respected as a matter of principle. To the many "unsubdued borderers" of the empire went forth the healing message : "The king desires that they should not be afraid of him but should trust him, and would receive from him not sorrow but happiness" [K.E. II]. Nor was subjection forced on the ruder peoples on the plea of civilising them : "Even upon the forest folk in his dominions His Sacred Majesty looks kindly" [R.E. XIII]. So rang through the country the message, loud and clear, repeated on rock and pillar, the message of freedom, of peace on earth and goodwill among men. Silenced was the war-drum : the *bherī-ghoṣa* was drowned in the *dharma-ghoṣa* ! [R.E. IV]. But we must note that Asoka attached a condition to his gift of freedom. Freedom must go with morality. While anxious "to secure the confidence of the borderers," he was equally anxious " to set them moving on the path of piety " [K.E. II]. The forest folks are distinctly " bidden to turn from their evil ways that they be not chastised " [R.E. XIII]. Secondly, while military conquest was forsworn, the moral conquests of the good king grew apace. These were undertaken as parts of the daily work of administration. And they were spreading not merely among his own peoples, but also in the foreign countries on his borders and beyond. Thus his international relations were governed by principles that still remain to be recognised. The barriers that divide nations could not stand before his sense of universal brotherhood. Thus we find this good king, centuries ahead of his times, carrying on welfare work among the citizens of other states by the expenses borne by his own state ! [R.E. II].

CHAPTER IV

RELIGION

WE shall now discuss Asoka's religion. At the outset, we must distinguish what was his personal religion from the religion he sought to preach and introduce among his people by his public measures.

His personal religion may be taken to be Buddhism, although there is a view that it was Jainism. That he was a Buddhist is apparent from several of his Edicts and other proofs. In the Minor R.E. I, he tells us of the stages in his progress towards Buddhism; and, according to the reading of M.R.E. I, Maski and Rupnath, by Hultzsch, he also openly declares himself in that Edict to be a "Śākya," and a "Buddha-Śākya," i.e., a Buddhist; in the Bhabru Edict he speaks with an air of authority over the church, pointing out several passages from the scriptures to be recited and meditated by the monks and nuns, and also by the laity, male and female, and declaring his faith in the Buddhist Trinity · in the Minor Pillar Edicts at Sārnāth, Kauśāmbī and Sāñchī, he stands out as the Defender of his Faith, and proclaims the penalties for schism; while, according to tradition,[1] he himself held a

[1] Tradition also testifies to Asoka's devotion to the Buddha by his seizure of his relics by opening the stūpas in which they were enshrined and redistributing them among the 84,000 stūpas of his own creation. The relics were originally in the possession of the Mallas of Kusinārā, where the Buddha died, but they were forced to share the relics with seven other claimants who made a hostile combination for the purpose. These seven claimants were: Ajātaśatru of Magadha, the Lichchhavis of Vaiśālī, the Śākyas of Kapilavastu, the Bulis of Allakappa, the Koliyas of Rāmagrāma, a Brahman of Veṭhadīpa, and the Mallas of Pāvā. This "War of the Relics"

PLATE IV.

Figure of Elephant carved on Stone at Kālsi

Council which defined the canon under the presidency of Moggaliputta Tissa, who produced the *Kathāvatthu* treatise for the purpose. There are also other facts pointing to the same conclusion: his pilgrimage to the holy places of Buddhism, his various measures for protecting animal life, his abolition of meat diet for the royal household, and abjuration of all amusements connected with the pain, or slaughter, of animals; his abolition of bloody sacrifices [R.E. I], his observance of the Uposatha Buddhist holidays [P.E. V], and his appointment of the Dharma-mahāmātras to look after "the interests of the Saṁgha" (*Saṁghaṭhasi*), as distinctly specified, and not for their supervision, as is implied by the expression used for the other sects [P.E. VII]. Lastly, we may note Asoka's attachment to a definite Buddhist symbol in the Edicts, the symbol of the White Elephant,[1] indicated by an inscription at Girnar at the end of R.E. XIII, and represented by a figure cut on the rock at Dhauli and incised at Kalsi with the label *gajatame*, "the most perfect elephant." The elephant recalls the Buddha descending in that form into the womb of his mother,[1] so

represented in the Sanchi sculptures, was settled by the intervention of Droṇa, the Brahmin. Centuries later, Asoka revived this war on the relics in another form by opening the stūpas in which they were deposited, but failed of his purpose at the Stūpa of Rāmagrāma against the defence of its heroic guardians, the Nāgas. The scene is depicted on one of the gateways of the Great Stūpa at Sanchi, showing the emperor approaching in his chariot with his army of cavalry, infantry and elephants. Other proofs of Asoka's Buddhism are the numerous stūpas said to have been erected by him all over the country from Kapis to Orissa to enshrine the Buddha's relics or mark the places hallowed by his visit or association, as mentioned in Yuan Chwang's account (noticed later); or his daily practice of offering worship at the stone at Pāṭaliputra bearing the Buddha's footprints, as related by Yuan Chwang [Watters, ii. 92].

[1] The descent of the Bodhisattva into the womb of his mother is referred to in texts like *Dīgha Nikāya*, II. (pp. 12-13, 55), or the *Jātakas* [" Bodhisatto setavaravāraṇo hutvā . . ." (Fausboll, i. 50)], and in the Bharhut inscription, *Bhagavato ūkraṃti*, and is represented in sculpture at Bharhut [Plate XXVIII. 2 of Cunningham's *Stūpa of Bharhut*] and Sanchi [Eastern Gate, top sculpture on the interior face of the right jamb], and later at Amarāvatī, and most correctly in Gandhāra [see Plate III. of Foucher's *Beginnings of Buddhist Art*].

that there is here an attempt on the part of Asoka to dedicate his Edicts, as it were, to the Buddha. Along with this association of the inscriptions with the Elephant, we should also note the association of the Asokan Pillars with the four animals of the Elephant, the Bull, the Horse, and the Lion, figuring as their capitals, and chosen for the purpose as symbols of different stages in the life of the Buddha. Thus the Elephant typifies the Conception, the Bull (as presiding over) the Nativity, the Horse the Great Departure (Renunciation), and the Lion, " the lion among the Śākyas " (*Śākya-siṁha*), the appellation by which the Buddha was known.

Asoka, however, did not inherit, but was a convert to, Buddhism. Like his predecessors, he freely allowed the slaughter of animals in the royal kitchen every day, prior to his conversion. It may be noted that he did not become an absolute vegetarian even after his conversion. His meat diet was limited to the flesh of antelopes and peacocks even in 258 B.C., some six years after his conversion, and, though the antelope was discarded later, it is not definitely known if the peacock was given up finally as an article of his food. It is interesting to note that, according to Buddhaghosa [*Sāratthappakāsinī*, the commentary on *Saṁyutta Nikāya*], the flesh of the peafowl was considered a delicacy in the Middle Country.[1] The exhaustive list of animals and birds specified for protection in the Pillar Edict V, issued as late as 243 B.C., does not include the peacock. Similarly, he indulged in all the customary merry-makings of kings before his conversion. And he has been described in all tradition as being up to usurping the throne by violence against his eldest brother, hardly a less legitimate claimant. Lastly, even as a Buddhist lay disciple, he did not desist from a bloody battle fought to the bitter end [R.E. XIII]. Thus no stories such as those anxiously invented by the Buddhist theologians are needed to prove the miraculous power of Buddhism in converting an ordinary king into the saintliest of men. The facts speak for themselves.

Tradition gives different versions of the story of Asoka's conversion. The Ceylonese legends ascribe it to the young

[1] I owe this reference to Mr. C. D. Chatterji.

PLATE V.

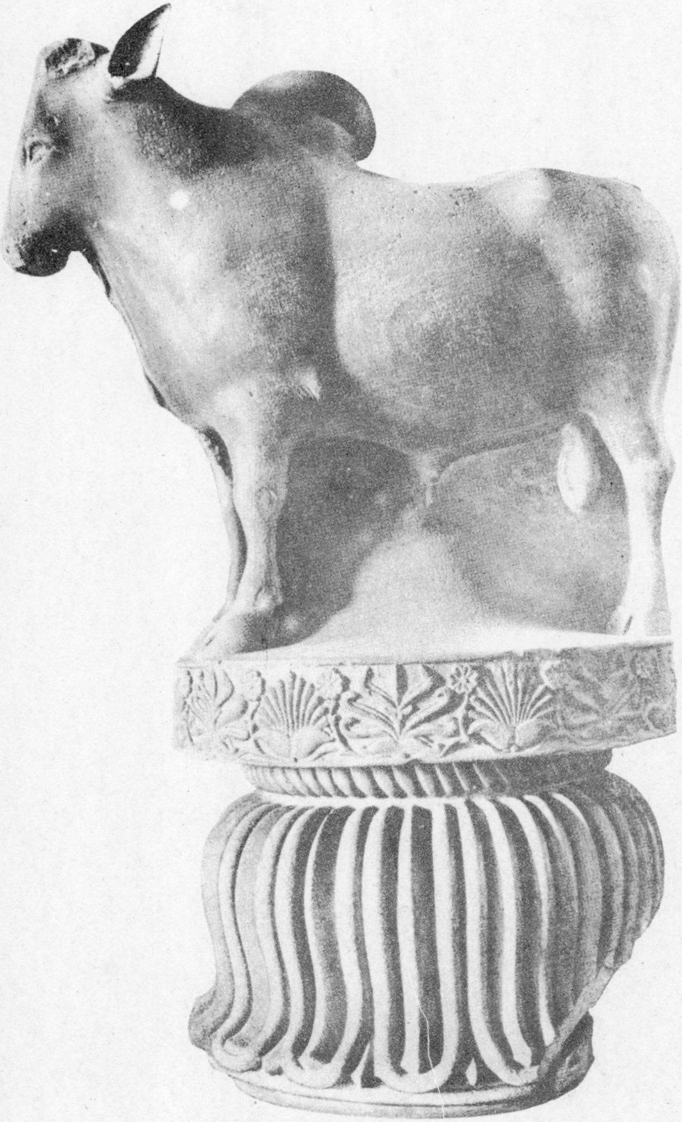

Rampurwa Bull Capital.

son of his eldest brother Sumana, the boy's name being Nigrodha. Next Tissa, son of Moggali, is mentioned as his preceptor. This divine is reckoned as the fifth Vinaya teacher from the time of the Buddha, his predecessors being Upāli, Dāsaka, Sonaka, Siggava, and Chandavajji [Geiger's *Mahāvaṁsa*, p. xlvii, f.]. Tissa was sixty years old at the time of Asoka's coronation, and he died at eighty, succeeded by Mahendra. Yuan Chwang names Upagupta as Asoka's preceptor in Buddhism, but Upagupta has been identified with Moggaliputta Tissa [Waddell in *JASB*, 1897, pp. 76-84]. The preceptor's first educative measure was to take his royal pupil out on a long pilgrimage already described. The emperor also lived under the influence of other Buddhist saints of the times. Among these are mentioned Sumitra and Tissa whose death is said to have been followed by much confusion in the church, due to the heretics outnumbering believers. At last the confusion had to be settled by convoking the Third Council under the king's spiritual director, Tissa, as already related. The Council sat for nine months.

It is not easy to define the degree of his devotion to his new faith. It is partly proved by his own statement in the M.R.E. I that he had intimately associated himself with the Saṅgha, and also by his dedication of his son and daughter to the direct service of the Saṅgha.[1] The legends

[1] The *Mahāvaṁsa* [Geiger's tr. pp. 42-43] represents Asoka (then called Dharmāsoka for his benefactions) as allowing his son and daughter to take orders instead of himself taking orders. By this measure his status in the Saṅgha was nevertheless improved. Formerly, he was only a *Pachchayadāyaka*, i.e., an upāsaka or a lay devotee, who supplied *bhikṣus* with their four necessaries of food, clothing, shelter, and medicine. Now he was promoted to the rank of a *Śāsanadāyāda*, i.e., a kinsman of the Saṅgha, a status he had himself desired. Against this definite tradition which represents Asoka as deliberately refraining from the adoption of monkhood, it is not reasonable to infer that Asoka *did* become a monk from the expression—*saṁghaṁ upagate*—in M.R.E. I. It may also be noted in this connection that the supposed representation of the incident of Asoka's visit to the stūpas at Rāmagrāma in one of the sculptures of Sanchi represents Asoka not in the garb of a monk, but as emperor coming in his chariot with his full retinue of elephants, horsemen, and footmen, while the same thing is repeated in two other sculptures showing Asoka with his

go much farther to prove his devotion by relating the story that on completion of one of his religious edifices he made a gift of the empire to the monks and bought it back from them three times. This tradition is repeated by Fa-hien who refers to a great tope built by Asoka at Pāṭaliputra and to a stone pillar near it, fifteen cubits in circumference, and more than thirty in height, "on which there is an inscription, saying, 'Asoka gave the Jambudvīpa to the general body of all the monks, and then redeemed it from them with money.' This he did three times" [Legge's tr. p. 80]. But the few references in the Edicts to the Saṅgha breathe rather a spirit of authority than of submission, while his civil officers, the Dharma-Mahāmātras, were asked to control the Saṅgha as much as the *pariṣads* of other sects. Buddhaghosa records a tradition that Asoka so far controlled the church as to personally expel schismatics, "giving them white garments." His stern attitude towards schism in the church, as expressed in his Sarnath, Sanchi, and Kosambi Edicts, of course, demonstrates his zeal for its welfare.

This brings us to the question of Asoka's toleration as permitted by his zeal for Buddhism. In the first place, he did not choose to impose his personal faith on his people, although he was so zealous in its service. In the second place, he held the scales evenly between the competing claims of different religious sects to the royal patronage, as shown by his grant of cave-dwellings to the Ājīvikas,[1] or

two queens visiting the Deer Park and Bodh Gayā [see Marshall's *Guide to Sanchi*, pp. 47, 50, 51, 61].

The theory of Asoka's monkhood is suggested by a statement of It-sing [*JRAS*, 1908, p. 496] that he saw an image of Asoka dressed in the garb of a Buddhist monk, and by a passage in the *Divyāvadāna* stating that Asoka died, divested of all power, renouncing the world, and becoming a Buddhist monk [see *JRAS*, 1913, p. 657].

[1] This is generally taken as an example of Asoka's partiality towards the Ājīvikas, as compared with other sects of the times. This partiality he seems to have inherited from his parents, if we may believe in the legends. The *Mahāvaṁsaṭīkā* (p. 126), as has been already noticed, refers to the family-preceptor of his mother, Queen Dharmā, being an Ājīvika of the name of Janasāna (deviyā kulūpago Janasāno nāma eko Ājīvako), whom King Bindusāra summoned to interpret the meaning of the Queen's dream before the

promoting the interests of Brahmans, Ājīvikas and Nirgranthas equally with the Buddhists through the instrumentality of his officers, the Dharma-Mahāmātras, superintending their affairs at state expense. He also favoured the sect of worshippers of the previous Buddhas by doubly enlarging the stūpa of Buddha Koṇākamana and paying a personal visit to the shrine. In the third place, his own Edicts breathe consistently a lofty spirit of toleration. Liberality to Brahmans and Śramaṇas is always emphasised as a public duty [R.E. III, IX] and unseemly behaviour to them equally condemned [R.E. IV, P.E. VII]. In his own "pious tours," he made it a point of "visiting ascetics and Brahmans, with liberality to them" [R.E. VIII]. He passed a special decree removing the previous distinction obtaining between sects in respect of their rights of residence [R.E. VII]. In another Edict it is stated that "the king does reverence to men of all sects, whether ascetics or householders, by gifts and various forms of reverence." While encouraging discussion among different religious schools—a time-honoured feature of Indian intellectual life—he deprecated criticism "without reason," "because the sects of other people all deserve reverence for one reason or another," and "he who does reverence to his own sect, while disparaging the sects of others, wholly from attachment to his own, with intent to enhance the splendour of his own sect, in reality by such conduct inflicts the severest injury on his own sect." Thus the king's only care was "that there should be growth in the essence of the matter in, and respect for, all sects" [R.E. XII]. In a later Edict [P.E. VI] he asserts: "I devote my attention to all communities, for the followers of all denominations are honoured by me and the honour is paid in various forms. Nevertheless, showing personal regard for them is the chief thing in my opinion."

It is, however, to be remembered that Asoka's toleration

birth of Asoka; while in the *Divyāvadāna* (ch. xxvi) Bindusāra himself summons the Ājīvika ascetic, Piṅgalavatsa, for the examination of all his sons to find out who was the best to be his successor on the throne.

was easy enough among the different denominations of his time, which were all but offshoots of the same central faith, and did not differ among themselves so completely as the religions of Jesus, Zoroaster, or Mahomet introduced later into the country. Thus it was not difficult for the emperor, with due credit to the liberality of his views, to discover " the essence of the matter in all sects " and honour it duly. There are a few other facts which take away from his toleration to some extent. The prohibition of sacrificial slaughter of animals was another interference with a prescribed form of Brahmanical religious worship.[1] He openly expresses his disapprobation of certain rites and ceremonies the performance of which is an essential feature of Brahmanical religion [R.E. IX]. The sacredness of the lower animal life was disproportionately emphasised, while the sacredness of human life was not recognised by abolishing capital punishment. The only concession in this regard shown by Asoka was the three days' reprieve granted to convicts condemned to death, which might be utilised by their relations to get them a revision of the sentence [P.E. IV], as well as the institution of jail-deliveries on the anniversary days of his coronation [*Ib.* and P.E. V]. Perhaps the responsibility of man for his actions accounts for the hard treatment prescribed for him and leniency towards the lower forms of life.

In connection with his personal religion of Buddhism of which he was such a zealous follower, we may note that

[1] It is, however, to be noted that in interdicting the slaughter of animals at sacrifices, and in his general attitude towards rituals and ceremonies, Asoka is at one with the highest Brahmanical thought as represented in the Upaniṣads, some of the teachings of which are, indeed, echoed in his Edicts [see note under M.R.E. II]. Some of the Upaniṣads frankly stand up for the *parā-vidyā*, the knowledge of the Ātman, as the only and ultimate Reality, and brands as unworthy of attention all other study condemned as *aparā-vidyā*, in which were included even the four Vedas and the six Vedāṅgas [cf. *Muṇḍaka*, i, 1, 4-5 ; *Chhāndogya*, vii. 1 ; *Bṛihadāraṇyaka*, iii. 5, 1 ; etc.]. The *Muṇḍaka* [i. 2, 7] openly brands as fools those who perform mere rites and ceremonies. The *Bṛihadāraṇyaka* [i. 4, 10] likens those who offer sacrifices to the gods without knowing the Ātman to domestic animals ministering to the comforts of their owners !

what appealed most to the essentially spiritual mind of Asoka were not its external elements, its rituals and regulations, so much as its aids to inner development or self-realisation. As a Buddhist, Asoka takes more interest in the regulations for the life spiritual than in those for the collective life of the Saṅgha, though as emperor he was keenly interested in its prosperity and preventing and punishing disunion in the Saṅgha.

The particular cast of his mind is, indeed, envisaged in the different canonical texts selected by Asoka for the religious instruction of his co-religionists of all classes in the Bhabru Edict. He shows a preference for the ideal of the *Muni*, as set forth in two of the texts cited by him, viz., the *Muni-gāthā* and *Moneya-sute*, the recluse who is free from all desire, has renounced the world, and lives to himself in solitude and meditation leading up to *nirvāṇa*. In the *Aliya-vasāni* is emphasised the need of simplicity and asceticism as regards food, dress, dwelling, and the need of meditation. The necessity for strenuous self-exertion in spiritual life is emphasised against the unforeseen hindrances to it from the *Anāgata-bhayāni*, such as disease, decay, famine, war, or schism. No less are the internal hindrances to it, which are to be guarded against by constant self-examination, scrutiny of every act of the body, mind, and speech, as laid down in the *Lāghulovāda*. Thus it is apparent from these citations of the texts that what appealed most to Asoka in Buddhism was its ideal of purity and asceticism, and the aids it prescribes for the life spiritual, rather than its external rituals and regulations or those special and sectarian elements which distinguished Buddhism from other systems.

This also leads us to infer that by the word *Saṅgha* as used in the Edicts, Asoka meant the entire Buddhist Order, which in all probability remained undivided up to his time, so that Asoka's Buddhism was not the particular Buddhism of any of its special sects or schools. This view, though borne out by the Edicts (e.g., the P.E. VII and Bhabru Edict, where the Saṅgha does not denote any sect of Buddhism, but the whole Order), is not in consonance with tradition according to which, by the time of the third

Buddhist Council held at Pāṭaliputra in the tenth year of Asoka's reign, there were already in the Saṅgha not only its two divisions, called *Theravāda* and *Mahāsaṅghika*, but also two subdivisions of the former and four of the latter [see Kern's *Manual of Indian Buddhism*]. But the tradition may be brought into conformity with what we find in the Edicts, if we suppose with some scholars [1] that the second Buddhist Council at Vaiśāli really came off at the time of Asoka (called Kālāśoka in tradition) when the Saṅgha was for the first time threatened with a schism, due to the Ten Points about Discipline raised by the Vṛijian monks who were, however, defeated in the controversy, and the split in the Saṅgha was averted. This explains Asoka's fear of schism, and his measures to prevent it, and his references in the Edicts to the Saṅgha as an undivided unity which must be preserved at all costs. His intolerance towards dissent or schism was only due to his desire to nip it in the bud before it was too late : the intolerance could be commended if it had anticipated, and had not followed, the schism.[2]

We shall now treat of his public religion which he sought to present before his people. Negatively, we may say that it was not to be identified with any of the then prevailing faiths of the country. It was certainly not Buddhism, his own religion. " We hear from him nothing concerning the deeper ideas or fundamental tenets of that faith ; there is no mention of the Four Grand Truths, the Eightfold Path, the Chain of Causation, the supernatural quality of Buddha : the word and the idea of *Nirvāṇa* fail to occur ; and the innumerable points of difference which occupied the several sects are likewise ignored " [*Cambridge History*, p. 505]. As also pointed out by Vincent Smith : " the zeal of Asoka for Buddhism is proved not by his presentation of Dharma, but by his references to the canon, by the cast of his language, by his pilgrimages to Buddhist holy places, and by his

[1] E.g., Dr. D. R. Bhandarkar who forcibly advances this view in his *Asoka* [pp. 93-96].

[2] Asoka's attitude towards schism is determined by the canonical injunctions on the subject, of which an account is given in the annotation of Sarnath Edict below.

active control of the church" [*Asoka*, third ed. p. 60], i.e., by what does not appear in the principal Edicts.

The *dharma* of the Edicts is not any particular dharma or religious system, but the Moral Law independent of any caste or creed, the *sāra* or essence of all religions [R.E. XII]. It has a two-fold aspect: (1) practical and (2) doctrinal. In its practical aspect, it prescribes a comprehensive code of conduct embracing the various relations of life. It is described as comprising:

(1) *Śuśrūṣā*, obedience, to
- (*a*) Father and mother [R.E. III, IV, XI, XIII, and P.E. VII];
- (*b*) Elders [R.E. IV.; (*anupaṭīpati*) P.E. VII];
- (*c*) Teachers (*gurus*) [R.E. XIII, P.E. VII];
- (*d*) Men of high caste or pay [*agrabhuti* (or *bhuta*) -*suśruṣā* in R.E. XIII].

(2) *Apachiti*, respect,
- (*a*) Of pupils (*antevāsī*) towards their *gurus* [M.R.E. II];
- (*b*) Towards *gurus* [R.E. IX].

(3) *Sampratipatti*, proper treatment, towards
- (*a*) Ascetics, both brāhmaṇa and śramaṇa [R.E. IV, P.E. VII];
- (*b*) Relations [M.R.E. II, R.E. IV, and XIII];
- (*c*) Servants and dependants (*dāsa-bhataka*) [R.E. IX, XI, XIII, P.E. VII];
- (*d*) The poor and miserable (*kapana-valāka*) [P.E. VII];
- (*e*) Friends, acquaintances, and companions [R.E. XIII].

(4) *Dānam*, liberality, towards
- (*a*) Ascetics, brāhmaṇa and śramaṇa [R.E. III, VIII, IX and XI];
- (*b*) Friends, comrades, and relatives (*mita-śaṁstuta-ñātikā*) [R.E. III and XI];
- (*c*) The aged ("*thairānaṁ hiraṁṇapatividhāno*," "gift of gold to the aged," in R.E. VIII).

(5) *Prāṇānāṁ anāraṁbha*, abstention from slaughter of living beings [R.E. III, IV, XI, and P.E. VII]; *praṇanaṁ*

saṁyamo, restraint of violence towards living beings [R.E. IX] ; *avihīsā bhūtānaṁ,* non-violence towards life [R.E. IV, P.E. VII] ; *savra bhutana akṣati saṁyamaṁ* [R.E. XIII] ; *prāṇēsu drahyitavyaṁ* [M.R.E. II].

By the inclusion of these duties, the emperor no doubt aimed at the purity of domestic life so essential to the well-being of society, of which the family is the basis and unit. The circle of domestic relations embraced even the Brāhmaṇas and Śramaṇas, thereby recognising the duty of householders to support the ascetics who left their households in the interests of their spiritual life. It also embraced the lower animals, whose claims to kind treatment by their human masters are established and even enforced [R.E. III, IV, IX, XI, XIII, and P.E. VII].

Sometimes, again, this Code of Duties, or practical *Dharma,* is more generally described as comprising the following virtues, viz.,

(1) *Dayā,* kindness [P.E. II and VII].
(2) *Dānam,* liberality [*Ib.* and R.E. VII].
(3) *Satyam,* truthfulness [M.R.E. II, P.E. II and VII].
(4) *Śaucham,* inner and outer purity [P.E. II and VII].
(5) *Mārdavam,* gentleness [R.E. XIII, G. and K., and P.E. VII].
(6) *Sādhutā,* saintliness [P.E. VII].
(7) *Apa-vyayatā* and *apa-bhāṇḍatā,* moderation in spending and saving [R.E. III].
(8) *Saṁyama,* self-control [R.E. VII].
(9) *Bhāva-śuddhi,* purity of heart [*Ib.*].
(10) *Kṛitajñatā,* gratitude [*Ib.*].
(11) *Dṛiḍhabhaktitā,* firm devotion [*Ib.* and R.E. XIII, l. 5].
(12) *Dharma-rati,* attachment to morality [R.E. XIII].

In R.E. XIII, the *Dharma* is described in a nutshell as the right attitude towards all, manifesting itself in (1) *akṣati,* non-injury ; (2) *saṁyama,* restraint ; (3) *samācharaṇaṁ,* equal treatment ; and (4) *mārdavaṁ,* mildness, in respect of all creatures, human beings, as well as beasts and birds (*sarvabhūtānāṁ*). In P.E. I, again, the following requisites are mentioned for attaining happiness in this world and the next :

(1) *Dharmā-kāmatā*, love of dharma; (2) *Parīkṣā*, self-examination; (3) *Śuśrūṣā*, obedience; (4) *Bhaya*, fear (of sin); (5) *Utsāha*, enthusiasm (for *dharma*). The *practical* side of *dharma* is also emphasised by defining it *positively* as consisting in an abundance of good deeds (*bahu kayāne*) [P.E. II], and also *negatively* as *apāsinavaṁ*, i.e., freedom from *āsinavaṁ* [*Ib.*], or *pāpam*, sin [P.E. III], the incentives to which are also pointed out, viz, *chāṇḍyam*, rage or fury; *niṣṭhūryam*, cruelty; *krodhaḥ*, anger; *mānam*, pride; and *īrṣā*, envy. In R.E. X, the *dharma* is also negatively defined as *aparisravam*, i.e., freedom from *parisrava*, or *apuṇya*, evil.[1]

For his own part, Asoka proved by his personal example the value he attached to his precepts. We have already seen

[1] We may note that Jainism mentions 18 kinds of *pāpa*, and 42 of *āśrava* [Mrs. Stevenson, *Heart of Jainism*, pp. 302-305 f.], of which three, viz., *krodha*, *māna*, and *īrṣā* or *dveṣa* are also mentioned among the five *āsinavagāminis* by Asoka [P.E. III]. The Jaina work, *Praśnavyākaraṇa Sūtra*, I. 7, mentions five kinds of *āśrava*, viz., *hiṁsā* (violence), *mriṣāvāda* (lying), *adattadravyagrahaṇam* (stealing), *abrahmacharya* (incontinence), and *parigraha* (greed). *Āśrava* is also defined as *bhavahetu*, the cause of existence, as contrasted with *saṁvara*, self-control, the cause of *mokṣa* or emancipation.

Buddhism also has its own list of *āsavas*, comprising, as shown by Childers, (1) *Kāmāsava*, the lust of flesh; (2) *Bhavāsava*, attachment to existence; (3) *Avijjāsava*, the sin of ignorance (of the Four Great Truths, *ariyasachchāni*); and (4) *Diṭṭhāsava*, the sin of heresy.

It is thus clear that Asoka has followed the Jain rather than the Buddhist view of the *āsavas*. Dr. D. R. Bhandarkar [*Asoka*, pp. 129-30] finds a further borrowing of Asoka from Jainism in his use in the Edicts of the terms *jīva*, *pāṇa*, *bhūta*, and *jāta*, corresponding to the *pāṇā-bhūyā-jivā-sattā* of the *Āchāraṅga Sūtra*. In this way, Asoka, true to his own theory, has tried to include the *sāra* of the different religions, Brahmanism, Buddhism, and Jainism, in his own *Dharma*.

With the above conception of Asoka's *Dharma* as set forth in his Edicts, it is interesting to compare that given in the Buddhist Canonical text, *Sigālovāda Suttanta* [*Digha N.* iii. xxxi], according to which the following are to be avoided, viz., (*a*) The Four *Vices* (*Kamma-Kilesā*), viz.,—(1) Destruction of Life (*pāṇātipāto*), (2) Theft, (3) Lying (*musāvādo*), and (4) Adultery; (*b*) The Four *Motives* to Evil Deed—(1) Partiality (*chhandā*), (2) Enmity (*dosā*=*dveṣā*), (3) Fear, and (4) Folly; (*c*) The Six Means of Enjoyment (*bhogānāṁ apāyamukhāni*)—viz., (1) Intoxicating liquors, (2) Frequenting streets at unusual hours, (3) Haunting fairs (*samajjābhicharaṇaṁ*), (4) Gambling, (5) Evil Company, and (6) Laziness, from each of which result six *Ādīnavas* (cf. Asoka's *āsinava*) or Dangers.

how much he cherished all his domestic relations, brothers and sisters, sons and grandsons, his wives and other female relations of his, in whose affairs, charities, moral welfare, and happiness, both in this world and the next, he was keenly interested. Those outside his own family, the people at large, he regarded and declared as his own children for whose welfare he was constantly working. In P.E. VI, he says: "I devote my attention alike to my relatives, to persons near, and to persons afar off, if haply I may guide some of them to happiness, and to that end I make my arrangements." Thus arose his many public works of utility already described, together with his grants to Brahmans and ascetics of different orders. In P.E. II, Asoka himself refers to his many and various kindnesses and good deeds (vividhe *anugahe* and bahūni *kayānāni*) in respect of both man and beast, birds and aquatic creatures. To man his highest gift has been *dharma-dānam* [R.E. XI], the gift of dharma, or *chakṣu-dānam* [P.E. II], the gift of spiritual insight, while to the lower brute creation it was *prāṇa-dakṣiṇā* [*Ib.*], the gift of life. Asoka also insists on *dharmānuśāsanaṁ*, preaching of morality, or *dharmānuśasti* [R.E. IV, XIII, and P.E. VII], as the supreme duty of a king (*seste kaṁme*, R.E. IV), and, accordingly, he himself undertook a part of this public instruction in morality by moving among his people in the different provinces (*jānapadasya janasya darśanaṁ*), instructing them in morality and questioning them also about morality (*dharmānuśasti* and *dharmaparіprichchhanaṁ*), as stated in R.E. VIII. In R.E. VI, he asserts the promotion of the good of all (*sarvaloka-hita*) as the most important duty of the king, which could only be duly discharged by "exertion and despatch of business" (*utthānaṁ* and *artha-saṁtīraṇaṁ*), qualities which he so pre-eminently cultivated, as will appear from the same Edict.

But the *Dharma* of the Edicts was not merely practical. It is distinguished by several characteristic doctrines and philosophical positions, bringing out the originality of Asoka's ideas of moral reform. The sanctity of animal life was to be recognised on principle. *Toleration* was insisted on as an absolute duty in a land of many faiths. The root of Toleration (tasya tu idaṁ *mūlaṁ*) is restraint of speech (*vachaguti*), "refraining from speaking well of one's own sect and ill of others." On that basis Toleration among the followers of different faiths will grow, and it should be further promoted by making them know of one another's doctrines, so that the follower of one sect may be able to appreciate the doctrines of other sects, and be a *Bahu-śruta*. Out of this width of knowledge will spring the width of outlook (*bahukā*), charity and toleration, and purity of doctrines (*kalyāṇāgama*), the essence or *sāra*, of all religions [R.E. XII]. The essentials of religious life are recovered from the many accidents enshrouding them, and are brought out as the several virtues already noticed. Among a people whose religion was dominated by rituals, and moral life expressed in the performance of too "many, manifold, trivial, and worthless ceremonies" connected with sickness, marriage, birth, or even journey, it was appropriate to point out the *True Ceremonial* as consisting only in the good and moral conduct in all relations of life [R.E. IX]. Similarly was it specially appropriate to emphasise that the gift of Dharma was the only *True Gift* ! We may compare Cromwell's message : "Building of hospitals provided for men's bodies ; to build material temples is judged a work of piety ; but they that procure spiritual food, they that build up spiritual temples, they are the men truly charitable, truly pious" [R.E. XI and V. Smith's *Asoka*, p. 182]. In Rock Edict IV also is stated : "For this is the best of deeds—even the inculcation of the Law." Next is emphasised the need of *self-exertion* as a means of moral progress. The need, he frankly admits, is all the greater for a man of "high degree" [R.E. X] He further points out : "Difficult, verily, it is to attain such freedom (from the peril of vice), whether by people of low or high degree, save by the utmost exertion (*parākrama*), giving up all other aims (*sarvaṁ parityajya*). The Minor Rock Edict I publishes the declaration : "Let small and great exert themselves (*parākrameyuḥ*)." One method of this exertion is *self-examination*. This must mean examination of one's bad deeds with his good ones [P.E. III]. In P.E. I, he emphasises intense self-examination (*parīkṣā*) and intense effort (*utsāha*) as among the aids to moral life. In another Edict [P.E. VII], *reflection* (*nijhati*) is pointed out as another form of self-exertion. Here reflection on the Duty is regarded as a more powerful moral force than its regulations. Lastly, for kings and administrators, two appropriate doctrines are propounded. One is the Doctrine of *True Conquest*, a conquest causing pleasure, and not pain, achieved not over men's bodies, against their wishes, by physical force, but over their hearts and wills by the force of moral persuasion. The other is the Doctrine of *True Glory* or Fame for the king, which does not depend upon the physical extent of his dominion, but upon the moral progress he can help his people to achieve [R.E. X]. It is evident that by these and other similar doctrines, Asoka tried to instal Morality as the governing principle and force in every sphere of life, and to spiritualise politics and, indeed, all life's activities. His new ideals and doctrines express themselves in a new language, a variety of terms invented by him to indicate the new measures and institutions in which these had materialised. Among these terms, the significance of some of which has been already considered, may be mentioned here the following : (1) *Dharma-mahāmātra*, (2) *Dharma-yātrā* [R.E. VIII], (3) *Dharma-lipi*, as distinguished from the secular royal messages, (4) *Dharma-niyama* [P.E. VII], the restrictions dictated by Morality, (5) *Dharma-śrāvaṇa* [*Ib.*], (6) *Dharma-ghoṣa* [R.E. IV], religious proclamations as distinguished from military proclamations (*bherī-ghoṣa*), (7) *Dharma-staṁbha* [P.E. VII], pillars of piety as distinguished from the usual pillars of military victory and fame (vijaya or kīrti-staṁbha), (8) *Dharma-saṁbandha*, (9) *Dharma-saṁstava*, (10) *Dharma-saṁvibhāga* [R.E. XI], (11) *Dharma-nugraha* [R.E. IX], and (12) *Dharma-dāna*, (13) *Dharma-maṅgala*, and (14) *Dharma-vijaya*, referred to above. In P.E. I, he sums up his intentions by saying that he wants the maintenance, governance, happiness, and protection of the people to be regulated by Dharma, and the people to grow day by day in their dependence upon Dharma and devotion to Dharma (*dhaṁmena pālanā dhaṁmena vidhāne dhaṁmena sukhiyanā dhaṁmena gotīti; dhaṁmāpekhā dhaṁma-kāmatā*).

We may, lastly, note that an article of Asoka's faith was his belief in the other world (*paraloka*) repeated in several of his Edicts, and also in the attainment of *svarga* or happiness in that world as the result of the pursuit of Dharma in this world [K.E. I, P.E. I, IV, VII, and R.E. VI, IX, X, XIII. He also believed in the eternity of heaven and, consequently, in the immortality of soul [cf. "*anaṁtaṁ puṇaṁ prasavati*" in R.E. XI]. In his scheme of values, he considered the other world as of supreme consequence and as the objective of life ["*paratrikameva maha-phala meñati Devanaṁpriyo*" in R.E. XIII]. In R.E. X, he plainly declares that *all* his endeavour (*parikamate*) is for the sake of the other world (*savaṁ pāratrikāya*). The belief in *svarga* is common to both Brahmanical and Buddhist systems. The Buddha himself has said that a virtuous householder will be born as a god in the next world [*Majj. N.* I. 289, 388], while the blisses of *svarga* or heaven are described in the *Vimānavatthu* as comprising the *Vimāna* or a movable palace always at the disposal of the denizens of heaven, a completely white celestial elephant, and a radiant body shining like fire. As a believer in the *svarga*, Asoka also says in his R.E. IV how he tried to stimulate his people to virtue by presenting before them pictures of such blisses awaiting them after death. In P.E. IV, Asoka also hints at his belief in the forgiveness of sins when he holds that by fasts criminals condemned to death might obtain happiness in the other world.

The *dharma* that is thus presented in these Edicts is but another name for the moral or virtuous life, and takes its stand upon the common ground of all religions.[1] It cannot

[1] That the *Dharma* in this sense was not Asoka's original conception, but was known in earlier times, he himself hints at in two of his Edicts. In R.E. XIII, we are told that, prior to his conquest of Kalinga, and preaching of this dharma, there *were* people in Kalinga who conformed to this *dharma*. The Kalinga society was following this *dharma* as laid down in the Brahmanical system. The P.E. VII also indicates how Asoka's forefathers were anxious that the people

be called sectarian in any sense, but is completely cosmopolitan, capable of universal application and acceptance as the *sāra*, essence, of all religions [R.E. XII], and is thus worthy of the sovereign of a vast empire comprising peoples in various stages of development and following different religions. Thus in the moral interests of the diverse peoples committed to his care, Asoka was at pains to think out a system which might be imposed upon all his subjects irrespective of their personal faith and beliefs. Thus he laid the basis of a universal religion, and was probably the first to do so in history. We can now easily understand how the *Dharma* propounded by him could be introduced equally among the wild tribes, the unsubdued borderers of his empire, among all classes and ranks of society, followers of

should grow in *dharma*. The same Edict also points out that what Asoka did for this *dharma* was to define, publish, and preach it. His originality lay not in the idea of the *dharma* but in the practical measures for its adoption by the people. These measures he distinguishes as (1) his religious messages (*dharma-śrāvaṇāni*), (2) his religious injunctions (*dharmānuśāsanāni*), and (3) his appointment of officers (the Puruṣas, the Rājūkas, and the Dharma-mahāmātras) to give effect to these messages and injunctions and help the people in their religious practice (e.g., gifts).

Asoka's efforts after *Dharma* date from his conquest of Kalinga. His mental reactions from its violence increased his cultivation of *Dharma*, his devotion to *Dharma*, and his instruction of the people in *Dharma* [R.E. XIII]. The reason for his moral propagandism is indicated to be that he feels bound to promote the real welfare of his subjects, as "a father does of his children" [K.R.E]. The reason is further indicated in the following statement: "And whatever efforts I am making is made that I may discharge the debt which I owe to living beings, that I may make them happy in this world and that they may attain heaven in the other world" [R.E. VI]. Thus Asoka takes to moral propagandism (*dharma-vijaya*) as an absolute duty of a ruler towards his subjects, one of the obligations ("debts") of kingship. Such a duty must needs be wide and catholic in its outlook and scope, such as the promotion of happiness of all sections of the people both in this world and the next.

The Edicts use the word *Dharma* in two senses, firstly, and usually, in its wide sense acceptable to all religions, Brahmanical or Buddhist; and, secondly, but very rarely, to indicate Buddhism, Asoka's personal religion, as in the Bhabru Edict.

different sects and denominations, males and females, householders and ascetics, among Indians and non-Indians, nay, even among the civilised peoples of Hellenistic kingdoms in the West. Therefore, to dismiss Asoka's reference to the foreign missions he sent to the Western countries as nothing but "royal rodomontade"[1] smacks of prejudice and a superficial view of the matter. In organising such missions to foreign countries at the expense of India, Asoka perhaps felt that India also would be benefited along with them. These were the countries with which India had active intercourse in those days, and it was desirable that they should conform to common codes and ideals of conduct and thought. The influx of foreigners to India in those days is apparent from the statement of Megasthenes that there was a separate department of administration, a sort of a Foreign Office, to deal with their special interests. The history of the Western Greek countries does not preserve any record showing how Asoka's missionaries fared there, but we need not assume on *a priori* grounds that those countries did not welcome the Indians who brought to them only a message of peace and goodwill and the means of medical aid for man and beast. The Indians came to serve them, and not to teach them any new religious truths: the Greeks were not called upon "to discard their gods at the bidding of the Hindus." These came to them on innocent and peaceful propaganda of social service and not on any offensive and aggressive religious propaganda. It is undeniable that Buddhist thought has left its marks upon some phases of Western thought,[2] notably "the heretical Gnostic sects and some of the more orthodox forms of Christian teaching" [V. A. Smith's *Early History of India*, 3rd ed., p. 188], and it was through the instrumentality

[1] As was done by the late Dr. Rhys Davids in his *Buddhist India*.

[2] E.g., the sects of the *Essenes*, a small Jewish community on the shores of the Dead Sea, existing before Christianity, and of the *Therapentae*, a similar order existing near Alexandria [see *Encyclopaedia of Religion and Ethics*, v. 401, and xii. 318-9 quoted in Bhandarkar's *Asoka*, p. 165].

of such foreign missions from India that these results were achieved.[1]

[1] It may not be amiss to recall in this connection that while Asoka used to despatch his "*dūtas*," the messengers of peace and goodwill, to the western Hellenistic States, these states also used to reciprocate by sending to the Mauryan Court their own envoys. The treaty with Seleukos of about 302 B.C. was followed by the despatch to the court of Asoka's grandfather of the famous envoy, Megasthenes, an officer of Arachosia, while Asoka's father, Bindusāra, received at his court the homage of the next envoy, Deimachos, from Antiochos Soter. A third envoy named Dionysios was sent to the court of Pāṭaliputra by Asoka's contemporary, Ptolemy Philadelphos of Egypt (285-247 B.C.), called *Turamāyo* in R.E. XIII, either in his time, or in that of his father.

CHAPTER V

MONUMENTS

WE shall now discuss the greatness of Asoka as a builder. The greatness has been somewhat exaggerated, if we are to consider only the tangible evidence proving it. Tradition, however, makes Asoka a mighty builder, the builder of cities, of innumerable stūpas, vihāras or monasteries, and pillars and rails of stone, bearing inscriptions or artistic sculptures The *Divyāvadāna* [ch. xxvii] ascribes Asoka's building activity to the desire which he expressed to his preceptor, Upagupta, in the following words : " Those places which were inhabited by the Lord Buddha—those I shall visit, worship, and mark with memorials for the benefit of remote posterity." The testimony of tradition is confirmed to some extent by that of Asoka's own words in his Edicts.

Tradition ascribes to Asoka the foundation of two cities. The first is Śrīnagara, the capital of Kashmir, where Asoka is said to have built 500 Buddhist monasteries together with other edifices, some of which were consecrated to Brahmanical worship. The tradition is recorded by Kalhana in his *Rājataraṅginī* [Book I, vv. 101-7], but, earlier than Kalhana, by Yuan Chwang who makes the additional statement that " Asoka gave up all Kashmir for the benefit of the Buddhist church " [Watters' tr., p. 267]. The Chinese pilgrim saw about 100 Buddhist monasteries then still existing in the country, and also saw " four Asoka topes." The second city built by Asoka was in Nepal which he is said to have visited with his daughter, Chārumatī, and her Kṣatriya husband, Devapāla, who chose to settle there, building respectively a nunnery and a monastery. In commemoration of the royal visit were built the city of Deo-Pātan (Deva-pattana), and four stūpas still standing in their archaic style [Sylvain Levi, *Le Nepal*, quoted in *Cambridge History*, p. 501].

More than the builder of cities is Asoka the builder of monasteries or stūpas, according to the legend which describes them to be as high as hill-tops (" *stūpair vichitraiḥ giriśṛiṅgakalpaiḥ* " in the *Div.*). The *Mahāvaṁsa* relates that the emperor once asked his preceptor, Moggaliputra Tissa, the question, " How great is the content of the Dharma taught by the Master ? " to which the divine replied : " There are 84,000 sections of the Dhamma." Then Asoka said : " Each one of them will I honour with a *vihāra*." Thus he proceeded to have 84,000 vihāras built by all his subordinate kings in 84,000 towns selected all over India [*Ib.* v. 78-80], including the Asoka monastery built by himself at Pāṭaliputra. This tradition is, however, differently told by Fa-hien. According to him, Asoka " wished to destroy the eight topes [1] (i.e., those built over the relics of the

[1] The story of Asoka's treatment of the Buddha relics has had different versions. Originally, as we read in the *Mahāparinibbāna Sutta*, the relics were divided among eight claimants, as already related. Besides these, Droṇa the Brahman, who made the division, received the vessel in which the body was cremated, while the Moriyas of Pipphalivana, who had arrived too late, had to content themselves only with the ashes of the funeral pyre. All these ten parties also promised each to put up a cairn or stūpa over their portion. Of these, Fa-hien saw what he calls the " Charcoal tope," the tope attributed to the Moriyas of Pipphalivana, but locates it, like Yuan Chwang, not at Pipphalivana, but near Kuśinagara. The *Buddhacharita*, indeed, assigns the ashes and the ashes-stūpa to the Mallas of Kuśinagara and not to these Moriyas. Fa-hien also saw Ajātaśatru's original stūpa at Rājagṛiha and not the one over the collective deposit of the relics mentioned below, which was seen by Yuan Chwang [Watters, ii. 158]. The third stūpa seen by Fa-hien was that at Rāmagrāma. Yuan Chwang saw the stūpa of Droṇa also at a place called Mahāśāla, near Arrah. Of all these stūpas, however, only *one* has been supposed to be discovered up to now, the stūpa of the Śākyas at Piprahwa, containing an urn bearing the following inscription : " This shrine for relics of the Buddha, the august One, is the pious foundation (*sukiti*) of the Śākyas, his brethren, in associa-

Buddha's body distributed at his death among eight different peoples), and to build instead of them 84,000 topes" on the theory that the bones of the human body comprised 84,000 atoms [Legge's tr., p. 69]. But archaeological evidence makes us sure about only a few of the stūpas or vihāras ascribed to Asoka. From his own words in the Edicts, we only learn that he enlarged to twice its size the stūpa of Koṇāgamana, the previous Buddha, at Niglīva and built for the sect of Ājīvikas three sets of cave-dwellings in the Barabar hills of Bihar, while archaeological inference ascribes to Asoka the great stūpa at Sanchi (forming the nucleus of the structure built round it a century later and to be seen now), as also a stūpa at Bharhut with elaborately carved railing bearing inscriptions in Asokan scripts. The latter stūpa has now disappeared, and parts of its richly sculptured railing on view at the Indian Museum in Calcutta

tion with their sisters, their children, and their wives." A reason, however, for doubting this identification of the Piprahwa stūpa, and for explaining, indeed, the non-discovery of any of the old ten stūpas, is sought to be found in a late legend that Asoka broke open seven of these and carried off the relics for distribution among his own stūpas. This story is first given in a passage in the *Divyāvadāna*, but a passage of which the historical value is weakened by the fact that it is much later than Asoka, besides being rather curt, self-contradictory, and enigmatic. This story we then find repeated by Fa-hien and, later, in the *Sumaṅgalavilāsinī* of Buddhaghosa, where, however, it is not Asoka but Ajātasattu who first gets the relics out of all the eight stūpas (except that at Rāmagāma guarded by the Nāgas). He is led to this step [twenty years after the Buddha's death (Bigandet, ii. 97)] by the advice of the sage Mahākassapa, who, afraid of the safety of the relics, collects them and gets them deposited in a subterranean chamber specially built for the purpose by the king. It is here that Asoka, after opening all the seven stūpas in vain, finds the relics, which he deposits in his own 84,000, not stūpas, but vihāras. Rhys Davids, who has discussed this subject [*JRAS*, 1901, p. 397], observes that this legend of Asoka breaking open the stūpas is not mentioned in any one of the twenty-nine canonical Buddhist writings from the time of Buddha to that of Asoka, though there is a reference to the *stūpabhedaka*, the violator of stūpas, in an isolated verse in the *Mahāvastu*, in which one may, but should not, find a reference to Asoka [see Fleet's articles on "The Corporeal Relics of Buddha" in the *JRAS*, 1906, for the legends in full].

are all that now remain of that ancient structure. We may note that Yuan Chwang in the seventh century A.D. made definite mention of more than 80 stūpas [1] and vihāras [2] associated by tradition with Asoka, besides the 500 vihāras of Kashmir and other large groups of same in different

[1] Yuan Chwang noticed the following Asokan Topes: Kapis (Kafiristan)—1 (containing the Buddha's relics); Nagar (Jalalabad) —2; Udyāna—1 (where the Buddha, as king Śivi, sliced his body to ransom a pigeon from a hawk); Taxila—2 (the tope where the Buddha gave his head away in charity, and the tope marking the spot where Prince Kuṇāla had his eyes torn out by the guile of his stepmother); Sinhapur—3 (including the one where the Buddha fed the hungry tigress by his body); Uras—1; Kashmir—4 (with the Buddha's relics); Sthāneśvara—1; Srughna—1; Govisana—1 (where the Buddha preached); Ahichchhatra—1; Pilosanna—1; Kanauj—2 (where the Buddha preached); Hayamukha—1 (where the Buddha preached); Prayāga—1 (where the Buddha defeated his opponents in controversy); Kosambī—3 (where the Buddha preached); Śrāvastī—1 (with relics); Kapilavastu—3 (to mark places where the Buddha was born, had the first bath, and met and taught his father after his Buddhahood); Rāmagrāma—3 (to mark the places where the Buddha cut off his hair and stopped to turn back his groom Chandaka); Kuśinagara—2 (the second to mark the place of the division of the relics among the eight kings); Sarnath—2; Ghazipur —1 (with relics, and where the Buddha had also preached); Mahāśāla (near Arrah)—2 (the second to mark the place where were deposited the relics and jar of the Brahman Droṇa, also called the Kumbha Stūpa); Vaiśālī—2; Vajji—1 (where the Buddha preached); Gayā—1 (where the Buddha uttered the Ratnamegha Sūtra); Bodh-Gayā—1 (to mark the place where the grass-cutter gave the Buddha grass for his seat); Pāṭaliputra—1 (for relics); Rājagṛiha—2; near Nalanda—3 (one marking the place of Mudgalaputra's birth and death, and the other of the Buddha's preaching); Tāmralipti—1; Karṇasuvarṇa—several topes to mark the places where the Buddha preached; Orissa—more than 10 topes to mark places of Buddha's teaching; South Kosala—1 (where the Buddha defeated the Tīrthikas in argument); Chola country—1; Dravida and Kāñchi—several topes; Mahārāṣṭra—5; Valabhī—several topes; Pofato (near Multan)—4; Afantu (in Sindh)—1; and Sindh with "some tens of topes as memorials of the Buddha's visits."

[2] E.g., the Asokārāma or Kukkuṭārāma at Pāṭaliputra, which was large enough to accommodate, according to the tradition recorded by Yuan-Chwang, an assembly of 1000 monks; according to other authorities [Watters, ii. 98], 300,000 monks assembled there to attend Asoka's first "quinquennial festival of the holy priesthood."

localities vaguely indicated. One of the stūpas found by Yuan Chwang to the north-west of Vaiśālī, which was erected to mark the place where the Buddha in one of his previous births ruled as a Chakravartī, may be identified as the stūpa now found at Kesariya, the stūpa of the Rāja-keśarī, if it may be so taken.

Asoka was also a great builder of monolithic pillars, of which but few are now extant and can be definitely ascribed to him. Fa-hien noticed only *six* pillars, of which two were on each side of the door of the Jetavana Vihāra at Śrāvastī with a *wheel* and *ox* on their tops ; one at Saṅkāśya, " about 50 cubits high, with a *lion* on the top of it," and niches containing shining images of the Buddha on its four sides ; the fourth, an inscribed one, on the way to Vaiśālī from Kuśinagara ;[1] the fifth, also an inscribed one, at Pāṭaliputra, already described, and the sixth in the same locality, " more than 30 ft. high with a *lion* on the top of it " [*Ibid.* p. 80].

Yuan Chwang noticed fifteen of such pillars of which four or five can now be identified with existing examples, some of which, on the other hand, escaped the notice of the two Chinese pilgrims. Yuan Chwang had noticed pillars at the following places :

(1) The Pillar at Sankassa " of a lustrous violet colour, and very hard, with a crouching *lion* on the top (also noticed

[1] At a distance of 12 *yojanas* from Kuśinagara towards south-east, and of 10 *yojanas* from Vaiśālī [Legge, pp. 71, 72]. The *yojana* of Fa-hien has been variously estimated at from 4½ or 5 to 7 or more miles. Considering the location of the pillar on the highway leading from Pāṭaliputra through Vaiśālī to Kapilavastu and Kuśinagara, on which stands no less than five of the Asokan Pillars, I am tempted to hazard the conjecture that this particular pillar must have been one of these Asokan Pillars, though it is not described as such by Fa-hien, and that it may be identified with what is called the Lauriya-Ararāj Pillar of Asoka bearing P.E. I-VI. Fa-hien also testifies to the inscription on the Pillar, though he could not read and understand its contents himself. He relies upon the local report about them, and states that the inscription gives an account of the event of the Buddha's sending back the Lichchhavis when they insisted on following him to his *pari-nirvāṇa*. As noticed below, Yuan Chwang also has recorded wrong accounts of the substance of the inscriptions on Asokan Pillars he had noticed.

by Fa-hien) and quaintly carved figures on sides." [1] [Watters, i. 334.]

(2) and (3) The two Pillars on the two sides of the east gate of the Jetavana Vihāra at Śrāvastī, one surmounted by a sculptured *wheel*, and the other by an *ox* (as noticed by Fa-hien), and both 70 ft. high [*Ib.* i. 383].

(4) The Pillar near Kapilavastu, commemorative of the previous Buddha, Krakuchhanda, " with a carved *lion* on the top and an account of his decease on the sides," and above 30 ft. high [*Ib.* ii. 5].

(5) The Pillar near Kapilavastu, commemorative of the previous Buddha, Kanakamuni, " with a *lion* on the top, and a record of the circumstances of this Buddha's decease on the sides," and above 20 ft. high [*Ib.* ii. 6].

This is probably the same pillar as was discovered near Niglīva with an inscription which, however, does *not* give particulars of the decease of the Buddha, but only states that Asoka had enlarged to double its size the tope of Kanakamuni and offered it worship. The *tope* with bodily relics of that Buddha was also noticed by Yuan Chwang. It is thus probable that Yuan Chwang could not read the

[1] Cunningham found at a village called Sankisa in the Farrukhābād District a pillar with a well-carved elephant on the top, without its trunk and tail [Plate VI]. He supposed this pillar to be the pillar seen by Fa-hien who, according to him, must have mistaken a lion for the elephant as its top. It is, however, strange that an accurate observer like Yuan Chwang also fell into that optical illusion by noticing " a crouching lion " instead of the elephant on the top of the same pillar. Cunningham has further supposed that the modern village of Sankisa should be identified with the ancient Sankāśya [*ASR*, i. 274]. Both the suppositions about the pillar and its place are vigorously opposed by V. A. Smith [Watters, ii. 338] who asserts : " The ' elephant-pillar ' at Sankisa cannot be the ' lion-pillar ' seen at Kapitha (i.e., Saṅkāśya) by Yuan Chwang. I do not believe in Cunningham's identification of the little village called Sankisa in the Farrukābād District with Kapitha or Saṅkāśya." He places Saṅkāśya somewhere in the N.E. corner of the Etah District.

It may be further noted that Yuan Chwang may be taken as capable of distinguishing the lion from the elephant on the tops of these pillars when he mentions both ' lion-tops ' and ' elephant-tops.' He mentions the ' elephant-top ' of the Rājagriha Pillar.

PLATE VI.

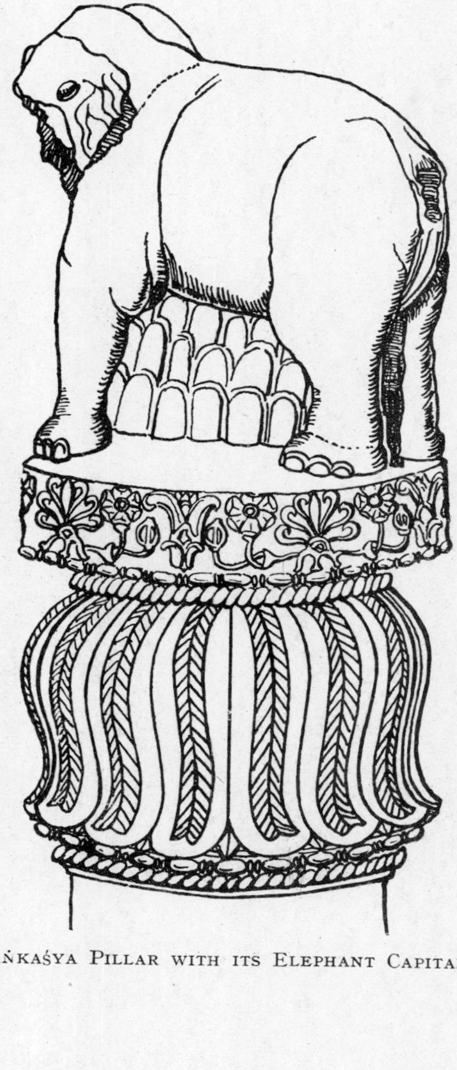

Saṅkāśya Pillar with its Elephant Capital.

Asokan inscription and depended on the local people, who could not read it either, for its meaning.

(6) The Pillar in Lumbini grove (modern Rummindei in Nepal and about six miles from Dulhā in Basti District) " with the figure of a *horse* on the top," which Yuan Chwang saw broken in the middle and laid on the ground, being struck by lightning [*Ib.* ii. 14]. P. C. Mukharji, also, who first discovered the Rummindei Pillar, describes how " its upper portion is gone, and of what remains the top is split into two halves, the line of fissure coming down to near the middle height. The capital was of the usual bell-shaped form, of which the base, broken into two halves, exists." But the horse-capital has not been traced. Yuan Chwang does not refer to the inscription on the pillar, but the *Fang-chih* tells us that the Pillar recorded the circumstances of the Buddha's birth, which is not also quite correct.

(7) The Pillar at Kusinārā on " which were recorded the circumstances of the Buddha's decease " [*Ib.* ii. 28]; not yet discovered.

(8) A second pillar at Kusinārā recording the circumstances of the division of the Buddha's relics among the eight claimants [*Ib.* ii. 42]; not discovered.

(9) The Pillar on the way to Sarnath, " of polished green stone, clear and lustrous as a mirror in which the reflection of the Buddha was constantly visible " [*Ib.* ii. 48]. This pillar is identified by V. A. Smith as the pillar now known as Lāṭ Bhairo in Benares which was smashed during a riot in 1908.

(10) The Pillar at Sarnath, " above 70 ft. high,[1] which had the softness of jade and was of dazzling brightness "; it was erected " at the spot at which the Buddha, having obtained enlightenment, first preached his religion " [*Ib.* ii. 50]. This pillar has been discovered together with the inscription it bears, as well as the beautiful capital of four lions for which it is so deservedly famous.

(11) A pillar " surmounted by a lion " in front of the

[1] The height is overestimated by Yuan Chwang, unless he is referring to a different pillar. The Sarnath Pillar discovered measures only 37 feet above ground.

Asokan tope at Mahāśāla, with an inscription stating " how the Buddha here subdued and converted certain cannibal demons of the wilderness " [*Ib.* ii. 60].

(12) The pillar at Vaiśālī " about 50 ft. high, and surmounted by a *lion* " [*Ib.* ii. 65]. This pillar is identified by Cunningham [*ASR*, i. 60] with the Asokan Pillar (uninscribed) discovered near the village of Bakhra. It may be noted that the pillar is really located at the village now called Koluha (from ancient *Kollāga*) near the ruins of old Vaisālī, modern Basarh. It is to be observed that this locality was famous in those ancient times as the birthplace of Vardhamāna Mahāvīra, the founder of Jainism [*ASR*, 1903-4, p. 88], and this might explain the location of this pillar. Thus we might rename Bakhra Pillar as Koluha Pillar.

(13) The Pillar at Pāṭaliputra " above 30 ft. high, with an inscription much injured," the gist of which, as given by Yuan Chwang, is the same as that given by Fa-hien [*Ib.* ii. 93]. Fragments of this pillar have been found.

(14) A second pillar at Pāṭaliputra, " some tens of feet in height," marking Asoka's " hell " or prison [*Ib.* ii. 88].

(15) The Pillar at Rājagṛiha,[1] above " 50 ft. high, surmounted by an *elephant*, and having an inscription " [*Ib.* ii. 162].

Up to now, the so-called Asokan pillars have been discovered at Topra, Meerut (both removed to Delhi by Sultan Firoz Tughlak in 1356 A.D.), Allahabad (probably removed by Emperor Akbar from Kauśāmbī),[2] Lauriya-Ararāj, Lauriya-Nandangarh (with lion-capital), Rampurwa (with bell-capital crowned by a lion), Sanchi (with four lions

[1] Before coming to Rājagṛiha, to the east of the Bodhi tree, across the Nairanjana river, Yuan Chwang had noticed *two* pillars, one " erected where the Buddha Kāśyapa had sat in meditation," and the other associated with a Tīrthika [Watters, ii. 141]. These pillars Yuan Chwang does not connect with Asoka.

[2] Recently what is believed to be an uninscribed Asokan Pillar has been discovered without its capital at Kosam (Kauśāmbī), but with the characteristic Mauryan polish [*ASR*, 1922-23, p. 13]. There are already found three other uninscribed Pillars taken to be Asokan, viz., those at Bakhra (Vaiśālī), Rampurwa (with bull capital) and Sankisa (with elephant capital).

PLATE VII.

BAKHRA PILLAR WITH ITS LION CAPITAL.

forming the capital), Sarnath (with capital of four lions), Rummindei (with bell-capital) and Niglīva. All these ten pillars ascribed to Asoka on the ground that they bear his inscription cannot, however, be ascribed *en bloc* to him. His own words forbid that inference : in the Minor Rock Edict I (Rupnath text) he orders that the Edict is to be " engraved upon stone pillars wherever there are stone pillars in my dominions " ; while the last of his Edicts [P.E. VII] concludes with the sentence : " This scripture of the Law, wheresoever pillars of stone or tables of stone exist, must there be recorded so that it may be everlasting." One of the most refreshing features of Asoka's character is his scrupulous truthfulness in carefully distinguishing the achievements of his predecessors from those of his own. Thus he does not claim that all the pillars to bear his inscription were his own creation. Some of them were already found in his dominion, presumably the work of his predecessors.[1] These were not always

[1] The question of the existence of pre-Asokan Pillars has not received attention. Some light is thrown on the subject by Yuan Chwang who distinctly describes some of the pillars he had seen as being built by Asoka, but is silent about others. For instance, in the list of Pillars seen by him as given above, Nos. (1)-(6) and (13) are definitely mentioned as Asokan, while Nos. (7)-(12) and (15) are merely mentioned as standing before Asokan topes, and No. (14) on the site of Asoka's " Hell." Pre-Asokan might be supposed the two pillars Yuan Chwang had seen on his way to Rājagṛiha from Bodh-Gayā, as referred to above. To the same category might perhaps belong the pillar discovered by Cunningham at Bakror near Bodh-Gayā with two stumps *in situ* and part of the main shaft above 16 ft. in height. It was made of sandstone bricks of size $15\frac{1}{2} \times 10\frac{1}{4} \times 3\frac{1}{2}$ in., the standard Asokan brick being $16 \times 10 \times 3$ in. in size. The main shaft was removed to Gayā [*ASR* i. 12]. Cunningham saw two other similar and uninscribed pillars, one at Taxila and the other " with an eight-lion capital " at Latiya near Ghazipur, while he also saw " the capitals of six other large pillars still lying at Sankisa, Bhilsa, Sanchi and Udayagiri " [near Bhuvaneśvara, Orissa) [*Corpus*, p. 3]. In this connection one is tempted to hazard the conjecture that perhaps the Bhitari Pillar, famous for the Gupta inscription it bears, was originally a Mauryan Pillar some of whose characteristic marks it shows, viz., its reddish sandstone material, its capital, 3 ft. 2 in. high, which is bell-shaped and reeded like an Asokan capital, and its lower rectangular part or pedestal on which

utilised for his purposes by Asoka. Thus at Rampurwa one of the two pillars is uninscribed, as one was sufficient for the inscription of his edict and fulfilment of his desire. But evidence is wanting to show how and why they had been constructed before Asoka's time.

Even with regard to the stūpa, the history of that type of structure does not begin with Asoka. For instance, he "enlarged to twice its size the stūpa of Buddha Koṇākamana," as stated in the Niglīva Pillar inscription, which shows that the construction of the original stūpa was not due to Asoka.

After their location, a description may now be given of these monuments with reference to their structure and other characteristic features.

Of the *stūpa*, the Sanchi stūpa, as it now stands, is a segment of a sphere of which the proper height should have been $77\frac{1}{2}$ ft., while the diameter at the base of the dome is 110 ft. The original structure of Asoka, the nucleus of the present one, had somewhat smaller dimensions, and was evidently made of bricks. The other Asokan stūpa at Bharhut, also in brick, was nearly 68 ft. in diameter.

The Mauryan structures in brick are sought to be distinguished by the size of their bricks, but the size, it must be noted, is not at all a very reliable indication of architectural chronology. There is revealed as much variety of dimension among bricks of the early strata and periods as of the obviously later ones. Bricks belonging to the Mauryan levels at Bhitā measured $19\frac{1}{2} \times 12\frac{1}{4} \times 2\frac{1}{4}$ in. and $17\frac{1}{2} \times 11\frac{3}{4} \times 2\frac{3}{4}$ in. The bricks at Mathurā, at the Ganeśa Mound, measured $13\frac{1}{2} \times 10\frac{1}{4} \times 3$ in., and at Katra $11 \times 8\frac{1}{2} \times 2\frac{1}{3}$. The bricks found round the base of the Asokan Pillar at Sarnath were $16\frac{3}{4} \times 11 \times 2\frac{3}{4}$ in., but at other places the dimensions ranged from $15\frac{1}{2} \times 6\frac{1}{2} \times 2\frac{1}{2}$ to $8 \times 6\frac{1}{2} \times 2\frac{1}{2}$, the bricks used at the base being the largest. A much later monument, like the Bhitargaon Temple, again, showed bricks as large as the

the shaft stands. Its location is no less suspicious, being on the highway between Benares and Ghazipur (Chenchu) trodden by Yuan Chwang, while there is a precedent of an Asokan Pillar being seized by another Gupta emperor for his inscription at Allahabad !

Mauryan bricks, being 18 × 9 × 3 in. Thus the size of the brick is no certain criterion for determining the chronology of the monument concerned.

Of *cave-dwellings*, there are found in all seven, excavated in the Barabar and Nagarjuni hills near Gayā. These are all cut out of the hard and refractory syenitic granite. Three of these bear an inscription of Daśaratha, Asoka's grandson, and belong to the Nagarjuni group. Of all the caves, the largest is known as the Gopikā Cave, with its both ends semicircular. It has a length of 40 ft. 5 in., and width of 17 ft. 2 in., with walls 6 ft. 6 in. high, and the vaulted roof of 4 ft. above them. The caves bearing Asoka's inscription are also three in number and belong to the Barabar group. The first is known as the Karṇa Chaupar Cave, which has a plain rectangular hall, 33 ft. 6 in. long and 14 ft. broad, with walls of the height of 6 ft. 1 in. long and the vaulted roof of 4 ft. 8 in. above them. The next is known as the Sudāmā Cave, with an outer and inner chamber. The inner chamber is circular, with a hemispherical domed roof. The outer chamber is oblong, with a length of 32 ft. 9 in., breadth of 19 ft. 6 in., walls of the height of 6 ft. 9 in., and a vaulted roof above them of 5 ft. 6 in. The third cave of this group is known as the Lomaśa Ṛiṣi Cave. It does not bear any inscription of Asoka but of a later king, the Maukhari Anantavarman. The fourth cave is known as the Viśvajhopri (Viśvāmitra) Cave, and consists of two chambers somewhat unfinished. The outer chamber is more like a verandah than a chamber.

All these caves are marked by the Mauryan architectural characteristic of a bright polish shining from their walls as well as roofs, while the inscribed ones are dedicated in common to the Ājīvikas. It may be noted that Yuan Chwang mentions " some tens of cave-dwellings given by Asoka to his preceptor, Upagupta, at Pāṭaliputra, and also to other arhats " [Watters, ii. 95], but these are not yet traced.

The *pillars*, however, represent the high-water mark of Mauryan achievements in the domain of the fine arts. They generally consist of a round and a monolithic shaft tapering from the base with a diameter ranging from about

$35\frac{1}{2}$ in. to $49\frac{1}{2}$ in. to a total height of between 40 and 50 ft., the diameter at the top ranging from 22 in. to about 35 in.[1] The capital of the columns has the shape of a bell [supposed by Havell to be lotus, " the blue lotus of the sky, Vishnu's flower " (*Aryan Rule*, p. 106)], and is surmounted by an abacus and crowning sculpture in the round. One of the pillars in the best condition is that at Lauriya-Nandangarh, of which the crowning figure is a *lion*, while the abacus is adorned by a row of Brahmani geese or *haṁsas* pecking their food, shown in relief, symbolising the flock of which the Buddha is the shepherd. A single *lion* also adorns the top of the Asokan Pillars at Koluha (Bakhra), and Rampurwa. Instead of a single lion, there are *four lions* set back to back on the tops of the pillars at Sanchi and Sarnath. The column at Sankisa has an *elephant* as its capital, and that at Rampurwa a *bull*, while the capital of the Lauriya-Ararāj pillar had a *Garuḍa* according to V. A. Smith, but my local inquiry on the spot convinced me it was a single *lion*. It may be noted again in this connection that of the pillars seen by Fa-hien and Yuan Chwang, they noticed *lion*-capitals at Sankisa, at Kapilavastu on both its pillars, at Mahāśāla, at Vaiśālī (Bakhra ?), and at Pāṭaliputra ; *wheel*-capital and *ox*-capital at Śrāvastī ; *horse*-capital at Lumbini ; and an *elephant*-capital at Rājagṛiha.[2] The next noticeable feature

[1] The Delhi-Topra Pillar is 42 ft. 7 in. in length, the Lauriya-Ararāj Pillar $36\frac{1}{2}$ ft. above the ground, the Lauriya-Nandangarh 32 ft. $9\frac{1}{2}$ in., with its capital 6 ft. 10 in. high, the Rampurwa 44 ft. $9\frac{1}{2}$ in., the Allahabad Kosam Pillar 42 ft. 7 in., the Sarnath 37 ft. above ground, and the Rummindei about 21 ft. above ground.

[2] It is interesting to note that these Asokan Pillars had their imitations in later times. We find them, for instance, among the sculptures and bas-reliefs of Sanchi and Bharhut. The imitation is shown in the capitals of the pillars, such as four lions seated back to back, four elephants standing back to back and carrying riders, four dwarfs, three elephants, a wheel of sixteen spokes, one elephant between two lions, or two men in a pair-horsed chariot. Cunningham had noticed forty of such pillars at Sanchi. But the best of these was that crowned by a human figure, one of the finest specimens of sculpture, supposed by Cunningham to be the figure of Asoka himself ! It was 45 ft. high, and of fine polish too. There are also some pillars showing " false capitals," with figures of goats, horses,

PLATE VIII

RAMPURWA LION CAPITAL.

of these pillars is the decoration of their abacus, which shows a variety, sometimes a lotus and honeysuckle, or sometimes wheels and animals, alternating. The Sarnath Pillar follows a special decorative design: besides its capital surmounted by four lions standing back to back, it shows in their middle a large stone wheel, the symbol of the *dharma-chakra*, of which only fragments remain. The lions again stand on a drum showing figures of four animals [1] carved on it, viz., a lion, an elephant, a bull, and a horse, placed between four wheels. These sculptures Sir John Marshall [*ASR*, 1904-5, p. 36] considers as " masterpieces in point of both style and technique—the finest carving, indeed, that India has yet produced, and unsurpassed, I venture to think, by anything of their kind in the ancient world." Over and above the variety of spirited bas-reliefs and living statues of men and animals, the pillars show a brilliant polish which reflects the greatest credit on the craftsmanship concerned. Dr. Vincent A. Smith [*Asoka*, p. 136] remarks: " The skill of the stone-cutter may be said to have attained perfection, and to have accomplished tasks which would, perhaps, be found beyond the powers of the twentieth century. Gigantic shafts of hard sandstone, thirty or forty feet in length, were

bulls, camels, elephants, and lions. The Bharhut remains bring to light three bas-reliefs showing pillars with Persepolitan bell-capital surmounted by (1) an elephant (taken by Bloch [*ASR*, 1908-9, pp. 144 f.] to be a typical Asokan pillar), (2) three lions, and (3) garuḍa. See Plate X.

[1] It may be noted that these four animals also constitute the tops of the Asokan Pillars as discovered up to now, or noticed by the Chinese pilgrim, Yuan Chwang. The reason for Asoka's selection of these animals might perhaps be that they are traditionally associated with the four quarters as their guardians, viz., the elephant with the east, the horse with the south, the bull with the west, and the lion with the north. These four animals on the Sarnath column are thus intended to show that the Dhamma was proclaimed to all the four quarters. As regards the lion, Asoka might also have taken it to be a symbol of the Buddha [see V. A. Smith's *History of Fine Art in India and Ceylon*, p. 60]. According to Foucher [*Beginnings of Buddhist Art*], the bull is also associated with the Buddha as incarnating the traditional date of his birth, the full moon day of Vaiśākha.

dressed and proportioned with the utmost nicety, receiving a polish which no modern mason knows how to impart to the material." The polish [1] has deceived some observers into thinking that it was metallic. Tom Coryate in the seventeenth century described the Delhi pillar as 'a brazen pillar,' while Bishop Heber, writing early in the nineteenth century, recorded his impression that it was "a high black pillar of cast metal" [quoted in V. Smith's *Oxford History*, p. 113].

It is to be noted that this polish of the pillars did not extend to the parts that were below the surface of the ground. Thus of the total length of 42 ft. 7 in. of the Delhi-Topra pillar, the polish is visible down to the length of 35 ft., while the part below that level is left quite rough. Similarly, of the lion-pillar at Rampurwa, of which the shaft alone is 44 ft. 9½ in. long, fully 8 ft. 9 in. are left undressed and unpolished. Again, of the Lauriya-Nandangarh pillar, which is 39 ft. 7½ in. above the ground, a length of 10 ft. is below the ground. When its foundations were dug up, a ring-like projection, 2 in. thick, was seen round the shaft at a depth of 2 ft. below the ground. Up to this projection the pillar is polished, but below it, the stone was rough, bearing marks of the chisel. A little farther down was discovered the figure of a peacock, 4 inches in length, which is no doubt symbolical of the Mayūra ensign of the so-called imperial house of the *Moriyas* or Mauryas. Ten feet below the ground, the shaft was joined on to a square stone basement extending to a length of about 2 ft. on its four sides [see Cunningham, *ASR*, xxii. 46, 47]. A square pedestal was also found as the basement of the Koluha Pillar [*Ib.* i. 60].

In connection with the location of these Asokan pillars, the late Dr. V. A. Smith raised an engineering enigma which defies solution unless we are prepared to concede very much more to ancient Indian engineering than is usually done. The average weight of these pillars of the height up to 50 ft., and circumference up to 50 in., is estimated by Cunningham

[1] My photograph of the Lauriya-Ararāj Pillar shows the polish in the form of a whitish line along a part of its shaft.

PLATE IX.

LAURIYA NANDANGARH PILLAR.

to be about 50 tons. The handling of such enormous monoliths for purposes of their appointed location was a problem in transport. Their locations were, moreover, determined on a deliberate design. Four of them mark stages on the royal road frequented by pilgrims from Pāṭaliputra to the Buddhist holy places along the foot of the Himalayas in the Nepalese tarai, while the others are planted at important centres of population, whether cities or sacred places, like Sanchi, Sarnath, or Kauśāmbī, to enable the proclamations inscribed on them to be widely read. Then we must consider the location of the central workshop which turned out these pillars of a uniform, standardised, pattern, polish, and finish. The material of the pillars points to the Chunar hills out of which it was quarried. Thus they were "erected at localities hundreds of miles distant from any quarry capable of supplying the exceptionally choice blocks required for such huge monoliths. Their fabrication, conveyance, and erection bear eloquent testimony to the skill and resource of the stone-cutters and engineers of the Maurya age" [V. A. Smith's *Asoka*, p. 121]. Fortunately, we can realise the difficulties which Asoka's engineers had to face and overcome in transporting the pillars to their prescribed positions, from a description of an attempt at removal made about sixteen centuries later under the orders of the then Indian king, Sultan Firoz Shah Tughlak. The nearest place where an Asokan pillar was to be found being Topra, the Sultan wanted it to be removed as a trophy to Delhi. The arrangement for the removal involved the construction of a special carriage with 42 wheels, to each of which was fastened a rope. At each of these ropes pulled 200 men, so that the carriage with the weight of the pillar on it had to be drawn by as many as 8400 men. "When labour so great was required to move one a distance of 120 miles we may imagine how much energy was expended in setting up thirty pillars, some of which were much heavier than that removed by Firoz Shah, and were transported to distances still greater" [*Ibid*. p. 123].

The success of Mauryan engineering was also manifest in the domain of irrigation. The inscription of Rudradāman

(A.D. 150) relates how the beautiful Sudarśana lake [1] was constructed on the mountains Raivataka and Ūrjayat (near Girnar or Junagadh) by artificially damming up the course of their streams, Palāsinī, and others. It is also stated further in the inscription that the reservoir was "ordered to be made by the Vaiśya Puṣyagupta, the provincial governor (*Rāṣṭrīya*) of the Maurya king, Chandragupta, and adorned with conduits (*praṇālī*) for Asoka the Maurya by the Yavana king, Tuṣāspha, while governing (*adhiṣṭhāya*)." Thus the lake was equipped "with well-provided conduits, drains and means to guard against foul matters." We are in this connection reminded of the remark of Megasthenes that there were officers in Mauryan administration whose duty was "to measure the land and inspect the sluices by which water is distributed into the branch canals, so that every one may enjoy his fair share of the benefit."

Lastly, the Mauryan engineers were good at town-planning, too. Pāṭaliputra, the capital of the Magadhan empire since the days of Udaya, the grandson of Ajātaśatru (as stated in the *Vāyu Purāṇa*), who first laid its foundation at which the Buddha made a prophecy of its future greatness, had become developed by the time of Chandragupta Maurya into a mighty city fulfilling that prophecy. As seen and described by Megasthenes, "it stretched in the inhabited quarters to an extreme length on each side of 80 stadia (=about 9 miles), with breadth of 15 stadia (=$1\frac{1}{2}$ miles), in the shape of a parallelogram, encompassed all around by a ditch for defence and receiving the sewage of the city, which

[1] The history of the lake is carried down to the time of Skandagupta in one of his inscriptions [No. 14 of Fleet's Gupta Inscriptions] dated A.D. 458. It was situated in the western province of his empire, the land of the Surāṣṭras, under his governor Parṇadatta, who appointed his son, Chakrapālita, in charge of a city called in the earlier Rudradāman inscription, *Girinagara* or Girnār. The lake suddenly burst, owing to "much water raining down unceasingly for a long time," with the result that the rivers, which "dwelt so long in captivity" within the bounds of the lake, "went again to their lord, the sea." Of these rivers, only one is named, viz., *Palāsinī*. The reservoir (*taṭākam*) was, however, promptly restored by Chakrapālita at an "immeasurable expenditure of wealth" on "masonry work."

was 600 ft. in breadth and 30 cubits in depth." [1] Its inner line of defence was formed by a massive timber palisade, "pierced with loopholes for the discharge of arrows, crowned with 570 towers, and provided with 64 gates." Megasthenes further notes that of the cities of India, of which "the number is so great that it cannot be stated with precision," those on the banks of rivers or on the sea-coast are built of wood instead of brick to escape from floods, while those "on commanding situations and lofty eminences are built of brick and mud." This wooden city was dominated by the royal palace which excelled in splendour the palaces of Susa and Ekbatana, with its gilded pillars adorned with golden vines and silver birds, and its extensive grounds studded with fish-ponds, and beautified by many ornamental trees and shrubs. Thus with his empire, Asoka inherited all that won it, and made it great—a large army, an efficient administrative organisation, and, last, but not least, its wealth of artistic and architectural achievements and traditions. Thus some of the polished pillars are rightly ascribed by Asoka to his predecessors who could build a great city, and the most gorgeous palace of the East.

Asoka also made important contributions to the expansion of the city and palace, the magnitude of which made Fa-hien attribute them to supernatural agency. Seriously and sincerely does Fa-hien observe: "The royal palace and halls in the midst of the city, which exist now (i.e., about 650 years later) as of old, were all made by spirits which he employed, and which piled up the stones, reared the walls and gates, and executed the elegant carving and inlaid sculpture-work,—in a way which no human hand of this world could accomplish" [Legge's trans. p. 77]. This passage

[1] It is interesting to note that the river Ganges from the sea up to Pāṭaliputra was navigable in those days. Strabo [xv. i. 11] speaks of "the ascent of vessels from the sea by the Ganges to Palibothra," while in an earlier legend [*Vinaya*, iii. 338 (*Samantapāsādikā*)], Mahendra, the younger brother of Asoka, is represented as travelling by ship from Pāṭaliputra to Tāmalitti and thence to Ceylon. A Jātaka story [*Jāt.* iv. 159] even describes a company of carpenters as sailing from Benares, so far up the Ganges, right up to an island in the ocean!

hints that Asoka replaced much of the old wooden material of the palace by stone which was so successfully utilised in other monuments of Asoka in the different parts of his empire.

Archaeological exploration has been able partially to unearth a few remnants of the Mauryan palace. The work was begun by P. C. Mukharji who dug up several fragments of polished stone that could not be mistaken as parts of an Asokan column.[1] It was resumed many years later by Dr. D. B. Spooner whose excavations have brought to light polished Chunar sandstone pillars (each about 20 ft. high with a diameter at the base of 3½ in.) in parallel rows, 15 ft. apart, indicative of a hall of 100 pillars in the Mauryan palace showing a similarity of design [2] to the Achaemenian palaces of Persia. There was also discovered, 17 ft. below the surface, a wooden floor, on which there is a deposit of eight

[1] An Asokan Pillar at Pāṭaliputra was seen, it may be remembered, by both Fa-hien and Yuan Chwang.

[2] On this subject, which has excited much controversy, the following remarks of Havell, an authority on Indian Art and Artistic History, may be considered [*Aryan Rule*, p. 75]: "Excavations recently made on the site of Pāṭaliputra have revealed what are supposed to be the foundations of the palace, and an arrangement of pillars similar to that of the Apadana at Persepolis, whence it has been somewhat hastily assumed that Chandragupta sent for foreign builders to build him a palace on the Persian model, just as in modern times Anglo-Indian builders copy the plans of European buildings. Doubtless the fame of Chandragupta would have attracted craftsmen of all kinds from far and near, especially master-builders of repute, who were always accustomed to seek employment wherever it might be found when royal capitals were in the making. But Indian History did not begin with Chandragupta, and the Indo-Aryan building tradition was an ancient one when Pāṭaliputra was founded. The inference to be drawn from the fact that an Indo-Aryan imperial palace resembled an Iranian one in its general scheme is merely that Aryan culture in India and Iran inherited the same traditions, not that Chandragupta was of set purpose imitating the palace of Darius. So great a champion of the Indo-Aryan cause and the founder of the greatest Indo-Aryan dynasty known in history would hardly be likely to celebrate the freedom of Āryāvarta from the Macedonian yoke by imposing on it the intellectual dominion of Persia. The *Kauṭilīya-arthaśāstra* shows that Chandragupta's statesmanship was wholly inspired by Indo-Aryan traditions."

or ten feet of soil, followed by a layer of ashes in which lie the broken fragments of the columns. At the site of each column there is a tubular shaft of ashes descending through the soil to the level of the floor. Dr. Spooner's assumption is that the deposit of silt is indicative of a flood, and that of ashes a fire, and, between the *flood* and the *fire*, the work of the destruction of the palace was complete.[1] There have been also unearthed, lying parallel to one another, seven wooden platforms to the south of the assumed pillared hall, each of which is 30 ft. long, 6 ft. wide and 4½ ft. high. Dr. Spooner comments on "the absolute perfection" of the carpentry displayed in the making of these platforms.

Besides examples of architectural achievements, we may also consider some of the minor arts of the period. At Parkham near Mathurā was found a colossal statue of a man, 7 ft. high, in grey and highly polished sandstone, and bearing an inscription in Asokan script. A complementary female statue was also found at Besnagar, and quite lately two statues were discovered at Patna and Didarganj. These statues in their unifacial images betray the primitiveness of the art. Dr. A. K. Coomaraswamy [*History of Indian and Indonesian Art*, p. 16] considers these as examples of the "folk art" of the times, as distinguished from the *court* or official art. Similarly, the art of coining was not very advanced, considering the crude punch-marked coins of the period with their unsymmetrical forms and symbols stamped indiscriminately upon their surface. Likewise some of the contemporary terra-cottas discovered show only "coarse primitive reliefs." "Indeed, so far as is known at present, it was only in the jewellers' and lapidaries' arts that the Maurya craftsman attained any real proficiency, and in this domain his aptitude lay, not in the plastic treatment of form, but in the high technical skill with which he cut and polished refractory stones or applied delicate filigree and granular

[1] It is interesting to note that the *Mahāparinibbāna Suttanta* [i. 28] puts into the mouth of the Buddha the following prophecy about the destruction of Pāṭaliputra from the same natural calamities: "But three dangers will hang over Pāṭaliputra, that of *fire*, that of *water*, and that of dissension among friends."

designs to metal objects. The refined quality of his gold and silver work is well illustrated in two pieces of jewellery which were discovered on the site of Taxila in company with a gold coin of Diodotus, a large number of local punch-marked coins, and a quantity of other jewellery and precious stones. Of the stone-cutter's art, also, some beautiful examples are furnished by the relic caskets of beryl and rock crystal from the stūpas of Bhattiprolu and Piprahwa, the latter of which is probably to be assigned to this epoch" [*Cambridge History*, p. 623]. We may add to these examples the very inscriptions of Asoka which are executed with perfect accuracy in very well-cut letters.

From the archaeological we may now proceed to consider the artistic aspect of these monuments of Asoka. That in their best examples they exhibit a high level of technical and artistic accomplishment is admitted on all hands. But there is a doubt as to how far this art is Indian in its origin and character, and especially in some of its finished forms which we see among the Asokan monuments. As its excellence is seen mainly in the treatment of animals, of their muscles, veins, and claws, and also of plants, and birds, the art has been taken as naturalistic, and, to that extent, as foreign to Indian artistic traditions and ideals. It is taken to be inspired by Greek Art which alone in that epoch of world's history distinguished itself in the modelling of living forms. A negative evidence for the foreign inspiration in Asokan Art is sought to be found in the fact that its best examples belong to the same epoch which witnessed crude and primitive examples already mentioned, such as the statues in the round found at Mathura, Besnagar, and Patna, of which the indigenous origin cannot be disputed, so that we are forced to account for the evolution of an art that could produce at the same time such an extreme difference in the quality of its examples. Thus the best examples, the Asokan Pillars, are traced to foreign influence. While some of their elements are traced to Greece, others are traced to Persia. Their so-called bell-shaped capitals, their smooth unfluted shafts, their polish, and even their inscriptions are traced to Persia.

This, however, does not seem, on a closer examination, to be a completely correct view of the subject. Even V. A. Smith was not prepared to go so far in ascribing foreign origins to Asokan art. He considers, for instance, the treatment of the bull and the elephant in the Sarnath abacus as being entirely Indian in both subject and inspiration, and not as in any way the outcome of a half-caste art. According to Havell, the supposed Persepolitan bell-capital is a misreading of the Indian lotus. Further, Codrington points out that the Persian capital is not quite closely related to these early Indian bell-capitals, and does not show itself to be a necessary part of the structure of the Asokan pillar. "The Persian bell is conceived as part of a compound capital, and is always crowned by a further member, the lines of which curve upwards and outwards, the whole suggesting the flourishing head of a palm tree with a ring of drooping half-dead leaves clustering below round the stem. Above this comes a quadruple bracket-like member with upper and lower incurving volutes, between which and the final member is nothing but a bead-and-reel fillet. Above this, the head and bent-back fore-legs of the surmounting beast jut out, without any sort of abacus or intermediary platform. The typical Achaemenid pillar-shaft was also fluted, not smooth, whatever its rudimentary form may have been" [*Ancient India*, pp. 18, 19]. As regards the pillars themselves, it is to be noted that while those at Persepolis and elsewhere are structural, the Asokan ones are purely monumental. Nor is the idea of raising the pillars completely foreign to India. The raising of religious symbols for common reverence is a time-honoured Indian practice. Hindu temples have always before them their banner-torch or light-pillar, which are often adorned with the special symbol of the god, a wheel, or a trident. Vedic literature, itself, by its descriptions of the banner of Indra, and of sacrificial posts, points to far-distant origins of these pillars. The Asokan pillar is the descendant of those royal or tribal ensigns or standards which were set up to mark off the sacrificial areas for ancient Vedic ceremonies. The Indian purpose of these pillars is, again, declared in their very locations. Rummindei and Sarnath called for pillars commemorative respectively of the Buddha's Nativity and first teaching. The pillar at Nigliva associates itself with the fifth of the previous Buddhas. A group of pillars guides the pilgrim's progress towards the Buddhist holy places.

It is not, however, to be claimed that Asokan art does not reveal any trace of foreign influence. It is only difficult to trace it to a particular source or country in that age of frequent and fruitful intercourse between India and the outside world. The influx of foreigners to India for purposes of trade and business called for the institution of a Foreign Office in the chief cities of India under Asoka's grandfather, Chandragupta Maurya, as stated by Megasthenes, the Greek ambassador to his court. And we have already seen from Asoka's own words in his edicts how largely and religiously did he seek to cherish and cultivate these foreign relations with the then most prominent Western countries and seats of Hellenic culture and civilisation. The fact of the matter was that in that age of intercourse and interchange of ideals, the arts of different countries were bound to reveal some common elements and features which in the case of India and Persia might be traced to a common source from which the entire culture of the East or Asia has sprung.

CHAPTER VI

SOCIAL CONDITIONS

We may now present an account of the social conditions of the country, so far as they can be gathered from the evidence available.

Society is described as comprising religious and secular classes. The former are distinguished as "Brāhmaṇas, Śramaṇas and other Pāṣaṇdas," i.e., followers of different dissenting sects. Among these dissenters, the most prominent in Asoka's time were the Nirgranthas (Jains), and the Ājīvikas, who have been singled out as receiving the special favour of the emperor by his grant of rock-cut dwellings to them.

The religious life of the country was represented by a multiplicity of sects, of which the Edicts mention by name only the four aforesaid as being evidently the more influential ones, viz., the Brāhmaṇas, the Buddhists, the Ājīvikas, and the Nirgranthas. The interests of all these religions were promoted equally and impartially by the State through a special department created for the purpose under the enlightened religious policy of the emperor. That policy, it should be observed, was not one of religious neutrality, which is a policy of apathy and inaction, but a policy of active support of the "essence" and good to be found, in the opinion of the emperor, in all the religious denominations of the country.

Intellectual life centred chiefly in the monasteries and other institutions associated with the different denominations, and was very much quickened by the debates and discussions among these denominations which were really so many different schools of philosophy. Learning and culture at the higher levels of society seem also to have filtered down to the masses so as to produce a comparatively large percentage of literacy among them. This we can infer, as Dr. Vincent A. Smith was the first to point out [*Asoka*, p. 139], from the fact that the Edicts were composed in the vernacular dialects, and inscribed in the two principal scripts of the country on stone in places where they were accessible to the masses, only on the assumption that they would be able to read them [1] and lay to heart the meaning of the message which their beloved sovereign addressed to them for their own true well-being. Any other assumption would only represent Asoka as having embarked upon this costly and arduous adventure simply to satisfy his own whim or vanity. The popular literacy was the product of the numerous educational institutions and monasteries connected with the various denominations of the country. The efficiency of the monasteries as agencies of popular education may be inferred from the results achieved even in modern times, not the days of their glory, by the monasteries of Burma where the number of persons per 1000 able to read and write is 378 for males and 45 for females, as against 37 and 2 in the United Provinces of Agra and Oudh, with so many cities and historic capitals, according to the Census figures of 1901. Thus Vincent Smith comes to the conclusion : "I think it likely that the percentage of literacy among the Buddhist [?] population in Asoka's time was

[1] In considering, however, this apparently very reasonable inference advanced by Dr. V. A. Smith and other writers, we must note that it leads us to the position that there was some sort of *lingua franca* developed in Asokan India. For Asoka's inscriptions reveal a common language underlying its many local peculiarities and provincialisms in respect of the forms of words, grammar, and vocabulary, and this common language is assumed to have been understood by the north as well as the south Indians in the third century B.C., though South India so early became the fruitful mother of so many vigorous languages different from one another, and radically different from the languages of the north! The whole question should be considered from the standpoint of the history of the Indian languages and literature.

higher than it is now in many provinces of British India" [*Ibid.*].

The religious classes of society are distinguished from the secular classes designated as *grihasthas* or householders in the Edicts. Among the different castes or classes then existing in society, we have mention of the Brāhmaṇas and *Ibhyas* or Vaiśyas [R.E. V], soldiers and their leaders, corresponding to Kṣatriyas (*bhaṭamaya, ib.*), and servants and hirelings (*dāsa-bhaṭaka* in R.E. IX, XI, XIII, and P.E. VII), corresponding to the Śūdras. All these different castes and classes marked society in all the provinces of Asoka's empire, except the *janapada* or province of the *Yonas* who did not know of these *nikāyas* and *pāṣaṁḍas*, and were strangers even to Brāhmaṇas and Śramaṇas [R.E. XIII]. Thus the Yona province of the empire was not at all Hinduised in cult or custom.

An elevated and extended conception of the home or family life appears in the Edicts. Moral life is to be built primarily upon a proper system of domestic relations to be marked by a wide range of interests and sympathies, embracing not merely the relationships in blood, but also those due to pupilage, or even physical service, nay, even the service derived from the domesticated animals whose claims to kind treatment are recognised.

The popular religious life of the times seems to have been dominated by too many and trivial ceremonies, as stated in R.E. IX. There was also the universal belief in *pāpa* [R.E. V and P.E. III] and *puṇya* [R.E. IX and X], in *paraloka*, and *svarga*, i.e., in what may be called the doctrine of *Karma*. The popular Buddhism of the times seems also to have admitted of the worship of the previous Buddhas, as is apparent from Asoka's visit and repairs to the stūpa of *Koṇākamana*.

It was also the recognised duty of the householders to honour and support those who left their houses and chattels in their quest of Truth. Asoka's repeated insistence on respect for the ascetics points to their numerical strength in the country. The growth of asceticism is a compliment to the moral progress of a country which could produce a plentiful crop of men capable of renouncing the world and of utmost self-denial in the interests of the life spiritual.

Some of the ascetics could be induced to include social service as a religious duty. Out of these were recruited Asoka's missionaries who dedicated themselves to the service of their faith in distant and foreign lands.

Some facts about the social life of the upper classes and royalty may be gathered from the legends. Polygamy and early marriage seem to have been in vogue. Asoka had several wives. He first married at 18. He married his eldest daughter when she was 14. But it is remarkable how the Buddhist Church in those days provided a career for the aristocratic youths choosing to dedicate themselves to its service. Prince Mahendra and Princess Saṅghamitrā both renounced the world and entered the Saṅgha as its members. That is why Asoka shows a distinct predilection for ascetics in his Edicts.

The popular religious outlook was distinctly wide and catholic. Hindu missionaries working in " the country of the Yona " [*Mahāv.* XII. 6],—in the five Hellenistic countries of Syria, Egypt, Cyrene, Macedonia, and Epirus,—successfully solved the social problem of sea-voyage and foreign travel. Caste could not pit itself against religion. A further typical example of the same broadening religious outlook is furnished in the conversion of a Greek into a Hindu with his original name changed into Dharmarakṣita, and then by his selection as an evangeliser of the Aparāntaka country. After this, we need not be surprised at the gift of a monolithic column in honour of Lord Vāsudeva by a Hindu Greek named Heliodorus calling himself a Bhāgavata, in about 140 B.C. It was this kind of spirituality that, surmounting geographical boundaries and barriers, carried India's message and thought to other lands and laid the foundation of a Greater India across the northern mountains and the southern seas.

Though one of the greatest kings of history, Asoka has not received from posterity the tribute due to his memory, if we, of course, leave out of account the Buddhist literature of legends, Ceylonese and Indian, that have naturally gathered round one to whom Buddhism owes so much. An attempt was even made by some later Brahmin grammarians to bring into disrepute the very title by which he is known. They have explained his appellation *Devānāmpriya* as the standing epithet of a fool! But the Buddhist references are, of course, duly respectful. The *Milinda Pañha* [iv. 1, 47] refers reverentially to Asoka as "dhammarāja," the righteous king, holding his court at Pāṭaliputra, and moving out to see the river Ganges on which his city stands, with his retinue of urban and rural people (*negama-jānapada*), his officers (*amachcha*), his soldiers (*bhaṭa-bala*), and his ministers (*mahāmātras*). Other tributes to his memory are on stone. The Junagadh inscription of Rudradāman (about A.D. 150) contains the expression *Asokasya Mauryasya* [*Ep. Ind.* viii. 43], while in a much later inscription at Sarnath of Kumāradevī [queen of King Govindachandra of Kanauj (A.D. 1114-1154), *Ep. Ind.* ix. 321], we have the expression, "*Dharmāśoka-narādhipasya*," i.e., "of righteous Asoka, the ruler of men." A yet later inscription of Dhammacheti [*IA*, xxii.] also mentions Dharmāsoka. Lastly, there is a Burmese inscription at Bodh-Gaya of the date A.D. 1295-1298, which refers to "Śrī Dhammāsoka, the ruler of Jambudvīpa, who built 84,000 chaityas" [*Ep. Ind.* xi. 119]. Thus Indian historical judgment has rightly designated Asoka as Asoka the Righteous.

But the memory of Asoka has perhaps received a more fitting recognition and reverence in sculpture. According to Foucher, the Asokan Cycle has inspired even early Buddhist Art. He finds some of the texts of the *Divyāvadāna* bearing on the life of Asoka illustrated on stone at Sanchi. On the front face of the lower lintel of the eastern gate of the Sanchi stūpa, there may be traced a representation of the visit of Asoka to the Bodhi tree, the details of which seem to be borrowed from the description of the event in the *Divyāvadāna* (pp. 397-398). It tells of Asoka coming with his jealous queen, Tiṣyarakṣitā, in a procession to the Bodhi tree, which was withering under a spell cast by her upon it, to have it revived by "watering it with pitchers of scented water." Accordingly, we find to the left of the sculpture a crowd of musicians and devotees with water vessels ; in the centre, the temple and Tree of Knowledge (*Saṁbodhi*) ; and to the right, a royal retinue, a ḳing and queen descending from an elephant, and the same offering later their worship at the Tree. The association of this sculpture with Asoka is further indicated by the figure of pairs of peacocks at the ends of the architrave, the peacock (*mayūra* or Pali *mora*) being the dynastic symbol of the Mauryas. This scene is repeated on the top and second panels of the rear face of the left pillar of the south gate also. Then the story of the *Divyāvadāna* of Asoka's visit to the stūpa at Rāmagrāma is also represented, with its details, on stone, both at the south and the east gates. At the south gate, it occurs on the front face of the middle architrave, showing to the right Asoka approaching in his chariot with his royal retinue of elephants, horsemen, and footmen, and to the left, the worshipping Nāgas and Nāgīs, the guardians of the stūpa [*Div.* p. 380]. It may be noted that about a century earlier, at a few paces from this sculpture, Asoka himself had erected his pillar to bear the inscription of his Edict. At the east gate, back lower lintel, the Nāgas are represented as elephants bringing flowers and fruit as offerings. Lastly, the *Divyāvadāna* story of Asoka's visit to the Deer Park as the scene of the Buddha's first teaching is also represented at Sanchi. Sir John Marshall discovers it on the south gate, front face of its left pillar, of which the top panel shows Asoka with his two queens visiting the *Mṛigadāva* indicated by the symbols of the deer and the wheel, and the second panel showing Asoka in his chariot with his retinue around [*Guide to Sanchi*, p. 50]. Thus these sculptures constitute some of the best memorials which posterity has raised to the pious memory of Asoka.

CHAPTER VII

TRANSLATION AND ANNOTATION OF THE EDICTS[1]

A. Minor Rock Edicts

I

[Brahmagiri]

Under the instructions of the Prince (*āryaputra*) and Ministers (*mahāmātras*)[2] from Suvarṇagiri,[3] the Ministers of

[1] The Edicts here are arranged in the chronological order, so far as it may be inferred from, or is indicated by, them.

[2] Literally "great in measure," and hence a man of high rank, high official, prime minister. In the Edicts, the Mahāmātras are found in independent charge of cities, e.g., Isila, Samāpā [K.R.E. II], or Kosambi [M.P.E.], or associated with the Viceregal Princes as at Tosalī [K.R.E. II] or at Suvarṇagiri, as here; are placed in charge of over thousands of lives [K.R.E. II]; are sent out on quinquennial inspection of judicial administration, as on other duties (*Ib.*); are heads of Departments as Dharma-Mahāmātras, Strī-adhyakṣa-Mahāmātras, or as directors of different religious sects [R.E. V, P.E. VII, M.P.E.]; and are also members of the Mantri-Pariṣad or councillors to whom the king confides urgent matters [R.E. VI]. In the *Kauṭilīya*, the Mahāmātra figures as a minister [I. 10, 12, 13], and as the chief executive officer of a city under the title "Nāgarika-mahāmātra [IV. 5], while his power and influence will be evident from the fact that the seditious mahāmātra is a cause of much concern to the king, who even sends him out of the way [V. 1]! The Vinaya Piṭaka, as Dr. Thomas shows [*JRAS*, 1914, p. 389], knows of more varieties of Mahāmātras, the Vohārika Mahāmatta (for Law), Gaṇaka Mahāmatta (Finance), Senānāyakam (Army), Upachārakam (Court), and Sabbatthakam (Prime Minister).

[3] From its name, the "gold mount," the place might be in the ancient gold-mining areas, and this edict has been found at Maski

Isila [1] are to be wished good health and then addressed as follows: [2]

Thus ordains His Sacred Majesty: [3] For more than two

near Raichur, which shows numerous traces of ancient gold workings, a shaft of which is the deepest in the world known so far [*Hyderabad Arch. Series*, No. I.]. Hultzsch identifies it with Kanakagiri, south of Maski.

[1] The name Isila, strangely enough, appears in a Sanchi inscription [No. 4, p. 111, of *Ep. Ind.* ii.]. Isila may be taken to be the modern Siddapura Village in the Chitaldroog District of the Mysore Province.

[2] This paragraph appears only in the three Mysore versions of the Edicts.

[3] The Maski Edict uses the king's personal name, *Asoka*, and has settled a long controversy on the subject.

The formula, "Thus saith the king Piyadasi," is absolutely singular in Indian Epigraphy, without any precedent or imitation. It was, however, in use among the Achaemenian Kings of Persia. The inscriptions of Darius begin with the formula, "thātiy (Sans. śaṁsati) Dārayvaush (=Dhārayavasuḥ) kshāyathiya (=kṣetā)," "thus saith the King Darius." Thus the formula became known in India through the political connection of Darius with a part of the Panjab. It is also significant that the Persian word for inscription is the same as the Asokan word *dipi, lipi* [see Senart, *Inscriptions of Piyadasi*, ii. 100]. It is, however, to be noted that the formula, "*evam āha*," "thus saith," may be also taken to be of indigenous origin, considering that it is mentioned as one of the set phrases prescribed for what is called a *prajñāpana-śāsana* (writ of information) by Kauṭilya. Another variety of *rāja-śāsana* (royal writ) is called by Kauṭilya *ājñā-lekha* (writ of command), of which we have also examples in this Edict, as well as in R.E. III and IV, where Asoka addresses his *ājñā* or decree to his various officers and to his *pariṣad* or council respectively.

For the expression *Devānāṁpriya Priyadarśī*, V. A. Smith's translation, "His Sacred and Gracious Majesty," seems to me to be the most appropriate, and is accordingly adopted here. The form *Devānāṁ-priya* instead of *Deva-priya* would be an epithet of contempt under a rule of Pāṇini [vi. 3, 21], but is mentioned among the exceptions to the rule by Kātyāyana (about 350 B.C. according to Sir R. G. Bhandarkar), supported by Patañjali (150 B.C.) and even the *Kāśikā* (A.D. 650). The exception is not, however, allowed by the later grammarian, Bhattojidīkṣita, who insists on taking *Devānāṁpriya* as a term of-contempt, implying a fool (*mūrkha*) devoid of the knowledge of Brahma, and hence addicted only to sacrifices and offerings by which they please gods, as cows please men by offering milk (vide *Tattvabodhinī* and *Bālamanoramā*). Thus a title which was complimentary during the Nandas, Mauryas, and Śuṅgas, suffers

years and a half that I had been a lay-disciple (upāsaka),[1] I had not exerted myself well.[2]

But a year—indeed, for more than a year that I visited the Saṁgha,[3] I exerted myself greatly.

a deterioration in sense under later Brahminical prejudice against the most distinguished Buddhist monarch !

The rule of Pāṇini referred to above is " Ṣaṣṭhyā ākrośe," i.e., the genitive affix is to be retained for compounds denoting affront or insult, e.g., *Chaurasya Kulam*, but *Brāhmaṇa-kulam*, where no contempt is meant, and, similarly, *Devānāṁpriya*, as instanced in the *Vārttika*. Patañjali, in his gloss on Pāṇini's v. 3, 14, mentions *Devānāṁpriya* as a form of benedictory address, along with forms like Dīrghāyuḥ and Āyuṣmān. In Bāṇa's *Harṣacharita*, the epithet is twice used as an honorific.

[1] Ya hakaṁ upāsake. . . .
Ya sumi pākā sayake . . . (Rūpnath),
(or) prakāsa Sake (as read by Hultzsch) ;
Yaṁ aṁ sumi buṁpāśake (Maski).
Aṁ sumi Budha-Śake (Maski, as read by Hultzsch).

Thus, according to Hultzsch, the Rupnath text states : two and a half years and somewhat more (have passed) since I am openly a ' *Śākya*," or a " *Buddha Śākya*," according to Maski text. The word *Śākya* means a Buddhist. Kauṭilya has the expression *Śakyājīvakādīn* = the Śākyas, the Ājīvakas and others [III. 20], while the Buddha is called *Śākyamuni* in the Rummindei Pillar Inscription.

[2] *Prakaṁte* from verb *prakram*.

[3] This passage has to be read, as explained in the body of the book, along with that in R.E. XIII which refers to Asoka's increased devotion to Buddhism following the Kalinga war. This increased devotion practically meant his entering upon a higher stage than that of the idle and indifferent *upāsaka*. This might indicate the stage of the *Bhikkhu-gatika* or some other stage as explained in the text.

Asoka had been in this stage " for more than a year " when he issued the first Minor Rock Edict, of which the date must thus be about 260 B.C., i.e., about two years later than his Kalinga conquest with which commenced his real religious progress (*prakrama*). This is one of the grounds for considering this edict as the earliest of the edicts, the Rock Edicts on their own evidence being issued between 258-57 B.C.

The original has the following readings :

Saṁghe upayīte [Brahm. and Siddap.] or *upete* (Ru.) or *upayāte* (Bair.) or *upagate* [Maski]. The commentary on *Niddesa* explains *upeto* as *āsannam gato* (approaching), and *upagato* as *upagantvā thito* (approaching stayed there).

Thus the expression does not point to the permanent monkhood

Thus during this time the people in Jambudvīpa who had remained unassociated with the gods became associated with the gods.[1]

of the emperor, as has been usually assumed. It may merely mean his actual visit to the Saṅgha, such as is related in the legends.

Indeed, the legends seem to throw some light on this obscure passage in the edict. Like the edict, they mark out two *stages* in Asoka's progress towards Buddhism, the stage of inaction followed by that of exertion. The *period* of the first stage is also represented in tradition to be three years, as in the edict. The *Mahāvaṁsa* and *Samantapāsādika*, for instance, relate that for three years from his coronation, Asoka remained in his ancestral faith, a follower of non-Buddhist sects (Rājākira abhisekaṁ pāpuṇitva tīṇi yeva saṁvachchharāni bāhiraka pāsaṇḍaṁ parigaṇhi). During this time he also came under the influence of Nigrodha who taught him the Doctrine of *Appamāda* (=*parākrama* of the edict) and gradually introduced to him a growing number of Bhikṣus, until in the fourth year Asoka was moved to visit the Saṅgha (*gantvā Saṁghaṁ*) and invite them to the palace under their leader, Moggaliputta Tissa. From a follower of an individual teacher, Asoka now became the follower of the Saṅgha. This second stage is referred to in the legends by the expression *Sāsanappaveśo*, which corresponds to *Saṁghe upagate* of the edict. The edict calls this stage as one of active pursuit of the Dharma (*parākrama*). Tradition gives the details and events of such activity, viz., (1) *Vihārakamma*, construction of religious edifices [the *dhaṁmathaṁbhas* of P.E. VII] for three years; (2) his brother, Tissa, and son-in-law, Agnibrahmā, ordained in the fourth year of his reign; (3) his son, Mahendra, and daughter, Saṅghamitrā, ordained in the sixth year, whence Asoka is promoted to the status of *Sāsanadāyāda*. The tradition is somewhat differently told in the northern text, *Divyāvadāna*, according to which Asoka was in the first stage drawn towards Buddhism by the monk Bālapaṇḍita, or Samudra, and the second stage was marked by (*a*) his acceptance of Upagupta as his preceptor, and (*b*) his pilgrimage to the Buddhist holy places under Upagupta. Even in the first stage, the stage of an ordinary *upāsaka*, the *Div.* makes Asoka declare his taking refuge in the Teacher, the Buddha and the Dharma (*Śaraṇaṁ ṛiṣiṁ upaimi taṁ cha Buddhaṁ gaṇavaraṁ āryaniveditaṁ cha dharmam*), and his readiness to sacrifice everything—children, home, wives, and wealth—for the sake of the kingdom of righteousness (*dharmarājyasya śāsane*). Dr. B. M. Barua considers the expression—*saṁghaṁ upagate* or *upete*—as a shortening of the usual formulae for an upāsaka, such as *Saṁghaṁ saraṇaṁ gato* or *saraṇattham upeto* or *Saṁghassa sissabhāvūpagato* [*Sumaṅgalav.* I. 230-236]. He has also found the more allied expression, *saṅgha-gata*, in *Visuddhimagga* [*PTS.* ed., Vol. I, p. 18].

[1] This passage has not been adequately explained. Its different

readings are given below :

Rūpnath Text : Yā imāya kālāya Jaṁbudipasi
Sahasram Text : Etena cha aṁtalena Jaṁbudīpasi
Brahmagiri Text : Iminā chu kālena
Maski Text : Pure Jaṁbudīpasi
Rūpnath Text : Amisā devā husu te dāni misā kaṭā
Sahasram Text : Aṁmisaṁ devā saṁta munisā misaṁdeva kaṭā
Brahmagiri Text : Amisā samānā munisā Jaṁbudīpasi misā devehi
Maski Text : Ye amisā devā husu te dāni misibhūtā

The different translators of the passage up to Hultzsch have all taken it to refer to the commingling of gods with men or men with gods, but have not taken the trouble to explain what exactly the "commingling" means. According to Dr. F. W. Thomas [*Cambridge History*, p. 505], the meaning is to the following effect: "Asoka claims that in little more than a year he had brought the Brāhman gods to the knowledge of those people in India, i.e., the wild tribes, who had formerly known nothing of them." I suggest the following further and more probable interpretations :

(1) Within this interval, in Jambudvīpa, men who were "unmingled with gods" (i.e., had no gods or no religion) came to be "mingled with gods" (i.e., became religious, or worshippers of gods).

By Asoka's missionary activities following a closer contact with the Saṅgha, the cause of religion had made a considerable advance among the peoples of India.

(2) Within this interval, in Jambudvīpa, men whose gods were disunited had become men whose gods were united.

In other words, within this interval of time, the strife of gods and their worshippers (i.e., of the jarring sects) had largely ceased in the country.

In other edicts, Asoka inculcates religious toleration, and respect for Brāhmaṇas as well as Śramaṇas ; here he states that as the consequence of religious discipline, he reached the stage at which he perceived that the divers religions and the various gods worshipped by different sects could (and ought to be) harmonised. The harmony of religions now became to him a conscious pursuit.

Of these two interpretations, the first is inapplicable to the Rūpnath and Maski inscriptions, which speak only of the union of gods previously disunited, and have no reference to men or to the progress of religion or godliness among men. The Rūpnath inscription definitely states that the gods were disunited before and are now united, i.e., religious strife, the war of sects, had largely ceased ; the Maski inscription is equally clear in its reference to the harmonisation of gods and religions.

The only remaining inscription which has preserved this passage intact is that at Brahmagiri, and it mentions both men and gods. And it can be interpreted in either of the two ways, (1) and (2). "*Misā devehi,*" if construed as "mingled with the gods," would give the same meaning as (1) ; if rendered as "united along with their gods," or "united by or through their gods," it would give the same meaning as (2). Indeed, "*amisā samānā munisā*" can hardly mean "disunited with the gods," as it must under the interpretation (1); the natural meaning is "disunited among themselves," which agrees with (2).

Accordingly, (2), which suits all the readings, must be the correct rendering.

Asoka then proceeds to point out that the promotion of religious unity among the sects is not the monopoly or special privilege of princes or other highly placed men; amity and toleration in religion can be equally promoted by other men, however low their station in life. Everyone can, and ought to, practise this virtue.

After dilating on a man's obligation in relation to the followers of other religions, this edict (in its latter part called M.R.E. II) teaches a man's duties in other relations of life, e.g., towards parents, preceptors, kinsmen, neighbours, animals, etc. The theme of the edict is a man's duties towards his fellow-men or fellow-creatures in different relations of life.

Besides the above two interpretations, a third interpretation may also be suggested as a very plausible one from the context of the passage. It would appear from the context that Asoka says in effect: "By a little more than a year's exertion, lo! I have made such progress (*bāḍhaṁ cha me pakaṁte . . . pakamasa hi iyaṁ phale*): it is, indeed, the men in Jambudvīpa (the best country, according to the sacred texts, for spiritual life) who could thus have 'commerce with gods' in such a short time. But let it not be understood that such progress is only for the great like me. 'It is easier for a camel to enter the eye of a needle than for a rich man to enter heaven.' Great or small, all must exert themselves. Then alone will the Pilgrim's Progress (*prakrama*) lead to the Promised Land (*vipula sarga*)." In this interpretation, the exertion and its results are personal to the king, and are not objective in their reference. Asoka is here making an appeal to his people for the moral life on the strength of his own experience, the success of his personal self-exertions. The other interpretations would assume the impossible, viz., that Asoka by a year's propagandist work had made the entire people godlike, or the wilder tribes acquainted with the gods, or had harmonised the warring creeds. Therefore the subjective reference of the passage would make a better sense. As regards the superior spiritual potentialities of the people of Jambudvīpa, on which the Indian sacred works are fond of dwelling, we may refer to Manu's definition of Brahmāvarta as "the land created by the gods," or to a typical passage in the *Viṣṇupurāṇaṁ* where it is stated that birth in India is the final felicity rewarding spiritual merit accumulated in a thousand lives, that those born in India can surpass even the gods in spiritual progress, and that, accordingly, the gods themselves seek birth in this holy land. This sentiment we find first expressed in the *Atharvaveda*. [See my *Nationalism in Hindu Culture*, Asian Library Series, London, 1921].

Of exertion, indeed, is this the result! But this cannot be attained by the great [1] alone. For the small, too, can attain to a wide heaven of bliss [2] by sustained exertion.[3]

For this purpose has this message been proclaimed that (the small) along with the great may exert themselves in this manner, and that even my frontagers,[4] may know (it), and that this exertion may be of long duration. Nay, it shall increase, shall immensely increase, it shall increase by at least [5] one and a half times.[6] And this message has been caused to be proclaimed 256 times by the king on tour.[7]

[1] *Mahātpeneva* (i.e., Mahātmanaiva). Kauṭilya [I. 13] uses the words *pradhāna* and *kṣudraka*. Maski and other versions use the form *uḍālake* or *uḍālā* from Sans. *udāra*.

[2] Notice that the result of religious exercise (*parākrama* or *prakrama*) is described, firstly, as communion with the gods, secondly, as attainment of heaven.

[3] *Paka[m]i . . . ṇeṇa=pakamaminenā* [R.], *palakamaminenā* [S.], but in Maski, the word is *dhamayutena*, i.e., by devotion to dharma. This should settle the meaning of the word *dhaṁmayuta* used in other edicts [R.E. V, P.E. VII].

[4] These frontagers (*antas*) are *named* in R.E. II and XIII. It may be noted that these Minor Rock Edicts meant for the people on the borders of Asoka's empire were consequently located on the borders of that empire, in Mysore. Thus their location was determined not by accident but by design.

[5] *Avaradhiya=avaladhiyenā* [S.]=*avarārddhena*, i.e., by the least part or minimum (cf. Pāṇini, v. 4, 57).

Cf. *Aparārddhya*=without a maximum.

[6] The Rūpnath text (as well as Sahasram) adds: "This very message is to be inscribed on rocks, and also, where there are pillars of stone here (*hadha*), on such pillars also is it to be inscribed."

This statement shows that some pillars had existed before Asoka's time, and been fashioned and erected by his predecessors.

It also proves the priority in time of these Minor Pillar Edicts to all other edicts by referring to the issue of edicts by Asoka as being only *intended* at this time, and not as accomplished facts.

[7] This passage is one of the notorious cruxes of Asokan Inscriptions, and can be best explained on the basis of a comparative study of its different readings, viz.,

Br. Iyaṁ cha sāvaṇe sāvāpite vyūthena 200 50 6.

Ru. Vyuṭhenā sāvane kaṭe 200 50 6 sata vivāsā ta.

Sa. Iyaṁ cha savane vivuthena duve sapaṁnā lāti-satā vivuthā ti 200 50 6.

(1) From the above readings it is evident that *vyūthena* or *vyuṭhenā*

and *vivuthena* may be equated, as also *vivuthā* and *vivāsā*. Here *vivutha* is also common to the two equations: therefore the words *vyūtha, vyuṭha, vivutha*, and *vivāsa* are cognate. Now *vivāsa* means, literally, "dwelling out (or away from home)." It may apply to a tour, or a mission, and the days of such a tour (or mission) may be numbered as so many *vivāsas*. And *vyūtha* or *vyuṭha* [=Sans. *vyuṣita* or *vyuṣṭa*, "absent from home," or "one who has passed (e.g., *rātrim*, a night)" (Monier Williams' Dictionary)] may mean one who is on a tour or mission.

No doubt we have other uses of *vyuṣṭa* in the *Kauṭilīya* [II. 6 and 7] in the sense of "the regnal year, month, fortnight and day"; in the *Varāha Śrauta Sūtra* [Akulapada, Khaṇḍa III] in the sense of the fourth *yāma* or last part of night-time; or in the *Baudhāyana Dharma Sūtra* [IV. 5, 30] in the sense of "having spent the night (in prayer)"; but in these inscriptions of Asoka, *vyūtha* or *vyuṭha* has to be derived from *vivāsa*, and must be connected with a tour or mission, away from home or headquarters.

(2) Next consider the numerals 200 50 6.

The Rūpnath reading "200 50 6 sata vivāsā ta" (or *ti*, as proposed by Hultzsch) and the Sahasram "duve sapaṁnā lāti satā vivuthā ti" both show that this is the number of *vivāsas* or *vivuthas*.

If *vivāsa or vivutha* stands for "days away from headquarters," then we have 256 such days.

If *vivāsa* or *vivutha*, like *vyūtha*, means "officer on a mission or expedition," or "officer despatched," then we have 256 such officers (by whom the proclamation is despatched to as many quarters). In the South Indian inscription of Brahmagiri, the figures 200 50 6 immediately following "sāvāpite vyūthena" indicate customary particulars about the proclamation, and from the Rūpnath and Sahasram inscriptions, we find that these particulars relate either to the date or the method of despatch. In fact, these inscriptions tell of all the methods by which Asoka sought to give publicity to his proclamations. He would first have them inscribed (*lekhāpetavālata*) on rock (*pavatisu*) and pillar (*silāṭhaṁbhasi*), fixed and permanent; he would also have them circulate in different local areas by despatching his Publicity Officers, or *copies* of his proclamations. Indeed, we must find a difference of meaning in "sāvaṇe sāvāpite" of Brahmagiri text and "sāvane kaṭe" of Rūpnath. For while "sāvāpite" refers to the *hearing* of the proclamation, *kaṭe = kṛita* refers to the *drafting* of the proclamation, according to Paṇini's rules "Adhikṛitya kṛite granthe" and "Kṛite granthe" [IV. 3, 87, 116].

(3) In the Sahasram inscription, "duve sampaṁnā lāti-satā" gives in words the meaning of the figures "200 50 6." The expression may be taken as equivalent to Sanskrit "dve ṣaṭpañchāśadadhike śate." Here *lāti* cannot, as generally supposed, stand for *rāti* (night), because in that case we have "two (fiftysix nights) hundred" or "two fiftysix (nights hundred)," meaning "nights two hundred

fiftysix," but for this to mean 256, we must have the place-value, if not the full decimal scale of notation. Before the device of place-value came to be in vogue, "fifty-six (added to) two hundred" would be necessary, i.e., there must be *ati* (in the sense of *adhika*) between fifty-six and two hundred to express 256. Hence *lāti* contains *ati*. It cannot possibly stand for *rāti*, *rātri*. It is true that the place-value is mentioned in Vasubandhu and the *Vyāsa-bhāṣya* as in common use, and this may take us back on the most favourable supposition to the second century A.D. as the era of its introduction, but as regards the Asokan inscriptions, the very figures 200 50 6 show that the device of the place-value was not yet in existence. Nor can it be said that "duve sapaṁnā lāti-satā" simply reads in words the figures 200 50 6; this cannot explain *sapaṁnā* for 50 6; nor the intervention of *sapaṁnā* between *duve* and *satā*.

Turning to the question, what is *la* in *lāti* ? we have two possible interpretations :

(i) Sapaṁnālāti = sapaṁnāsāti = sapaṁnāśa + ati = fifty-six (added to). Here *la* must be taken to be the scribe's mistake for *sa* or *śa*, or *paṁnāla* is a dialectical variant of *paṁnāśa* (though not phonetically sound).

(ii) (Originally) sapaṁnā + ati = sapaṁnāyati (or sapaṁnāyāti) = sapaṁnālāti.

Now in the Rūpnath inscription itself, we find *la* for *ya*, either by the scribe's mistake, or (though this is a phonetic heresy) by a dialectic variant, as in the expression "pavatisu lekhāpeta vā*l*ata," l. 4, which must be "pavatisu lekhāpetavā*y*ata," as we find by comparison with "silāṭhambhasi lākhāpetavayata" of l. 5. We may note that in Rūpnath we have both the forms *vāya* and *vaya*, e.g. *vivasetavāya ti* of l. 5.

But perhaps a third, and in my opinion, the best, interpretation of "*sa-paṁnā-lāti*" is suggested by the Pali grammatical rule—"Yavamadanataralā chāgamā," "the consonants, *ya*, *va*, *ma*, *da*, *na*, *ta*, *ra*, and *'a* should be placed between the final vowel of the preceding word and the initial vowel of the succeeding word, if a *sandhi* between those two vowels takes place." The examples cited for this rule include chha + asīti = chhalāsīti, whence we may also derive chha-paṁnālāti by sandhi from chhapaṁnā + ati = chha-paṁnālāti. (The Pāli rule was found for me by Mr. C. D. Chatterji.)

(4) *Sata* in Rūpnath and *satā* in Sahasram appear at first sight to mean the same thing, but this is not so. In 200 50 6 *sata vivāsā* (Rūpnath), *sata* cannot mean hundred, for it would give 25600; and *satā* in "duve sapaṁnā lāti-satā" must mean "hundred," as otherwise we do not get 256. In *sata vivāsā*, therefore, *sata* stands for *santaḥ*.

In the light of the above explanations (1), (2), and (3), the following interpretations of the text are possible :

[*Note continued on next page.*

II [1]

Thus saith again His Sacred Majesty: Father and mother must be properly served; [2] likewise, a respect [3] for all life should be an established principle,[4] truth must be spoken. These religious requisites or virtues must be promoted.

Likewise the preceptor must be reverenced by his pupil [5] and proper treatment should be shown towards relations. This is the traditional [6] rule of conduct, and this makes

---

1. The proclamation has been issued by (me) on tour, when 256 days had been spent.

Naturally a diary of the tour would be kept, and this proclamation was dated the 256th *vivāsa* or day of absence on tour.

2. Taking *vivuthā*, *vivāsā* = missioners (for despatch) [cf. *vivasetavāya* of Rūpnath], the proclamation has been issued by (me) on tour and 256 officers have been despatched (to as many districts or quarters) with the proclamations.

It may be noted in passing that $256 = 16 \times 16$ or $4 \times 8 \times 8$. It may be an auspicious number, or may stand for 32 subdivisions of 8 quarters, or for the number of districts in the particular administrative area.

[1] This Edict appears only in the three Mysore places.

[2] *Susūsitaviye* = śuśruṣitavyaḥ.

[3] *Garuta* = gurutā; according to Bühler, *gurut*(*vam*) but Hultzsch reads *garusu* = " to elders."

[4] *Drahitavyaṁ*, lit., = should be made firm; but, according to Hultzsch, the passage means " firmness (of compassion) must be shown "; gerundive of *darhyati* from root *dṛih*.

[5] *Antevāsinā*, i.e., a pupil who dwells in the house of his teacher.

[6] *Purāṇa*: the appropriateness of the epithet will be evident from the fact that the rule of conduct herein preached is taken by Asoka from a well-known passage in the *Taittirīya Upaniṣad* [i. 11] giving the teacher's valedictory exhortations to his retiring pupil. Asoka bases his statement of Dharma on the following sentences of the *Upaniṣad*: " Satyaṁ vada, dharmaṁ chara, mātṛidevo bhava, pitridevo bhava, āchāryadevo bhava, atithidevo bhava." The same code of conduct is also prescribed in the *Sigālovāda-sutta* (which, according to some scholars, is one of the texts cited in the Bhabru Edict). Seeing the householder's son, Sigāla, worshipping the six quarters, the Buddha said that the six quarters to be daily worshipped are (1) mother and father, (2) teachers, (3) wife and children, (4) friends and kin, (5) servants and working folk, and (6) Brahmans

for long life. Thus should one act.[1] Written by the scribe[2] Chapaḍa.

B. The Bhabru or Bairat No. 2 Rock Edict[3]

His Gracious Majesty,[4] King of Magadha,[5] saluting the Saṅgha, and wishing them all health and happiness, addresses them as follows:

Known is it to you, Reverend Sirs, to what extent is my reverence as well as faith in the Buddha, the Dharma and the Saṁgha.[6]

and recluses. The *Mahābhārata* is also never tired of repeating the same duties of life. A passage selected at random states them thus:

" Vṛiddhopasevā dānañcha | Śauchamutthānameva cha | Sarvabhūtānukampā cha. . . ." [Śānti. Rājadh. P., ch. 59, v. 142.]

This edict gives the first of Asoka's definitions of the Dharma he preaches to his people—the " *dhaṁmaguṇā*," i.e., the *guṇas*, or distinguishing marks, of the dharma. This proves the chronological priority of this edict to the Rock and Pillar Edicts where the Dharma is more fully elaborated.

[1] The Jaṭiṅga Rāmeśvara version has here the following sentence —" Hevaṁ dhaṁme Devāṇaṁpiyasa," i.e., " this is the Dharma of Devānaṁpriya."

[2] *Lipikareṇa*: this word occurring in the southernmost edict is, however, written by the scribe in the northern Kharoṣṭhī script, probably to show off his knowledge of different styles of writing. The script also indicates that the *lipikara* had come all the way from the northwestern frontiers to serve in the southernmost parts of the empire.

[3] This edict was engraved on a small block of granite which it was not difficult to remove to Calcutta where it is now in the Aṣiatic Society's building. It lay near the rock at Bairat bearing the M.R.E. I, and may therefore be taken of the same date.

[4] *Priyadasi*, lit., " one who *sees* to the agreeable (*priya*), i.e., the good, of others; who wishes well of others"; and thus an appropriate title for the *Rājā* who is so called *prakṛitirañjanāt*, i.e., from satisfying his people; also interpreted as " one who looks with kindness upon everything," " one of pleasing countenance."

[5] *Māgadhe*: the full expression *Priyadasi lājā Māgadhe* should be taken as " Piyadasi, Rājā of Magadha," in which case the edict would be addressed to the Saṅgha in general, and not to the Saṅgha of Magadha (as has been sometimes interpreted), to whom it need not be addressed from distant Rajputana.

[6] This declaration of his faith in the Buddhist Trinity may be connected and compared with his statement in the M.R.E. I—*Saṁghe upagate*—which has created so much controversy as to its meaning.

Whatsoever has been said, Reverend Sirs, by the Lord Buddha, all that has of course been well said.[1] But of such, what has been selected by me that the True Dharma may be everlasting[2] I may be privileged to state.

The following, Reverend Sirs, are the passages of the scripture:

1. The excellent treatise on Moral Discipline (*Vinaya-samukasa*).[3]
2. The course of conduct followed by the sages—modes of ideal life (*Aliya-vasāṇi*).[4]
3. Fears of what may come about in future (*Anāgata-bhayāni*)[5]—dangers threatening the Saṅgha and the doctrine.
4. Poem on "Who is an hermit?"[6] (*Muni-gāthā*).
5. Discourse on Quietism[7] (*Mauneya-sūte*).
6. The Questions of Upatiṣya[8] (*Upatisa-pasine*).

[1] Identified with a passage in *Aṅguttara* [IV. p. 164] by Poussin.

[2] The passage occurs in *Mahāvyutpatti* and the *Aṅguttara*.

[3] Cf. *Sāmukkaṁsikā-dhammadesanā* [*Udāna*, v. 3], an expression applied to the Four Truths expounded by the Buddha in his First Sermon at Sarnath, which Asoka must have in mind here, according to A. J. Edmunds [*JRAS*, 1913, p. 387]. Dr. B. M. Barua identifies it with the *Sigālovāda-Suttanta* [*Dīgha Nikāya*, iii. 180-194] on the ground that, as stated in the commentary of Buddhaghosa, it applies to householders (whence it is called *Gihivinaya*) and, indeed, to all classes, to monks, nuns, and the laity, for whose study Asoka intended it. The *Suttanta* further deals with "*Ariyassa Vinaya*," i.e., same as "*Vinaya-samukasa*," Ideal Discipline, as phrased by Asoka [*JRAS*, 1915, p. 809]. Dr. Barua's translations are partially utilised here. Another identification has been proposed by Mr. S. N. Mitra [*IA*, xlviii., 1919, pp. 8-11], viz., *Sappurisasutta* [*Majjhima*, iii. pp. 37-45], which uses the words *Vinayādhāra* and *attān ukkaṁseti* = *sāmukkaṁso*.

[4] *Aṅguttara*, II. p. 27, as pointed out by Dharmānanda Kosambi and Lanman in *IA*, 1912, pp. 37-40; *Ang*. V. p. 29 (*Sangīti-sutta*) according to Rhys Davids [*JRAS*, 1898, p. 640]; Hultzsch takes the expression to mean *ariya vaṁsāni*, "lineages or traditional ways of the holy."

[5] *Aṅguttara*, III. p. 103, *Sutta*, 78 [*Ib.*].

[6] *Sutta Nipāta*, i. 12, p. 36 [*Ib.*].

[7] Same as Nālaka Sutta of *Sutta Nipāta*, iii. 11, pp. 131-4.

[8] Same as Sāriputta-Sutta [*Ibid.* iv. 16, pp. 176-9]. Rhys Davids [*JRAS*, 1893, p. 639] identifies it with *Vinaya*, i. 39, 41.

7. The Sermon to Rāhula [1] beginning with the Sermon on Falsehood, as delivered by the Lord Buddha (*Lāghulovāde musāvādaṁ* [2] *adhigichya* [3]).

These sections of the Dharma, Reverend Sirs, I desire that most of the reverend monks and nuns should repeatedly listen to [4] and meditate, and in the same way, the lay-disciples, male as well as female (should act).

For this reason, Reverend Sirs, am I causing this to be inscribed that they may know of my intention.[5]

[1] *Majjhima Nikāya*, i. 414-420. Regarding these various identifications of these texts, a clue may also be found in the story related by Buddhaghosa in his *Visuddhimagga* of an ideal monk who followed the code of conduct prescribed by the Buddha in the following Suttas, viz. (1) *Ratha-Vinīta-sutta* (same as No. 6 of Asoka), (2) *Nālaka-sutta* (Asoka's No. 5), (3) *Mahā-Ariyavaṁsa* (corresponding to No. 2, *Aliyavasāṇi*, of Asoka), and (4) *Tuvaṭaka-sutta*, in which the Buddha discourses on *paṭipadā* (religious practices), *pāti-mokkha*, and *samādhi*, and these may well make up the cream of the Vinaya, *Vinaya-samukase* or Vinaya *par excellence*. What Buddhaghosa, therefore, selected as the most important and representative texts for a Bhikṣu might well have been cited by Asoka too. I owe this very important reference to Mr. C. D. Chatterji.

[2] The form *musā* for *mṛiṣā*, false, used in this edict at Bairat, should make it certain that the *amisā* used in the other edict at Bairat [M.R.E. I] must be a different word which has thus been rightly connected with Sanskrit *misra*.

[3] The original is read by some (e.g., Kern) as *adhigichya* = *adhikṛitya* (*Ib.*), and by some (e.g., Michelson) as *adhigiḍhya* = *adhigṛihya* (?)

[4] *Sunayu* or *suneyu* (Hultzsch) = *śṛiṇeyuḥ*; this shows, as remarked by Senart [*Inscriptions of Piyadasi*, p. 70], how learning was still being handed down by oral tradition and not by written books.

[5] This edict, as is evident, throws great light upon the history of the Buddhist canonical literature. It also definitely makes out Asoka as a Buddhist and, more than that, as having some authority over the church, from his injunctions to all its classes, lay or monastic, male or female. Senart [*Inscriptions*, ii. 103] finds it strange that, if the Buddhist canon was defined and closed by the time of Asoka, as stated in southern legends, he should select for indicating the Buddha's lessons "pieces so little characteristic, so short, and so devoid of dogmatic importance as those which he cites appear to be, and that, too, without even alluding to the great collection of which the title alone would have been infinitely more significant, and to which it would be so natural to appeal," when addressing the Saṅgha.

It may also be noted that this edict, dealing only with matters

C. The Kalinga Rock Edicts

I

[Dhauli] [1]

The High Officers of Tosalī [2] in charge of the administration of the city, are to be addressed as follows at the command of His Sacred Majesty :

Whatsoever I view (as right) I want to see how it

concerning the Saṅgha, is also addressed directly to the Saṅgha, whereas there are three others, the Minor Pillar Edicts at Sarnath, Sanchi, and Kosambi, which, though similarly dealing with matters affecting the Saṅgha, are not, however, addressed to the Saṅghas, but to the Mahāmātras concerned, those officers whom Asoka appointed to look after the different religious sects, as stated in R.E. V. Thus it is reasonable to infer that the Bhabru Edict is not addressed to the Mahāmātras because it was issued prior to their very creation or institution, and, therefore, this is another proof showing that the Bhabru Edict was prior to the main body of the Rock Edicts.

[1] The inscription on the Dhauli rock appears in three columns, R.E. I-VI in the middle, R.E. VII-X and XIV in the right, followed by K.R.E. II, while K.R.E. I occupies the whole of the left column.

[2] Instead of *Tosalī*, the Jaugaḍa text has *Samāpā*. The term used for these officers of the cities is *Mahāmātānagala-viyohālaka* = Nagaravyāvahārika-Mahāmātras, corresponding to the term *Paura-Vyāvahārika* used by Kauṭilya [I. 12] for one of the eighteen chief officers of the state (*tīrthas*). Elsewhere [IV. 5] Kauṭilya uses the expression "*Nāgarikamahāmātra*" corresponding to the expression "*Mahāmātānagalaka*," as used in l. 10 of the Jaugaḍa text of this edict, showing how both Asoka and Kauṭilya are at one in giving the city-magistrate the rank of a Mahāmātra. The *Nāgarika* of Kauṭilya as the chief executive officer of the city was to the *nagara* or city what the *Samāhartā* was to the *janapada* or province. The administration of both was modelled on a common plan : the city as well as the province was divided into four parts, of which each was under a *Sthānika*, who had the *Gopa* as his subordinate officer, in charge of ten to forty households in the case of the city, and of five to ten villages in the case of the province [II. 35, 36]. Kauṭilya also calls the prefect of the city *pura-mukhya* [I. 16].

Regarding Tosalī, Hultzsch refers to two copperplate inscriptions found in the Cuttack district, where northern and southern Tosalī are mentioned [*Ep. Ind.* ix. 286].

can be carried out in practice and fulfilled by proper means.

And this is regarded by me as the principal means to this end, viz., (to give) instructions to you.

For you are placed over thousands of souls [1] with the object of getting to the people's [2] affection.

All men are as my children.[3] As, on behalf of my own children, I desire that they may be provided with complete welfare and happiness both in this world and the next, the same I desire also for (all) men.[4]

Now you do not understand how far this matter goes.[5]

Some individual person understands this, but he, too, only a part, not the whole.

See to it then, although you are well provided for.[6] In administration,[7] it happens that some individual undergoes imprisonment or torture, which accidentally becomes the cause of his death,[8] and many other persons are deeply

[1] The charge of these city-magistrates is quite an extensive one, next to a governorship.

The *Rājūka* or Governor in P.E. IV is described as being set over " many hundred thousands of people."

[2] *Su munisānaṁ* : here *su* = Sans. *svit* (Hultzsch).

[3] The king's fatherly relationship to his subjects is also emphasised in the *Kauṭilīya* : " Nivṛitta-parihārān pitevānugṛihṇīyāt," the king shall favour like a father those who have passed the period for remission of taxes [II. 1]; " sarvatra chopahatān pitevānugṛihṇīyāt," the king shall always protect the afflicted among his people as a father his sons [IV. 3].

The *Mahābhārata* [Śānti-P. Rājdh. ch. 56, vv. 44, 46] compares the king's relationship to his subjects to the mother's relationship to her son. Like the mother, the king should sacrifice for the good of his subjects whatever he may personally like.

[4] Hultzsch quotes Aśvaghoṣa's *Buddha-Charita*, ii. 35 : " Svābhyaḥ prajābhyo hi yathā tathaiva sarvaprajābhyaḥ śivamāśaśaṁse."

[5] *Āvagamuke* = *Yāvad gamakaḥ.*

[6] *Suvihitā.*

[7] *Nitiyaṁ* = daṇḍa-nītyām ; J. has *bahuka*, " frequently."

[8] *Badhanaṁtika*, one whose *bandhana* becomes his *anta* or end. The severity of judicial torture in Mauryan administration which Asoka tried only to mitigate by prevention of its arbitrary application is fully described in the *Kauṭilīya* [IV. 8, 9, 11]. We have accounts of mutilation, and fines in lieu thereof, of trial and torture to extort confessions, and arbitrary applications of torture which

aggrieved [1] over it. There must you demand that the Middle Path (i.e., moderation or justice) be observed. But one cannot achieve success through the following traits: envy, volatility, cruelty, impatience, want of application, laziness, and lethargy. "That these traits be not mine" is to be wished for. The root of the whole matter is, indeed, Steadiness and Patience. He who is tired in administration will not rise up; but one should move, advance and march on. [2]

He who will look after this [3] must tell you: "See to the discharge of your obligations [4] (to the king). Such and such is the instruction of His Sacred Majesty."

Observance of same produces great good, non-observance great calamity. For if one fails to observe this, there will not be attainment of either heaven or royal favour. The reason why (there is) my excessive thought (is) that of this duty (there is) a twofold gain, [5] for by properly fulfilling it

were punished. Hultzsch, following Lüders, takes *badhanaṁtika* = baṁdhanāṁtika and the sentence as "tena baṁdhanāntikaḥ (prāptaḥ)," i.e., an order cancelling the imprisonment is obtained by him.

[1] *Daviye dukhīyati*; the Jaugada text has *bahuke vedayati*.

[2] *Etaviye*, after which the J. text adds the word *nītiyaṁ*, i.e., make progress in administrative work.

[3] *Hevaṁmeva e dakheya* = *eve dakheyā* (Jaugaḍa), i.e., evaṁ e dakheyā. It refers to the Mahāmātras mentioned at the end of the inscription as "overseers" of the administration.

[4] *Ānaṁne* = *āṇṛiṇyam*; previously it was read as *aṁnaṁ ne* = Sans. ājñāṁ naḥ (Bühler) or anyat + naḥ (Lüders). Hultzsch now has settled the correct reading. Jaugaḍa reads as follows: "*Ānaṁne ṇijhapetaviye.*"

[5] V. A. Smith translates it thus: "Ill performance of this duty can never gain my regard." The difficulty is about the word *duāhale* = dvāhara, "yielding a double profiṭ" (*āhara*) or procuring two, nom. sing., neut. adj. The word *ahāle* occurs in the Rūpnath text of M.R.E. I. But Hultzsch, following Franke, takes it as *dur* + *āhara*, imperfect carrying out, and translates the passage thus: "For how (could) my mind be pleased (me kute mano-atileke) if one badly fulfils this duty?" But should not *duāhale* in this sense be *dulāhale*? Then, again, the proper meaning of the word *atileka* = excess is not taken into account in this translation. Thus the interpretation of Bühler and Senart is followed here.

you will win both heaven and release from your obligations to me.

And this edict is to be listened to on (every day of) the Tiṣya,[1] and in the intervals between the Tiṣya days, on auspicious[2] occasions, it may be listened to even by individuals.

Thus doing you will be able[3] to accomplish (this object).

For this purpose has this edict been inscribed here that the city Magistrates[4] may strive all the time that there might not be the imprisonment of the citizens or their torture without cause.[5]

And for this purpose shall I depute every five years [a Mahāmātra (Jaugaḍa text)] who would be neither harsh nor violent but considerate in action,[6] (in order to ascertain whether (the Judicial Officers) understanding this purpose are acting thus, as (is) my injunction.[7]

But from Ujjayinī, too, the prince[8] (governor) will, for

[1] This day might have a special significance in the life of Asoka.

[2] *Khanasi khanasi*; on frequent occasions (Hultzsch).

[3] *Chaghatha* connected with the root *śak*, whence *chakiye* in K.R.E. II, Dh., M.R.E., Sah. and Bair.

[4] *Nagala-viyohālakā*; *mahāmātā-nagalaka* in J. Cf. Kautilya's *Nāgaraka-mahāmātra* already cited.

[5] *Palikilese*; the word *parikleśa* also occurs in the *Kauṭilīya* [IV. 8], where the Superintendent of the Jail is forbidden under a penalty to cause *parikleśa* to prisoners.

See on this subject R.E. V.

[6] *Sakhinālaṁbhe* = ślākṣṇāraṁbhaḥ: I am not taking the word "āraṁbha" in the sense of slaughter, because there is no reference in this edict to the subject of the sanctity of animal life.

This passage, as explained in the book, is important for determining the chronological order of the edicts. We find here Asoka's first conception of his scheme of Quinquennial Tours for his officers, which is fully elaborated in some of his Rock Edicts which are therefore later than these Kaliṅga Edicts.

[7] As read, restored, and translated by Hultzsch.

[8] "*Ujenite pi chu Kumāle* . . ." followed by "*hemeva Takhasilā te pi*," with which may be compared the expression "*Tosaliyaṁ Kumāle*" in K.R.E. II, l. 1, Dhauli text, and the expression "*Suvaṁṇagirite ayaputasa*." These expressions show that *Kumāras* or *Aryaputras*, princes of the royal family, were posted as viceroys or

the self-same purpose, depute a similar[1] body of officers[2] and will not allow (more than) three years to elapse.[3]

governors in the cities mentioned, viz. Ujjayinī, Takṣaśilā, Tosalī and Suvarṇagiri, but that these princes are *not* mentioned as being Asoka's *sons*. Where Asoka refers to his *own* sons and descendants, he uses the definite expression like "putrā cha potrā cha prapotrā cha Devānaṁpriyasa . . ." as in R.E. IV, Girnar, or "*me* putrā potā cha prapotrā cha" in R.E. VI, *Ib*. Thus the princes that are referred to here as viceroys must be taken to be Asoka's brothers, and not his sons. That one of his brothers named Tissa was appointed by him as his viceroy in 270 B.C., and continued as such up to 266 B.C., we know from the *Mahāvaṁsa* [v. 33, 171]. According to Asokan chronology as worked out here, the date of this edict would be 259 B.C. when Asoka would be 45 years old, but not the father of so many sons old enough to be appointed as his viceroys. The only known son of Asoka who was old enough to be his viceroy then was Mahendra, but he became a monk as early as 264 B.C., as recorded in the *Mahāvaṁsa*, after having officiated as viceroy in the place of Tissa for a very short time. The other known son of Asoka who was appointed as his viceroy and posted to Taxila is Kuṇāla according to the *Divyāvadāna*, but the date of his birth is worked out to be 263 B.C., and of his appointment as Viceroy of Taxila, 235 B.C. No doubt Asoka might have one or two sons who in 257 B.C. were eligible by age for viceroyalty, taking the minimum viceregal age to be 18, at which age Asoka himself was sent out by his father as his viceroy to Ujjayinī. But who these sons were we do not know, though Asoka might have had children born to him between 282 B.C. and 263 B.C., the dates of birth respectively of Saṅghamitrā and Kuṇāla. Perhaps these children might be *Tīvara* mentioned in an edict and *Chārumatī* of Nepal tradition. At any rate, the princes of his inscriptions whom he refers to as his viceroys need not be taken to be all his own sons.

[1] I.e., with similar moral qualifications.

[2] *Vagaṁ*: Kauṭilya also uses the word *varga* in the same sense [I. 7]. The usual meaning of *varga* in Sanskrit is "class." But earlier in this edict, in l. 9, the word *jane* is used where the Jaugaḍa text uses the word *varga*. Similarly, the word *varga* is used in R.E. X, where Girnar reads *jana*. Thus the expression *hedisameva vagaṁ* may be translated as "a person of the same description" [Hultzsch]. Cf. the term *nikāyā* used for classes of officials in R.E. XII.

[3] It is difficult to understand why the Viceroyalties of Ujjain and Taxila needed a more frequent inspection in regard to their criminal administration than the newly-annexed province of Kaliṅga. Perhaps it was because they were so distant from the imperial headquarters and "the master's eye." Later, when R.E. III was issued, the rule was that this administrative tour or *anusaṁyāna*

So also from Takhasilā.[1]

When . . . these High Officers [2] would thus set out on tour,[3]

should be undertaken every five years in *every* province of the empire (*sarvata vijite mama*) without any exception.

[1] According to *Divyāvadāna* [ch. xxvii.], Taxila belonged to the people called the *Svaśas* (*Svaśarājyam*, p. 372), and was always in a state of revolt. In the time of Bindusāra, the revolt could not be checked by his first viceroy, Prince Susīma, who was then replaced by Asoka. Towards the latter part of Asoka's own reign, when Tiṣyarakṣitā was his Chief Queen, i.e., about 236 B.C., according to *Mahāvaṁsa*, xx. 3, report was received by Asoka of hostility at Taxila (*Rājñośokasya Uttarāpathe Takṣaśilā nagaraṁ viruddham*), whereupon Asoka deputed his son Kuṇāla, then 28 years old, to Taxila for its subjection [*Div.* p. 407]. But, as already explained, this edict refers to the early part of Asoka's reign when there was no such trouble at Taxila, and hence to some brother of Asoka as his viceroy, or some unknown son of his who must be old enough for the post, one who should be born about 275 B.C. at the latest to be 18 years old in 257 B.C.

[2] The officers sent out on inspection were of the rank of *Mahāmātras*, as indicated here in the Dhauli text and above in the Jaugaḍa text.

[3] Officers would be sent, each according to his turn (*anu*), once every five years, on tour through their charge (and not transferred out of it, as understood by V. A. Smith) in prosecution of their ordinary, as well as these new and special duties. The ordinary sense of the word *anusaṁyāna* seems quite suitable. Besides, Buddhaghosa defines *anusaṁyāna* as follows: "Tato tato gantvā pachchavekkhanam," i.e., going here and there for purposes of inspection [*Samantapāsādikā*]. This last passage I owe to Mr. Charan Das Chatterji. He has also found a passage in *Aṅguttara*, i. pp. 59-60, where it is stated that *anusaṁyāna* in frontier districts (pachchantime janapade anusaññātum) is not easy for kings at a time when raiders are abroad. The commentary explains the expression as follows: "pachchantime janapade anusaññatuṁ ti—gāmāvāsa-karaṇatthāya, setu-atthāya, pokkharaṇi-khaṇāpanatthāya, sālādīnaṁ karaṇatthāya pachchantime janapade *anusāsitum* pi na sukhaṁ hoti"; i.e., "it is not easy to go into the frontier districts to see to the construction of residences in the villages, of public works, halls, and similar works, or excavation of tanks." Asoka's full purpose in instituting *anusaṁyāna* for his officers is both administrative (including *judicial* as here) and religious, as defined in R.E. III.

It may be noted that Kautilya [II. 9] provides for transfer of government servants (*yuktas*) from one post to another to prevent embezzlement (*viparyasyāt cha karmasu*). He also uses the word *niryāṇa* for *anusaṁyāna* for the king's tour [I. 21].

then they would, without neglecting their own duties, will ascertain this as well, viz., whether (the Judicial Officers) are carrying out this also thus, as is the king's injunction.[1]

II[2]

[JAUGAḌA]

His Sacred Majesty thus says: At Samāpā[3] the High Officers entitled to receive the king's messages[4] are to be addressed as follows:

Whatsoever I view (as right) I want to see how it can be executed in practice and fulfilled by proper means.

And this is regarded by me as the principal means to this end, viz., to give my instructions to you.

All men are as my children; as, on behalf of my own children, I desire that they may be provided with complete welfare and happiness both in this world and the next, the same I desire also for all men.

It might occur to the unconquered borderers (to ask): "What does the king desire with regard to us?"[5]

This alone is my desire with regard to the borderers (that) they may understand that the king desires this (that) they should be free from fear of me, but should trust in me;

[1] As translated by Hultzsch.

[2] The fourteen Rock Edicts were not all published in Kaliṅga. R.E. XI, XII, and XIII were omitted, and in their place were added these two special edicts after R.E. XIV, of which this one comes first upon the rock and should have been described as first, but the usual editions of the edicts reverse the order, and this reversed order is accordingly followed here also.

The two separate Kaliṅga Edicts appear on the Jaugaḍa rock apart from the main edicts within a space enclosed by lines. The upper portion of this space is marked by the *Svastika* symbol figured at the two corners, while the lower portion by the letter *ma* figured four times along the line of its separation. According to Harit Krishna Deb [*JASB*, 17, 232 f.], the supposed *Svastika* symbol may be taken as a monogram made up of two Brāhmī *O*'s and the *ma* the final letter of the sacred syllable *Om*.

[3] In the Dhauli text the edict is addressed to "the Prince, and the Mahāmātras of Tosalī."

[4] *Lājavachanika*. [5] As translated by Hultzsch.

(that) they would receive from me only happiness and not sorrow;[1] that they should further understand (this) that the king will tolerate in them what can be tolerated;[2] that they may be persuaded by me[3] to practise Dharma or morality; (and that) they may gain both this world and the next.

And for this purpose am I instructing you, (viz. that) by this do I render myself free from debt[4] (to animate beings), that I instruct you, and make known to you my will, my determination, and promise, not to be shaken.

Therefore acting thus,[5] should you perform your duties and assure them that they may understand that "the king is to us even as a father; (that) he feels for us even as he feels for himself; we are to him as his children."

By instructing you, and making known to you my will, my determination and vow inviolable, I shall have (i.e., post) for this end officers in all provinces.[6]

[1] *Khaṁ = dukhaṁ* (Dh.).

[2] The king's gift of freedom to these border peoples is conditional upon their conformity to his moral code.

[3] *Mamaṁ nimitaṁ*, i.e., by my instrumentality.

[4] *Anane*, which is explained here in the light of the expression *bhūtānaṁ ānaniyaṁ yehaṁ* of R.E. VI, Dhauli.

[5] *Sa hevaṁ kaṭū* (i.e., kṛitvā).

[6] *Desā āyutike, desāvutike*, Dhauli; *Āyuti* = Sans. Āyuktin; while *Āvuti* = Sans. Āyukti, an order, is used in P.E. IV. The term *Yukta* is used in R.E. III for government servants. Here the term *Āyukta* indicates the provincial officers, the Mahāmātras, whom Asoka would depute on inspection duty from Pāṭaliputra, and also from Ujjayinī and Takṣaśilā under the princely viceroys, as stated in K.R.E. I. In P.E. I, these officers are called *Anta-mahāmātras*, as they had to deal with the "unconquered *antas*" as described here, who might also include the "forest folks," the *aṭaviyo* of R.E. XIII, but Kauṭilya [I. 16] mentions a special class of officers for them, called the *Aṭavīpāla*.

Kauṭilya uses the term *yukta* for the lower government servants with their assistants, called *upayuktas*, and their subordinates (*puruṣas*) [II. 5]. He considers them as not above embezzlement of public funds [II. 9]. Manu also, while giving to the *Yuktas* the charge of stolen property, does not consider them above theft [VIII. 34]. Kauṭilya, instead of *Yuktas*, sometimes uses the terms *Yogapuruṣa* (p. 245) or *Yugyapuruṣa* for "employees," from the root *yuj*, to

For you have the capacity to produce their confidence, their good and happiness both in this world and the next. Thus doing you will also win heaven and release from your obligations to me (or win me release from my debts).

And for this purpose has this edict been inscribed in this place that the High Officers may be all the time at work for the confidence and practice of religion of these frontier peoples.

This same edict is also to be proclaimed at the commencement of every quarter of the year on the Tiṣya day, and also in the intervals between the Tiṣya days and even to individuals, when an occasion offers.[1]

Thus working should you strive towards accomplishment.

D. The Fourteen Rock Edicts

I

[Shahbazgarhi]

This religious edict[2] has been caused to be inscribed[3] by His Sacred and Gracious Majesty.

Here[4] not a single living creature should be slaughtered

employ (whence *Yukta* and *Yoga*). A commentator on Kauṭilya explains the term *upayukta* [II. 8] as an officer placed above the *Yuktas* (yuktānāṁ upari niyuktaḥ).

[1] *Khane saṁtaṁ.*

[2] The term *dhrama-dipi* or *dhaṁma lipī* applies to the entire series of the fourteen Rock Edicts issued in one corpus, as also to that of the seven Pillar Edicts. Senart remarks: "The whole has been considered as forming one *ensemble*, and must have been engraved at the same time" [*Inscriptions of Piyadasi*, vol. ii. p. 81].

[3] The Jaugaḍa text, of all other texts, mentions the very hill appointed for the inscription—"*Khapiṁgalasi* [Khepiṁgalasi = brown in the sky (Hultzsch)] *pavatasi likhāpitā*"; while in the Dhauli text the name of the hill is lost in "... si pavatasi," and this hill must have been a different hill too.

[4] *Hida*, i.e., here, at Pāṭaliputra, as stated in R.E. V, Girnar; it is, however, used in the sense of "in my dominion" in R.E. XIII (*hida raja-viṣavaspi* in l. 9) and M.R.E. (*hadha*, l. 4) Rūpnath. I prefer the former meaning to limit the operation of Asoka's new ordinance, which is far too sweeping in its scope, to his own city,

and sacrificed. Nor should any Samāja be held.[1] For His Sacred and Gracious Majesty sees much objection in such *samāja*.

where it might be more justifiable than if it had been applied all over his empire against the religious usage of the majority of its subjects, and against even his own ordinance as published in his P.E. V, which protects from slaughter only a few specified "living beings."

[1] See notes on the word of Dr. D. R. Bhandarkar [*IA*, xli. pp. 255-7] and Thomas [*JRAS*, 1914].

The objectionable kind of *Samajjā* is described in the *Dīgha Nikāya* [vol. iii. p. 183, P.T.S.] as comprising the six features of "dancing, singing, music, story-telling, cymbals, and tam-tams." Again, in the Brahmajāla Sutta [*Dīgha*, i. p. 6], there are mentioned several objectionable shows (*visuka-dassanam*) marked by some of the above features. One of these is called *Pekkham*, which Buddhaghosa has explained as *naṭa-samajjā*, thereby indicating that the other shows mentioned in this passage are to be taken as so many varieties of *samajjā*, some of which would be highly objectionable from Asoka's standpoint: e.g., the fights arranged between animals such as "elephants, horses, buffaloes, bulls, goats and rams," and even between "birds like cocks and quails." Another kind of *samajjā* is described in the *Commentary on Dhammapada* [vol. iv. p. 59, P.T.S.], where it is stated how it was organised by a company of actors (*nātakā*) numbering even 500, who would give yearly or six-monthly performances before the king at Rājagṛiha for large rewards. These performances would last for seven days, at which the chief feat shown was that of a damsel walking, dancing, and singing on a horizontal bar. The mischief caused by this *samajjā* was that one of the spectators in the amphitheatre (*mañchātimañche ṭhita*), Uggasena, the son of a rich merchant, fell in love with that performing damsel. The same passage tells us how in those days these actors used to exhibit their arts at villages, towns, and the capital cities of the country (*gāmanigamarājadhānīsu*). This joy of popular life was now being restricted by a puritanical emperor!

In the *Vinaya*, we read of a *samāja* held on a hill at Rājagṛiha with dancing, singing and music [ii. 5, 2, 6], and another for a feast [iv. 37, 1]. Several uses of the word also occur in the *Jātakas*: e.g., *Jāt.* iii. 541, 20 (club fight); 318; 545.

The epigraphic uses of the word are seen in the expression "usava-samāja-karapanāhi" in the Khāravela Inscription, and also in "usava-samāja-kārakasa" in a Nasik Cave Inscription.

The form *samajyā* is also known in Sanskrit, but the usual form is *samāja*. In the *Mahābhārata*, the *samāja* figures as a Śaiva festival [Hopkins, *Epic Mythology*, pp. 65, 220] accompanied by drinking, song and dance. But the secular *samāja* is held in an amphitheatre

But there are also certain varieties of same which are considered commendable [1] by His Sacred and Gracious Majesty.

Formerly in the kitchen of His Sacred and Gracious Majesty, daily many hundred thousands [2] of living creatures were slaughtered for purposes of curries. But now when this religious edict is being inscribed, only three living creatures are slaughtered, two peacocks and one deer, and the deer, too, not regularly. Even these three living creatures afterwards shall not [3] be slaughtered.

(*raṅga* or *prekṣāgāra*) with *śibikās*, camps, and *mañchas*, platforms, for the accommodation of different classes and corporations (*śreṇis* and *gaṇas*) assembling (1) for a public feast with varieties of meat dishes, or to witness (2) a joust at arms [*Harivaṁśa*, vv. 4528-38, 4642-58], (3) a display of military manoeuvres [*Ādi. P.* chh. 134 f.], or (4) a *svayamvara* ceremony accompanied by dancing, singing and music [*Ib.* ch. 185 ; cited by Dr. Bhandarkar].

Thomas quotes *Mbh.* i. 185, 29, which refers to a game being held in an arena, *samājavāṭa*, surrounded by platforms, *mañcha*, and hence the game might be animal fights. For its derivative sense, the *samāja* may be compared with the English sporting term, " a meet."

Kauṭilya in one passage [II. 25] refers to *utsava, samāja* and *yātrā*, where the drinking of wine was unrestricted for four days, and in another passage [XIII. 5] points out the conqueror's duty of conciliating the conquered people by respecting their national devotion to their country, their religion (*deśa-daivata*), and their institutions, viz., their *utsava*, *samāja* and *vihāra*.

The word also occurs in *Vātsāyana Kāmasūtra* [Bk. i. ch. iv. 26], not in a technical but a general sense, of a gathering at the temple of Sarasvatī once a month or a fortnight to hear the songs of local or outside musicians with dancing.

Lastly, we may note that Asoka's grandfather Chandragupta, used to hold annually a great festival for animal fights. There were butting contests between rams, wild bulls, elephants, and even rhinoceroses, and also races between chariots drawn by two oxen with a horse between [Ælian]. These public shows organised by his predecessors Asoka now rules out.

[1] These are the shows organised by Asoka himself, as described in R.E. IV.

[2] Probably an exaggeration, from which the edicts are not free sometimes, like the literary works much maligned on that ground. The *Mahāvaṁsa* relates how Asoka's father entertained 60,000 Brahmans daily, and Asoka did the same for three years [v. 34].

[3] This was not done for the poor peacocks which do not figure in the list of protected animals and birds given in P.E. V. The *Rāmāyaṇa*

II

[GIRNAR]

Everywhere within the dominion [1] of His Sacred and Gracious Majesty the King, and likewise among the frontagers such as the Cholas,[2] Pāṇḍyas,[3] the Satiyaputra,[4] the

[ii. 91, 70] mentions the *mayūra* as a food of kings, while Buddhaghosa states that the "flesh of a pea-fowl is delicious" to the people of Madhyadeśa (including Magadha). [*Sāratthappakāsini*, Commentary on *Saṁyutta Nikāya*, cited for me by Mr. C. D. Chatterji.]

[1] *Vijitamhi* or *vijitasi* as contrasted with *prachaṁtesu* or *aṁtā*, i.e., peoples, not his subjects, but of countries outside but bordering on the limits of his dominion. Cf. the reference to *aṁtā*, frontagers, in M.R.E. I, to *aṁtānaṁ avijitānaṁ* (i.e., independent neighbours) of K.R.E. II, to *aṁtesu* of R.E. XIII and to *Aparāntas* in R.E. V. The terms *anta* and *pratyanta* have a political, and the term *Aparānta*, a purely geographical, reference. Kauṭilya [I. 17] uses the term *pratyanta* which the commentator explains as *mlechchhadeśa*, to which a king should deport his disloyal sons.

[2] The plural form, according to Bhandarkar [*Asoka*, p. 38], indicates two Choḍa kingdoms, one of which he identifies with Ptolemy's Soretai (Tamil, soṛa = choṛa), with its capital Orthoura = Uraiyur near Trichinopoly, and the other, the northern kingdom, with Sora, with its capital Arkatos = Arcot.

[3] Ptolemy also speaks of the *Pandinoi* with their city of Modoura = Madura, while Varāhamihira (sixth century A.D.) knows of the Uttara-Pāṇḍyas, showing there were two Paṇḍya kingdoms, northern and southern [*Ib.* 40].

[4] Identified by V. A. Smith with "the Satyamaṅgalam Taluk of Coimbatore district along the Western Ghats and bordering on Mysore, Malabar, Coimbatore and Coorg. A town of the same name commands the Gazalhatti Pass from Mysore, formerly of strategical importance. The Satyamaṅgala country was also included in the territory colonised by the Great Migration (*Bṛihadcharaṇam*), possibly that led by Bhadrabāhu in the days of Chandragupta Maurya" [*Asoka*, p. 161, and *JRAS*, 1919, p. 584 n.]. A writer in *JRAS* [1918, p. 541] argues for identifying Satiyaputra with the people of Kāñchipura, the place of Asokan stūpas as recorded by Yuan Chwang and known to the orthodox as the Satyavrata country. Another writer in the *JRAS* [1923, p. 412] thinks it is the same as *Satyabhūmi*, the name of the country north of Kerala, as mentioned in some early Tamil works composed on the western coast. Satiya is taken by Hultzsch to be Sattiya = Satviya, with which we may compare the *Satvats* of the *Aitareya Brāhmaṇa* [viii. 14] or Pāṇini, v. 3, 117, referring to a Kṣatriya clan of that name in Southern India.

Keralaputra,[1] what is (known as) Tāmraparṇī,[2] the Greek King, Antiochos, and those kings, too, who are the neighbours [3] of that Antiochos—everywhere have been instituted by His Sacred and Gracious Majesty two kinds of medical treatment [4]—medical treatment of man and medical treatment of beast. Medicinal herbs also, those wholesome for man and wholesome for beast, have been caused to be imported [5] and to be planted in all places wherever they did not exist.

Roots also, and fruits, have been caused to be imported and to be planted everywhere wherever they did not exist. On the roads, wells also have been caused to be dug and trees caused to be planted for the enjoyment of man and beast.[6]

[1] I.e., Chera or Malabar. The ending *putra* denotes " the children of the soil." The original *Ketalaputo* is a mistake for Keralaputra.

[2] In Kauṭilya's *Arthaśastra* it is a river in the Pāṇḍya country, according to the commentator Bhaṭṭasvāmī. But in the Pāli literature, it is the name of Ceylon, *Taṁbapaṁniya* in R.E. XIII also definitely denoting the people of Ceylon (as shown also by Monier Williams in his Dictionary). Besides, the ruler of a large empire cannot be expected to think of a petty boundary like a river in Tinnevelly to indicate the peoples beyond his frontiers. Finally, Ceylon, to which his son gave its religion, must naturally figure prominently as the objective of his " moral conquests," his humanitarian work. *Ā Taṁbapaṁṇī* of the text = *yā Tāmraparṇī*.

[3] Named in R.E. XIII.

[4] *Chikīchha, chikitsā,* medical treatment, which implies the provision of (*a*) physicians (including those for animals, veterinary surgeons), (*b*) medicines, and (*c*) places equipped for treatment, i.e., hospitals. Thus all the three—men, materials, and place—are conveyed by the term. The supply of medicines depended upon special botanical gardens for their cultivation, and pharmaceutical works for their manufacture.

[5] In the description of the palace of Chandragupta Maurya as given by Ælian [c. xviii.], there is a reference to trees " native to the soil " and others which are " with circumspect care brought from other parts."

The evidence of the edict on Asoka's supply of medical aid is echoed in the legends which trace the origin of this measure to the death of a monk for want of medicines, whereupon Asoka had four tanks filled with medicines at the four gates of the city, as related by Buddhaghosa [*Samantapāsādikā*, p. 306].

[6] Kauṭilya [II. 21] also encourages the import of seeds of useful and medicinal plants by exempting such import from tolls (mahopakāram-uchchhulkam kuryāt vījam tu durlabhaṁ].

III

[GIRNAR]

His Sacred and Gracious Majesty thus saith : By me consecrated twelve years [1] was the following ordained : Everywhere within my dominions, the *Yuktas* [2] the *Rājūka* [3] and

[1] Kauṭilya [II. 6] applies the term *rājavarṣa* to the year counted from the king's coronation.

[2] A general term for government employees. It is also found in the *Arthaśāstra* [II. 5]: "*Sarvādhikaraṇeṣu Yuktopayukta-tatpuruṣānām*," e.g., "among the *Yuktas*, *Upayuktas* and their subordinates [*puruṣas* (a term occurring in P.E. I, IV and VII)] of all departments." Here the *Yuktas* must mean the subordinate secretariat staff accompanying the higher officials on tour [Thomas, *JRAS*, 1914, p. 391]. In II. 9, Kauṭilya refers to the *Yuktas* being employed in the collection of revenue which they may embezzle unnoticed. The terms *āyuktaka* and *viniyuktaka* frequently occur in the Gupta Inscriptions.

[3] *Rājūke* or *raju* (Manshera) is probably connected with the word *Rājā* which in Pāli might mean even a *Mahāmatta*, *Mahāmātra*, and "all those who have power of life and death" [Childers]. In the *Mahāvaṁsa*, there is even the term *Rājako* for a king. The functions of these *Rājūkas* are indicated in P.E. IV, where it is stated that they were in charge of "many hundred thousands of people" and are invested with some of the powers of the sovereign, viz., independence as regards *daṇḍa*, i.e., justice, and *abhihāra*, i.e., rewards (or attack), as well as *anugraha*, i.e., privileges and pardons. Thus the *Rājūkas* ranked next to the king and the viceroys, and were like the provincial governors.

Bühler thought that the word was connected with the word *rajju* and the same as the Pāli word *rajjūka*, ropeholder, and hence signifying "Revenue and Settlement Officer" [*Ep. Ind.* vol. ii. p. 466 n.]. Dr. F. W. Thomas agrees with Bühler in thinking that while the *Rājūkas* represented the highest local officials, their chief functions were connected with "survey, land settlement and irrigation" [*Cambridge History*, p. 487]. Megasthenes also speaks of high officers who "superintend the rivers, *measure the land*, inspect the sluices by which water is let out from the main canals into their branches, have charge of the huntsmen with power of *rewarding* or *punishing* them, *collect the taxes* and superintend the occupations connected with land."

The *Kauṭilīya* has the expression *rajjūśchorarajjūścha* [II. 6], of which the meaning is not clear. But in IV. 13, Kauṭilya

the *Prādeśika* [1] must, every five years, go out on tour by turns [2] as well for other business too [3] as for this purpose,

mentions an officer called *chora-rajjuka*, whose duty was probably to apprehend thieves. He was made liable to make good the loss by theft within his jurisdiction to traders who had declared to him the value of their goods. [The commentator explains *chora-rajjuka* =*choragrahaṇa-niyukta*.] But Jacobi has found in the Jaina work *Kalpasūtra* the word *rajjū* which he explains as "a writer, a clerk."

[1] These might be higher officers than the *Rājūkas*, if they are mentioned in an ascending order. Dr. F. W. Thomas identifies them with the *Pradeṣṭṛis* who were in charge of "the executive, revenue and judicial service" [*JRAS*, 1914, pp. 383-6, and *Cambridge History*, pp. 488, 508]. The *Pradeṣṭṛi* figures as the head of one of the traditional eighteen *tīrthas* or departments of the state in the *Kauṭilīya* [I. 12]. The name signifies a distinct department or branch of public service. The *Pradeṣṭṛi* is in charge of criminal administration and justice (*Kanṭaka-śodhana*), as the *Dharmastha* was of civil justice [IV. 1]. Like the *Dharmastha* and, indeed, other *Adhyakṣas*, the *Pradeṣṭā* was himself also subject to espionage under the direction of the *Samāhartā* [IV. 4]. He figures also as the chief officer of the police, with his own staff of *Gopas* and *Sthānikas* to assist him in tracking thieves from outside the province [IV. 6]. Like the *Samāhartā*, he is also to check the work of the *Adhyakṣas* and their subordinates (*puruṣas*) [IV. 9]. With the *Dharmastha*, again, he is empowered to make awards of penalties like fines and corporeal punishment [*Ib.*]. Lastly, he also helped the local administrations by inspecting the work, and the means employed for it, by their officers, the *Sthānika* and *Gopa*, and also by collecting the religious cesses [II. 35]. The *Prādeśika* in its literal sense would indicate the ruler of a *pradeśa* or local area, and is similar to the term *Rāṣṭra-pāla* used by Kauṭilya [V. 1] or to the term *Rāstriyena* applied to the provincial governor in the Junāgaḍh Inscription of Rudradāman. Dr. Thomas [*JRAS*, 1915] also now proposes to derive the word from *pradeśa* in the sense of "report" [as in the *Kauṭilīya*, p. 111]. The term *Prādeśikeśvara* = provincial chief occurs in *Rājataraṅginī*, iv. 126.

In this connection we may note the following terms used in the Edicts to indicate local officials having independent charge: *Nagaravyāvahāraka-Mahāmātras* ("set over thousands of souls," K.R.E. II), *Lājavachanika-Mahāmātras* [*Ib.*], *Rājūkas*, and *Prādeśikas*.

[2] *Anusaṁyānaṁ niyātu* (*nikramatu*, S., and *nikhamāvū*, D. and J.). See the note on the words occurring in K.R.E. I.

[3] *Yathā aññāya pi kaṁmāya*: cf. "*atane kaṁmam ahāpayitu etaṁ pi*," "without neglecting their own duties, while on tour, in undertaking this new duty" [K.R.E. I]. This repetition con-

for this religious instruction : Commendable [1] is the service of father and mother [2] ; commendable is liberality to friends,[3] acquaintances, relatives, Brahmans and Śramaṇas ; [4] commendable is abstention from the slaughter of living creatures ; [5] commendable also is not to spend or hoard too much.[6] The Council [7] will also similarly instruct the *Yuktas*

clusively shows that ordinary administrative tour is meant by the term *anusaṁyāna*, and not the transfer of officials as suggested by some.

[1] *Sādhu.*

[2] Cf. *Sigālovāda Suttanta* : " In five ways a child should minister to his parents (*mātā-pitaro-pachchupaṭṭhātabbā*) : ' Once supported by them I will now be their support (*bhato nesaṁ bharissāmi*) ; I will perform duties incumbent on them ; I will keep up the lineage and tradition (*kula-vaṁsaṁ*) of my family (i.e., by " not dissipating property, restoring, if need be, the family honour and integrity, and maintaining gifts to religieux ") ; I will make myself worthy of my heritage (*dāyajjaṁ patipajjāmi*).' " This is the full meaning of the expression " mātari cha pitari cha śuśrūṣā," as so often used in the Edicts.

[3] There are mentioned five ways in which these friends and companions (*mittāmachchā*) may be served [*Ib.*]; viz., " by generosity (*dānena*), courtesy (*peyyavajjena*), benevolence (*attha-chariyāya*), by treating them as one treats himself (*samānattatāya*), and by being as good as his word (*avisaṁvādanatāya*)."

[4] " In five ways should one minister to the Samaṇas and Brāhmaṇas: by friendliness (*mettena*) in act, speech, and mind, by keeping an open house for them (*anāvaṭa-dvāratāya*), and by supplying their temporal needs (*āmisānuppadānena*) " [*Ib.*].

According to Kauṭilya [II. 1], the royal liberality to a Brāhmaṇa, whether a *ṛitvik*, an *āchārya*, a *purohita*, or a *śrotṛiya*, should take the form of the gift to him of tax-free lands.

[5] *Prāṇānaṁ sādhu anāraṁbho'.*

The *Sigālovāda Suttanta* includes as one of the four vices (*kamma kilesā*) *pāṇatipāto* or destruction of life.

[6] *Apavyayatā apabhāḍatā* ; this moderation in spending or hoarding is thus defined [*Ib.*] :

" One portion let him spend and taste the fruit.
His business to conduct let him take two
And portion four let him reserve and hoard (*nidhāpeyya*),
So there'ill be wherewithal in times of need."

[7] *Parisā*, interpreted by Mr. K. P. Jayaswal as the *Mantripariṣad* as described in the *Kauṭilīya*, Bk. I. ch. 15.

for purposes of accounts [1] in accordance with my order [2] and its grounds.

IV

[GIRNAR]

For a long period past, for many hundreds of years, have increased the sacrificial slaughter of animals, cruelty towards living beings and improper treatment of relatives, of Brahmans and Śramaṇas. But to-day, in consequence of the practice of morality [3] by His Sacred and Gracious Majesty the King, the sound of the war drum has become [4] the call (not to arms but) to *Dharma*, exhibiting [5] to the people [6] the sight of the cars of the gods, of elephants,[7]

[1] *Gaṇanāyam, gaṇanasi,* which I take in the ordinary sense and not in the technical sense of the Department of Accounts (as taken in V. Smith's *Asoka*). Hultzsch takes it to mean "for registering (these rules)."

The *gaṇanā*, as has been very aptly suggested by Dr. D. R. Bhandarkar [*Asoka*, p. 280], might refer to the accounts of each household which should be examined by the *yuktas* to see how far they conformed to the principle of moderation in both spending and saving (*apavyayatā apabhāṇḍatā*) laid down by the emperor.

We may also refer in this connection to the principle of Public Finance laid down by Kauṭilya [II. 6], which requires the Collector-General, *Samāhartā*, to see to the increase of revenue by taxation and decrease of expenditure by checking the spending authorities and by retrenchments. Perhaps Asoka had some such principle in view in this passage in his edict.

[2] *Vyaṁjanato.*

[3] *Dhaṁmacharaṇena.*

[4] *Aho = abhavat*, became.

[5] *Draśayitu* (S.), *draśeti* (M.), *dasayitpā* (G.), *dasayitu* (K.).

[6] *Janaṁ* ; *janasa* and *munisānaṁ* in other texts.

[7] *Hastidasaṇā* ; other texts have *hathīni* or *astina*. The elephants may be actual elephants in procession (instead of those for war) or figures of celestial elephants, the vehicles of the *Lokapālas*, or the white elephant symbolising the Buddha (suggested by Dr. Bhandarkar and Hultzsch).

Instead of the sights of the war chariots, war elephants, and destructive fires, Asoka was presenting to his people the edifying sights of the chariots of the gods, divine elephants, and radiant shapes of celestial beings, or inoffensive bonfires.

masses of fire[1] and other heavenly shows.[2]

As were not seen before for many hundreds of years, so now have increased through the religious ordinances of His Sacred and Gracious Majesty the king cessation of slaughter of animals, non-violence towards living beings, proper treatment of relatives, of Brahmans and Śramaṇas, obedience[3] to mother and father and to the seniors.[4]

This and other practice of morality of many kinds has been increased. And His Sacred and Gracious Majesty the king will further increase this practice of morality.

And the sons, grandsons, and great-grandsons,[5] too, of His

[1] *Agikhaṁdhāni*; Shahbazgarhi has *jotikaṁdhani*; translated as bonfires, fireworks or illuminations, or "fiery" balls and other signs in the heavens. Hultzsch [*JRAS*, 1913, p. 652] quotes *mahantā aggikkhandhā* to signify the guardians of the quarters, Indra and Brahma, appearing as "great masses of fire." In that case, the word in the edict would refer to radiant figures of the gods—*divyāni rūpāni*. Dr. D. R. Bhandarkar, however, interprets the passage in the light of the *Vimānavatthu* which describes the bliss of *Svarga* awaiting a virtuous man after death as comprising (1) the *vimāna*, a movable palace, (2) the *hastī*, all-white celestial elephant, (3) shining complexion, resembling star, fire, or lightning. These blisses were objectively presented before the people as stimulus to virtuous life.

[2] *Divyāni rūpāni*: Asoka's idea seems to have been that by seeing these exhibitions about the gods, the people might try to be like the gods, as indicated in M.R.E. I (*amisā samānā munisā misā devehi*).

[3] *Susrusā*: Mr. and Mrs. Rhys Davids do not approve of Childers' translation of the word as "obedience." They point out that "obedience does not occur in Buddhist ethics. It is not mentioned in any one of the 227 rules of the Buddhist order. It does not occur in any one of the clauses of this summary of the ethics of the Buddhist layman (viz., the *Sigālovāda Suttanta*), and it does not enter into any of the divisions of the Eightfold Path nor of the 37 constituent qualities of Arahantship. Hence no member of the Buddhist order takes any vow of obedience; and the vows of a Buddhist layman ignore it. Has this been one of the reasons for the success of Buddhism? It looked beyond obedience" [*Dialogues of the Buddha*, part 3, p. 181, n. 4]. They translate the word by "eagerness to learn," which is specially appropriate for the word used in reference to teachers in P.E. VII.

[4] *Thaira* = *sthavira*; or *vuḍhanaṁ*, i.e., *vṛiddhānām* in other texts.

[5] *Potrā* (or *nati*) *cha prapotrā* (or *pranatika*); it is an interesting question whether Asoka lived to see his *prapautra*.

Sacred and Gracious Majesty the King will increase this practice of morality up to the end of time (" the aeon of universal destruction ") [1] and will preach the Dharma, themselves abiding in [2] Dharma and righteous conduct. For this is the highest work, viz., preaching of the Dharma.

The practice of morality, too, is not of one devoid of virtue. The increase of this work, nay, even its non-diminution, is laudable. For this purpose has this been inscribed [3] that they (i.e., Asoka's successors) may apply themselves to the promotion of this object, and that its decline should not be entertained.

By His Sacred and Gracious Majesty the King consecrated twelve years [4] was this caused to be inscribed.[5]

[1] *Āva savaṭakapā = yāvat saṁvartakalpam.* The *Mahābhārata* refers to the *saṁvartaka* fire of destruction, appearing at the end of 1000 *yugas* [see V. A. Smith's *Asoka*, 3rd ed. p. 167]. Other texts read *āva kapaṁ = yāvat kalpam.*

[2] *Tisṭaṁto.*

[3] *Lekhāpitaṁ ;* S. has *nipistaṁ* as read by Hultzsch. Bŭhler read it as *dipista.*

[4] Both this edict and the previous one state that they were issued in 258 B.C., while the next edict states it was issued a year later, when the *Dharma-Mahāmātras* were appointed. Thus the entire body of the fourteen Rock Edicts took a year, 258-257 B.C., for their publication on their own showing.

[5] *Lekhāpitam* or *lekhitā* (K.), but Shah. has *dipapitaṁ*, and in R.E. V has the form *dhramadipi dipista* in place of *dhaṁmalipi lekhitā* of K.

Pāṇini [iii. 2, 21] uses the forms *lipikara* and *libikara* for the scribe, and we have also in Sanskrit the word *dibira* for *lipikara.* Thus *dipapitam* or *dipista* is from root *dipa* or *diba,* to write. Hultzsch reads *nipista* for *dipista,* which Mr. K. P. Jayaswal would take to be *nīvīstha,* i.e., filed, or recorded, from the word *nīvī* = a cord for tying. [Cf. the word *nibandha* ; the word *nibaddha* for " registered " is used in a Nasik Inscription (see my *Local Government in Ancient India,* 2nd ed. p. 119).] But the word *nīvī* in Sanskrit more usually means a piece of cloth wrapped round the waist, and as money was generally carried in such cloth (the old images of Kubera show bags of cloth hanging from his neck !) the word came to signify the money thus carried, one's capital or saving. The word is used in this sense by Kauṭilya [II. 6 and 7] and also in the significant expression, *akṣaya-nīvī,* used in several inscriptions to distinguish the capital or principal to remain untouched from the interest yielded by it to be utilised [cf. my *Local Govt.,* p. 116 n.]. [I owe this note to that of Rai Bahadur

V

[MĀNSEHRĀ]

Thus saith His Sacred and Gracious Majesty the King: The good deed [1] is difficult of performance. He who is the first performer [2] of a good deed achieves something difficult of performance. Now by me many a good deed has been achieved.

Therefore should my sons, grandsons, and my descendants after them [3] up to the end of time follow in my footsteps, they will do really meritorious deeds. But he who in this matter will cause even a portion [4] to diminish [5] will perform an evil deed indeed. Sin must be trodden down.[6]

Now in times past the *Dharma-Mahāmātras* were non-existent previously. But now the *Dharma-Mahāmātras* have been created by me consecrated for thirteen years. They have been employed among all sects for the establishment and growth of Dharma and for the good and happiness

G. H. Ojhā in his valuable Hindi edition of Asoka's Edicts (p. 52 n.).] Hultzsch [*JRAS*, 1913, p. 634] takes *nipista*, however, to be *ṇiṣpiṣta* (stamped ground), and hence "engraved." He now thinks [*Corpus*, p. xlii.] that the word should be connected with the ancient Persian *nipish*, to write, and quotes the inscription of Xerxes at Van—"*yanaiy dipim naiy nipishtām*," "where Darius did not cause an inscription to be written."

Instead of *idaṁ lekhāpitaṁ*, S., according to Hultzsch, reads *ñanaṁ hida nipesitaṁ* which he translates thus: "(This) conception (*jñāna*) was caused to be written here."

[1] *Kalaṇaṁ, kayāne* (K.) = *kalyāṇam*.

[2] *Adikare* = *ādikaraḥ*, i.e., originator.

[3] The manner of the statement seems to indicate that Asoka had lived to see his grandsons and no later descendants [cf. the dedications naming Daśaratha *Devānaṁpiya*].

[4] *Deśa*: the word also occurs in Kalinga R.E. I (*se pi desaṁ no savaṁ*). Cf. *ekadeśam*, a part.

[5] *Hapeśati* = *hāpayiṣyati*; cf. *hini* = *hāniḥ* in R.E. IV.

[6] *Supadarave* or *supadālaye* (K.) = *supradalitavya*, i.e., to be trampled on foot, to be destroyed. The Shahbazgarhi version, as well as Girnar, uses the word *sukaraṁ*, in which case the sense of the passage will be: "sin is indeed easily committed."

of those devoted to religion [1] (even) among the Yonas,[2] Kambojas, Gandhāras,[3] Rāsṭrikas,[4] Pitinikas [5] and whatever other peoples of Aparānta [6] or western borderers (of mine

[1] *Dhramayutasa* : I take the meaning of the word as intended clearly in the Maski Edict and not in the accepted sense of "subordinate officials of the Law of Piety."

[2] The Yonas are to be distinguished from the "*Yona-rājās*" of R.E. II and XIII. According to Senart, these peoples who are termed *Āparāntas* are somewhat different in status from the peoples called *Āntas* : the former are more closely related to the king through the *Dharma-Mahāmātras* he deputes for work among them; the *Āntas* [R.E. II], on the contrary, receive a different kind of benefit from the king—viz., supply of medical aid. To this category would belong all the foreign peoples under the Greek kings named. In R.E. II the word *anta* alternates with the word *pratyanta* in the different versions.

[3] Hultzsch [*Arch. S.*, S. I., i. 223] takes them to be "Greeks, Kabulis, and N.W. Panjabis."

[4] The terms *Mahā-raṭhis* and *Mahā-bhojas* occur in some inscriptions of the Āndhra or Sātavāhana period in the Deccan to indicate feudatory chiefs, while the word *petenika* is explained as "hereditary" by the commentator on *Aṅguttara*, iii. 70, and 300, where occurs the expression *Raṭṭhika Pettanika*. This is the suggestion of Dr. D. R. Bhandarkar who would interpret Pitinika-Rāṣṭrikas or Bhojas [R.E. XIII] as hereditary chieftains. The equation *Peteṇika* = *Pettanika* is, however, rejected by Michelson as "defying known phonetic shifts." He thinks *Peteṇika* can be derived only from *Paitrayaṇika* [*JAOS*, 46. 257]. Hultzsch takes *Rāṣṭrika* = *Āraṭṭas* of the Panjab = *Arattioi* of the *Periplus*.

Hultzsch [*Corpus*, p. xxxviii.] further suggests that the Raṭhikas or Rāṣṭikas might refer to the people of Kathiāvār, from the fact that its governor is given the title of *Rāṣṭrīya* in the Junāgarh Inscription of Rudradāman.

[5] *Raṭhika-Pitinikana*; *Raṭhikanaṁ Pitinikanaṁ* (S.), *Risṭika-Peteṇikānaṁ* (G.), *Laṭhika-Pitenikesu* (Dhauli).

In R.E. XIII we have the compound *Bhoja-Pitinikeṣu* or *Pitinikyeṣu*.

[6] The term *Aparānta* in Sanskrit literature seems to be a stock word for Western India. The *Purāṇas* for instance, call the five Divisions of India as (1) Madhyadeśa (central), (2) Udīchya (north), (3) Prāchya (east), (4) Dakṣināpatha (south), and (5) Aparānta (west). The five divisions are thus described in the *Kāvyamīmāṁsā* : (1) Pūrvadeśa, eastern country, from Vārāṇasī, (2) Dakṣināpatha, stretching southwards from Māhiṣmatī, (3) Uttarāpatha, north of Pṛithūdaka (= Pehoa, west of Thanesar), (4) Antarvedī, middle

there are). They are also employed among the soldiers and their chiefs,[1] Brahmanical ascetics [2] and householders, the

country, defined as the land between Vinasána and Prayāga, Gaṅgā and Yamunā, and (5) *Paśchātdeśa*, western country, the Aparānta of the Purāṇas, which is defined as comprising the following sub-divisions, viz., Devasabhā, Surāṣṭra, Daśeraka (Malwa), Travaṇa, Bhṛigukachchha, Kachchhīya, Ānarta (Gujarat), Arbuda (round Mount Abu), *Yavana* and others. Thus the peoples named by Asoka would come well within Aparānta. The Aparānta is also one of the regions to which the third Buddhist Council despatched a missionary, as stated in the text. The capital of Aparānta was Sūrpāraka in Pāli works, which is modern Sopārā in Thana District, where occurs a version of the Rock Edicts. Jayaswal, however, takes the word *Aparānta* as an antithesis to *Anta*, and interprets the two words as meaning peoples *within* and *outside* the limits of Asoka's empire respectively. See note under R.E. XIII. It may also be noted that Kauṭilya also uses the word Aparānta for Western India, and refers to this region as being known for its elephants though only of middle quality [II. 2], and for its excessive rainfall, whence the commentator identifies it with Konkan [II. 24].

[1] *Bhaṭamayeṣu* = *bhṛita-m* (euphonic) *-āryesu*; *bhaṭa* (= a soldier) is not the same word as *bhaṭaka* (= a servant) in the expression *dāsa-bhaṭakasi*, "in slaves and servants," occurring in R.E. IX. The expression *Bhaṭa-chāṭa* (regular and irregular troops) frequently occurs in the Gupta Inscriptions.

[2] *Bramaṇibhyeṣu*: the Brahmans are here contrasted with those who are called *ibhyas*, i.e., persons possessed of wealth and family, and hence householders, as distinguished from ascetics. P.E. VII, l. 15, in the same context has the expression *pavajītānaṁ gihithānaṁ*, "ascetics and householders." The other juxtaposition, *Brāhmaṇa-Śramaṇeṣu* occurring in other edicts (e.g., R.E. IV), also shows that the term *Brāhmaṇa* does not denote the caste, but the Brahmanical orders of ascetics, as the term *Śramaṇa* denotes the other orders of ascetics. There were in that age numerous sects of Brahmanical ascetics designated as Titthiyas, Ājīvikas, Nigaṇṭhas, Muṇḍaśāvakas, Jaṭilakas, Paribbājakas, Māgaṇḍikas, Tedaṇḍikas, Eka-Sātakas, Aviruddhakas, Gotamakas, Devadhammikas, Charakas, Āchelakas, etc. [see *JRAS*, 1898, p. 197, and *Sutta Nipāta*], while the *Śramaṇa* ascetics were also of different varieties known as Magga-jinas, Magga-desins, Magga-jivins, and Magga-dusins, disputes among whom split them into more sects. Thus the term *Brāhmaṇa-Śramaṇa* would bring under it all classes of ascetics in that age, manifold as they were. The respect for Brahman and Śramaṇa ascetics is not Asoka's innovation: it is as old as the Buddha, who was full of it. As the passage already cited shows [*Dīgha Nikāya*, iii. p. 191, P.T.S.], the Buddha points to "*Samaṇa-Brāhmaṇā*" as objects of highest

destitute, and the infirm by age, for the good and happiness, and freedom from molestation, of those [1] who have applied themselves to Dharma. They are also employed for taking steps against [2] imprisonment,[3] for freedom from molestation,

respect to be shown in five ways, viz., by friendliness of action, speech and thought, keeping open door for them (*anāvaṭa-dvāratāya*), and by supply of needs (*āmisānuppadānena*). Thus Asoka's insistence on respect for Brahman ascetics is due to his Buddhism, and its traditions in that regard.

It may be noted that Megasthenes also had noticed two classes of ascetics he calls " Brachmanes and Sarmanes." The former lived in simple style, using beds of rushes or skins, abstaining from animal food, always studying and discoursing up to the age of 37, when they returned to the world. Thus these must have been the Brahmachārī Brāhmaṇas. But Arrian noticed other classes of ascetics whom he calls *Sophists*, who " go naked, living in the open air under trees, and eating only fruits and barks of trees." These must have been the Brāhmaṇas of the fourth *āśrama*, i.e., those who renounced the world and became *Sannyāsis*. The other class of ascetics whom the Greek writers call *Sarmanes*, i.e., *Śramaṇas*, " lived in the woods, subsisting on leaves and fruits, and wearing barks of trees."

[1] *Apalibodhaye*, but the Girnar text reads *aparigodhāya*. Dr. Thomas, in a long and learned article [*JRAS*, 1915, pp. 99-106], has shown the meanings of both the words, *paligodha* and *palibodha*, from their uses in different texts. From root *gṛidh*, we get *parigṛiddha* used in the sense of " desire," " greed " or " worldliness " in several passages in the *Śikṣā-samuchchaya* and also in the *Divyāvadāna* (p. 351: parigṛiddho viṣayābhirataścha). The word *palibodha* is derived from root *budh*, " to be aware," but its various uses in the *Vinaya*, the *Jātakas*, and other texts, show that its established meaning is " anxiety," " trouble," or " worldly cares." These fine shades of difference in the meanings of the two words were lost in popular usage, and the inditer of the edict may be pardoned if he has missed them.

It may be noted in connection with these duties of the *Dharma-Mahāmātras* to give state help to the destitute and the infirm by age (*anātheṣu vṛiddheṣu*), that Kauṭilya also recognised the same duty of the state : " Bāla-vṛiddha-vyādhita-vyasanya-anāthāṁścha rājā bibhṛiyāt," " the king shall maintain the orphan, decrepit, diseased, afflicted and destitute (II. 1)."

[2] *Paṭividhanaye* ; *paṭividhānāya* (G.) : Sanskrit *pratividhānam* = precautionary or remedial step. Hultzsch, however, takes it in the sense of a gift, in which sense the word is used in R.E. VIII, and explains it as " in supporting."

[3] *Badhana-badhasa* ; *baṁdhana-badhasa* (G.), " of one bound in chains." Cf. *baṁdhana-badhānaṁ* in P.E. IV.

and for granting release, on the ground that one has numerous offspring [1] or is overwhelmed by misfortune [2] or afflicted by age. Here,[3] and in all the outlying towns, in all the harems [4]

[1] *Pajāva ti vā* in K. settles the meaning of the expression; = " prajāvān iti vā "; one who is encumbered with too many children and is thus deserving of clemency. As regards these *anubandhas* or grounds for relief, Jayaswal was the first to explain them in the light of Smṛiti texts [*Manu*, viii. 126; *Gautama*, xii. 51; *Vasiṣṭha*, xix. 91; *Yājñavalkya*, i. 367; and *Kauṭilya*, IV. 85; cited in *JBORS*, IV. pp. 144-46] referring to the various grounds for revision of judicial sentences.

[2] *Kartabhikara* or, according to Hultzsch, *Kaṭrabhikara*; *Kiṭabhikaro* (S.); *Kaṭābhikāle* (K.); nom. sing. m.; " one overwhelmed by misfortune," as explained by Bühler from the use of the word *abhikirati* in the sense of " oppresses, overpowers " in *Jāt.* iv. 125, v. 72. *Abhikāra*, according to Woolner, may also mean (1) charm, incantation, in which sense it is taken by Senart and Hultzsch who explain *kaṭābhikāle* as " victims of a trick," and " bewitched " respectively; (2) means of livelihood, and hence *kaṭābhikāle* = the bread-winner [citing *Deśīnāmamālā*, i. 2].

On the whole subject of the unjust imprisonment (*bandhana*), execution (*vadha*), and torture (*palibodha*) of prisoners, it is interesting to note that Kauṭilya [IV. 8] also warns the Superintendent of Jails against these. He is liable to fines for confining persons in lock-up without declaring the reason (*saṁruddhakamanākhyāya chārayataḥ*); for putting them to unjust torture (*karmakārayataḥ*); for denying them food and drink; for molesting them (*parikleśayataḥ*); and for causing their death (*ghnataḥ*). Thus the work of Asoka's *Dharma-Mahāmātras* in respect of these matters lay with the superintendents of different jails in his empire, who were responsible for much unjust suffering for the people.

[3] The Girnar text reads here " *Pāṭalipute*," i.e., " at Pāṭaliputra," which settles the meaning of the word, wherever it occurs in the edicts [e.g., R.E. I]. Pāṭaliputra is also mentioned in the Sarnath Pillar Edict. As regards residence of members of the royal family in the provincial towns, we may mention those where the princes lived as viceroys, viz., Taxila, Ujjain, Tosalī, Suvarṇagiri. Kauṭilya also speaks of Mahāmātras being appointed in charge of the royal places of pleasure (*vihāra*), both in the capital and outside (*vāhyābhyantara*) [I. 10].

[4] The Dhauli text reads: " hida cha bāhilesu cha nagalesu savesu s[a]vesu olodhanes[u] [me] e vā pi bhāt[ī]naṁ me bhaginīnaṁ va. . . ." The expression " *me olodhanesu*," " *my* harems," does not occur in the other readings. This shows that Asoka had his own harems in the Mufussil towns, and in this connection we may instance the case of his wife, Devī of Vedisagiri, who, according to the Ceylon

of my brothers and sisters [1] and whatever other relatives (of mine there are), everywhere are they employed. These *Dharma-Mahāmātras* are employed among those devoted to Dharma in all places within my dominions,[2] whether one is eager for Dharma or established in Dharma or properly devoted to charity.[3]

For this purpose has this religious edict been inscribed that it may be everlasting and that my descendants [4] may follow in this path.

VI

[GIRNAR]

Thus saith His Sacred and Gracious Majesty the King:

In times past, there was not before at all hours [5] discharge

legends, permanently resided there, instead of coming to Pāṭaliputra to live there with her royal husband and children. Similarly, a second *avarodhana* or harem of Asoka must have been maintained for his second queen, Kāruvākī, the mother of Prince Tīvara, at the city of Kauśāmbī, as will appear from her edict inscribed on the Allahabad Pillar, which was originally located at Kauśambī. As regards the harems of his brothers, they were, as already explained, at the four cities where the brothers were posted as Asoka's viceroys.

The nature of the work of these *Dharma-Mahāmātras* in the royal harems is indicated in P.E. VII, viz., to stimulate their inmates to morality and gifts.

[1] *Spasuna*.

[2] *Vijitasi* or *vijite*, also used in R.E. II and III; but the Dhauli text uses the significant word *puṭhaviyaṁ*, i.e., *pṛithivyām*, signifying the extent of his dominions. That his empire was extensive is also stated by Asoka in another place—*Mahālake* (or *mahaṁte*) *hi vijitaṁ* [R.E. XIV].

[3] "*Dhramaniśito to va dhramadhithane ti va danasaṁyute,*" of which I take the translation of Hultzsch.

[4] *Praja* = sons or descendants in this edict, as also in the two Kalinga Edicts; not *subjects*, as translated by V. Smith.

[5] This statement is not in keeping with the heavy programme of daily duties and engagements to which the king is required to attend in all *Nīti-Śāstras* [*Kauṭilya*, I. 19; *Manu*, vii. 145, 146, 222-226; *Yājñavalkya*, vii. 327-333; *Agni-Purāṇa*, ccxxv. 1-17]. Asoka's stricture against his predecessors does not apply even to his grandfather whose devotion to public work is thus described by Megasthenes: "The king may not sleep during the daytime. He leaves his

of administrative business or the receiving of reports. So by me has thus been arranged: at all hours, when I am eating,[1] or in the harem, or in the inner apartments,[2] or even in the ranches,[3] or in the place of religious instruction,[4]

palace not only in time of war, but also for the purpose of judging causes. He then remains in Court for the whole day without allowing the business to be interrupted, even though the hour arrives when he must needs attend to his person" [McCrindle, p. 72]. Curtius [viii. 9] also adds: "The palace is open to all comers, even when the king is having his hair combed and dressed. It is then that he gives audience to ambassadors and administers justice to his subjects." [*Ib.*, *Ancient India*, p. 58 n.].

[1] *Bhuṁjamānasa, adamānasā* (Kalsi), *aśamanasa* (Shah.), and *aśatasa* (Man.).

[2] *Orodhanamhi*, but the Kalinga texts have "*aṁte olodhanasi*," "within the harem."

[3] *Vachamhi, vachasi*, or *vrachaspi*, connected by the Prakrit grammarian Hemachandra with Sanskrit *vraja* = enclosure for cattle and herdsmen. Kauṭilya [II. 6] includes in a *vraja* the following animals: cows, buffaloes, goats, sheep, asses, camels, horses, and mules. He also makes attending to the business of his cattle the king's personal work [I. 19]. Michelson [*JAOS*, 46. 259] points out the phonetic difficulty of deriving *vacha* from *vraja*, and of explaining the change of *ja* to *cha* in Girnar. But Girnar has *vacha-bhūmikā* in R.E. XII which is evidently *vraja-bhumikāḥ*. Shah. has the forms *vracheyam* (in this edict), *vracha-bhumika* [R.E. XII] and *vrachaṁti* [R.E. XIII], all connected with *vraja*.

[4] *Vinītamhi, vinītasi*. I adopt the meaning of Senart, in accordance with the idea that all these words single out the different places with which are associated the different functions of his domestic and private life, viz., eating, sleeping, company of females, walking about in the gardens (*udyāneṣu*) or his farm, and last, but not least important, for Asoka, his religious exercise. In this edict, Asoka declares that public work has, however, the right to encroach upon the domain of his private life, and can pursue him even into his home, and leisure and privacy. Some scholars [Vidhuśekhara (*IA*, xlix. 53) and Ojhā] take *vraja* to mean a short journey, and *vinīta*, a long one, involving a succession of conveyances and relays of horses, *paramparāvāhana*, as Amarakoṣa puts it. Prof. Vidhuśekhara cites an apt passage from the *Rathavinīta Sutta* of *Majjhima Nikāya* where it is stated that for King Pasenadi's journey on urgent business from Sāvatthi to Sāketa, seven *ratha-vinītas* [lit., "the chariots to which are yoked the horses that are well trained and of good race" (Buddhaghosa)], i.e., seven changes of horses (and perhaps of vehicles too) were arranged for. It may be noted that Kauṭilya [II. 33]

or in the parks,[1] everywhere, *Prativedakas*[2] are posted[3] with instructions to report on the affairs of my people. In

mentions a class of chariots called *vainayika* or training chariots. I still adhere to my own meaning which is supported by Kauṭilya's statement of the king's duties which included *svādhyāya.* (religious study), evening prayers (*sandhyāmupāsīta*), and receiving benedictions from preceptors, etc., and solitary meditation (*śāstramiti kartavyatām chintayet*), for which the *Vinīta*, the place for such religious duties, was necessary. Kauṭilya and the edict agree in other points, too, e.g., *orodhane* of the edict corresponding to *śayīta* of Kauṭilya ; *bhuṁjamānasa* to *snānabhojana* ; *uyānesu* to *svairavihāra* ; and *vraja*, which is implied in the king's inspection of his horses, elephants, chariots and infantry (*hastyaśvarathāyudhīyān paśyet*). Corresponding to *Vinīta*, Kauṭilya also refers to the *Upasthāna* (sanctuary) and *Agnyāgāra* (room of sacred fire), where the king with his preceptors would deal with religious and other matters [Kauṭilya, I. 19]. Instead of "Svādhyāya," or worship of Agni, Asoka would study *Vinaya* in his *Vinīta* !

[1] That the Mauryan palace at *Pāṭaliputra* was set in a beautiful park is recorded by Ælian [xiii. 18, McCrindle] : "In the parks, tame pea-cocks are kept, domesticated pheasants. There are shady groves and pasture grounds planted with trees, some of them ever in bloom, and while some are native to the soil, others are with circumspect care brought from other parts, and with their beauty enhance the charms of the landscape. Parrots keep hovering about the king and wheeling round him. Within the palace grounds there are also artificial ponds of great beauty in which they keep fish of enormous size but quite tame, providing sport for the king's sons who also try boating on the water."

The *Udyāna* of the edict probably corresponds to the *Mṛiga-vana* which Kauṭilya [II. 3] provides for the king's pleasure. This game forest, protected by a surrounding ditch, and equipped with delicious fruit trees, bushes, bowers, and thornless trees, was rendered more secure and entertaining for the king by admitting into it all wild animals—tigers, elephants, bisons, and the like—with their powers for mischief, their claws and teeth, cut off.

[2] The sixth among the seven castes mentioned by Megasthenes who calls them "overseers or inspectors." "It is their province to enquire into and superintend all that goes on in India, and make report to the king" [Megasthenes, p. 43]. Arrian adds that "it is against use and wont for these to give in a false report, but, indeed, no Indian is accused of lying." Strabo also states : "The best and most trustworthy men are appointed to fill these offices" [McCrindle, p. 53]. This confirms the statement of Kauṭilya [I. 11] that they should be recruited from the highest ranks of civil service (*amātya*) and be men tried and tested. Kauṭilya calls them *Gūḍhapuruṣas*

all places do I dispose of the affairs of the people. And if perchance by word of mouth I personally command a donation [4] or a proclamation; [5] or again, if an urgent matter has been assigned to the *Mahāmātras* [6] and if in connection therewith a debate or deliberation [7] takes

making up the Intelligence Department of Government. The Department had a stationary (*saṁsthā*) as well as a travelling (*sañchāra*) branch [I. 11-13].

The *Prādeśikas* of R.E. III may be the same as the *Prativedakas*, if we derive the word with Thomas [*JRAS*, 1915, p. 112] from *Pradeśa* = not a district, but a " report," in which sense it is used, for instance, by Kauṭilya [p. 111], " *tena pradeśena rājā . . upadiśet* " [cf. also *etinā cha vayajanenā* of M.R.E. I (R.) and M.P.E. (Sarnath)].

[3] *Stitā.*

[4] *Dāpakaṁ* : e.g., Asoka's inscriptions recording his grant of cave dwellings to the Ājīvikas.

[5] *Srāvāpakaṁ*, e.g., the edicts (cf. *śrāvāpitam, śrāvaṇam* of M.R.E. I). Ojha suggests that the two words might mean the officers connected with the royal benefactions (the Almoners), and with the proclamation of the royal messages. Kauṭilya [II. 7] also mentions an officer called *Dāpaka* who fixes and collects the amount of taxes to be paid by the *dāyaka* or tax-payer. It may also be noted that some of the Gupta Inscriptions mention an officer called *Ājñā-dāpaka*, and Asoka might have had such an officer in view to receive his orders from his mouth (*mukhato āñapayāmi svayaṁ dāpakaṁ vā srāvāpakaṁ*). *Srāvāpakam* might then mean *Ājñā-srāvāpakam*, the officer to proclaim the king's orders.

[6] The clause is repeated by a mistake in the Shāhbāzgarhi text—one of the few clerical errors of the edicts.

[7] *Nijhatī* ; Sanskrit *nidhyānam* ; variously interpreted as " meditation, reconsideration, amendment, adjournment, and appeal." There is a reference here to the king's *oral* orders as distinguished from his more usual written orders. Jayaswal [*Hindu Polity*, II. 141] cites a passage from the *Śukranītisāra* showing that the oral orders of a king were not binding on his *pariṣat* or council, whence there arises in the council a *vivāda* or a *nijhati*, which may even mean a reversal of the king's oral order. The passage in the *Sukranīti* is: " *Alekhyamājñāpayati hyalekhyaṁ yat karoti yaḥ* ¦ *rāja kṛityamubhau chorau tau bhṛitya-nṛipatī sadā* ; a king who orders any business without writing, and an officer executing it, are both thieves in Law " [II. 291].

Dr. B. M. Barua cites a passage from the commentary on the Kosambika Sutta of *Majjhima-Nikāya* in which *nijhati* or *nijjhāpanaṁ* is defined as " atthañ cha kāraṇañ cha dassetvā aññamaññaṁ jānāpanam," i.e., as coming to an agreement after considering the

place [1] in the *Parisat,*[2] then without a moment's interval should it be reported [3] to me in all places, at all hours.

Thus has been ordered by me.

For there is no satisfaction of mine in exertion [4] and despatch of business. My highest duty is, indeed, the promotion of the good of all. Of that, again, the root is

facts and reasons ; and another passage from the *Aṅguttara*, Part I, " Parisā-vagga," p. 66, where *saññatti* is used almost as a synonym for *nijjhatti*. In the *Manoratha-Pūraṇi* [*Aṅguttara*—Commentary], *saññatti* is explained as " making the matter known " (*saññāpentīti jānāpenti*) and *nijjhatti* as " getting the matter examined " (*nijjhāpenti pekkhāpenti*) [*Asoka Edicts in New Light*, pp. 78, 79].

[1] *Saṁto* ; *saṁtaṁ* (K.), *saṁta* (M.), *sataṁ* (S.). See note on the word in P.E. IV.

[2] Also used in R.E. III in the same sense. Entrusting urgent matters to ministers, attending to them promptly, and summoning the *Pariṣad* or Council for the purpose, are all mentioned by Kautilya as the duties of the king. " Summoning the ministers and their council (*mantripariṣadaṁ*), the king shall speak to them on urgent matters (*ātyayike kārye*=*atiyāyike* or *āchāyike* of the Edict) " ; " all urgent matter should the king attend to, but never put off ; when postponed it will be difficult or impossible of achievement (*Sarvamātyayikaṁ kāryaṁ śriṇuyānnātipātayet*) " [Kauṭilya, I. 15 and 19].

It is interesting to note that Kauṭilya [*Ib.*] has even defined the classes of business to which the king must personally attend, and the order in which he should attend to such business in accordance with its importance or urgency (*ātyayikavaśena*), viz., that concerning (1) religion, (2) ascetics, (3) different sects, (4) learned Brāhmaṇas, (5) cattle, (6) sacred places, (7) orphans, (8) the helpless by age, disease or misfortune, (9) the destitute, and (10) women.

Among the king's duties, Kauṭilya also mentions (*a*) activity (*utthānam*), (*b*) performance of religious rites (*yajñaḥ*), (*c*) administration, (*d*) liberality (*dakṣinā*), (*e*) impartial justice (*vṛitti-sāmyam*).

[3] According to Kauṭilya [I. 15, 19], the king usually consulted his council of ministers by means of correspondence (*mantrapariṣadā patrasaṁpreṣaṇena mantrayeta*). It was only on urgent matters that they were summoned to his presence. At such meetings of the council, the opinion of the majority was accepted by the king (*tatra yad-bhūyiṣṭhāh brūyuḥ tat kuryāt*). The meeting-place of the council is called by Kauṭilya [I. 20] *mantra-bhūmi*.

[4] *Ustānamhi* : Kauṭilya [I. 19] uses the same word *uttiṣṭhamānam* or *utthānam* in almost the same context, pointing out the need of a king to be always active and energetic. The whole passage is indeed an echo of Kautilya : " In the happiness of his subjects lies the king's

this: exertion and despatch of business.[1] There is no higher work than the promotion of the commonweal. And if I am at all making any exertion, it is in order that I may obtain the discharge of debt to all living beings,[2] and make them [3] happy in this world, while they may attain heaven in the world beyond. Now, for this purpose is this religious edict inscribed that it may last for ever, and that my sons,[4] and grandsons, and great-grandsons may follow [5] it for the good of all. But this is difficult of achievement except by great [6] and sustained effort.[7]

VII

[SHAHBAZGARHI]

His Sacred and Gracious Majesty desires that in all places should reside [8] people of diverse sects.

happiness, in their good his good; the satisfaction of his subjects, and not his own, he should seek."

[1] An exact echo, almost a literal translation, of Kautilya [*Ib.*]: *arthasya mūlamutthānam*—" the root (of success in government) is to be up and doing."

[2] Asoka adds a fourth debt for the king, over and above the three debts to the fathers, gods and ṛiṣis—according to the Śāstras.

[3] *Nāni* and *kāni* in some texts from Sans. *ena*, and *ṣe* in other texts from *eṣa*.

[4] The Kalsi text reads *putadāle*, with which may be compared the word *dālakā* for the king's sons used in P.E. VII.

[5] *Anuvatarav̇ṁ*; cf. *anuvatatu* in R.E. V. Other texts use the word *parakramaṁtu*, and its correspondents i.e., may exert themselves [cf. M.R.E. I.].

[6] *Agena*.

[7] The Dhauli text adds an isolated word *seto* at the end. The word may mean *śveta*, i.e., white, with which may be compared the isolated sentence at the end of R.E. XIII in the Girnar version.

[8] This is apparently against Kautilya's injunction that "*pāṣaṇḍas* and *chaṇḍālas* are to dwell near the cremation ground (beyond the city)" [II. 4]. Elsewhere [II. 36] Kautilya also rules that no *pāṣaṇḍas* could be accommodated in a *dharmaśālā* without the permission of the city officer, *Gopa*, and their abode should be searched for suspicious characters.

For they all desire restraint of passions and purity of heart.

But men are of various inclinations and of various passions. They may thus perform the whole or a part [1] (of their duties). But of him whose liberality is, too, not great, restraint of passion, inner purity, gratitude and constancy of devotion should be indispensable [2] and commendable.[3]

VIII

[SHAHBAZGARHI]

In past periods, Their Sacred Majesties [4] used to go out [5] on so-called *Vihārayātrās* [6] (excursions for enjoyment). In these were hunting [7] and other similar

[1] *Ekadeśam* : the word occurs also in R.E. V and K.R.E. I.

[2] *Niche* (S., M. and K.) ; *nīche* (D. and J.) ; *nichā* (G.). Interpreted by Senart and Thomas as *nityam,* i.e., " always, permanent, indispensable." But the word for *nityam* is *nikyam* in the Kalsi text of R.E. XIV. Bühler took *niche* as locative singular =" in a lowly man." Luders and Hultzsch take it in the sense of " low or mean," i.e., as nom. sing. masc., in which case the passage will be translated thus : " But he whose liberality is great, but whose restraint, inner purity, gratitude and firmness of faith are non-existent—such a man is very mean."

The word *nichā* for " low " or " down country," " in the south," is also used in R.E. XIII.

[3] *Padhaṁ* ; *bāḍhaṁ* (G.).

[4] *Devanampriya,* which is thus seen to have been the title of Asoka's predecessors too ; in the Girnar and Dhauli versions, it is *rājāno* and *lājāne.*

[5] *Nikramiṣu* ; G. has *ñayāsu* which Michelson [*JAOS,* 31. 245] takes as equivalent to *nyayāsuḥ* in the sense of *nirayāsuḥ.*

[6] Kauṭilya [II. 2] provides for a reserved forest for the king's *vihāra* or pleasures of sport.

[7] According to *Mahāvaṁsa* [v. 154], Asoka's own brother, Tissa, had indulged in hunting as his *uparāja,* so that hunting was permitted by him as a royal pastime down to at least 266 B.C., when Tissa left the world and became a monk. The statement of Asoka about the pleasures of sport indulged in by his predecessors is also confirmed by what the Greek writers tell us about Chandragupta Maurya. The chase is one of the three things (the two others being

diversions.[1] But His Sacred and Gracious Majesty the present King, when he had been consecrated ten years, went out to the place of Sambodhi,[2] whence these *Dharma-*

" sacrifice " and administrative work) which draw the king out of the palace. He goes to the chase like Dionysos : " crowds of women surround him, and outside of this circle spearmen are ranged. The road is marked off with ropes, and it is death for man and woman alike to pass within the ropes. Men with drums and gongs lead the procession. The king hunts in the enclosures and shoots arrows from a platform. At his side stand two or three armed women. If he hunts in the open grounds he shoots from the back of an elephant. Of the women, some are in chariots, some on horses and some even on elephants, and they are equipped with weapons of every kind, as if they were going on a campaign " [Megasthenes, *Fragm.* xxvii.]. The merits of *mrugaya*, i.e., *mṛigayā*, are also discussed by Kauṭilya [VIII. 3]. While Piśuna condemns it as a *vyasana*, or indulgence, chiefly for its physical dangers from robbers, enemies, wild animals, forest fires, accidents, hunger, thirst, and even mistake about direction and destination, Kauṭilya approves of it as a *vyāyāma* or healthy physical exercise, destroying the excess of phlegm, bile, fat, and perspiration, and improving one's marksmanship and knowledge of the tempers of wild beasts. This opinion is, indeed, worthy of the minister of Chandragupta, a warm lover of the chase.

[1] Perhaps the animal fights already referred to under R.E. I.

[2] *Nikrami* or *Ayāya Saṁbodhiṁ*, lit., proceeded towards Enlightenment ; cf. the expression *Saṁghe upayīte* of M.R.E. I. The events referred to in these two expressions are similar in character and took place also about the same time, 260 B.C. The term *Saṁbodhi* is used in the *Mahāvaṁsa* [v. 266] in the sense of Buddhism which was taught Asoka by Upagupta after 262 B.C. [*Ib.* 227]. The *Vṛihat Svayambhū Purāṇam* also represents Asoka as approaching Upagupta for instruction as regards "*Saṁbodhi-vrata, saṁbodhi-sādhana,* or *Bodhi-mārga* " [*Fasciculus*, I. p. 20].

" Going to Saṁbodhi " may, however, mean a physical process, as Dr. D. R. Bhandarkar has suggested ; it indicates a journey to the *place* of Enlightenment, i.e., to Bodh Gayā. This meaning follows from the statement that this journey is designated as, and included among, the *Dharma-yātrās*, the royal pilgrimages through the country, which were fraught with so much good for it. The " going to Saṁbodhi " or Gayā was the first of Asoka's *Dharma-yātrās*, which afterwards became the order of the day, as definitely stated in the Edict in the expression, *tenesā dharmayātā* (G.). The *Divyāvadāna*, however, makes Lumbini-vana as the first of the holy places visited by Asoka on his pilgrimage with Upagupta, and his visit to *Bodhi-mūla* following afterwards. The *Div.* dates Asoka's pilgrimage as following the construction of his

yātrās in which are the following: visits and gifts to Brahmans and Śramaṇas; visits and gifts of gold [1] to the elders; visits to the people of the country,[2] instructing them in morality, and discussions with them on same as suitable thereto.[3]

vihāras and *stūpas* which, according to the *Mahāvaṁsa* [v. 173], were completed after the seventh year of his coronation, i.e., after about 262 B.C., and so the legends may be taken to be at one with the inscription on this point. The *Divyāvadāna* further states that after his first visit to the Bodhi-tree, Asoka became so much attached to it that it roused the jealousy of his then Chief, but wicked, Queen, Tiṣyarakṣitā who had a spell cast upon the tree to destroy it. Eventually she had to yield to the king's devotion to the tree, and to accompany him on his anxious visit to the tree with elaborate measures to revive it.

In place of *ayāya* (Saṁbodhiṁ) are used in other versions *nikrami*, *nikhamithā*, a word already used in R.E. III and K.R.E. II to indicate the sending out of officers on *tour*.

[1] *Hirana-prativividhane*: cf. *baṁdhanabadhasa paṭividhānāya* in R.E. V. This statement about Asoka's journeys being attended with gifts of gold is supported by the *Divyāvadāna* where, on the occasion of his visit to each Buddhist holy place, Asoka is said to have given away 100,000 gold pieces (*śatasahasraṁ dattam*). He is also said to have built at each such place a *chaitya* or shrine as a memorial of his visit. That he must have built such a shrine at Bodh-Gayā is inferred from the fact that it must have served as the prototype of the representations of the Bodhi-tree with its stone surround and temple figured among the sculptures at Sanchi and Bharhut where, moreover, there is the identifying inscribed label, "*Bhagavato Sākamunino Bodhi* (Asatho)," "Aśvattha, the Bodhi-tree of Bhagavān Śākyamuni" [see Foucher's *Beginnings of Buddhist Art*, p. 102, and Marshall's *Guide to Sanchi*, pp. 51, 61, 65, 71]. Bloch, however, thinks [*ASR*, 1908-9, pp. 146 f.] that the Bharhut relievo cannot be taken to be the representation of the supposed Asokan fencing round the Bodhi-tree in the absence of any remains, while of the extant remains, the railing, the oldest part, from its inscriptions naming the kings, Indrāgnimitra and Brahmamitra, is clearly post-Asokan, of the Śuṅga period, and the other part is of the Gupta period, with its figures of Garuḍas, Kīrtimukhas, stūpas, etc.

[2] *Janapadasa janasa* as distinguished from the *Paurajana*, or townspeople.

[3] *Tatopayaṁ* = tadopayā (G.), akin to Sanskrit *tadaupāyika* or *tadupayogī*, suitable for that; some take it as *tataḥ param*.

PLATE X.

BHARHUT SCULPTURE SHOWING THE BODH-GAYA TEMPLE AND AN IMITATION ASOKAN PILLAR WITH ELEPHANT CAPITAL.

This becomes a great delight,[1] an additional [2] portion,[3] of His Sacred and Gracious Majesty the King.

IX.

[KALSI]

Thus saith His Sacred and Gracious Majesty the King: People perform various ceremonies.[4] In troubles,[5] marriages of sons [6] and daughters,[7] birth of children, departures from home—on these and other (occasions) people perform many different ceremonies. But in such (cases) mothers and wives [8]

[1] *Rati*, *lāti*, and *abhilāme* (Dhauli text) = *abhirāma*. Cf. Sans. *rati* = delight.

[2] *Aṁñi*, *aṇe* (M.).

[3] *Bhago*. The meaning is that Asoka derived from the *dharma-yātrās* an additional pleasure, such as his predecessors could not derive from their *vihāra-yātrās*.

Usually *bhāge aṁñe* (G.) have been taken as locatives = Pāli and Sans. *apara-bhāge*, "on the other side." But the locative in the eastern dialect would add to the two words the ending *-asi*, as shown by Hultzsch [*Corpus*, p. 15, n. 6]. Hultzsch, however, translates the passage differently: "This (*esā*) second (*aṁñe*) period (*bhāge*) (of the reign) of King Devānāṁpriya Priyadarśin becomes a pleasure in a higher degree" [*Ibid.*].

[4] *Maṁgalaṁ*, the meaning of which is indicated, as Mr. K. P. Jayaswal has pointed out [*JBORS*, vol. iv. p. 146], in the *Mahā-maṁgala Jātaka*. It indicates the special ceremonies which are performed to secuie some good or avert some evil, and involved sacrifice of animal life, the real reason for Asoka's objection to them. The idea of this Edict is suggested by the *Mahāmaṇgala Sutta* [*Sutta Nipātā*, ii. 4], where among the best of *maṅgalas* the Buddha instances "waiting on father and mother, protecting child and wife, giving alms, looking after relatives, patience, and pleasant speech, intercourse with samaṇas, and so forth."

[5] *Ābādhasi*, illness or troubles.

[6] *Āvāha*, "bringing in the married couple."

[7] *Vivāha*, "sending out the daughter."

[8] *Abakajaniyo*, i.e., *arbhakajananī*; *mahidāyo* (G.) (*mahilā*), *ithī* (strī) (D.), *striyaka* (S.) and *balikajanika* (M.) (*abaka*, according to Hultzsch).

perform numerous and diverse, petty [1] and worthless ceremonies.[2]

Now ceremonies should certainly be performed. But these bear little fruit. That, however, is productive of great fruit which is connected with Dharma. Herein are these: Proper treatment of slaves and employees,[3] reverence to

[1] *Khudā*; also *chhudaṁ* (G.) (*kṣudram*) and *putika* (S.) (*pūtika*, stinking, foul).

[2] Dr. Bloch regards the worship of the Bodhi Tree as one of such ceremonies, and finds in Asoka's contempt for these, as expressed here, the reason for believing in the truth of the tradition, already narrated, that Asoka once made " a determined effort to destroy the Bodhi Tree " as recorded by Yuan Chwang [*ASR*, 1908-9, p. 140]. That is why no remains whatever have been brought to light so far in Bodh Gayā, which might be ascribed to Asoka, as further concluded by Dr. Bloch [*Ib.*].

[3] *Dāsa-bhaṭakasi samyā* (*samma* in S.) *-paṭipati*. According to the *Sigālovāda suttanta* [cited under R.E. III] the master (*ayiraka*) should minister (*pachchupaṭṭhātabbā*) to his servants and employees (*dāsa-kammakarā*) in five ways, viz., " by assigning them work according to their strength (*yathā balaṁ kammanta saṁvidhānena*); by supplying them with food and wages (*bhatta-vettana*); by tending them in sickness (*gilānupaṭṭhānena*); by sharing with them unusual delicacies (*achchhariyānaṁ rasānaṁ saṁvibhāgena*); by granting leave at times [*samaye vossaggena*: i.e., 'by constant relaxation so that they need not work all day, and special leave with extra food and adornment for festivals, etc.' " (*Commentary*)]. It is also to be noted that Kauṭilya in his *Arthaśāstra* has two chapters dealing with the rights and duties of *dāsas* and *karmakaras* or *bhṛitakas*, slaves and hirelings [III. 13 and 14]. According to him, a man became a slave as a captive in war (*dhvajāhṛitaḥ*), or for inability to pay off debts incurred to meet domestic troubles, or government demand for fines and court decrees. But such slavery for an *Ārya* could always be redeemed. What Asoka means by " proper treatment " of these slaves and paid servants is, therefore, the treatment to which they were entitled under the law as expounded by Kauṭilya. The law made penal the following offences against slaves, viz., (*a*) defrauding a slave of his property and privileges; (*b*) mis-employing him (such as making him carry corpses or sweep) or hurting or abusing him. As regards the *karmakara*, the law secured to him his wages under the agreement between him and his master, which should be known to their neighbours (*karmakarasya karmasaṁbandhamāsannā vidyuḥ*). The amount of the wages was to be determined by the nature of the work and the time taken in doing it. Non-payment of such wages was fined. The *bhṛitaka* was also entitled to his *vetana* or legal wages,

teachers,[1] restraint of violence towards living creatures and liberality to Brahman and Śramaṇa ascetics.[2] These and such others are called *Dharma-maṁgalas*.

Therefore should it be said by a father, or a son, or a brother, or a master, or a friend, a companion, and even a neighbour : " This is commendable ; this is the ceremony to be performed until the purpose thereof is fulfilled ; this shall I perform." [3] For those ceremonies that are other than these [4]—they [5] are all of doubtful effect. It may achieve

and to some concession if he was incapacitated for work (*aśaktaḥ*), or put to ugly work (*kutsita karma*), or was in illness or distress (*vyādhau vyasane*). In another chapter, Kauṭilya [II. 1] lays down as the king's duty to correct (*vinayaṁ grāhayet*) those who neglect their duty towards slaves and relatives (*dāsahitakabandhūnaśṛiṇvato*), and punishes with a fine the person of means not supporting his wife and children, father and mother, minor brothers, or widowed sisters and daughters.

[1] *Gurūnaṁ apachiti* (G.) ; teachers (*āchariyā*) are to be served by their pupils (*antevāsinā*) in five ways : " by rising (from their seat in salutation, *uṭṭhānena*) ; by waiting upon them (*upaṭṭhānena*) ; by eagerness to learn (*sussūsāya*) ; by personal service (*pārichariyāya*) ; and by attention when receiving their teaching (*sakkachchaṁ sippa-paṭiggahaṇena*) " [*Ib.*].

[2] In R.E. III and Girnar texts of other edicts where the expression occurs, it is of the form Brāhmaṇa-Śramaṇa, but elsewhere it is Śramaṇa-brāhmaṇa. According to Pāṇini [ii. 2, 34], the correct Sanskrit form should be *Śramaṇa-brāhmaṇam*, but, according to *Vārttika*, the order of the two words in such compounds is the order of social precedence conveyed by them. Thus in this view it may be inferred that the expression *Śramaṇa-brāhmaṇa* must have been used in places or by writers preferring Buddhism to Brāhmanism. Later, this interesting compound came to be cited by Patañjali as an example under Pāṇini's rule [ii. 4, 9] to indicate standing enmity, as between the cat and the mungoose, between the Brāhmaṇa and the Śramaṇa, and Patañjali is supported also by the later *Kāśikā*. Thus the sense of both the Asokan compounds, *Devānāmpriya* and *Śramaṇa-brāhmaṇa* has deteriorated in course of history.

[3] Hultzsch reads " imaṁ kachhāmi ti." Buhler reads here " *ka [tha] miti.*"

[4] *E hi itale magale* ; *ye hi etake magale* (Shah.) ; *ehi itare magale* (Man.).

[5] *Se* ; *taṁ* (S.).

that purpose or may not. And it is only for this world. But this ceremonial of Dharma is not of time. Even if one does not achieve that object in this world, in the world beyond is produced endless merit. But if one achieves that purpose in this world, the gain of both results from it—that object in this world, and endless merit is produced in the other world by this *Dharma-maṅgala*.[1]

X

[Kalsi]

His Sacred and Gracious Majesty the King does not regard glory or fame as bringing much gain except that whatever glory or fame he desires, it would be only for this that the people might in the present time and in the future [2] should practise obedience to Dharma and conform to the observances of Dharma. For this purpose does His Sacred and Gracious Majesty the King wish for glory or fame. And what little he exerts [3] himself, that is all for the hereafter, and in order that all may be free from confinement (or

[1] Instead of this paragraph, the Girnar, Dhauli, and Jaugada texts have the following: "And this, too, is stated that liberality is commendable. But there is no such liberality or favour as the gift of religion (*dharma-dānam*), or the favour of religion. Therefore should a friend, lover (*suhṛidayena*), relative, or patron, exhort, on such and such occasions, thus: 'This should be done; this is laudable; by this one is able to attain heaven.' And what is more worth doing than the attainment of heaven?"

The words *dhamma-dāna* and *dhammānuggaha* occur in the *Itivuttaka*.

[2] *Ayatiye*; the Girnar text reads *dighāya* = *dīrghāya*, i.e., long time to come. The word for "the present" is *tadātpano* (Girnar) or *tadatvāye* (Kalsi), which is explained by Thomas [*JRAS*, 1916, p. 120] in the light of the words *tadātvānubandhau*, "immediate and future effects," and *tādātvika*, "one who lives in the moment and spends as he gets" (*yo yad yad utpadyate tad tad bhakṣayati so tādātvikaḥ*), used by Kauṭilya [II. 9; IX. 4]. Kauṭilya also uses the expression *tadātve cha āyatyām cha* in V. 1 and 4.

[3] *Lakamati, parakramati* (S.), a favourite word of Asoka in his Edicts [M.R.E. I, R.E. VI].

bondage).[1] And this is bondage, viz., sin.[2] This is, indeed, difficult of achievement by the lowly or high [3] in rank [4] except by strenuous preliminary [5] effort, renouncing all.[6] But among these [7] (two), it is the more difficult of achievement by the person of superior rank.

XI

[SHAHBAZGARHI]

Thus saith His Sacred and Gracious Majesty the King: There is no such gift as the gift of Dharma,[8] acquaintance in Dharma,[9] or the distribution of Dharma, or kinship in

[1] *Apapalāṣave*; *aparisrave* (S.); *apaparisrave* (G.); from root *śri*, to surround, encircle, enclose. Literally, it might mean "in little peril" = *alpa-pariśrave*.

[2] Cf. the expression *vaddha-jīva*, i.e., soul that is "cribbed, cabined, and confined," and not free.

[3] *Uṣuṭena* = *uchchhritena*, "of high degree."

[4] *Vagenā* = *vargena*, i.e., by status; the word also occurs in K.R.E. I, but in a different sense, which is by some supposed to be the sense here too. In that case, the meaning would be "officers of low and high rank."

[5] *Agenā*; cf. R.E. VI.

[6] *Savaṁ palitiditu* [also *parichajitpā* (G.) and *paritijitu* (S.)]. This makes more definite the idea first expressed by Asoka in M.R.E. I by the expression *parākramamānena* or *dhamayutena* (Maski text), which refers ultimately to concentration of effort, renouncing all other interests. Hultzsch notes: "the usual translation, 'renouncing everything,' is improbable because Asoka nowhere advocates absolute poverty, though he recommends 'moderation in possessions' in R.E. III." He translates it as "laying aside every (other aim)." Cf. *savachati rati* in R.E. XIII, Shah., l. 12.

[7] *Heta*; *atra* in Mansehra text.

[8] The expression *dhammadānam* and the sense of the whole passage are to be found in the *Dhammapada*, verse 354, as shown by Senart —*Sabbadānam dhammadānam jināti*, "the gift of Dharma prevails over all gifts."

[9] Interpreters of this Edict have not explained how the items that follow are to be taken as illustrations of what have been called (1) *Dharma-dāna*, (2) *Dharma-saṁstava*, (3) *Dharma-saṁvibhāga* (4) *Dharma-saṁbandha*. Unless this is understood the sense of the Edict will be missed. These four expressions may be taken to refer

Dharma. It is as follows: proper treatment of slaves and servants, obedience to mother and father, liberality to friends, companions, relations, Brāhmaṇa and Śramaṇa ascetics, and abstention from slaughter of living creatures for sacrifice.

This is to be preached by father, son, brother, master, friend, comrade, or neighbour—that this is commendable, this should be accepted as duty. Thus doing, one gains [1] this world while infinite merit occurs in the world beyond by this *dharma-dāna*.

XII

[GIRNAR]

His Sacred and Gracious Majesty the King is honouring all sects,[2] both ascetics, and house-holders; [3] by gifts and

to the different relations and activities of life, such as those connected with gifts, acquaintance, kinship or distribution of riches (*saṁvibhāga*). These Asoka wants to be based on, and regulated by, morality. If a man has to give, he should preferably give to Brāhmaṇas and Śramaṇas, and thereby support Dharma and make his gifts a *Dharma-dāna*, a righteous gift as distinguished from *adharma-dāna*, gift to unlawful objects. Similarly, the proper relationship (*Dharma-saṁbandha*) with one's parents is obedience to them. Friendship must be based not on mere sentiment, but on liberality, and then alone will it be *Dharma-saṁstava*. Lastly, the blessings of Dharma should be widely distributed so as to reach the lowly members of the household, its slaves and servants, nay, even the dumb animals, so that they may be spared improper treatment and violence. This is implied by *Dharma-saṁvibhāga*.

To these four terms, expressive of the application of morality to domestic life and relations, may be added the fifth term used by Asoka in R.E. XIII, viz., *Dharma-vijaya*, which applies to the conduct of a king. We have also the expressions *dharma-yātrā* in R.E. VIII; *dharmānugraha*, *dharma-dāna*, and *dharma-maṅgala* in R.E. IX; *dharma-staṁbha*, *dharma-śrāvaṇa* in P.E. VII; and the well-known word *dharma-mahāmātra* in so many Edicts.

[1] *Aradheti*: Senart quotes *ārādhaye maggam* from *Dhammapada*, verse 281.

[2] *Pāsaṁḍāni*; also *praṣaṁḍani* (S.); paṣaḍani (M.); below K. has the form *pāśada* and S. *praṣaḍa*; the word is also used in R.E. VII and XIII.

[3] The various *pāṣaṇḍas* or sects are made up of two classes of people—the ascetics and the householders.

offerings of various kinds is he honouring them. But His Sacred Majesty does not value such gifts or honours as that how should there be the growth of the essential elements [1] of all religious sects. The growth of this genuine matter is, however, of many kinds. But the root of it is restraint of speech, that is, that there should not be honour of one's own sect and condemnation of others' sects without any ground. Such slighting [2] should be for specified grounds only. On the other hand, the sects of others should be honoured for this ground and that.[3] Thus doing, one helps his own sect to grow, and benefits the sects of others, too. Doing otherwise, one hurts [4] his own sect and injures the sects of others. For whosoever honours his own sect and condemns the sects of others wholly from devotion to his own sect, i.e., the thought, "How I may glorify [5] my own sect,"—one acting thus [6] injures more gravely his own sect on the contrary. Hence concord [7] alone is commendable, in this sense that all should listen and be willing to listen to the doctrines professed by others. This is, in fact, the desire of His Sacred Majesty, viz., that

[1] *Sāravadhī* = *sāra-vṛiddhi*. Asoka's meaning is that the greatness of a sect does not depend so much upon the external support or reverence it can command, the number of its followers, as upon its inner essence, its vital principles. The vital and essential principles no doubt themselves differ among different sects, but Asoka discovers the common root of them all, which is a wide-hearted toleration recognising that there is an element of truth in every sect, to be respected by all sects.

[2] *Lahukā* from *laghu*.

[3] *Tena tana prakaraṇena* ; the Shah. and Mans. texts have *akarena* = *ākāreṇa*, i.e., "in every way."

[4] *Chhaṇati* ; *ksaṇati* (S.), hurts.

[5] *Dīpayema*.

[6] *So cha puna tatha karāto* or *karaṁtam* (S.) ; the Shahbazgarhi text shows another mistake in writing by repeating this clause.

[7] *Samavāyo* ; but Shah. reads *sayamo*, i.e., *saṁyamaḥ*, restraint of speech. Bhandarkar [*Asoka*, p. 299] translates the word by "concourse" in the sense of "coming together, assembling." But for the Shah. correspondent *saṁyama*, this meaning would have been more suitable in view of the next phrase which implies "hearing" and is suggestive of an *assembly*.

all sects should be possessed of wide learning [1] and good doctrines. And those who are content in their respective faiths, should all be told that His Sacred Majesty does not value so much gift or external honour as that there should be the growth of the essential elements, and breadth,[2] of all sects.

For this purpose are, indeed, employed the *Dharma-mahāmātras*, *Strī-adhyakṣa-mahāmātras* [3] (Mahāmātras in charge of, or who were, the superintendents of women), the officers in charge of pastures [4] and other

[1] *Bahusrutā*: this is suggested by the previous exhortation that the sects should not remain self-contained, but should know each other's doctrines. Such knowledge will promote harmony. The term "Bahuśruta" is mentioned as a technical academic title for Buddhist monks by Itsing (Takakusu's tr., p. 180).

[2] *Bahakā*, breadth of outlook and sympathies, the result of *bahuśruta*. Hultzsch takes it in the sense of many, i.e., as an adjective qualifying the officers mentioned in the sentence following.

[3] *Ithījhakha-mahāmātā*; *ithidhiyakha-mahāmātā* (Kalsi); *istrijakṣa-mahamatra* (Mansehra). It is usually translated as simply "censors of the women," ignoring the word *adhyakṣa*. It is possible to take the Mahāmātras as being themselves the *adhyakṣas* or superintendents of the women. That the *Mahāmātras* were in charge of women is stated in R.E. V.

[4] *Vachabhūmikā*, also *vrachabhumika* (Shah. and Mans). The word *vracha* (also used in R.E. VI) means *vraja* or pasture, and *bhūmi* denotes office. It is not, however, clear how officers dealing with pastures and women can promote the cause of toleration among the different sects. The passage as interpreted up to now does not fit in with the context, unless we suppose that the expression might indicate the officers in charge of the high roads along which travelled the people and pilgrims, and these *vrajabhūmikas* could usefully work among the travellers. There is also a suggestion that the *vraja-bhūmika* might be the native of Vraja-bhūmi (i.e., the sacred land of Mathura and Brindāban), fond of pilgrimage and religious discussions, for which such officers could be profitably employed by government. But the other supposition is more likely. There were needed special officers to be in charge of roads, and rest-houses, which Asoka was so liberal in providing. It may be noted that Kauṭilya [II. 1] lays down as the king's duty the protection of the highways of commerce (*vanik-patham*) from molestations by courtiers, tax-collectors (*kārmika*), robbers, and wardens of the marches (*Anta-pāla*), and from damage by herds of cattle, and of the live stock of the country (*pasuvrajān*) from robbers, tigers, poisonous creatures, and diseases. Thus an

bodies.[1] And the fruit of this is that the promotion of one's own sect takes place as well as the glorification[2] of the Dharma.[3]

officer like the *vraja-bhūmika* might very well be needed for discharging this duty and obligation of the king in respect of the *paśuvraja* and *vanikpatha*, an officer in charge of cattle and communications [including trade-routes by both land and sea—" sthalapatha vāripathaścha " (Kauṭilya, II. 37)]. The *Vivitādhyakṣa* of Kauṭilya [II. 34] corresponds to such an officer. His duty was to establish wells and tanks, and groves of flowers and fruit-trees in arid tracts (*anudake*), to keep the roads in order, arrest thieves, see to the safety of caravans of merchants, and to protect cattle. Lastly, it may be noted that Kauṭilya [II. 6] has also used the term *vraja* to denote a subject of administration under the *Samāhartā*, defined as comprising the interests of the live-stock of the country such as kine, buffaloes, goats, sheep, asses, camels, horses, and mules.

Regarding women, perhaps it was necessary to preach the *dharma* of toleration to them as a class! That there were *Mahāmātras* attached to the royal harem is also indicated by Kauṭilya [I. 10]: because they had to deal with ladies, their special qualification emphasised is sexual purity (*kāmopadhāśuddhān*), and they are to be placed in charge of the places of pleasure both in capital and outside (*vāhyābhyantara-vihārarakṣāsu*). The word *vāhya* of Kauṭilya occurs also in the R.E. V in the expression " Hida cha (or Pāṭālipute cha) bāhilesu cha nagalesu." Again, in the *Vinaya* [vol. iv. p. 158], there is a reference to the appointment of religious preachers for the royal harem (*itthāgāram dhammam vachehīti*). Hultzsch compares *ithījhakha* with the *gaṇikādhyakṣa* of Kauṭilya [II. 27]. The women are dealt with by the *Dharma-Mahāmātras* in R.E. V, but here by a special class of officers. Thus R.E. XII must have been a later production than R.E. V—another proof that all the Edicts were not composed simultaneously. [See note under R.E. IV]

[1] *Nikāyā*. Cf. the word *varga* in K.R.E. II. Officials in charge of different sects are mentioned in R.E. VII.

[2] *Dīpanā*.

[3] The *Dharma* here may be taken to refer to the essence or vital element, the *sāra*, of each sect, which this Edict emphasises, and not to the *Dharma* as defined in other Edicts.

It may be noted that this Edict appears by itself on a separate rock at Shahbazgarhi as at Mansehra. Probably the conditions in these localities called for special attention being drawn to the lessons of toleration preached in this Edict. Kauṭilya [XIII. 5] also insists that the king who conquers a country should respect its religion and its festivals.

XIII [1]

[Shahbazgarhi]

By His Sacred and Gracious Majesty consecrated eight years was Kalinga conquered. One hundred and fifty thousand in number were those carried off from there, a hundred thousand in number were those who were slain [2] there, and many times as many those who were dead.[3]

Thereafter,[4] now,[5] the Kalingas being annexed, became

[1] It is interesting to note that this Edict describing the conquest of Kalinga and its attendant cruelties and evils was not allowed by the emperor to appear among the other Edicts in Kalinga, probably out of his own sense of remorse, and respect for the feelings of the conquered people.

[2] *Hate*. G. reads "*tatrāhataṁ = tatra āhatam*." If so, the word *hate* should mean *āhata* or "wounded," but below *hate* is again used in the sense of "slain." The expression "vadha va maraṇaṁ va apavaho va" is used a little below, corresponding to "apavuḍhe, hate, and muṭe" as used here.

[3] It may be that this Edict is guilty of an exaggeration here. If the number of those who died (of wounds received in the fight) be taken to be at least thrice that of the killed, the total number of casualties would be something like four lacs, and, adding to these the number of deportees, the total number of the army that fought on the battlefield would be at least 5½ lacs. If, with Goltz [*The Nation in Arms*, p. 148, quoted by Mr. K. P. Jayaswal in *JBORS*, vol. iii. p. 440], we assume that "every 15th soul of the population can take up arms in defence against a foreign invasion," the population of Kalinga in Asoka's time would number at least 75 lacs, as against the present population of 50 lacs. According to the famous Khāravela inscription of about a hundred years later, the population of Kalinga is stated to be 38 lacs, if the reading of Mr. Jayaswal [*Ib.*] is accepted. We may arrive at that figure by slightly altering the proportion of its fighting strength to its total population from six per cent., as stated by Goltz, to say eight per cent., which is quite reasonable. The heavy casualties in this war with the Kalingas were, no doubt, due to the heroism of their defence as well as to the number of the army. The interesting fact is given by Megasthenes [*Fragm.* l. vi] that the king of the Kalingas had himself a standing bodyguard of "60,000 foot soldiers, 1000 horsemen, and 700 elephants."

[4] *Tatopacha, tataḥ paśchāt.*

[5] *Adhuna.*

intense [1] His Sacred Majesty's observance of Dharma,[2] love of Dharma,[3] and his preaching of the Dharma. There was the remorse [4] of His Sacred Majesty having conquered [5] the Kalingas. For where an independent country is forcibly reduced, that there are slaughter, death, and deportation of people has been considered very painful and deplorable by His Sacred Majesty. But this is considered even more grievous by His Sacred Majesty in as much as there [6] dwell Brāhmaṇa and Śramaṇa ascetics, or followers of other sects,[7] or householders, among whom are established (the following virtues), viz., obedience to elders,[8] to parents, and preceptors, proper conduct towards friends, companions, supporters and relatives, servants and dependents and steadfastness of devotion, whom befalls there injury or slaughter or removal [9] of their loved ones.

Or, if there are then incurring misfortune [10] the friends, acquaintances, helpmates, and relations of those whose affection (for them) is unabated, this becomes the affliction [11]

[1] *Tivre*, also *tīvo* (G.). The significance of this word has been generally missed to the misreading of an important phase of Asoka's history, as explained in the body of the book. The view taken here is that the Kalinga conquest was followed by the *increase* of Asoka's faith in Buddhism, not by his conversion which took place earlier. Because he had already been a lay-Buddhist, he felt all the more keenly the cruelties of the war.

[2] *Dhramapalanam*; *dhaṁma-vāyo* in other texts. Hultzsch reads *Dhramaśilana* = study of morality.

[3] *Dhrama-kamata*; *dhaṁma-kāmatā* (K.).

[4] *Anusochana*; also *anuṣaye* (K.).

[5] *Vijiniti*; *vijinitu* in K. [6] *Tatra*.

[7] *Amñe va praṣaṁda*; the Buddhists call all non-Buddhist sects as *pāṣaṇdas*, heretics.

[8] *Agrabhuṭi*; cf. the use of the word *agra* in other Edicts [R.E. X, VI]. K. reads *agabhuti* which Bühler took to mean *agrajanman*, a member of a higher caste, or a Brāhmaṇa. But Hultzsch thinks that *bhuṭi* in *agrabhuṭi* corresponds to Sans. *bhṛiti*, and takes *agrabhuṭi* to mean "those who receive high pay."

[9] *Nikramaṇaṁ*; cf. the use of the word in other Edicts [R.E. III (K.)., R.E. II].

[10] *Vasana*; *vyasanaṁ* (G.); misfortune, due to their bereavement.

[11] *Apaghratho*, also *upaghāto* (G.).

of them, too, though they are (themselves) well provided for.[1]

Thus these (ills) are of all men in equal shares [2] but felt most by His Sacred Majesty.[3] [There is, again, no country where do not exist these classes,[4] viz., Brāhmaṇa and Śramaṇa ascetics, except among the Yonas.[5]] There is no (place) in any country where there is not a faith of people in one or other of the sects.

Therefore, even a hundredth or the thousandth part of all those people who were wounded, slain, or carried off captives, in Kalinga, would now be considered grievous by His Sacred

[1] *Suvihitanaṁ*: the expression points to the non-combatant civilian population, who nevertheless felt hit by the war, though indirectly, through the sufferings it caused to their near and dear ones. Their very virtue of fellow-feeling (*sneha*) brings them to grief. Asoka thus repents the war (1) for the sufferings of the soldiers, (2) for the sufferings of the families of soldiers that were mostly virtuous people, and (3) the sufferings of the general body of citizens connected with the bereaved families by ties of affection, dependence, or kinship. Thus the suffering of the war is not localised, but becomes general, affecting all classes of people in the country.

[2] *Pratibhagaṁ*.

[3] The king who regards " all men as his children " [K.R.E.] has to take a share of the suffering of all.

[4] *Nikāyā*: this sentence does not appear in the Shah., but only in the Kalsi, Girnar and Mansehra texts.

[5] An echo of the canonical passage addressed by the Buddha to Assalāyana : " *Sutante : Yonakambojesu aññesu cha pachchantimesu janapadeṣu dveva vaṇṇā, ayyoch' eva dāso cha ; ayyo 'hutvā dāso hoti, dāso hutvā ayyo hotīti* ? " " Have you heard this : that in the Yona, Kamboja, and other border countries, there are only two *varṇas* or social classes, *ārya*, master, and *dāsa*, servant ; that an *ārya* may become a *dāsa* and a *dāsa* may become an *ārya* ? " This passage shows that as early as the time of the Buddha and Āśvalāyana these Yonas, Kambojas, and other peoples on the Indian frontier, were outside the pale of Indian society with its characteristic divisions into castes and sects. The only divisions they had in their society were the economic ones, the divisions between the class of employers and that of the employees, and these divisions were more or less elastic and interchangeable, unlike the castes of Indian society which were rigidly fixed, so that one could not pass from one caste to another. [*Majjhima-Nikāya* ii. 149, P.T.S.] (I owe this reference to Mr. C. D. Chatterji.)

Majesty. Nay, even if any one does mischief, what can be forgiven is considered as fit to be forgiven by His Sacred Majesty. Even those forest peoples [1] who have come under the dominions of His Sacred Majesty—even these he seeks to win over to his way of life and thought.[2] And it is said unto them how even in his repentance [3] is the might [4] of His Sacred Majesty, so that they may be ashamed (of their crimes) and may not be killed. Indeed, His Sacred Majesty desires towards all living beings freedom from harm, restraint of passions, impartiality and cheerfulness.[5]

And what is *Dharma-vijaya*,[6] moral conquest, is considered

[1] *Aṭavi*; also *aṭaviyo* (G.). It may be noted that Kauṭilya [XIII. 5] mentions two kinds of conquests, viz. (1) the conquest of the *Aṭavyas* or foresters, and (2) the conquest of settled territory (*grāmādi*). He places the *aṭavyas* under the administration of special officers called the *Aṭavīpāla* [I. 16, etc.].

[2] *Anuneti*, also *anunayati* (M.). I take the words in their literal sense: *anu-nayati* = brings them to the same discipline; *anunijapeti*, *anunijhapayati* (M.) = *anunidhyāpayati*, i.e., make them follow the same line of thinking.

[3] *Anutape*: cf. *anuśochanam* used above.

[4] *Prabhave* = *prabhāva*, power. It is connected with the word *hamñeyasu* which follows. Provided the wild tribes behave decently, they will be kindly treated: otherwise they will feel the compelling power of the emperor.

[5] Another definition of the Dharma specially meant for these ruder peoples who must first be trained in the elementary virtues of life specified here. They must first get over "the state of nature" in which they live, the state of war among themselves, and form themselves into a "civil society" resting on self-restraint, fellow-feeling, and the joy of a communal life. Thus Asoka does not place before these ruder folks his usual definition of Dharma involving the cultivation of proper domestic and social relations.

The word for "cheerfulness" is *rabhasiye* as taken by Buhler from Sans. *rābhasya*. But *rābhasya* may also mean "violence," in which sense it is taken by Luders and Hultzsch, who explain *samachariyaṁ rabhasiye* as "impartiality in case of violence," taking *rabhasiye* as locative case. Instead of *rabhasiye*, G. and K. read *mādava* and *madava*, i.e., mildness, compassion.

[6] It is interesting to note that the term *dharmavijaya* is not newly coined by Asoka, though he gives it his own, and a new, meaning. The term has been used by Kautilya [XII. 1] who distinguishes three classes of conquerors as (*a*) *Dharmavijayi*, who is satisfied with the

by His Sacred Majesty the principal conquest. And this has been repeatedly won by His Sacred Majesty both here (in his dominions) and among all the frontier peoples even to the extent of six hundred yojanas where (are) the Yona king, Antiochos by name, and, beyond that Antiochos, the four kings named Ptolemy, Antigonos, Magas and Alexander [1]; below,[2] the Cholas, Pāṇḍyas, as far as Tāmraparṇī.[3]

mere obeisance of the conquered; (*b*) *Lobha-vijayī*, whose greed has to be satisfied by the surrender of territory and treasure; and (*c*) *Asura-vijayī*, who would be satisfied with the surrender of not merely territory and treasure, but even the sons and wives of the conquered, and even taking away his life. According to this characterisation of conquerors, probably Asoka, as conqueror of the innocent Kalingas, had behaved like the *Asura-vijayī*, the unrighteous conqueror! This transition from an *Asura-vijayī* to a *Dharma-vijayī* had no doubt followed the transformation of *Chaṇḍāsoka* to *Dharmāsoka*!

It may be noted that the *Mahābhārata* also [Śanti P., Rajadharma, ch. 59, v. 38] refers to three kinds of conquest or *vijaya*, viz. (1) *Dharmayukta-vijaya*, (2) *Artha-vijaya*, and (3) *Asura-vijaya*.

[1] Historically perhaps the most important passage of the Edicts, as it helps the working out of Asoka's chronological history. The five Greek contemporaries of Asoka were all alive up to 258 B.C. when one of them died, and if Asoka could not hear of it till a year later, then the date of this reference would be 257 B.C. We know from R.E. III, IV and V that the Rock Edicts were issued in the twelfth and thirteenth year of his consecration which took place in 270 B.C., whence his accession should be dated in 274 B.C. The Greek kings referred to were (1) Antiochos II. Theos of Syria (261-246 B.C.), also mentioned in R.E. II (2) Ptolemy II. Philadelphos of Egypt (285-247 B.C.) (3) Antigonos Gonatas of Macedonia (278-239 B.C.) (4) Magas of Cyrene (west of Egypt), (300-258 B.C.) (5) Alexander of Epirus (272 ?-258 B.C.). The identification of these kings was due to Lassen [*Indische Alterthūmskunde*, Bd. ii. p. 256 f.]. The view of Asoka's chronology as taken here (which is also that of *Cambridge History*) does not admit of the suggestion of Bloch that No. (5) might be the Alexander of Corinth who reigned between 252-244 B.C. [see *JRAS*, 1914, p. 944]. The dates of the other kings are those accepted in the *Cambridge History of India*, vol. i. p. 502.

[2] *Nicha*, i.e., in the south, down country; the meaning of the word does not seem to be satisfactorily settled. Is it in any way connected with some western peoples called *Nīchyas* in the *Aitareya Brāhmaṇa* [viii. 14, 2, 3]?

We may here note that by the expression "*iha cha saveṣu cha*

Likewise, here in the king's dominion,[4] among the

aṁteṣu," in l. 8, Asoka distinguishes the *Āntas* from his subject peoples. The *Āntas* are also described as *avijita*, unsubdued, in K.R.E. I, and referred to in R.E. II, where the alternative term *pratyanta* is also used, and also in M.R.E. I, R.E. II, and this Edict shows that by the term *Āntas*, Asoka meant peoples outside his dominion, both in India and beyond, viz., the Cholas, Pāṇḍyas, Satiyaputra, Keralaputra, *in* India, and, *beyond*, up to the limit of 600 yojanas, the peoples under the five Greek kings named here. Then there is another class of peoples referred to by the term *Āparāntas*, the peoples belonging to the definite geographical region called *Aparānta*, among whom are named the following, viz., the Yonas, Kambojas, Pitinikas (in both R.E. V and here), the Nabhapaṁtis, Bhojas, Andhras and Pulindas, in this Edict, and the Gandhāras and Rāṣṭrikas in R.E. V. The term *Āparānta* is, however, used for the peoples named in R.E. V. only, while in this Edict they are described as living "idha-rāja-visayamhi" (G.), i.e., in the king's territories but not within his direct jurisdiction (*vijitasi*, R.E. II). Thus the *Āparāntas* were like protected peoples, while the *Āntas* were absolutely independent. It is also to be noted that the *Āparānta* Yonas were the Greeks who were settled in India. A *Yona-rājā* named Tuṣāspha even entered the service of Asoka as his provincial governor at Girnar (in Aparānta ?).

[3] See the note on the word in R.E. II.

[4] *Hida rajaviṣavaspi* ; *raja-viṣavasi* (M.) ; *rājavisayamhi* (G.) ; and *lājaviśavaṣi* (K.). The expression "*rājaviṣaya*," king's dominion, is to be taken as an antithesis to the expression "*aṁtesu*" of l. 8. The meaning is that while, among the *Āntas* or foreign peoples the king was achieving his *dharma-vijaya*, or moral conquest, within his empire, among the semi-independent peoples, his *dharmānuśāsti*, or moral instruction, was being followed. Those within the empire were naturally subject to his *anuśāsana* or instruction, and those outside and independent of it, to his *vijaya*, or conquest, of Love. Ojha takes the expression to be "*itaḥ rājye Viṣa* (unknown people)—*Vrajjisu* (i.e., the Vṛijis)." Jayaswal in his *Hindu Polity* [I. 144] takes it to mean "here among the *rāja-viṣayas*," and *rājaviṣayas* = ruling or sovereign states which were, according to R.E. V, *āparāntas*, i.e., countries inside the limits of the empire, as distinguished from the *āntas*, i.e., countries outside those limits. He does not explain *rāja-viṣaya* in the sense of Asoka's *own* dominion, because "Asoka *always* refers to his territories in the first person possessive." But this assumption is not correct: of the *three* references to his territories, *two* are without the first person possessive, viz., "savratra vijite Devanaṁ-priyasa" of R.E. II (S.), and "mahalake hi vijite" of R.E. XIV (S.), and *one* only is with it, viz., "sarvata vijite mama yutā . . ." of R.E. III (G.), but even here the first person possessive

Yonas[1] and Kambojas, among the Nabhakas[2] and Nabhitis, (Nābhapaṁtis in K.), among Pitinikas,[3] among the Andhras

might go with *yutā* instead of *vijite*. Secondly, Mr. Jayaswal's interpretation takes *rājaviṣaya*, which is in the singular number in the text, as plural.

[1] These Yonas must have been the Greeks (Ionians) who had settled in the Aparānta provinces of Asoka's empire. Their exact place may be inferred as being contiguous to that of the Kambojas with whom they are associated in the Edicts, as also by Manu. The Kambojas were the people on the Kabul river, and so also those Yonas. This Greek colony is ingeniously identified by Jayaswal [*Ib.* p. 147] with the city state of Nysa, where Alexander and his army felt themselves at home for its Hellenic ways, while the name of its president, Akoubhi, he derives from the Vedic name *Kūbhā* of the Kabul river. Lassen identified it with one of the countries to the west of the Indus which was ceded by Seleucus to Asoka's grandfather. It may also be noted that *Yona-raṭṭha*, the country of the Yonas, was one of the countries to which, according to the *Mahāvaṁsa*, a Buddhist missionary was despatched by the Third Buddhist Council under Asoka. The immigration of these Yonas, Ionians, or Greeks into these regions must have taken place as early as the days of Cyrus, Darius, and Xerxes, and of the war between the Persian Empire and Hellas. The earlier references to these Yonas outside the Indian borders are in the expression *Yavanānī lipi* of Pāṇini [iv. 1, 49] and the passage quoted above from the *Majjihima Nikāya*.

[2] Bühler cites a passage from the *Vaivartta Purāṇa* which mentions a city called Nābhikapura as belonging to the Uttara-kurus, so that the *Nābhapaṁtis* might be a Himalayan people towards the north-west, the neighbours of the Kambojas. R.E. V mentions the Gandhāras in place of the Nābhapaṁtis who might be connected with them. The names, *Nābhāka* and *Ūrṇa-nābha*, occur as names of peoples in the *gaṇa-pātha* for a sūtra of Pāṇini [iv. 1, 112; also cf. iv. 2, 53], and Jayaswal thinks that the *Ūrṇa-nābhas* might be connected with Gandhāra famous for its *wool* since the Rigvedic times. Instead of *Nābhapaṁtis*, S. reads "Nabhitina," which Jayaswal interprets as the *three* Nābhas, there being three divisions of the same people like the three *Yaudheyas* or the five sections of the *Yuechis*.

[3] The context shows that these names are those of peoples outside Asoka's direct authority, and not of hereditary *chiefs*, as is taken by Dr. D. R. Bhandarkar to be the meaning of the word *peteṇika* [see note under R.E. V]. Bühler places the Bhoja country in Vidarbha, but Hultzsch somewhere in the western regions. A king of the Bhojas is mentioned as a contemporary of Śaṅkaravarman of Kashmir by Kalhana.

and Palidas,[1] everywhere are (people) following the religious injunction of His Sacred Majesty. Even those to whom the envoys of His Sacred Majesty do not go,[2] having heard of His Sacred Majesty's practice, ordinances, and injunctions of Dharma, themselves follow, and will follow, the Dharma. The conquest that by this is won everywhere, that conquest, again, everywhere is productive of a feeling of Love. Love is won [3] in moral conquests. That love may be, indeed, slight,[4] but His Sacred Majesty [5] considers it productive of great fruit, indeed, in the world beyond.

For this purpose has this religious edict been indited that my sons and great-grandsons [6] that may be, should not think that a new conquest ought to be made; but that if a conquest is theirs (or pleases them),[7] they should relish

[1] It is significant that along with the Nīchyas, the *Aitareya Brāhmaṇa* [vii. 18] also mentions the Andhras and the Pulindas. The *Kāśikā* on *Pāṇini* [v. 3, 144] mentions the Pulindas as a republican people (*Pulinda-gaṇa*). The Girnar text reads *Pārimdesu*, and Kālsī *Pāladeṣu*. Hultzsch [*Corpus*, p. xxxix] thinks that, like the Andhras, they should be an eastern people. The Pulindas are mentioned along with the *Vindhyamūliyas*, i.e., people at the foot of the Vindhyas, in the *Vāyu Purāṇa*, and as near the Chedis in the *Mahābhārata*, *Sabhā P.* [29, 11]. Thus their country might have included Rupnath of the Minor Rock Edict.

[2] This shows that Asoka was already in the habit of sending his *dūtas* or envoys to the Greek states, just as these sent their own envoys like Megasthenes, Deimachos, and Dionysios, to the Mauryan Court. Asoka now utilises these *dūtas* for the preaching of his Dharma in these Greek kingdoms whither they were hitherto sent on purely political business, just as in his R.E. II he entrusts his purely civil officers with the work of moral propagandism in addition to their usual administrative duties. Kautilya [I. 16] speaks of three grades of *Dūtas*.

[3] *Ladhā* (G.), but K. has *gadhā* = San. *gāḍhā*, i.e., profound, deep, which Bühler connected with Pāli *gādhati*, "to stand fast."

[4] *Lahuka*: the word also occurs in R.E. XII.

[5] The Kālsi text uses the word *pine* for *piye*, perhaps another clerical error in the Edicts. It shows another error in repeating the word *piti* twice in the preceding sentence.

[6] The Edict curiously omits to mention *potrā*, the grandsons.

[7] *Spakaspi yo vijaye kṣaṁti*; *ṣayakaṣi no vijayaṣi khaṁti* (K.); *spakaspi*, *ṣayakaṣi* = *svakīye*, own; G. reads: "*Sarasake eva vijaye*,"

forbearance and mildness of punishment,[1] and that they should consider that only as conquest which is moral conquest. That is of both this world and the next. And be their pleasure in the renunciation [2] of all (other aims), which is pleasure in morality. That is of both this world and the next.[3]

i.e., if a conquest does please them (from *sva* + *rasa*, pleasure). Thus the word *sarasake* has no connection with Sans. *śara-śakyaḥ* as supposed, nor does it mean "*śarākarṣiṇaṁ vijayaṁ*," a violent conquest. For *spaka* = *svaka*, cf. *spagram* [R.E. VI] = *svargam*.

[1] The K.R.E. I, l. 10, also insists on moderation of punishments (*majhaṁ paṭipādayemā ti*).

[2] Hultzsch explains *chati* in *savachati-rati* as corresponding to Sans. *tyakti* = *tyāga*. K. and M. here read differently: "*ṣavā cha ka nilati hotu uyāma-lati*" (K.), "and all (their) pleasure be the pleasure of exertion" [*cha ka* = *cha kaṁ*, same as *cha* as in "*putā cha kaṁ natāle chā*" in R.E. IV, K.; *uyāma* = *udyāma*, same as *utthāna* and *parākrama* of R.E. VI and X]; "*sava cha ka nirati hotu ya dhramarati*" (M.), "and all (their) pleasure be the pleasure in dharma."

[3] The Girnar text adds at the end on the right side the following isolated sentence: *(sa)rvasveto hasti sarva-loka-sukhāharo nāma*, "the perfectly white Elephant, bringing happiness, indeed, to all the world." The passage probably "refers to the lost figure of an elephant, such as is incised on the rock at Kālsi with the legend, *Gaj(o) tame*, i.e., *gajottama*, 'the most excellent elephant.' At Dhauli an elephant carved in relief looks down upon the inscriptions. The elephant was a familiar symbol of the Buddha" [V. Smith's *Asoka*, 3rd ed., p. 189 n.]. The word *seto* also occurs at the end of R.E. VI of the Dhauli text.

Below the Girnar inscription, on the left side, Hultzsch has traced two defaced lines, and the words *teṣa* and *p·pā* in the first and second line respectively. He suggests these might be connected with the well-known Buddhist formula—*hetuṁ teṣāṁ Tathāgato hyavadat | teṣāṁ cha*, etc. [*Corpus*, p. 26].

PLATE XI.

ROCK-CUT ELEPHANT AT DHAULI.

XIV

[GIRNAR]

These religious edicts have been caused to be inscribed by His Sacred and Gracious [1] Majesty the King in abridged,[2] medium,[3] or expanded form.[4]

Nor, again,[5] was all executed (or suitable) [5] everywhere.[6] Vast is the conquered country,[7] much is already written and much shall I get written.[8] There is also here something [9] said again and again for the sweetness [10] of the topics concerned that the people should act accordingly.

There sometimes might also be writing left unfinished,[11]

[1] The Shah. text uses the strange form *Priśina* for *Priyadasinā*, which is nowhere to be found in the Edicts. Thus it may be taken as another clerical error of the Edicts, especially when the standing form in this text is *Priyadraśisa* [cf. R.E. II].

[2] The Maski Edict is perhaps an instance of an abridgment.

[3] E.g., omission of certain words in the Shah. text of R.E. XIII (see note) : S. also omits the word for "*majhamena*" in other texts.

[4] E.g. addition of several words in the Rūpnath text of M.R.E. I not to be found in other texts ; also in the Shah. text of R.E. VI.

[5] *cha* ; *hi* in other texts, in which case the translation will be: "For all was not executed everywhere." Hultzsch translates the word *ghaṭitam* by "suitable."

[6] No copy of the Minor Rock Edicts, for instance, has been executed in places where the fourteen rock edicts appear. At Sopara, again, only the eighth edict was perhaps incised, of which but a few words have been traced.

[7] Implying that his dominion was so extensive that his Edicts could not be inscribed in all its different parts or provinces (*na cha sarvaṁ sarvata ghaṭitam*).

[8] E.g., the Pillar Edicts issued later. K. has: "Much shall I also get written constantly—*lekhāpeśāmi cheva nikyaṁ*."

[9] "*Asti cha eta kaṁ . . .*," which Hultzsch translates as "and some of this has been stated again and again." In other versions there is *atra* instead of *eta kaṁ*. This suggests that *eta kaṁ* should correspond to *atra kiṁchit*.

[10] E.g., the repeated definitions of the Dharma in the Edicts; *vutaṁ* = *uktam* ; *lapitaṁ* (S.).

[11] *Tatra ekadā* ; S. has: "*so siya va atra kiche*," i.e., there might also be here something (incompletely written).

taking into account the locality,[1] or fully considering the reasons,[2] or by the lapses [3] of the scribe.[4]

E. The Seven Pillar Edicts

I

Thus saith His Sacred and Gracious Majesty the King: By me consecrated twenty-six years was this religious edict [5] caused to be inscribed. Both this world and the next are

[1] E.g., the two Kalinga Edicts are substituted for R.E. XI, XII and XIII at Dhauli and Jaugada. The original expression used here is—*desaṁ* (*diṣā* in Kālsi text) *va sachhāya* (or *ṣaṁkheye*). Cf. *Sutta Nipāta* [i. 12, 208]: *Saṁkhāya vatthūni*, "having pondered over things." Kauṭilya has also the phrase, *Saṅkhyātārtheṣu karmasu niyuktā ye*, i.e., "those who understand their duties" [I. 8]. "*Diṣā*" in K. in the sense of "*deśa*" must be a clerical error for "*deśaṁ*." Cf. *disāsu* in P.E. VII, l. 27. Senart took *sachhāya* or *saṁkhaya* to be connected with Sans. *saṁkṣepa* or abridgment, and the meaning of the passage to be "by reason of mutilation of a passage." Bühler translated it as "It is due to lack of space." For *saṁkhaya* from *saṁkṣepa* or abridgment, cf. "*Mūlaṁ papañchasaṁkhāyā*," "let him completely cut off the root of *prapañcha* or delusion" [*Tuvaṭaka Sutta*, v. 2].

[2] *Kāraṇaṁ* [*karaṇa* (S.), *kālanaṁ* (K.)] *va alochetpā* [*alocheti* (S.), *alochayitu* (K.)]; the word *alochetpā* is taken here in the sense of *ālochya*, deliberating. But some take it in the sense of the word "*alochayiśu*," as used in R.E. IV [*hīni cha mā alochayisū* (Dh.) = that they might not countenance decrease]. Hence Hultzsch translates the whole passage thus: "either on account of the locality, or because my motive was not liked." Taking the word *sachhāya* in the sense of abridging, the translation would be: "myself having deleted one passage, and not finding good reason for another." To this Woolner rightly objects, saying that "the king's subordinates would hardly be allowed to dislike his motives, and omit passages as they pleased" [*Asoka Text and Glossary*, p. 138].

[3] Some of these lapses have been already noticed. This Edict shows that the whole series of the Rock Edicts was definitely closed by Asoka without allowing the possibility of further additions.

[4] S. has the form *dipikarasa*.

[5] The series of Pillar Edicts was issued in 244 B.C. This date is repeated in P.E. IV, V (twice), VI and VII. The text adopted for the translation of the Pillar Edicts is that of the Delhi-Topra Pillar.

difficult of attainment [1] except by utmost love of Dharma,[2] utmost self-examination,[3] utmost obedience, utmost dread,[4] and utmost enthusiasm. But, indeed, by my religious instruction, this regard for Dharma, as well as love of Dharma, has day by day [5] become grown and will grow.

And my *Puruṣas*,[6] too, whether high, low,[7] or of middle ranks, act according to my injunctions, and enforce their proper practice, "being in a position to [8] recall to duty the fickle-minded." Thus also are my *Anta-mahāmātras* doing.[9]

[1] *Dusaṁpaṭipādaye = duḥ-saṁpratipādyam.* But this derivation is dismissed as phonetically inadmissible by Michelson [*JAOS*, 46. 259]. Hultzsch [*Corpus*, p. cxxii] considers it as a future passive participle in *-ya* like *dekhiya*, or *āvāsayiya*.

[2] *Agāyā dhaṁma-kāmatāyā*; cf. *dhaṁma-kāmatā* as used in R.E. XIII.

[3] *Palīkhāyā* = Parīkṣayā. The need of *pachchavekkhana* or self-examination is emphasised in the *Rāhulovāda Sutta* cited in the Bhabru Edict.

[4] I.e., dread of sin. [5] *Suve suve*; cf. Sanskrit *svaḥ* = to-morrow.

[6] Also used in P.E. IV and VII.

[7] *Gevayā* connected by Bühler with *gevekā* from root *gev*, "to serve," like *sevakāḥ* = menials, subalterns, lowly ones.

[8] Thus translated by Woolner; *samādāpayati* is to investigate; Pāli *samādāpeti* = instigate, encourage. Hence Hultzsch translates it as "to stir up."

[9] The principles of Asoka's Frontier Policy and administration are set forth in the Kalinga Rock Edict II. It may be noted that the *Anta-Mahāmātras* are not mentioned in K.R.E. II, although there was occasion to do so. Probably they were created later than that Edict. Kauṭilya [II. 4] knows of *Anta-pālas* whom he includes among the heads of eighteen administrative departments or *tīrthas* [I. 12]. The term *Anta-mahāmātras* is generally rendered as "wardens of the marches" (Bühler), "overseers of the frontier provinces" like Charlemagne's Markgrafen (Woolner), or "*Mahāmātras* of the *Āntas* or Borderers" (Hultzsch). These Mahāmātras might be very properly taken to be the Mahāmātras who were deputed to work among the *Āntas* such as those mentioned in M.R.E. I, R.E. II, and R.E. XIII, in prosecution of Asoka's *Dharma-vijaya* (R.E. XIII), or humanitarian missions (R.E. II). Since the institution of this special class of officers or Mahāmātras is referred to for the first time in this Pillar Edict, this Edict may be well taken to have been later in time than the Rock Edicts II, V and XIII, where their functions, and the functions of the *Dharma-*

And my injunction, too, is as follows: maintenance by Dharma, regulation by Dharma, causing happiness by Dharma, and protection by Dharma.[1]

II

Thus saith His Sacred and Gracious Majesty the King: Good is Dharma. But what[2] does Dharma include? (It includes) freedom from self-indulgence,[3] abundance

mahāmātras in general are mentioned. The definition of the functions evidently led up to the creation of the appropriate functionaries, as referred to in P.E. I. In this view of the *Anta-mahāmātras*, it is also clear that, as their work lay outside the empire, they are here distinguished from the *Puruṣas* whose work lay within the empire. Lastly, it may be noted that, akin to the *Anta-mahāmātras* must have been the *dūtas* of R.E. XIII, who were also sent out to distant and foreign countries for welfare work under Asoka's scheme.

[1] As indicated in K.R.E. II, Asoka's gift of protection or freedom to the frontier peoples was conditional on their observance of piety. Hultzsch, however, translates this as "to guard (their speech) according to morality," comparing *goti* with the expression *vachigutī*, *vachaguti* of R.E. XII.

[2] *Kiyaṁ* = *kiyām*.

[3] *Apāsinave*; from *apa* (or *alpa*) + *āsinavam*. *Āsinava* is called *pāpa*, sin, in P.E. III. The word *āsinava* is derived in two ways: (1) from *āsnava* from *ā* + root *snu*; cf. Jain word *aṇhaya* for sin; *taṇhā*, *taṣinā* = *triṣṇā*. (2) From *āsrava*, from root *sru*, to flow, whence a flowing of the soul from the senses towards their objects; the *Sarva-darśana-saṁgraha* defines it as "a door opening into water and allowing the stream to descend through it," and "with Jainas, the action of the senses which impels the soul towards external objects." In the *Āpastamba Dh. S.* [ii. 25, 19] the word is also taken to signify "external objects," *yaih puruṣaḥ āsrāvyate*, i.e., *vahiḥ ākriṣyate*, "those objects by which a person is attracted outwards." Lists of *āsravas* are given both in the Buddhist and Jain texts (as already mentioned in the body of the work). Michelson considers this latter derivation as against known phonetic laws [*JAOS*, 46. 257].

Akin to the word *āsrava* is the word *parisrava* used in R.E. X, which is also equated with the word *apuṇyam*, or sin. But the word *parisrava* suggests the word *pariśraya*, from root "*śri*," to surround, and hence may mean "bondage" (of sin). Cf. the expression "*dhaṁmaṁ parissaya-vinayaṁ*," "the Dharma that removes all dangers," in *Tuvaṭaka Sutta* [v. 7]. The *apa* of *apāsinave* may be taken as opposed to *bahu* of *bahukayāne*, in which case it should be translated as "few sins, many good deeds."

of good deeds, kindness, liberality, truthfulness, and purity.[1]

The gift of spiritual insight,[2] too, has been bestowed by me [3] in various ways, and for two-footed and four-footed beings, for birds and denizens of waters, I have ordained manifold kindnesses up to the boon of life.[4] Similarly, many other good deeds [5] have been performed by me.

For this purpose have I caused this religious Edict to be inscribed in order that (people) might follow it,[6] and that it might be of long duration. And he who will follow it completely will perform a meritorious deed.

III

Thus saith His Sacred and Gracious Majesty the King: one sees only his good deed, thinking, " this good deed has been done by me." But he sees in no wise [7] his sin, thinking, " this sin has been committed by me, or this indulgence of passions,[8] as it is called."

[1] Here is another definition of Asoka's Dharma.

[2] *Chakhudāne*, first understood by Bühler in its true meaning. Hultzsch [*Corpus*, p. 121 n.] quotes *Itivuttaka* which mentions three kinds of eye, the *maṁsa-chakkhu*, the *dibba-chakkhu*, and the *paññа-chakkhu*.

[3] Upon men. Asoka serves both man and beast; cf. R.E. II, P.E. VII.

[4] The detailed regulations on this are the subject of P.E. V.

[5] E.g., the many public works of utility referred to in R.E. II and P.E. VII.

[6] *Anupaṭipajaṁtu*: a word frequently occurring in the Pillar Edicts.

[7] *Mina* or *minā* is explained by Bühler as Sanskrit *manāk*, *nomanāk* =not in the least, in no wise. But to derive *mina* from *manāk* is considered phonetically impossible by Michelson [*JAOS*, 46. 261]. He considers the change of *a* to *i* impossible in view of the Pāli and Prākrit correspondents to *manāk* which have all *a*; e.g., Pāli *manā*, *manaṁ*; Prākrit *maṇā*, *maṇaṁ*; Jaina Mahārāṣṭrī *maṇāgaṁ*. So he would take *nomina*=*no amina*, and *amina*=Pāli *aminā*, " also." Cf. *iminā*, *amunā*. The translation of the passage will then be: " One does not *also* see an evil deed."

[8] *Āsinave*, also used in the preceding Edict.

Difficult, indeed, it is to see it fully.[1] But it has to be seen thus : " These are called the incentives to indulgence,[2] namely, ferocity, cruelty, anger, arrogance, jealousy ; and by these reasons [3] let me not ruin [4] (myself)." The following ought to be specially regarded : " this is for me for this world, that other [5] for me for the next."

IV

Thus saith His Sacred and Gracious Majesty the King : By me consecrated twenty-six years was this Document of Law caused to be inscribed.

The *Rājūkas* [6] have been placed [7] by me over many hundred thousand lives. What is their (administration of) Law [8]

[1] *Du-paṭivekhe* ; *paṭivekhe* = Pāli *pachchavekkhanam*. Hultzsch takes it as nom. sing. neut. = *duṣprativekṣyam*, " difficult to recognise." The word *paṭivekhāmi* occurs twice in P.E. VI, and the word *anuvekhamāne* in P.E. VII.

[2] *Āsinavagāmini*.

[3] *Kālanena* ; cf. *āsinavagāmīni* ; the passions are the causes of one's infamy.

[4] *Palibhasayisaṁ* : Bühler connects the word with Sanskrit *paribhraṅśayisyāmi*, cf. Sanskrit *bhraṣṭa*, fallen through sin. The sense of the passage will thus be : " even through these I shall bring about my downfall " or " may I not cause my downfall through them ? "

[5] *Iyaṁmana* is taken by Hultzsch as *idaṁ anyat*. For the *sandhi*, he instances *hevaṁmeva*, etc.

[6] See note under R.E. III. *Me* in this line may be taken as a *genitive* singular instead of *instrumental*.

[7] *Āyatā* = *Āyutā* = *Āyuktāḥ*, appointed, or from root *yat* = " be concerned for," " caring for," " occupied with " (Luders).

[8] *Abhihāle* = *abhihārāḥ*, occurring, as Bühler has shown, in one of the *Jātakas* [Vol. v., p. 58, verse 143 ; *ib.*, p. 59] in the sense of *pūjā*, honour, honorarium, as explained by the commentator. Cf. *ahāle* in M.R.E. I (Rup.). Jayaswal [*JBORS*, Vol. iv, p. 41] takes the word *abhihāra* in the sense of " attack," so that the *Rājūkas* would be like " Imperial High Ministers " exercising the sovereign's powers delegated to them as regards *Daṇḍa* and *Abhihāra*, Administration, or Peace, and War. But, as Senart has shown, *abhihāla* and *daṁḍa* are equated below with *viyohāla-samatā* and *daṁḍa-samatā*, whence *abhihāla* = *vyavahāra*, i.e., Law, while *daṁḍa* is Justice. Thus the *Rājūkas* are given independent charge of both judicial and executive functions, or rather of legislation and judicial administration.

or Justice[1] has been made by me subject to their own authority,[2] so that the *Rājūkas*, assured,[3] and without being afraid, may set about their tasks,[4] distribute[5] the good and happiness of the people of the country,[6] and also bestow favours.[7] They shall acquaint themselves with what causes happiness or misery,[8] and, with the help of the pious,[9] admonish the people of the provinces[10] that they may gain both here and hereafter.

The *Rājūkas*, too, are ready[11] to obey me.

They will also obey the *Puruṣas* who know (my) wishes;[12]

[1] *Daṁde* = daṇḍaḥ.

[2] *Atapatiye me kaṭe*, i.e., *mayā ātmapatyaḥ kṛitaḥ* (qualifying *abhihāra* and *daṇḍa*).

[3] *Asvatha*, i.e., āśvastāḥ. [4] *Pavatayevū*: Sans. *pravartayeyuḥ*.

[5] *Upadahevū* = *upadadheyuḥ* from *upa* + root *dhā*.

[6] *Janasa jānapadasā*; cf. the preceding "*Lajūkā me bahūsu pānasatasahasesu janasi āyatā*." This shows clearly that the *Rājūkas* were *Jānapada* or provincial officers of the highest rank, to whom the king has confided lacs and lacs of his subjects, as a man confides his child to an expert nurse, as stated below.

[7] *Anugahinevu* = anugṛihṇīyuḥ.

[8] *Sukhīyana-dukhīyanaṁ*. This sounds like Buddhism pure and simple, which is based on the analysis of the causes of *sukham* and *duḥkham*. In the Edicts the cause of suffering is sin, *āsrava* or *parisrava* [R.E. X], and that of happiness is *dharma*.

[9] *Dhaṁmayutena*, taken in the same sense here as in the Maski Edict.

[10] *Janaṁ jānapadaṁ*, the people of the country parts, the masses, with which the *Rājūkas* had to deal.

[11] *Laghaṁti* = Sanskrit *raṅghaṅte*, "they hasten, are eager" (Bühler). It might also be connected with *arhanti*, "must." Jayaswal [*Hindu Polity*, ii. 145], strangely enough, takes the sentence "*Lajūkā pi laghaṁti paṭichalitave maṁ*" = "And the Rājūkas disregard (*laghaṁti* = *laṅghaṅti*) my proclamations." But *maṁ* = *me*, accusative, *not* possessive, and *paṭichalitave* is a dative infinitive and taken by all scholars to be connected with Sanskrit *paricharitum*, to serve. Cf. *paṭibhogāya* of other texts = *paribhogāya* of Girnār text of R.E. II.

[12] *Chhaṁdaṁnāni*, i.e., *chhandājñāni*, but Bühler construes it from *chhandājñāḥ*, i.e., "those who know the king's will and order," qualifying *pulisāni*. Regarding the *Puruṣas*, it is apparent that those of high rank (*ukasā*, P.E. I) were higher than even the *Rājūkas* to be able to exhort the remiss among them to duty. Bühler identifies

they will also exhort those (people) [1] so that the *Rājūkas* may be able to please me.[2]

Indeed, just as a man, after having entrusted his child to a skilled nurse,[3] rests assured with the thought: " the skilled nurse will be able to keep my child well," even so the *Rājūkas* were created by me for the good and happiness of the country people.[4]

In order that these, being [5] free from fear, misgivings, and distracted mind, might apply themselves to their tasks, independence of the *Rājūkas* has been ordained by me in the matter of Law and Justice.[6]

them with *Prativedakas* of R.E. VI; the *Puruṣas* are, indeed, more in direct touch with the king and know his mind better than the *Rājūkas*, and they thus resemble the *Prativedakas*. Both the classes of officers are referred to again in P.E. VII.

[1] *Kāni*; according to Bühler it means " some," i.e., some people among the *Rājūkas* or the provincials. The sense of the passage will then be that the *Puruṣas* by exhortations to the undutiful *Rājūkas*, or to the people at large, will encourage the *Rājūkas* to do their duty by the dharma and king. *Kāni* occurs in R.E. VI, Kālsī, for *nāni* at Girnār, and for *ṣa* or *ṣe* at Shah. and Mansehra. Thus it should be taken as demonstrative, " those." The singular form is *kaṁ*, used in K.R.E. Jaug.

[2] Cf. *Lājāladhi* in K.R.E. II. The word *chaghaṁti* is to be compared with the word *chaghatha* in K.R.E. II, Dh., M.R.E. Sahs., and Bairat. Thus it corresponds to Sans. *śakṣante*.

[3] *Viyata*, i.e., *vyaktā*, " wise, learned, skilful."

[4] *Jānapadasya hitasukhāye*: this expression, along with the preceding metaphor about nurse, emphasises the high status and functions of the *Rājūkas*, to whom the king commits vast numbers of his subjects with the same confidence as the father commits his child to an expert nurse.

[5] *Saṁtaṁ*; taken by Hultzsch to be a nominative singular absolute on the analogy of the forms *kalaṁtaṁ* [K.R.E. I and II], *-patayaṁtaṁ* [K.R.E. I. (J.)], *saṁtaṁ* [R.E. VI, *saṁto* (G.)] and *-pajaṁtaṁ* [P.E. VII]. Michelson, however, [*JAOS*, 36. 205] would take *saṁtaṁ* as an adverb, *śāntaṁ*, "quietly." Lüders took *saṁtaṁ* to be a *plural* nominative on the analogy of Kalsi *saṁtaṁ* in R.E. VIII [Girnar *saṁto*, Sh. *sato*], but there it is clearly a *singular* nominative masculine qualifying *lājā*. *Saṁta* is plural in the Sahasram "*aṁmisaṁ devā saṁta*" in M.R.E.

[6] It may be noted that the administration of justice, and specially the correction of its abuses, were originally among the duties of the

Since it is to be desired that there should be uniformity in law as well as uniformity in justice,[1] from this time forward[2] is my injunction:[3] "To persons confined in chains,[4] already judged,[5] and sentenced to death,[6] a grace[7] of three days has been granted by me."

(During this period of grace) either (their relatives) will, for their[8] lives,[9] persuade[10] those (*Rājūkas*) to reconsider their judgment, or, if there be none[11] who persuades[12] (them),

Dharma-Mahāmātras, according to R.E. V. But here it appears that these duties were transferred to the *Rājūkas*, the provincial governors. Is not this another proof of the priority of the Rock Edicts to the Pillar Edicts?

[1] *Viyohāla* (*Vyavahāra*)-*samatā*, *daṁḍa-samatā*, uniformity of laws (procedure) and punishments. Asoka makes all men equal in the eye of the law.

[2] *Ava ite pi cha*; Hultzsch translates "even so far."

[3] *Āvuti* = *āyukti*. [4] *Baṁdhana-badhānaṁ*.

[5] *Tīlitadaṁdānaṁ*, i.e., *tīrṇadaṇḍānām*, "on whom judgment has been passed."

[6] *Pata* (*prāpta*)-*vadhānaṁ*.

[7] *Yote* = *yautakam*. The word *yautaka* conveys also the sense of a right which convicts might claim. The *Asokāvadāna* represents Asoka as abolishing capital punishment altogether on having put to death a monk who happened to be his own brother.

[8] *Tānaṁ*; cf. *teṣāṁ*. [9] *Jīvitāye*.

[10] *Nijhapayisaṁti*, "will cause to reconsider, or revise." Lüders found the word *nijjhapana* used in the technical sense in the *Ayoghara-Jātaka* in a passage stating that "of Death's sentences there is no *nijjhapana*, remission or revocation" [cited in *JRAS*, 1916, p. 120, by Thomas]. Dr. B. M. Barua cites from the commentary to show that in the case of *Yama* or Death, the *nijjhapana* might come through *balikamma* or sacrificial offerings by which he might be induced to forgive (*khamāpenti*) or relent (*pasādenti*), while in the case of an earthly king it might come through proof of innocence by witnesses (*sakkhīhi attano niraparādha-bhāvaṁ pakāsetvā pasādetvā*) [*Asoka Edicts in New Light*, p. 77].

[11] *Nāsaṁtam* = "not being, if there are none"; to be taken with *kāni*; Bühler took it as *nāśyantam*, "dying, about to die," i.e., *nāśyamānam*; Senart took it to mean *nāśa* + *antam*, "limit of their execution." Luders and Hultzsch give the meaning adopted here.

[12] *Nijhapayitā*, while the other three versions read *nijhapayitave*. It means "one who persuades," and refers to the absence of his relatives to intercede on behalf of the prisoner. Hultzsch remarks

they (i.e., the prisoners) will give alms for the sake of the other world or will perform fasts.

For my desire is that even when the time (of grace) has expired,[1] they may gain the hereafter, and that various kinds of religious practice increase, together with self-restraint and distribution of alms on the part of the people.

V

Thus saith His Sacred and Gracious Majesty the King: By me consecrated twenty-six years, the following creatures[2] were declared as not to be killed, such as[3]—Parrots, mainas, adjutants[4] (?), ruddy geese,[5] wild geese, nandī-mukhas,[6]

that the means of such persuasion must have been payment of ransom which is also mentioned by Kauṭilya [II. 36] as one of the grounds for the release of prisoners (*hiraṇyānugrahena vā*).

The reading *nijhapayitave* would make the meaning different: "If there is none to persuade (the *Lājūkas*)," i.e., "if the convict must die, he should try to be better off in the next world by gifts and fasts in this!"

[1] *Niludhasi pi kālasi*, formerly interpreted as *nirodhakālepi*, "even in the time of their imprisonment" (Bühler), "or in a closed dungeon" (Senart). Dr. F. W. Thomas takes the word *nirodha* in the sense of stoppage, and *kāla* = *maraṇa-kāla*, so that the sense is: "though their hour of death is irrevocably fixed (there being no *nijhati*)" [*JRAS*, 1916, p. 123 (Thomas)]. Hultzsch, however, refers the *kāla* to the three days' period of grace aforesaid, and "*niruddhe api kāle*" in the sense of that period being ended, the Pāli word *nirodha* meaning end or annihilation. Cf. Patañjali's *Yoga-sūtram*—"*yogaḥ chittavṛitti-nirodhaḥ*," i.e., *yoga* is the suspension of mental activity.

Thus the sense of the passage seems to be that Asoka would not shut out from the practice of morality any man, however condemned, even one who is forfeiting his very life for his crimes. When his hopes are ended in this world, Asoka holds out hopes for him in the other world. For when everything else deserts the man, *Dharma* does not desert him and is always open to him.

[2] *Jātāni*.

[3] *Seyathā* = Sans. *tad yathā*.

[4] *Alune*: perhaps some kind of red bird from *aruṇa*, red.

[5] *Haṁse*.

[6] An aquatic bird mentioned in the *Bhāvaprakāśa* (*St. Petersberg Dictionary*), and also in the *Therīgāthā Commentary* (p. 204 of P.T.S. edition), where we have the following expression: *machchha-makara-*

gelāṭas (probably cranes), bats,[1] queen ants, terrapins, prawns,[2] *vedaveyakas*,[3] *gaṅgāpupuṭakas* (a kind of fish), skate,[4] tortoises and porcupines,[5] tree-squirrels,[6] Bārāsing stags,[7] bulls set at liberty, *okapiṅḍas*,[8] rhinoceroses,[9] white

nandiyādayo cha vārigocharā, i.e., fishes, alligators, nandis, and such other aquatic creatures. (I owe this reference to Mr. C. D. Chatterjee.) Dr. B. M. Barua has, however, found me the following passage in the Jaina work, *Praśna-vyākaraṇa Sūtra*, I. 7, where the term *nandīmukha* has a different meaning: "Parippava-kīva-mayuna-dīviya (pīpīliya) . . . *naṁdīmuha* naṁdamāṇaga . . ." which the commentator explains as "pāriplavāścha kīvāścha śakunāścha pīpīlikāścha (i.e., pī-pītikārakā haṁsāścha) . . . sārikāviśesāḥ *naṁdīmukhāścha*." Thus in this passage the terms, *naṁdīmukha* and *naṁdamāṇa*, are names of varieties of *sārikā* or maina rather than of any aquatic bird. These are further described as being small birds measuring only two fingers in length and accustomed to rest on the ground at night.

1 Morris read *jalūkā = jalaukāḥ*, or leeches.

2 *Anaṭhikamachhe = anasthika-matsyāni*.

3 Sanskrit *vaidarvya*, from *vi-darvya* or *vidarvī*, without a hood, eel (Woolner).

4 *Saṁkuja-machhe*, a kind of fish, from Sans. *saṁkuch*, "contract."

5 *Kaphaṭa-sayake*, or *-seyake* (*kamaṭha + ṣālyaka*), tortoises and porcupines, which may be eaten according to *Yājñavalkya* [i. 77]. Morris takes it as from *kapāta-sayyaka*, "living in shells" (see Woolner).

6 *Paṁnasase = parṇa* (leaf) *-śaśa* (hare).

7 *Simale* = Sanskrit *sṛimara*; the word occurs in the *Kauṭilīya*, p. 100; also *Jātakamālā*, xxvi. 9.

8 I.e., *oke piṇdo yeṣām te*, "animals which find their food in the houses," such as "cats, mice, iguanas, and mungooses (*bilāla-mūsika-godhā-muṅgusā*), as the term is explained by Buddhaghosa commenting on *Mahāvagga* vi. 17 [*S.B.E.* Vol. xvii. p. 70]. According to Bühler, the creature meant here is the *godhā*, large lizard, which was an eatable five-toed animal according to the law-books [*Āpastamba*, i. 17, 37; *Baudhāyana*, i. 12, 5; *Gautama*, xvii. 27; and *Vasiṣṭha*, xiv. 39].

9 *Palasate* (Bühler). In the passages of the law-books quoted above, the rhinoceros figures as one of the eatable animals, whose meat satisfies the manes for an endless time when offered at the *Śrāddhas* [*Manu*, iii. 272]. Hultzsch suggests *palāpate* = Sanskrit *pārāvataḥ*, turtle dove. The rhino ill precedes the birds in the list indeed !

doves,[1] domestic doves, and all quadrupeds which do not come into use,[2] nor are eaten.[3]

Those she-goats, ewes, and sows, whether with young or in milk, are not to be killed, as also their offspring which are within six months of age.[4]

The caponing of cocks is not permitted. Husks with living things therein must not be burnt.[5]

Forests for nothing or for violence (to living creatures) must not be burnt.

The living must not be nourished with the living.

[1] *Seta-kapote.*

[2] *Paṭibhogaṁ no eti.* The economic use of animals is here meant, of animals yielding skins, furs, feathers, horns, teeth, etc.

[3] From the omission of *mayūra* from the list of protected creatures, we may infer that the prohibition of its slaughter as contemplated by Asoka in R.E. I did not *eventually* take place, and that it continued to furnish one of the delicacies for the royal table! But a similar inference from the omission of the cow in the list, as made by V. A. Smith, is untenable, because the cow had been protected by popular religious opinion long before Asoka, and would also come under the class of quadrupeds which are "not eaten" (*khādiyatī*). The omission of *mṛiga* or antelope is perhaps due to its exemption from slaughter announced in R.E. I.

It may be noted that the *Kauṭilīya* [II. 26] has also a list of protected creatures (*pradiṣṭābhayānām*) among which are included in common with this Edict the following: *haṁsa, chakravāk, śuka, śārikā*, and other auspicious creatures (*maṅgalyāḥ*). It is interesting to find that the *mayūra* is also included in this list, though omitted in the Edict, together with the *mṛiga*, deer. The *Kauṭilīya* in a general way lays down the principle that those creatures, beasts, birds, and fishes are to be protected which do not prey upon other living creatures (*apravṛittabadhānām*), as also those creatures that are regarded as auspicious, *maṅgalyāḥ*, among which the cow would figure first. Kauṭilya also generally forbids under penalty the killing of the calf, the bull, and the milch-cow even among the animals that were not protected. It is thus absurd to suppose that he does not forbid *cow-killing*! (*vatso vṛiṣo dhenuś-chaisāmavadhyāḥ*).

[4] Bühler quotes *Gautama* [xviii. 31] to show that sacrifices of animals that have not changed their teeth were forbidden.

[5] *Jhāpetaviye*; also *jhāpayitaviye*. Cf. Sans. *kṣāpayati*, causative from *kṣāyati*, burns; also Sans. *dhmāpita* = reduced to ashes. Perhaps both forms have suggested *jhāpita*.

On the three Chāturmāsīs [i.e., on the full-moon day which falls before (or after) the usual season of four months [1]], and on the *Tiṣyā* (i.e., *Pauṣa* month) full moon, fish shall neither be killed, nor sold, for three days, viz., the fourteenth, the fifteenth, of the first, and the first of the second, fortnight, as well as on all fasting days as a rule.[2]

[1] *Chātuṁmāsīsu*, " at the full moon of each season," from *chāturmāsī*, which is thus defined by Patañjali [on Pāṇini, V. 1, 94, quoted by Bühler]: " *Chatursu māsesu bhavā chāturmāsī, paurṇamāsī*," " the full moon day which falls after a period of four months is called *Chāturmāsī*," while the *Kāśikā* explains that there are three such full moon days, viz., those of Āṣāḍha, Kārttika and Phālguna. Thus there was a division of the year into three seasons of four months each, at the end [(*ṛitvante*) *Manu*, iv. 26] or at the beginning [*ṛitumukhe* (*Baudhāyana*)] of which the *Chāturmāsya* sacrifices were performed by Brahmans. The three seasons were, of course, the *Grīṣma*, summer, *Varṣā*, the rains, and *Hemanta*, winter, which respectively begin with Phālguna or Chaitra, Āṣāḍha (or Śrāvaṇa), and Kārttika (or Mārgaśīrṣa). Thus it is not clear which full moons are meant in this Edict, whether those of Phālguna, Āṣāḍha and Kārttika, or of the other series, or whether those at the beginning or the end of the seasons. Perhaps Asoka meant the former, following Manu and the Buddhist scriptures, too [e.g., *Sumaṅgalavilāsinī* on *Dīgha N.* ii. 1, p. 139, quoted by Bühler, stating that the full moon of Kārttika marks the end of a season].

[2] Bühler shows that the fish thus got relief for fifty-six days in the year, made up of (1) six in each of the months beginning with a season, and in *Pauṣa*, viz., the eighth of each fortnight, the full-moon days with those preceding, and following, them, and the new-moon days, totalling $6 \times 4 = 24$; (2) four in the remaining eight months, viz., the full and new moon days, and the eighth of each fortnight, totalling thirty-two days. In specifying these days for practice of abstention, Asoka only followed the popular Brahmanical practice which held the four days of the changes of the moon as sacred sabbath days, called *Parvan*. On the two chief Parvans, the full- and new-moon days, there were fasting and sacrifices. The Parvan days were to be marked by continence, worship, prayer, and abstention from violence even to plants [cf. " Let him not cut even a blade of grass," *Viṣṇu*, lxxi. 87, cited by Bühler], and observed as holidays in the Brahmanical schools [*Manu*, iv. 113-114]. Thus in fixing their *Uposatha* days, the Buddhists and Jains only took over the Brahmanical usages. Asoka also in this Edict shows respect for them. Besides the four Parvan days, the three *Chāturmāsī* full-moons were also holidays for Brahmans when sacrifices were performed and studies suspended. As regards the three days at full moon in *Pauṣa* or

On the same days, again, in the elephant-forests,[1] and in the preserves of the fishermen,[2] other classes of living creatures must not be killed.

On the eighth (*tīthi*) of every fortnight, on the fourteenth, on the fifteenth, on the *Tiṣyā*, and *Punarvasu* days,[3] on the full-moon days of the three seasons, and at festivals, bulls shall not be castrated,[4] nor he-goats, rams, and boars, nor other such animals as are usually castrated.

On the *Tiṣyā* and *Punarvasu* days, on the full-moon days of the seasons, and during the fortnights connected with the seasonal full-moons, the branding of horses and cows [5] is not permitted.

Until (I had been) anointed twenty-six years,[6] in this

Taiṣa, Asoka makes them sacred probably for their connection with the *Uttarāyana*, a great popular festival to this day. Regarding these prohibitions, it is curious to note that they follow the lines laid down by Kauṭilya [XIII. 5]: " the king should prohibit the slaughter of animals for half a month during the period of *Chāturmāsya* (from July to September), for four nights on the full-moon days, and for a night to mark the date of his birth, or celebrate the anniversary of his conquest. He should also prohibit the slaughter of females and young ones as well as castration."

[1] *Nāgavanasi*, also mentioned in the *Kauṭilīya* [II. 2 and 31] together with the *Nāgavanādhyakṣa*, Superintendent of Elephant-forests [see N. Law's *Studies in Ancient Hindu Polity*, ch. iv.].

[2] *Kevaṭabhogasi*: particular pieces of water were reserved by, and for, fishermen for their own *bhoga*.

[3] If we accept Bühler's reason for the sacredness of the *Tiṣya* day, we may infer that the reasons for excepting the *Punarvasu* day might be that *Punarvasu* was perhaps the birth-star of Asoka. Besides the limitation of violence against animals, the king's birth-day anniversaries were to be celebrated, according to Kauṭilya, by a judicious liberation of prisoners, as noted below.

[4] *Nīlakhitaviye* from Sanskrit *nirlakṣyate* (referring to the absence of *lakṣana* or sign of sex). *Gone* = bulls, from Sans. *go* = ox.

[5] For the branding of cows, the new-moon day of Phālguna was considered suitable by Brahmans [*Śāṅkh. Gṛihya Sūtra*, iii. 10, cited by Bühler].

[6] The twenty-sixth year is thus the current year, and not the year that has expired, since up to this time there have been only twenty-five liberations of prisoners. Thus we may take it as a general rule that all years mentioned in the Edicts are the current years of the reign of Asoka.

period, twenty-five jail-deliveries have been effected by me.[1]

VI

Thus saith His Sacred and Gracious Majesty: By me consecrated twelve years was caused to be inscribed a body of Religious Edicts [2] for the good and happiness of the people that they, making that their own,[3] might attain to that and that [4] (i.e., a corresponding) growth in Dharma.

(Thinking): "thus will be (secured) the good and happiness of people," I am attending not only to (my) relatives, but to those who are near, and far,[5] in order that I might lead them to happiness, and I am ordaining accordingly.

Thus do I also attend to all classes.[6]

All sects are also honoured by me with various offerings. But that which is one's own approach [7] (or choice) is considered by me as the most essential.

[1] Probably to celebrate the king's birthday, as pointed out by V. A. Smith [*Asoka*, p. 207 n.] from a passage in the *Kauṭilīya* [II. 36]. The prisoners to be thus occasionally liberated should be from "the juvenile, aged, diseased, and helpless, *bāla - vṛiddha - vyādhita-anāthānām*" [*ib.*]. Cf. the grounds of relief as stated in R.E. V. Good conduct in jail might also win release according to Kauṭilya [*ib.*].

[2] I.e., the Rock Edicts, in some of which this very date, 258 B.C., is given.

[3] *Apahaṭā*, i.e., *apahṛitya* or *apahṛitvā*, which may have the two opposite meanings of "taking away," or "giving up." Senart adopts the former, and Bühler the latter, meaning. Kern took the word to be *a+pra+hṛitva* = not injuring, not violating, not transgressing (Hultzsch), while *taṁ* = the *matter* of the Edicts.

[4] *Taṁ taṁ*; the people will advance in Dharma according to the parts of it they accept and cultivate.

[5] *Apakaṭhesu* = *apakṛiṣtesu*; Asoka serves all the peoples, relatives, the near and dear ones (specially mentioned in R.E. IV and VII), and others at a distance from him.

[6] *Nikāyesu*; the word also occurs in R.E. XIII and XII.

[7] *Atanā pachūpagamane*, i.e., *ātamanaḥ pratyupagamanam*, "one's own free choice of a creed." Hultzsch translates the passage differently: "But this is considered by me (my) principal (duty), viz., visiting (the people) personally." For *mokhyamate*, cf. *mukhamuta vijay e*of R.E. XIII; for "*e chu iyaṁ . . . se me*," cf. "*esa hi vidhi yā iyaṁ*" in P.E. I. For the duty of visiting the people, we may

By me consecrated twenty-six years was this Religious Edict caused to be inscribed.

VII [1]

Thus saith His Sacred and Gracious Majesty the King: The kings,[2] who were in the past ages, wished thus: How should the people grow with the growth of Dharma? But the people were not advanced with a corresponding [3] advance in Dharma.

Concerning this,[4] His Sacred and Gracious Majesty thus saith: This occurred to me: In ages past did thus wish the kings: How should the people advance with enough advance in Dharma? But the people were not advanced with enough advance in Dharma. By what means, then,[5] might the people be made strictly to follow it?

By what means might the people be made to advance with enough advance in Dharma? By what means could I uplift them [6] with advance in Dharma?

Concerning this, His Sacred and Gracious Majesty thus saith: This occurred to me: Religious messages shall I

compare the *dharma-yātrā* of R.E. VIII. The expression "*atanā pachūpagamane*" may be compared with *atana āgācha* of the Rummindei and Nigliva Pillar Inscriptions.

[1] This Edict was found only on one pillar, that of Delhi-Topra, and part of it is inscribed round the shaft and was formerly taken as a separate Edict.

[2] *Lājāne*: the plural shows that Asoka here refers to at least two of his predecessors without mentioning their title *Devānām-priya* which is mentioned in R.E. VIII. Asoka credits his predecessors with a desire for the moral well-being of the people, but takes credit to himself for devising the proper *means* of realising that desire. Asoka's *means* are two-fold: (1) *Dharmaśrāvaṇāni* (religious messages), and (2) *Dharmānuśāsti* (religious instructions or injunctions). The *means* are executed by his *agents*, the *Puruṣas*, the *Rājūkas* and the *Dharma-Mahāmātras*.

[3] *Anulupāyā* (Sans. *anurūpa*) = in proper proportion.

[4] *Etaṁ* = *atra*, as translated by Hultzsch both here, and in R.E. XI. Shah.

[5] *Kinasu* = Pali *kenassu* and Sans. *kena-svit* (Hultzsch).

[6] *Kāni*; cf. *kāni* in R.E. VI, Kālsi, P.E. IV, V and VI.

cause to be proclaimed [1]: religious injunctions [2] shall I enjoin: the people listening to this will follow strictly, will uplift itself, and will be made to advance considerably with advance in religion.

For this purpose have the religious messages been proclaimed by me, various kinds of religious injunctions have been ordained, so that my *Puruṣas*, too, appointed in charge of many people [3] will expound [4] and expand [5] (these). The *Rājūkas*, too, in charge of many hundred thousands of lives,—these, too, have been instructed by me: " thus and thus exhort ye the people who are devoted to Dharma." [6]

Thus saith His Sacred and Gracious Majesty the King: By me perceiving this have indeed been set up pillars of

[1] *Dhaṁma-sāvanāni sāvāpayāmi.* Hultzsch translates: " I shall issue proclamations on Morality " and takes the M.R.E. as examples of *dhaṁma-sāvanāni* by taking as equivalents the expressions " *iyaṁ sāvaṇe sāvāpite* " [Brahm.] and *sāvane kaṭe* of Rūpnath.

[2] *Dhaṁmānusathini*; instructions in morality which Asoka imparted personally [R.E. VIII], as well as through his officers in general [R.E. III], and, later on, by special officers, the *Dharma-Mahāmātras* [R.E. V]. This moral instruction or propagandism was carried on both within and outside the empire, among both subject and protected or independent and foreign peoples [R.E. V and XIII]. The propaganda in foreign countries had resulted in the establishment of the means of treatment of diseases (hospitals) of both men and cattle [R.E. II].

[3] *Yathā pulisā pi bahune janasi āyatā.* Instead of *yathā*, Dr. D. R. Bhandārkar reads *vyuthā*, the notorious word of M.R.E. I. This reading is also accepted by V. A. Smith. But the sense of the passage does not suffer without it. We have already seen how high were the status and functions of the officers called *Puruṣas* [see note under P.E. IV], and here we have a further fact to show it, viz., their authority over multitudes of people. P.E. I also refers to *puruṣas* of high rank (*ukasā*).

[4] *Paliyovadisaṁti* from *pari* + *ava* + *vad*, to instruct.

[5] *Pavithalisaṁti* = *pravistārayiṣyanti*.

[6] *Janaṁ dhaṁmayutaṁ.* This passage helps to clear up further the meaning of the word *dhaṁma-yuta* in the Edicts. It also repeats the statement in R.E. V that the virtuous section of his people claimed the special care of the king and received his moral ministrations.

piety,[1] *Dharma-Mahāmātras* created, and Religious Edicts composed.[2]

Thus saith His Sacred and Gracious Majesty the King: On the high roads, too, banyan trees were caused to be planted by me that they might give shade to cattle and men, mango-gardens[3] were caused to be planted, and wells were caused to be dug by me at each half-kos,[4] rest-

[1] *Dhaṁma-thaṁbhāni*; cf. *silā-thaṁbhāni* and *silā-phalakāni* below, *silā-ṭhaṁbhasi* [Rūp. R.E.], *silā-thaṁbhā* [Sa. R.E.], *silā-thabhe* [Rum. P.E.], *thube* [Nig. P.E. = Pāli *thūpo*, Sans. *stūpa*] and *silā-ṭhubhe* or *ṭhube* (*stūpa*) [Rūp. R.E.; Hultzsch reads it as *sālāṭhabhe* = pillar].

The reference to the Pillar Edicts is thus a reference to the first six of these, as pointed out by Bühler. Dr. B. M. Barua, however, has shown that the expression *dharma-stambhas* might be regarded as analogous to *Dharma-Mahāmātras*, i.e., as monuments of Dharma. The pillars of dharma should be contrasted with the pillars of victory (*vijaya-stambha*) [*Asoka Edicts in New Light*, p. 54]. These pillars or monuments might then include the Asokan topes with which, as stated in the *Divyāvadāna*, pp. 389-97, the emperor marked out the holy places for convenience of visitors.

[2] These are the three things, among others, which Asoka claims as his own innovations. The word for "composed" is *kaṭe*, also used in the Rūpnath text of M.R.E. I.

[3] *Aṁbāvaḍikyā*, i.e., *āmravāṭikā*. The Queen's Edict has the form *aṁbā-vaḍikā*. *Aṁbā* = *āmra* but *vaḍikā* is the Prākrit equivalent of Sans. *vṛitikā* (= *vṛiti*, "a hedge") and not of Sans. *vāṭikā* which presupposes the form *vartikā* [see Hultzsch, *Corpus*, p. 134 n].

[4] *Aḍhakosikyāni*. A *krośa* = 8000 *hastas* = 4000 yards = less than three miles. The objection that the wells would thus come too close to one another may be answered by the statement of Strabo that Chandragupta's mile-stones were set up at intervals of 10 stadia = 2022½ yards = about ½ kos. *Aḍha* must be distinguished from *aṭha* = 8 of Rummindei Pillar Inscription and may be compared with the form *diyaḍhiya* of Maski Edict and Sahasram. If the expression is taken to mean 8 *krośas*, the intervals between the wells will be too distant. Yuan Chwang measured 1 *yojana* = 8 *krośas*, and his *yojana* meant distances of 5, 10, and 14 miles = 100 *li*. The third *yojana* of 14 miles was applied by Yuan Chwang to his Indian travels, as shown by Fleet [*JRAS*, 1906, p. 1011] who explains the literal sense of a *yojana* as yoking distance up to which a fully-loaded cart can be drawn by a pair of bullocks. It was also, according to Yuan Chwang [Watters, I. 141 f.], a day's march for the royal army. The *yojana* in the ancient books is measured in terms of *hastas*, from which has been derived its measurement in yards and miles.

houses[1] were caused to be built; many watering stations[2] were caused to be established by me, here and there, for the comfort of cattle and men. Slight comfort, indeed, is this. For by various kinds of facilities for comforts, the people have been made happy by previous kings,[3] and myself. But, that the people might strictly follow the path laid down by Dharma, was this thus[4] done by me.

Thus saith His Sacred and Gracious Majesty the King:

[1] *Niṁsiḍhayā* = Sanskrit *niṣadyā*. The Khāravela inscription, l. 15, uses the expression, *Arahata-nisidiyā-samīpe*. Cf. the expression *vāṣa-niṣidiyā* (rain-retreat) in the Nāgārjunī Hill Cave Inscriptions. Luders, strangely enough, takes the word to mean "steps (down to the water)" from Sans. *niśrayaṇī*, and *śliṣṭi*. Hultzsch also follows Luders, but derives the word from Sans. *niśliṣṭakā*. But, as Woolner rightly remarks, "the real need of the pedestrian in India, however, is not steps to walk into a well or a river, but a shady place to *sit down* in, and water to drink, and these more frequently than every eight kos" (as interpreted by some)!

[2] *Āpānāni*.

[3] Asoka does not claim credit for these various public works of utility. These were equally promoted by his predecessors. The Brahmanical works on Law and Polity include it among the duties of kings. The *Śukranīti* mentions the names of the classes of trees to be planted along the roads, and in the villages and forests, and of the sources of water-supply—*kūpa*, *vāpī*, *puṣkariṇī* and *taḍāga*. The *Kauṭilīya* [II. 1] enjoins the king to provide sources of water-supply (*setu*), land-routes, and waterways (*vāri-sthala-patha*), groves (*ārāma*) and the like, and to maintain the public works of previous kings (*pūrva-kṛitān*) and create new ones [*Ib.*]. In the *Saṁyutta Nikāya* [i. 5, 7] also we find it stated that "folks from earth to heaven go" who are:

> "Planters of groves and fruitful trees,
> And they who build causeway and dam,
> And wells construct and watering-sheds
> And (to the homeless) shelter give."

[4] *Etadathā me* = etad yathā me (Michelson), but Hultzsch construes *atha* = *arthāya*. But *artha* in the Edicts is invariably *aṭha* and not *atha*, while the dative is *aṭhāye*. Hultzsch cites in support of his view *a*[*th*]*āye* of l. 31 of this edict, but the reading is doubtful, Bühler read it as *aṭhāye* [*JAOS*, 46. 263]. Hultzsch also relies on the Girnar form *etāya athā* (i.e., *arthāya*) in R.E. XII, l. 9, but in the Pillar Edicts the dative termination is always *-āye*. Girnar *yathā* = Kalsi *athā* in the same Edict.

Those [1] my *Dharma-Mahāmātras*, too, are employed in various kinds of business, in matters of royal favour, both of ascetics and of house-holders [2]; among all sects also are they employed. In the business of the *Saṁgha*, too, has it been ordained by me that these shall be employed: similarly has it been ordained by me that these shall be employed among Brāhmaṇa and Ājīvika [3] ascetics; among Nirgranthas, too, has it been ordained by me that these shall be employed; among the various sects, too, has it been ordained by me that these shall be employed. There were such and such *Mahāmātras* specially (employed) for such and such (sects), but my *Dharma-Mahāmātras* [4] were employed among these (congregations), as also among all other sects.

Thus saith His Sacred and Gracious Majesty the King: These, and many other principal [5] officials, are also occupied with the distribution of charities of myself and the queens.[6] And in all my female establishments, both here [7] and in the provinces,[8] they are carrying out in various kinds of forms

[1] *Te*, i.e., those *Dharma-Mahāmātras* who are referred to above in l. 13 of the text.

[2] *Pavajītānaṁ cheva gihithānaṁ*; in the same context in R.E. V occurs the expression "Brāhmaṇa-ibhyeṣu," where the word *ibhyeṣu* has been taken to mean householders, and not the Vaiśyas merely.

[3] While Asoka shows so much concern for the Ājīvikas and even builds them special cave-dwellings, Kauṭilya, with his usual Brahmanical orthodoxy, brands them along with the Buddhists (*Śākyājīvakādīn*), as being unworthy of entertainment at any ceremony connected with the gods or ancestors [*deva-pitṛi-kāryeṣu* in III. 20].

[4] These *Dharma-Mahāmātras* were thus different from, though associated with, the *Mahāmātras* referred to in the sentence previous.

[5] *Mukhā*, "heads of departments." Some of these are mentioned in R.E. XII. The term *Mukhya* in this sense occurs in the *Smṛitis* [e.g., Yājñavalkya, xvii. 20]. Dr. Thomas, however, takes the word in the sense of "heads of accounts or revenue" [*JRAS*, 1915].

[6] *Devinaṁ*.

[7] I.e., at Pāṭaliputra, as stated in R.E. V.

[8] *Disāsu*: this settles the meaning of the word *diṣā* or *desaṁ* used in R.E. XIV, which indicates the locality and not "a part." The corresponding word for *disāsu* in R.E. V is *bahireṣu cha nagareṣu*. It is noteworthy that the members of the royal family were not all settled in the capital city, Pāṭaliputra, only: some of them settled down at the provincial towns too. This shows that the royal family was a large one, with its branches or ramifications.

such and such measures productive of happiness.[1] (And besides the queens and myself) has it also been ordained by me that they shall be occupied with the distribution of charities of my sons [2] and other queens' sons [3] in order (to promote) noble deeds of Dharma,[4] and strict adherence to Dharma.[5] And these are the noble deeds of Dharma and adherence to Dharma whereby the following,[6] viz., compassion, liberality, truthfulness, purity, gentleness, and goodness of the people will thus increase.

Thus saith His Sacred and Gracious Majesty the King: Whatever good deeds have been done by me,[7] these the people have followed and these they will imitate and thereby they have been made to progress, and will be made to

[1] *Tuṭhāyatanāni* = *tuṣṭāyatanāni*, sources of contentment, opportunities for charity (Bühler). The verb used here is "*paṭī* . . ." which Bühler restored as "*paṭīpādayaṁti*" = "they point out," but I take it in the sense of "execute, carry out." Hultzsch, however, would restore the word as *paṭīvedayaṁti* in the sense of "reporting." Cf. *paṭivedakā* of R.E. VI, and *pratīvedayaṁtu*, [*ib.*] Jaugada text.

[2] *Dālakānaṁ*.

[3] *Devikumālānaṁ*; according to Bühler, these *Kumāras* or princes were not the sons of Asoka's queens or *devīs*, but of the queens and *devīs* of his father, and were hence his step-brothers [*Ep. Ind.* ii., 276]. The word *devī* for queen is also used by Kauṭilya [I. 10], as well as the word *kumāra* for a prince [I. 20].

[4] *Dhaṁmāpadāne*. Childers points out that the thirteenth book of the *Khuddaka Nikāya*, comprising tales of good deeds of Buddhas and Arhats, is called an *Apadāna* (Sans. *avadāna*).

[5] In R.E. V, while the royal harem is specified as one of the spheres of the work of the *Dharma-Mahāmātras*, some of the details of such work are given here. Kauṭilya [I. 20] acquaints us with the administrative arrangements for the royal harems of the day. The *antaḥpura* with its inmates, the *avarodhas*, was placed under a military guard, the *antarvaśika-sainya*, and civil officers, the *abhyāgārikas*, comprising both males and females, who regulated all communications between the harem and the outside world. It may be noted that Kauṭilya does not permit the *muṇḍa* and *jaṭila* ascetics (probably the Buddhists and Jains) any access to the harem. The officers in charge of the harems are called *Strī-adhyakṣa-mahāmātras* in R.E. XII. Kauṭilya calls the chief officer of the harem *Antarvaśika* [V. 3].

[6] Another definition of Asoka's Dharma.

[7] *Mamiyā*. With Asoka, "example is always better than precept."

progress in obedience to parents, teachers, in reverence for age, in proper behaviour towards Brāhmaṇa and Śramaṇa ascetics, the poor and the miserable,[1] even towards servants and dependents.

Thus saith His Sacred and Gracious Majesty the King: This advance in Dharma of the people has been promoted only by two ways, by regulation of Dharma, and by inner meditation.[2] But of these (two), regulation of Dharma is of little effect,[3] but by inner meditation (Dharma may be promoted) greatly. The regulation by Dharma is this that by me is thus ordained that such and such creatures are not to be killed, as well as many other regulations of Dharma,[4]

[1] *Kapana-valākesu*, a new expression in the Edicts.

[2] *Nijhatiyā*, also used in P.E. IV, where it is used once in a technical, and at another time in a general, sense. Cf. *nijjhati-balaṁ*, power of thought; Sans. *nidhyapti*.

[3] *Lahu* = *laghu*, slight, of small account, because it is something external. " The aids to noble life are all within " (Matthew Arnold).

[4] Asoka's *dharma-niyama* comprises both negative and positive precepts, prohibitions and exhortations. As examples of the former may be mentioned the following:

(1) Do not *kill* living beings [R.E. III, IV, XI, and P.E. VII].

(2) Do not *injure* living beings [R.E. IV, IX, XIII, and P.E. VII].

(3) Do not hold festive meetings with objectionable amusements [R.E. I].

(4) Do not observe social and superstitious ceremonies as bearing little fruit [R.E. IX].

(5) Do not praise your own, and dispraise other, sects [R.E. XII].

The positive precepts or exhortations, such as proper behaviour towards all relations and living beings, liberality, truthfulness, etc., have been already discussed fully.

Certain special precepts are laid down for kings, such as *dharma-ghoṣa*, *dharma-yātrā*, *dharma-vijaya*, *dharmānugraha*, *dharma-dāna*, *dharma-maṅgala*, promotion of public works of utility [R.E. II and P.E. VII], checking abuses of justice [K.R.E. and R.E. V], public instruction in morality, *dharmānuśāsti* [R.E. III, IV, XIII, and P.E. VII], attention to public business at all hours [R.E. VI], seeking glory or fame (*yaśa* and *kīrti*) only in the promotion of Dharma among the people [R.E. X], honouring all sects [R.E. XII and P.E. VI], and seeing to the growth of their essential elements [*sāra-vṛiddhi*, R.E. XII], protection of lower creatures [P.E. V], etc. Most of these have been already discussed.

such as have been ordained by me. But by inner meditation, indeed, has been much promoted the people's progress in Dharma in respect of abstention from injury to life and from slaughter of living creatures.

To this end was it ordained that it may last as long as (my) sons and grandsons, or moon and sun (will be), and that (people) may follow in this path. For if one follows in this path, (happiness) in this and the other world will be attained.

By me consecrated twenty-six years was this Religious Edict inscribed.

About this [1] says His Sacred Majesty: This rescript on morality must be engraved where there are stone pillars, or stone-slabs,[2] in order that [3] this may be everlasting.

F. The Four Minor Pillar Edicts

I [4]

[The Sarnath Edict]

(Thus ordains) His Sacred (and Gracious) Majesty [5] . . . Pāṭa(liputra) [6] . . . the Saṁgha cannot be torn asunder [7] by any one whatsoever. Whoever,[8] monk or nun, breaks up [9]

[1] *Etaṁ*, as translated by Hultzsch both here and in Shah. R.E. XI, l. 24. The word is also used in line 9.

[2] *Silā-phalakāni*, stone-tablets, referring to the inscriptions on the rocky surfaces.

[3] *Ena*, as used also in the K.R.E. I and II, Dhauli.

[4] The text is mutilated in the first three lines.

[5] Restored as *Devānaṁpiye ānapayati* from Kauśāmbī M.P.E.

[6] Perhaps this Edict is addressed to the Mahāmātras of Pāṭaliputra, as the Kauśāmbī Edict is to the Mahāmātras of that place.

[7] *Bhetave*, i.e., *bhetavyaḥ*, from root *bhid*; cf. "*bhindati.*" In the *Pātimokkha* there occurs the passage—"Samaggassa saṁghassa bhedāya." Buddhaghosa explains *Saṁgha-bhedaka* as "*Saṅghaṁ bhindati ayam iti.*"

[8] *E chum kho*, i.e., *yaḥ tu khalu*.

[9] *Bhākhati* = *bhanakti*.

the Saṁgha must be made to wear [1] white [2] garments [3] and to take up abode [4] in a place other than a monastery.[5]

Thus should this order be made known [6] in the *Saṁghas* of *Bhikṣus* as well as of *Bhikṣuṇīs*.

Thus directs His Sacred Majesty: Let one [7] such Edict be with you, deposited [8] in the cloister of the vihāra; [9] deposit ye another self-same Edict with the *Upāsakas* (lay-worshippers).

Those *Upāsakas* may come on each fast day in order to acquaint themselves with this very Edict. And on every fast day regularly [10] (will) each *Mahāmātra* go for the fast-

[1] *Saṁnaṁdhāpayiyā* from Sans. *saṁnahya*.

[2] *Odātāni* = Sans. *ava + dāta* (white).

[3] *Dusani* = Sans. *dūṣyam*.

[4] *Āvāsayiye* = Sans. *āvāsya*.

[5] *Ānāvāsasi*: an abode which is not fit for the saṅgha, "*abhikkhuko āvāsa*" as called by Buddhaghosa [*Samantapāsādikā*, Introduction], who also enumerates as examples of *anāvāsa* "*chetiyagharam* (cemetery), *bodhigharam* (bo-tree sanctuary), *sammañjaniaṭṭako* (bath-house or platform), *dāru-aṭṭako* (log-house), *pāniyamālo* (water-shed), *vachchakuṭi* (privy), and *dvārakoṭṭhako* (towers or battlements of a town gate)" [*Chullavagga*, ii. 1, 3].

[6] *Viṁnapayitaviye* = Sanskrit *vijñāpayitavyam*.

[7] *Ikā lipī*, as contrasted with the *dhaṁmalipi*.

[8] *Nikhitā* = *nikṣiptā*.

[9] *Saṁsalanasi*; taken by some to mean "remembrance," *saṁsmaraṇam*. Dr. Thomas [*JRAS*, 1915, pp. 109-112] takes the word to mean a place in the vihāra like a lobby or cloister where the Edict might be deposited to attract public notice. The word is used in this sense in the *Vinaya* [pp. 152-3; *Chullavagga*, vi 3, 4]. Thus the passage is to be translated thus: "In order that a similar Edict may be within your reach, it has been deposited in the *saṁsaraṇa*. Do you also deposit a similar Edict within reach (*antikaṁ*) of the *Upāsakas*." The *saṁsaraṇa*, which is a part of a vihāra [where one could walk about (*saṁkramana*)], is thus not mentioned in the case of the Upāsakas who do not live in a vihāra. The expression—*ikaṁ cha lipiṁ hedisaṁ*—thus means a second copy of the Edict for the Upāsakas.

[10] *Dhuvāye* = *dhruvāya*; cf. *dhuvaṁ* in Jaug. R.E. I, and *dhuvāye* in P.E. V. This passage indicates the kind of work the Mahāmātras had to do in connection with the Saṁgha and other sects among whom they were employed [R.E. V, P.E. VII].

day service [1] in order to acquaint himself with this Edict and understand it fully. And as far as your jurisdiction [2] extends, you are to get dispatched [3] everywhere (an order) to this effect.[4] In this manner, also, in all fortified

[1] *Posathāye* ; from *uposatha*, Sans. *upavasatha*, the day of fast and abstinence preceding the day of the Vedic *yāgas* or sacrifices called *Darśa* and *Pūrṇa-māsa*, i.e., sacrifices held on the new- and full-moon days. The *upavasatha* day was so called because it was believed that on that day the gods to be worshipped came down to *live with* (upa + vasa) the worshipper [*Śatapatha Br.* i. 1, 1, 7], or because the worshipper with his wife would live on that day with the god, *Agni*, in the room dedicated to him [*ib.* xi. ; 2, 1, 4]. In Vedic worship the eighth day of each fortnight was also similarly fixed as a holy and fast day along with the new- and full-moon days and the days preceding them.

On these three holy days of every fortnight, the ascetics of Brahmanical sects used to meet and hold religious discourses. This good custom commended itself at once to the Buddha, who enjoined his Bhikṣus to assemble on those days [*Mahāv.* ii. 1, 4], not to remain silent but to discourse on their religion [*ib.* ii. 2, 1]. This religious discourse was then specified to be the *Prātimokṣa* [*ib.* ii. 4, 1] which was thus held thrice every fortnight. Later, it was fixed for one day, the new- or full-moon day [*ib.* ii. 4, 2 ; 34, 1], and was confined also exclusively to the Bhikṣus. It was not accessible to householders (*gṛihasthas*), nor even to the śrāmaṇera, śrāmaṇerī and bhikṣuṇī [*ib.* ii. 11, 8 ; 36]. But except this Prātimokṣa, or the *mukhya* (principal) uposatha day, the other two uposatha days were fixed for general religious discourses which were thrown open to all, or the Upāsakas.

This is how Asoka can think of his civil officers, the Mahāmātras, attending on each uposatha day (*anuposatham*) for purposes of the uposatha service (*posathāye*) which must have meant the ordinary religious discourse held on the eighth and fourteenth days of each fortnight, and not the uposatha service proper, the Prātimokṣa, for which the monks alone were eligible. This distinction between the two classes of uposatha service is to be kept in view in order to understand Asoka's injunctions as following those of his religious scriptures.

[2] *Āhāle* also used in M.R.E. I, Rūpnath text.

[3] *Vivāsayātha*, taken here in the same sense as in M.R.E. (Rūpnath). Smith, following F. W. Thomas [*JRAS*, 1915, p. 112], now understands the meaning of the word to be "expel."

[4] "Dispatch ye (an officer) everywhere according to the letter of this (Edict)" [Hultzsch]. The dispatch of *officers* he infers from K.R.E. I, where *Mahāmātras* are sent out by the king.

towns,[1] and districts, have this order sent out [2] to this effect.[3]

[1] *Koṭa*=a fort or a stronghold, according to *Vāstuvidyā* [xi. 28]. It is curious that the terms *koṭṭam* and *viṣaya* as used in this Edict occur in some South Indian inscriptions to indicate administrative areas larger than the village (*uru*), town (*nagara* or *parru*), and *Nadū* or *Kurram*, but smaller than the *Maṇḍala* or *Rāṣṭra* [see my *Local Govt.* p. 206]. The *Viṣaya* is a well-known term in the Gupta Inscriptions for a District (*e.g.* Lāṭa viṣaya) under a Province called a *Bhukti*.

[2] *Vivāsāpayāthā*; the double causal is necessary to indicate that the circulation of the order was done not directly, but through the instrumentality of those who had independent jurisdictions, as pointed out by V. A. Smith. Lines 6-11 of the Edict show the means adopted by the king " for the proper circulation of his Edict among all the parties concerned. This the king tries to ensure (1) by communicating his Edict to the monks and nuns whom it chiefly concerns, and (2) by ordering that one copy of it should be retained by the *Mahāmātras*, and another by the lay-worshippers, to be studied by both of them respectively at the fast-day services. The two last sections of the inscription contain further provisions for ensuring a still wider circulation to the king's Edict. The preceding paragraphs had arranged for its publicity among the citizens of Pāṭaliputra. In sections I and J (i.e., ll. 9-11), the king orders the Mahāmātras of Pāṭaliputra to make it known in the district surrounding Pāṭaliputra and in the jungle tracts beyond this district " [Hultzsch, *Corpus*, p. 163, n. 10]. Hultzsch, however, has now changed his mind regarding the meaning of the last two sections, which he now takes to mean: " expel (*vivāsayātha*) ye (schismatic monks and nuns) " and " issue ye orders to expel (*vivāsāpayāthā*) (schismatic monks) or nuns " [*ib. Corrigenda*, p. 259].

[3] This Edict and the Pillar Edicts at Kauśāmbī and Sanchi form a group by themselves by their reference to the common subject of schism in the Saṅgha, and to the king's measures to prevent and punish it. In these Edicts, Asoka appears in the rôle of the " Head of the Church and Defender of the Faith," as it were, but it must be noted that this rôle was not assumed by Asoka by an autocratic exercise of his sovereign powers, but was forced on him by the injunctions of the very faith he followed. Indeed, Asoka's attitude towards schism is determined and dictated by the Buddhist canonical law on the subject. This law seems to have developed by stages which may be traced in some of the sacred texts of early Buddhism.

These texts describe different degrees in the offences leading up to schism, as well as degrees in their punishments. The *Mahāvagga* [x. 1, 6, etc.], for instance, mentions in an ascending order differences among the members of a Saṅgha as " altercation (*bhaṇḍanaṁ*) contention (*kalaha*), discord (*vigraha*), quarrel (*vivāda*), division (*saṅgha-bheda*), disunion (*saṅgharāji*), separation (*saṅghavavatthānaṁ*), and schism (*saṅghanānākaraṇaṁ*) or dissolution of the Saṅgha." Again, in *Chullavagga*, vii. 5, disunion (*saṅgharāji*) is distinguished from schism proper (*saṅghabheda*). Disunion can happen only in smaller Saṅghas of members numbering from four to nine, while schism means a break-up of a Saṅgha of more than nine members. It is caused by a difference of opinion on eighteen points concerning (*a*) what is or what is not Dhamma, (*b*) what is or what is not Vinaya, (*c*) what has or has not been (i) taught and spoken, (ii) practised, and (iii) ordained by the Tathāgata, and (*d*) offences and rules regarding them [*ib*. vii. 5, 2 ; *Mahāv*. x. 5, 4, 5]. The same points are mentioned again in *Chullav*. iv. 14, 2, as creating a *Vivāda*, but a distinction is made between *Vivāda* and *Saṅghabheda*. In a *Vivāda*, the point at issue was to be decided finally by the Saṅgha, and there the matter must rest. But sometimes a difference of opinion may be pressed too far, either honestly, or with an evil intention, knowing that it would in either case result in the *saṅghabheda*. The intention to cause a *saṅghabheda* is absent in a *vivādādhikaraṇa*.

There were also certain legal restraints imposed upon the attempts at causing *saṅghabheda*. These attempts were valid only from a member of the Saṅgha who was under no disability (*pakatatta*), who belonged to the same community (*samāna-saṁvāsaka*), and who resided within the same boundary (*samānasīmāyathitā*). Next, the *Vivāda* could not be placed before a Saṅgha of less than nine members, as already stated, i.e., the Saṅgha should be large enough to admit of four members to each side of the dispute, and of the ninth member who was the *Salāka-gāhāpako*. Thus to produce a schism there should be at least four regular bhikṣus to agree on the point raised, and bring it before a chapter of nine with purpose prepense to cause division, whether knowing that the point was wrong or doubtful [*Chullav*. vii. 5, 5], or believing it, without due deliberation, to be right [*ib*. 5, 6]. It appears from *Chullav*. vii. 5, 6 that the latter position was not condemned. Secession from conviction or conscientious objection was not condemned. There was no embargo laid on honest differences of opinion, on freedom of thought.

Along with the offences leading towards *saṅghabheda* or dissolution of the Saṅgha, and schism, the texts contemplate different degrees and grades of penalty corresponding to such offences. The first punishment inflicted on a schismatic is that of *Nissāraṇaṁ*, or his temporary removal from the Saṅgha [*Mahāv*. x. 5, 14], during which he was subjected to *Parivāsa*, or living apart, for five or ten days, and *Mānatta*, or living under restraint for six days, as laid down in the *Pātimokkha*, *Saṅghādisesa*, 13. His restoration, *osāraṇam*, was permitted, if the accused expressed his acknowledgment of the guilt [*Mahāv*. *ib*.].

We may also note in this connection that the *Pātimokkha* brings the promotion of *saṅghabheda* under the class of *Saṅghādisesa* offences, i.e., offences for which atonement from beginning to end can be granted only by the Saṅgha. The offence, according to the same text, is defined as (*a*) causing division (*bheda*) in the Saṅgha that is at union (*samagga*); (*b*) persistently raising issues calculated to cause division. The offence may be committed by a single bhikṣu or by a number of bhikṣus, as his partisans, who would then be equally guilty with him. Thus though the offence against the Saṅgha is sufficiently serious, it is not visited by the extreme penalty of permanent expulsion in the *Pātimokkha* which may be taken to lay down the earlier form of the law. The *Pātimokkha* would reserve the extreme penalty for *Pārājika* sins, the offences against morality, such as adultery, theft, murder, or fraud (by claiming superhuman powers).

The extreme penalty for schism is, however, laid down in *Mahāvagga* [i. 60, 67 and 69]. It is called *nāsanam*, which is definitive and permanent expulsion from the Saṅgha, and is to be distinguished from (*a*) suspension or temporary excommunication, *ukkhepanam*, for a bhikṣu refusing to admit or atone for the offence committed or to renounce a false doctrine [*ib*. i. 79; *Chullav*. i. 25; 27]; and (*b*) temporary banishment, *pabbājanam*, for bhikṣus guilty of causing by their conduct scandal to the Saṅgha. Both (*a*) and (*b*) may, however, be revoked on repentance [*ib*.; *Mahāv*. x. 6].

It is difficult to see what kind or degree of schism or *saṅghabheda* and of the punishment of expulsion is meant by Asoka in his use of the expressions *bhetave* and *ānāvāsasi āvāsayiye* in the Edicts in question. If he was for complete and irrevocable expulsion of the heretical monks, he must be understood to have taken his stand upon the three passages of the *Mahāvagga* cited above, together with a fourth passage [*Mahāv*. iii. 11, 5] which describes as a "grievous sin" the causing of divisions (*bheda*) in the Saṅgha, and permits the good bhikṣu to dissociate himself from the heretics who commit this sin.

Along with the deportation of the heretical monks to non-monastic residences (*anāvāsa*), Asoka inflicts upon them the further penalty of disrobing them, replacing their yellow by white robes. For this punishment there is no canonical sanction, unless it is implied in the mere fact of the expulsion of the monks from the monasteries. Some of the Asokan legends, however, relate actual cases of Asoka enforcing this penal code of his Edicts against schismatics. Thus the *Mahāvaṁsa* [v. 270] relates how Asoka once "arranged an assembly of the community of bhikkhus in its full numbers" in the Asokārāma. "He then called to him in turn the bhikkhus of the several confessions, and asked them: 'Cir, what did the Blessed One teach?' And they each expounded their wrong doctrine. And all these adherents of false doctrine did the king cause to be *expelled* from the Order (*upapabbajesi*)." In the *Samantapāsādikā*, Buddhaghosa records the further fact that Asoka expelled these heretical monks after giving them white robes (*setakāni vatthāṁ dattvā*). Thus

II [1]

[THE KAUŚĀMBĪ EDICT]

His Sacred Majesty commands (thus). The Mahāmātras at Kauśāmbī . . . is made united . . . should not be received into the Saṁgha. Also whosoever, monk or nun, breaks up the Saṁgha, after being clothed in white garments, shall take up abode in a place other than a monastery.

once more the legends have confirmed the inscriptions of Asoka by their mention of practical application of the law of the Edicts against schism to concrete cases.

It is interesting to note in conclusion that the Buddhist law relating to schism has its counterpart in the Brahminical law, according to which mischief-makers who tried to create or foment dissensions in the village communities and assemblies were punished by banishment. It was the traditional duty of the king to uphold the laws, agreements and the constitution (*samaya* or *saṁvit*) by which the various local bodies, groups, and communities, such as *Kula*, *Jāti*, *Janapada*, or *Saṅgha*, organised and governed themselves, and to punish those who violated them by deportation [see the Smṛiti texts quoted in my *Local Government in Ancient India*, 2nd edition, Oxford].

Thus the spiritual sovereignty assumed and asserted in these Edicts by Asoka was not something which he had arrogated to himself as an arbitrary autocrat, but had behind it the sanction of both Brahminical and Buddhist Law [see Sukumar Dutt's *Early Buddhist Monachism* for a good discussion of the subject of schisms].

[1] This Edict is to be found on the Allahabad Asoka Pillar below the P.E. I-VI and the Queen's Edict, and hence to be regarded as later than either. The pillar was located originally at Kauśāmbī, modern Kosam, on the Jamuna river. It is identified with the Yana or forest Kauśāmbī of Pāṇini by Fleet [*JRAS*, 1907, p. 511, note], and placed near Bharhut by V. A. Smith [*ib.* 1898, pp. 507-19]. Cunningham supposed that the pillar was removed to Allahabad by Firoz Shāh who had removed the two other pillars from their original locations to Delhi which was his capital. But the supposition does not seem to be likely, for Firoz Shāh had very little to do with Allahabad which was really founded two centuries later by Akbar who might be held responsible for the removal of the pillar on which are, moreover, incised the inscriptions of his favourite Bīrbal, and of his son Jahangir [see Hultzsch, *Corpus*, p. xx].

III[1]

[The Sāñchī Edict]

. . . (cannot) be divided. . . . the Saṁgha of the monks and nuns is made united as long as (my) sons and great-grandsons (shall reign and) as long as the sun and moon (shall shine). The monk or nun who shall break up the Saṁgha should be caused to put on white robes and reside in a non-residence. For what is my desire? That the Saṁgha may be united and be ever-lasting.[2]

IV

[The Queen's Edict]

The Mahāmātras of all places are to be instructed as follows at the word of His Sacred Majesty: Whatever gifts here[3] be of the Second Queen, whether mango-groves[4] or gardens[5] or alms-houses[6] or whatever else, these[7] must

[1] *Samage*: "united in both body and mind" (*samaggassāti sahitassa chittena cha śarīreṇa cha aviyuktassāti attho*), as explained in the *Samantapāsādikā*. In the *Suttavibhaṅga* we have the following explanation: "*samaggo nāma saṅgho samāna saṁvāsako samāna-sīmāṭhito*," i.e., "what is called the united Saṅgha is made up of members living together and within the same boundaries."

[2] Adapted from the translation by Hultzsch. It may be noted that true to his own plans as stated in R.E. V, and repeated in P.E. VII, Asoka appointed Mahāmātras in charge of the Saṁghas of different sects, and, therefore, these three Edicts are addressed to them, and *not* to the Saṁgha, as the Bhābra Edict *is*, although the Edicts deal with matters affecting the Saṁgha.

[3] *Hetā*, *atra*, probably in Pāṭaliputra.

[4] *Aṁbā-vaḍikā* occurring in P.E. VII.

[5] *Ārāma* (*ālame*).

[6] *Dāna-gahe*. These are the concrete examples of the gifts, *dānavisarga*, of the king and his queens as alluded to in P.E. VII.

[7] *Nāni*.

PLATE XII.

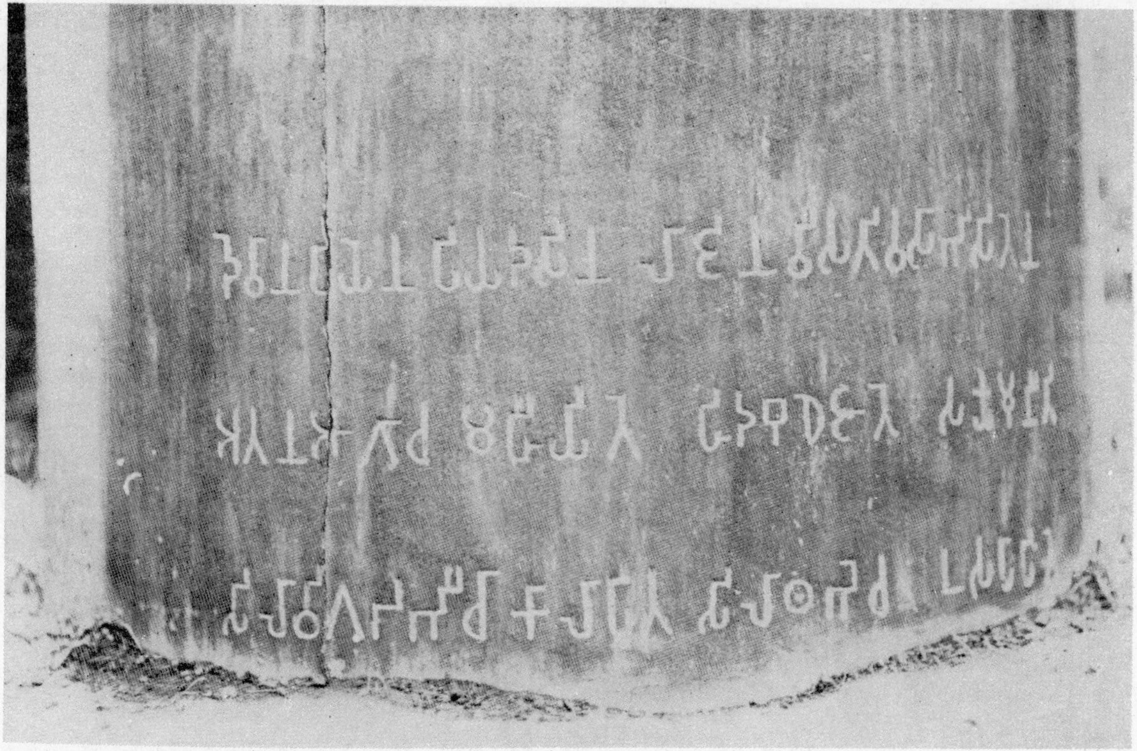

Lumbini Pillar Inscription.

be reckoned [1] as of that Queen. [This is the request [2]] of the Second Queen, the mother of Tīvara,[3] Kāruvākī.[4]

G. The Commemorative Pillar Inscriptions

I

[Rummindei]

By His Sacred and Gracious Majesty the King, consecrated twenty years,[5] coming in person, was worshipped (this spot), in as much as here was born the Buddha Śākyamuni.[6] A stone bearing a figure [7] was caused to be

[1] *Ganīyati.*

[2] Restored by Hultzsch as " [*He*] *vaṁ* [*vi*][*na*][*ti*] " ; *vinati* = Sans. *vijñapti.*

[3] The name is unusual, and occurs only in a Gupta inscription as that of a king of Kosala, as pointed out by Bühler [see Fleet's *Gupta Ins.* p. 293].

[4] The name is connected by Bühler with the Vedic gotra name of *Kāru.*

[5] I.e., 250 B.C.

[6] Hultzsch quotes *Mahāparinibbāna-sutta* : " āgamissanti kho Ānanda saddhā bhikkhu-bhikkhuniyo upāsaka-upāsikāya idha Tāthāgato jāto ti," and takes the first sentence of the inscription as extending up to this word. We may compare with the words of the inscription the following words which the *Divyāvadāna* puts into the mouth of Upagupta in addressing Asoka on their arrival at Lumbinī-vana : " *asmin Mahārāja pradeśe Bhagavān jātaḥ* " ; " in this place, O great king, tne Blessed One was born."

[7] *Silā-vigaḍabhī* ; *vigaḍa* is from Sans. *vikaṭa*, a variant of *vikṛita* which may mean a *vikāra*, a transformation of any given material, a carving, or figure carved on a stone ; or *vikaṭa* may mean a gigantic or grotesque figure as in an arabesque, tapestry, or coverlet. *Śilā-vikṛita* may be compared with the Pāli word *pāsādavikatikā*, a building with decorative figures. Buddhaghosa explains the word *vikatikā* as " *sīhabyagghādi-rūpavichitto uṇṇāmayo attharako,*" " a coverlet of linen decorated with figures of lions, tigers and the like." The *Mahāvaṁsa* [xxvii. 30] also refers to pillars bearing figures of lions, tigers and other animals, or figures of the gods (*sīhabyagghādi-rupehi devatā-rupakehi cha . . . thambhehi*). The *-bhī* is from Sans. root *bhṛit*, to bear, carry. Thus *silā-vigaḍabhī* means a stone carrying a figure, the capital of the pillar that was set up. The inscription

constructed and a pillar of stone was also set up, to show that the Blessed One was born here.

The village Luṁmini [1] was made free of religious

emphasises that not merely was the pillar of stone set up; there was also constructed (*kālāpita*) a figure of stone to decorate it as a fitting mark of a supremely holy place. This figure of stone, *śilā-vikṛita*, was seen to be the figure of a horse by Yuan Chwang, and Charpentier has sought to construe the word *vigaḍa* itself into a horse from *vigaḍa* = *agaḍa* for *agalitāśva*, a vigorous horse. Sir R. G. Bhandarkar took the expression as *śilā-vikaṭa* (of unusual size)-*bhityā* (*bhittikā* = wall). The meaning adopted here is from the suggestion of Dr. B. M. Barua [*Asoka Edicts in New Light*, p. 85 f.].

It is to be noted that the ending *-bhī* denotes the feminine, as well as *kālāpita*. Cf. such feminine forms as *daya*, *apekha*, *isya*, *sālika*, showing the shortening of the final *ā*, as used in the Pillar Edicts.

Besides deriving *vigaḍa* from *vikaṭa* = *vikṛita* (which is phonetically rather improbable), it is possible phonetically to derive *vigaḍa* from vigaḍha = vigarha = vigraha, while *bhī* might be taken to mean "also," as in Hindi *bhi*. *Vigraha* is, of course, the well-known word for a figure. The duplication "*bhī chā*" would then be for emphasis: "Silā-vigaḍa-bhī chā kālāpita silāthabhe cha usapāpite; not only was a figure of stone caused to be made—there was also a pillar of stone caused to be raised."

[1] This village is now known as Rummindei, but to the local people as Rupan-dehi, in the subdivision (*Māl*) Bithri, *Jilā* (district) Bithri, of the Nepal Government. I visited the place (with my pupil, Mr. P. P. Pande of Narharia, Basti, who kindly arranged for my visit) by travelling from the B.N.W.R. station, Nautanwa, for twelve miles on a pony to the village Khungai where I stayed for the night under the hospitable roof of Chaudhuri Sitaramji. Next morning (28th February, 1927), I rode through the village Padaria to the site of the Asokan Pillar about two miles distant. My photograph of the Pillar shows the fissure running along the entire length of the shaft which, according to Yuan Chwang, was caused by lightning.

Within a few paces of the Pillar stands a temple enshrining an ancient sculpture representing the Nativity of the Buddha, the figure of his mother, Mahāmāyā, standing under the sāl tree after her delivery with three attendants. The mutilated figure of the mother is now preserved and worshipped by the Hindus as the goddess "*Rupam Dehi*"!

In the illustration of the sculpture [Plate xiii.] (based on that of P. C. Mukharji in *ASR*, xxvi.), Māyādevī stands to the right in a graceful and easy posture, free from labour pains, holding with her right hand the branch of a sāl tree, and adjusting with her left hand her lower garments. The skill of a master-hand is shown in the delicate gradation of relief employed to indicate the branch and leaves of the tree, the contours of her head and hand, and her hair falling in wavelets. To her right, and below her right hand, stands a shorter female figure with her right hand raised to help her. The figure is supposed on the basis of the nativity legends of the Buddha to be that of her sister Prajāpati Gautamī, but P. C. Mukharji took it to be that of an attendant [*Ib.* 37]. The *third* tall figure is supposed by P. C. Mukharji [*Ib.*] to be that of Prajāpati, but by V. A. Smith [*Ib.*] to be a male figure, that of the god Indra who in the story receives the infant Bodhisattva on a cloth. The *fourth* female figure is that of an attendant. Lastly, there is the figure of infant Bodhisattva standing immediately after his birth, according to the story.

Regarding the possible age of this sculpture, Watters [*On Yuan Chwang*, ii. 17] remarks that " as it has not been closely examined, its age is quite uncertain." I have closely examined it, and found it to resemble the Sanchi and Bharhut sculptures on the same subject [Plate xxviii. of Cunningham's *Stūpa of Bharhut*]. V. A. Smith holds [*ASR*, xxvi. 6] that " probably the Rummindei group is the oldest known example of the nativity subject." P. C. Mukharji considers that it shows " that style of workmanship which is generally associated with the time of Asoka " [*Ib.* 37]. The material of the sculpture also shows it to be Asokan, because it is " the yellowish kind of stone which was employed in the edict pillars and in the two famous Yakṣa door-keepers of Pāṭaliputra, now in the Calcutta Museum " [*Ib.*]. The antiquity of the shrine is also shown by the fact that its original floor must have lain more than 20 feet below the present level of the ground, and the basement farther down, as calculated by P. C. Mukharji [*Ib.*]. Thus if this sculpture is held to be Asokan, the image of Māyādevī with her attendants and her son might be taken to be the very figure referred to in the expression *śilā-vigraha*, and would thus help to fix the meaning of that difficult passage in the inscription. The passage would then mean that Asoka marked out the birth-place of the Buddha by two *distinct* monuments, viz., (1) the pillar (*silā-thabhe*) and (2) a sculpture representing the Nativity (*silā-vigaḍa*). It is to be further noted that in the legendary texts such as *Asokāvadāna*, there is no mention of a stone pillar set up by Asoka. They record that Lumbini Garden is the first place to which Upagupta takes Asoka on his pilgrimage, and on his arrival there Upagupta tells the king that this is the place of the Buddha's birth, and points out *the particular tree under which Mahāmāyā stood when her child was born*. Then the king *sets up a shrine* at the place, makes a donation of 100,000 ounces of gold, and departs. Watters [*ib.*] rightly guesses that the *shrine* referred to is the one now discovered, and it actually shows us the representation on stone of the tree with Mahāmāyā standing under it. Such a representation was as appropriate a monument to mark the birth-place of the Buddha as the pillar announcing it by its inscription. Perhaps it had precedence over the pillar, for it is mentioned first in the inscription as being perhaps constructed first, the erection of the

cesses [1] and also liable to pay only one-eighth share [2] (of the produce).

pillar following later. That is why Asoka has mentioned the two undertakings as two distinct and separate ones in his inscription.

The inscription on the pillar has six lines, of which only the first three lines are visible and above the ground ; the last two lines are now buried beneath. Probably the entire inscription was hidden from view when Yuan Chwang came to the pillar. That is why he does not mention having seen any inscription on the pillar. But the Chinese work *Fang-chih* does refer to an inscription on the pillar recording the circumstances of the Buddha's birth.

Lastly, it may be noted that the Pillar and the Shrine are on a mound made up of the ruins of old structures accumulating through the ages. These structures must have included stūpas, though neither Fa-hien nor Yuan Chwang has mentioned any of these. "Yet we find mention of a great tope at the spot where the Buddha was born (in a Chinese work), and about the year A.D. 764, the tope was visited, we are told, by the Chinese pilgrim known as Wukung" [Watters, ii. 17].

The Nativity of the Buddha has been naturally a favourite subject of ancient Indian sculpture. We find it in sculpture of different styles, periods, and places, Sanchi, Bharhut, Gandhara, Amaravati, and Sarnath. The oldest is that of Sanchi and Bharhut, with which that of the Rummindei Temple agrees in style and form. At Bharhut the Nativity is represented by the Descent of the Bodhisattva into the womb of his Mother whose pose and form are similar to those of the Rummindei sculpture. At Sanchi, the Nativity is no doubt represented by a variety of symbols, such as the lotus, or a bunch of lotuses set in a vase, or Māyā herself seated on a full-blown lotus or flanked by two elephants pouring water over her (mistakenly taken to be *Śrī* hitherto), but the representation that is most in accord with the Buddhist texts is that of Māyā exhibited in a standing posture ready for her delivery, as shown at Rummindei. It is for this correspondence of the Rummindei to the Sanchi sculpture that I have taken it to be Asokan. [On Nativity in sculpture, see Marshall's *Guide to Sanchi,* p. 42, and Foucher's *Beginnings of Buddhist Art*, pp. 20, 21, 70, and plates i, iii, iv.]

[1] *Ubalike* = *udbalika* (Thomas) or *avavalika* or *apa-valika* (Bühler). The word *bali,* as well as *bhāga*, is used by Kauṭilya [II. 6].

[2] *Aṭhabhāgiye*: this means that the usual king's share of the produce as land-revenue, which was one-fourth in Chandragupta's time, according to Megasthenes, was reduced by half for this village as the birth-place of the Holy One. Bühler took *aṭha* = *artha,* and the meaning to be "sharer in wealth, partaking of the king's bounty"; deriving his suggestion from the legend that Asoka spent at Lumbinī-vana 100,000 gold pieces [*Div*. p. 390]. Pischel explained

PLATE XIII.

Nativity in Sculpture in the Rummindei Temple.

II

[NIGLIVA [1]]

By His Sacred and Gracious Majesty the King consecrated fourteen years was doubly [2] enlarged the stupa of Buddha Konākamana [3] and (by him) consecrated (twenty years), coming in person, and reverence being made, was set up (a stone pillar).

H. THE CAVE INSCRIPTIONS [4]

I

[NIGRODHA CAVE]

By His Gracious Majesty the King consecrated twelve years this Nigrodha Cave was granted to the Ājīvikas.

it as "with eight (*aṣṭa*) plots of assessable land." Kautilya uses the expression "*chaturtha-pañcha-bhāgikaḥ*" [II. 24] in the sense of "paying a fourth or fifth share of the produce."

[1] Called by Hultzsch the Nigālī Sāgar Pillar after the name of the tank on which the Pillar stood.

[2] *Dutiyaṁ vaḍhite*, enlarged to double its original size, as translated by Hultzsch who compares *diyaḍhiyaṁ vaḍhisati* of M.R.E, *Sahas.*

[3] Name of one of the twenty-four Buddhas and the third to precede Gautama Buddha.

[4] These cave-inscriptions occur in the hills called Barābar, which are isolated rocks of syenitic granite situated about fifteen miles north of Gayā. The hills contain two groups of caves called Barābar and Nāgārjunī The Nāgārjunī group is one of three caves, each containing an inscription of "*Daṣalatha Devānampiya*," the grandson of Asoka. The Barābar group is one of four caves, three of which bear an inscription of Asoka dealt with here. As stated in two of these inscriptions, the name of the Barābar Hill in the time of Asoka was Khalatika Hill According to an inscription in the fourth Barābar cave, known as the Lomaśa Riṣi Cave, of the Maukhari Anantavarman (A.D. 6th-7th century), the name of Khalatika was afterwards changed into Pravara hill. At some period between the times of Asoka and the Maukhari king, this same hill acquired another name, viz., *Gorathagiri*, which occurs in two inscriptions discovered by V. H. Jackson, one "on an isolated boulder over 100 yards N.W. of the ridge which contains three of the four Barābar caves," the other "cut on the western face of the ridge itself, only six or seven yards away from the entrance to the Lomaśa Riṣi Cave." The first inscrip-

II

[Khalatika Hill Cave]

By His Gracious Majesty the King, consecrated twelve years, this cave in the Khalatika Hill was granted to the Ājīvikas.

tion has the name as *Gorathāgiri*, and the second *Goradhagiri*. The name *Goradhagiri*, again, has been mentioned as the name of the same hill in line 7 of the Hathigumphā Cave Inscription of Khāravela, King of Kalinga, who " in the eighth year of his reign (about 165 B.C.) had stormed by his great army Goradhagiri." Thus between Maurya and Maukhari periods, in the second century B.C., the *Khalatika* Hill or a part of it was known as *Gorathagiri*. Very probably a change of name applied to a part of the Khalatika Hill, for the name was known enough in the time of Patañjali to be mentioned in his *Mahābhāṣya* [I. ii. 2] as an example of Pāṇini's rule [I. 2, 52] on which Kātyāyana (about 350 B.C.), too, cites the example—" Khalatikādiṣu vachanaṁ." This sentence Patañjali explains as " *Khalatikasya parvatasya adūrabhavāni vanāni Khalatikaṁ vanāni*." Thus in the second century B.C. the name Khalatika was known as the name of a famous hill.

According to the very ingenious suggestion of Dr. A. P. Banerji-Sastri, the connection of Kharavela with the Barābar Hills has left another mark on them. The last two Asokan Inscriptions in the Barābar Caves, as shown here, and the three Nāgārjunī Inscriptions of Daśaratha mention in common the grant of these caves to the *Ājīvikas*, but in three of these inscriptions there is detected an attempt to chisel away the word *Ājīvikehi*, as if the name of this sect was not tolerated by somebody who was at such pains to wipe it off. Now, who was this somebody ? Hultzsch conjectures it might have been the Maukhari Anantavarman who assigned one of the Barābar caves to Kriṣṇa, and two of the Nāgārjunī caves to Śiva and Pārvatī, and for his orthodox Hindu leanings did not favour the Ājīvikas. Dr. A. Banerji-Sastri puts forward a more convincing conjecture. He fastens the mischief on Khāravela, a Jain, with the traditional hostility of his community to the Ājīvikas, a mischief that was thus committed much earlier that the time of the Maukhari when the Asokan Brāhmī lipi was well-nigh forgotten. Besides, a Brahmanical Hindu would not be against the Ājīvika regarded as a follower of Viṣṇu or Kriṣṇa as shown by Kern [*IA*, xx. 361 f.], while he would be rather for defacing the name of *Devānaṁpiya Asoka*. Nor can the mischief be traced to a Buddhist who would regard it as a sacrilege against the most honoured Buddhist king to tamper with his sacred words. Thus Dr. Banerji-Sastri finds that the mischief-maker must have been a Jain [see Hultzsch, *Corpus*, p. xxviii ; *JBORS*, XII. pp. 49-52, 58-62].

III

[Khalatika Hill No. 2 Cave]

His Gracious Majesty the King being consecrated nineteen years, this cave in the very pleasant [1] Khalatika Hill was granted by me [2] against the coming of the rains.[3]

[1] *Supiye* = *supriya*.

[2] The donor may or may not be Asoka.

[3] *Jalaghosāgamathāta* = lit., "for the sake of the roar of waters." Cf. "*vāṣa-niṣidiyāye*," "for a shelter in the rainy season (*varṣā*)" as used in the three cave-inscriptions of Daśaratha.

APPENDIX B

ON THE CHRONOLOGY OF THE ASOKAN EDICTS

It is possible to trace a chronological sequence or relationship among the Edicts of Asoka from the evidence they themselves furnish. It is, however, to be noted that the date of the composition or issue of an Edict by the king must be different from the date on which the Edict was inscribed on rock or pillar in places far remote from headquarters. Thus it is quite reasonable to assume that different Edicts composed and issued by the king at different times, and exhibiting a process of evolution in the king's ideas on the subject, might be later on inscribed all together on the same remote rock or pillar on which they appear. We are here concerned with the inner chronology of the Edicts, which may be discovered from the data they themselves reveal. These may be indicated as follows :

1. *Appointment of Mahāmātras :* this subject is referred to in (*a*) the separate Rock Edicts at Dhauli and Jaugada (*b*) Rock Edict III (*c*) Rock Edict V and (*d*) Pillar Edict VII. The matter and manner of the reference to the same subject in these different Edicts betray their chronological connection.

In (*a*), Asoka announces his intention to appoint Mahāmātras for a particular purpose. It is that they may inspect the work of officers called *Nagala-viyohālaka* (=*Nagara-vyāvahāraka*) in the Dhauli text, and *Māhāmātā-nagalaka* (cf. Kauṭilya's *Paura-vyavahārika*, I. 12, and *Nāgarika-mahāmātra* in IV. 5) in the Jaugada text, l. 10], i.e., the judicial officers or city magistrates, so as to prevent " undeserved imprisonment and undeserved torture " (*akasmā palibodhe va akasmā palikilese va*). Thus Asoka thinks of appointing a special class (*vagam* in l. 24 of Dhauli) of Mahāmātras to check the abuses of his judicial officers. He also thinks that for this purpose he should send out (*nikhāmayisāmi*) every five years on tour (*anusaṁyānam*) these judicial inspectors of his. This rule about the quinquennial deputation and circuit of these special officers is, however, relaxed in the case of the Governors of Ujjain and of Taxila, who could make it triennial.

In (*b*), Asoka's intentions seem to have materialised into a standing order or a regular decree of the king, who ordains as follows :

"Everywhere within my dominions or conquered territory (*vijite*), the Yuktas, the Rājūka, and the Prādeśika, shall, every five years, go out on tour by turns (*anusaṁyānaṁ niyātu*, Girnar, *nikhamaṁtu*, Kalsi, and *nikramatu*, Shah.) as well for other business, too, as for this purpose, viz., for the following religious instruction."

It will be observed that Asoka's ideas and intentions on the subject, which were merely adumbrated or indicated in general terms in (*a*), have here attained to a much greater degree of definiteness and precision necessary to a government order on the subject. That (*b*) has thus developed out of (*a*) is further evident from the element common to them, viz., the rule about making the administrative tours quinquennial. This rule seems to be made absolute now, and does not refer to the exception or relaxation permitted in (*a*). Probably the exception of (*a*) did not work well and was withdrawn in the final government order. Further, while (*a*) merely refers to the need felt by the king for sending out, on periodical inspections of judicial administration, officers of the status of Mahāmātras, in (*b*) these Mahāmātras are particularised and specified. Lastly, while (*b*) confines the scope of the deputation to the judicial branch of the administration, (*a*) extends the scope so as to include the preaching of the Dharma by the king's superior administrative officers.

In (*c*) and (*d*) is to be seen a further development. Whereas (*b*) saddles the administrative officers with the duty of moral instruction, in (*c*) the duty of moral instruction is very properly thrown upon a special class of officers created for the first time by Asoka, viz., the *Dharma-Mahāmātras*, whose duties and responsibilities in this regard are conceived and defined on a generous scale, showing the progress the king's ideas had made since they first dawned on him when he spoke in (*a*). It may be noted that the checking by the Mahāmātras of injustices, such as undeserved imprisonment (*palibodhe*) and torture (*palikilese*) as mentioned in (*a*), is also included in the comprehensive definition of the duties of the *Dharma-Mahāmātras* as enumerated in (*c*), for they are employed to secure to deserving citizens (*dhaṁma-yutānaṁ*) freedom from molestation (*apalibodhāye*, *aparigodhāya* in Girnar), remedies against imprisonment (*baṁdhana-badhasa paṭividhānāya*), and release (*mokhāye*).

The final stage of the development is, however, registered in (*d*) which makes some additions to the duties of Dharma-Mahāmātras under (*c*). It is distinctly stated in l. 25 of Pillar Edict VII that these Dharma-Mahāmātras were to be " occupied also with all sects " (*sava-pāsaṁḍesu pi cha viyāpaṭāse*), such as the Buddhist *Saṅgha*, the Brāhmaṇas and Ājīvikas, the Nirgranthas, and others, different Mahāmātras thus working for different congregations. This Edict, indeed, unfolds fully the scheme of Asoka under which each class of functions pertaining to the propagation of his Dharma was administered by its own class of functionaries called by the general name of Dharma-Mahāmātras. Asoka's Ministry of Morals was made up of a large variety of officials in accordance with the variety of subjects and interests to be administered by them. Thus while (*c*) refers to the Dharma-Mahāmātras as a class of officers, (*d*) refers to the different classes under them to deal with such different interests as those of ascetics, householders, religious sects, the benefactions of the king, and of his queens, of the king's sons, and of other queen's sons and the like.

Thus the internal evidence of the Edicts (*a*), (*b*), (*c*), and (*d*) shows that they follow the chronological order in respect of their composition, as distinguished from their publication by inscription.

That the Kalinga separate Edicts are the earliest of these four is also indicated by the place of their incision on the rocks. For instance, in the Dhauli Rock, they appear separately, one on the left column of the inscribed surface, and the other below R.E. XIV. Of course, the time of the actual incision of the Edicts might have been the same, but not that of their drafting and proclamation by the king. We are here concerned, as already stated, with the chronological sequence of the contents and ideas of the Edicts.

(2) *Appointment of Strī-adhyakṣa-mahāmātras :* this is referred to in R.E. XII. It will be observed that in R.E. V there is the mention of the employment of the Dharma-Mahāmātras to look after the different harems of the king, of his brothers and sisters, and of his other relatives, at Pātaliputra, and in all the outlying provincial towns. The king's ideas on the subject show a further development in R.E. XII where he institutes a new and special class of officers called the Strī-adhyakṣa-mahāmātras to deal with women and the delicate task of looking after their morals.

(3) *The Saṅghas and Mahāmātras :* the Bhabru or the Calcutta-Bairat-Rock-Inscription is addressed by the " Māgadha King Priyadarśin " directly to the *Saṅgha*, but the king's messages to the Saṅgha are addressed to the *Mahāmātras* in charge at Sanchi,

Sarnath, and Kauśāmbī. The reason is that the king's appointment of Mahāmātras to take charge of the Saṅgha and other religious sects, which we find first mentioned in R.E. V, and repeated in P.E. VII, was subsequent to the time of the issue of the Bhabru Edict. Thus the Pillar Edicts of Sanchi, Sarnath and Kauśāmbī are addressed to the *Mahāmātras* in charge of the *Saṅghas* of those places in pursuance of the arrangements mentioned in R.E. V, and are, therefore, much later in time than either Bhabru or this Edict.

(4) *Appointment of Anta-Mahāmātras:* Asoka's solicitude for the welfare of his Antas or frontagers is expressed in several of his Edicts, viz., M.R.E. I, K.R.E. I (separate), R.E. II, V, and XIII, but the administrative machinery for the systematic promotion of their welfare is not thought of till P.E. I which is the only Edict that tells of the appointment of a special class of officers called the Anta-Mahāmatras to deal with the Antas. Thus P.E. I must be subsequent to the Rock Edicts mentioned.

(5) *Protection of lower life:* non-violence towards all living beings as a principle is preached in several Edicts, viz., M.R.E. II, R.E. III, IV, IX, and XI. But administrative action to secure the observance of this principle is first seen in R.E. I, and is fully developed in P.E. V which may be regarded as the Protection of Animals Act of Asoka. It may be noted further that while in R.E. I, Asoka contemplates the abolition of the slaughter of peacocks for the royal kitchen in the near future, P.E. V, which unfolds the full extent of Asoka's measures on the subject, omits to protect the peacocks. But the deer are protected in both the Edicts.

(6) *The Puruṣas:* this term applied to government servants of all ranks, high, low, or middle, is not used in any of the Rock Edicts, but is thought of later, and used in several Pillar Edicts, e.g., P.E. I, ıV, VII.

(7) *The Rājūkas:* they are merely mentioned in R.E. III, but their functions are defined in P.E. IV which indicates Asoka's administrative innovations in this regard, whereby some of the powers in respect of law and justice, which are given to the Dharma-Mahāmātras under R.E. V, are now transferred to these Rājūkas. Thus P.E. IV must be later than the Rock Edicts aforesaid.

(8) *The position of P.E. VII:* some scholars have recently gone against the received opinion by holding P.E. VII as prior to the Rock Edicts. They base their view chiefly on the ground that R.E. II, V, and XIII mention one of the most important innovations of Asoka, viz., his organisation of his welfare work and moral propagandism, not only in the countries

on his frontiers, but also in some remote countries, while P.E. VII knows nothing of it. That this view is not tenable, and the usual view is the correct view, will appear from the following considerations :

(*a*) Arguments from omission or silence are notoriously unreliable, and in the present case they seem to be specially so. It is assumed that P.E. VII was meant to give an exhaustive account of all that Asoka had done as a ruler. It is a mere assumption or inference from the contents of the Edict which itself reveals nothing about the scope of its contents. The contents would rather support the assumption that the Edict, which was issued by Asoka for the benefit of his own people, was naturally meant to be a resumé of the various *domestic* measures he had adopted for the moral uplift of his people, and not of what he had done for foreign peoples. A reference to the sovereign's foreign policy and measures would be clearly out of place here.

(*b*) Accordingly, all the domestic measures mentioned in the various Rock Edicts are mentioned in P.E. VII with a degree of elaboration and generalisation that can come only after an experience of those measures seen fully in operation. This will be evident from the following examples : (i) the chief officers mentioned in the Rock Edicts, viz., the Rājūkas, Mahāmātras, and Dharma-Mahāmātras, are also mentioned in P.E. VII ; (ii) the functions of these newly-created Dharma-Mahāmātras which are detailed in R.E. V are summarised in P.E. VII ; (iii) the public works of utility and comfort for both man and beast as indicated in R.E. II are fully mentioned in P.E. VII ; as instances of generalisations and references in P.E. VII to the R.E. may be mentioned : (iv) the statement that for the spread of Dharma Asoka has had religious messages (*Dhamma-sāvanāni*) proclaimed (*sāvāpitāni*), various religious injunctions (*Dhammānusathini vividhāni*) ordained (*ānapitāni*), officers, called Puruṣas and Lajūkas, set to exhort the people to morality, pillars of piety set up, Dharma-Mahāmātras appointed, religious messages composed (*kaṭe*) ; (v) the statement that the progress of the people in Dharma may be accomplished in two ways, by *dhamma-niyama*, by regulation, and by *nijhati*, by reflection or inner meditation.

(*c*) Above all, arguments from the inclusion or omission of certain matters in the two classes of Edicts cannot be conclusive as regards their chronological relationship. Does not Asoka himself in R.E. XIV address an emphatic warning on the subject ?—" *Na cha sarvam sarvatra ghaṭitam*," " all is not suitable in all places."

(9) *The position of M.R.E. I :* I agree with Hultzsch and many other scholars in thinking that this Edict is Asoka's earliest. As

pointed out by Hultzsch [*Corpus*, p. xliv], the Rūpnath and Sahasrām versions of this Edict (*a*) speak of inscriptions on rock and pillar as a task which it was intended to carry out, and not as a *fait accompli* (*lākhāpetavaya*) ; (*b*) contain, along with the Mysore records, the first elements of Asoka's Dharma, which we find more fully developed in his Rock and Pillar Edicts.

As regards (*a*), Dr. B. M. Barua has recently taken the objection, that Asoka's intention on inscription of his messages on rock and pillar is also expressed in a passage of his so-called last Edict, the P.E. VII, which is "*Iyaṁ dhamma libi ata athi silā-thaṁbhāni vā silā-phalakāni vā tata kaṭaviyā*," "this rescript on morality must be engraved there where either stone pillars or stone slabs are available," and that, therefore, no chronological conclusion can be based on such a passage, unless it be that P.E. VII is itself an earlier Edict like M.R.E. I, presaging both the R.E. and P.E. Against this objection it may be noted that the chronological position of P.E. VII has been established already on other grounds, while, so far as this particular passage is concerned, there is a difference between it and the corresponding passage in M.R.E. I. In the former, what is to be inscribed on pillar or slab of stone is the particular Edict, "*iyam dhaṁma libi*," whereas in the latter, what is to be inscribed is not the particular Edict but, as Hultzsch points out [*Corpus*, p. 168 n.], "the subject-matter or contents of Asoka's proclamations, viz., the Buddhist propaganda, '*iya cha aṭhe*,' instead of the usual '*iyam dhaṁma lipi lekhitā*.'" The other point of difference is the direct reference to the inscription of the king's message on *rocks* (*pavatisu*) in M.R.E. I, and not on slabs of stone (*silā-phalaka*) as mentioned in P.E. VII. Perhaps a difference of meaning was intended in these two expressions : a slab of stone might be found as much on a pillar as on a rock, and in that case the passage in question in P.E. VII might refer only to the Pillar Edicts.

There are other passages in the M.R.E. which are of great significance for the entire Asokan chronology. The significance will be realised by equating these passages with certain other passages occurring in R.E. XIII. These two sets of passages are given below :

(1) M.R.E. I : Aḍhikāni aḍhātiyāni vasāni ya hakaṁ upāsake no tu kho bāḍhaṁ prakaṁte huṣaṁ | ekaṁ savachharaṁ sātireke tu kho saṁvachhareṁ yaṁ mayā saṁghe upayīte bāḍhaṁ cha me pakaṁte [ll. 2-3, Brahmagiri text].

(2) R.E. XIII. : L.1.—Aṭha-vaṣa-abhisitasa Devanapriasa Priadraśisa raño Kaliga vijita. . . .

L.2—Tato pacha adhuna ladheṣu Kaligeṣu tivre dhrama-śilana dhramakamata dhramanuśasti cha Devanapriyasa.

In (1) Asoka states : " For more than two years and a half that I had been an *upāsaka*, lay-worshipper, I had not exerted myself well. But a year—indeed, for more than a year—that I approached the Saṅgha, I exerted myself greatly."

In (2) Asoka states : " In the eighth year of his coronation the king conquered the country of the Kalingas. Thereafter, now that the Kalingas were conquered, the king's cultivation of Dharma, love of Dharma, and preaching of the Dharma became intense (*tīvra*)."

The passage referring to the intensity of the king's zeal for the Dharma in (2) should be equated and considered along with the passage in (1) referring to his great exertions (*bāḍham cha me pakaṁte*) on behalf of the Dharma. In both (1) and (2), again, there is a reference to a stage in Asoka's life which was marked by a want of exertion and zeal for the Dharma.

On the basis of these two equations, we may obtain the following chronological results :

(1) The conquest of Kalinga took place about 262 B.C. (taking the *Cambridge History* date of 270 B.C. for Asoka's coronation).

(2) The conquest was preceded by a period of " more than two years and a half," when Asoka was a non-zealous *upāsaka* of the Buddhist Church. This takes us to 265 B.C. as the date of Asoka's entry into that Church as an *upāsaka*, the date of his conversion to Buddhism.

(3) After 262 B.C. began Asoka's active efforts on behalf of his new faith, and by 260 B.C., i.e., " within more than a year," he was conscious of the " results " (*phale*) of such efforts, as stated in M.R.E. I whose date must thus be 260 B.C.

(4) The second consequence of his efforts (*parākrama*) was the first of his religious tours (*dharma-yātrā*) to Bodh-Gayā, as stated in R.E. VIII. This took place in the " tenth year of his coronation," i.e., in 260 B.C.

(5) Issue of the two separate Kalinga Rock Edicts in 259 B.C.

(6) Issue of the other Rock Edicts, 258-257 B.C.

PLATE XIV.

BRAHMAGIRI MINOR ROCK EDICT.

CHAPTER VIII

TEXT OF THE INSCRIPTIONS

A. Minor Rock Edicts

I

[Brahmagiri]

LINE

1 [S]uv[a]ṁṇagirīte ayaputasa mahāmātāṇaṁ cha vachan[e] na Isilasi mahāmātā ārogiyaṁ vataviyā hevaṁ cha vataviyā [1]
Devāṇaṁpiye [2] āṇapayati [3]

2 Adhikāni [4] aḍhātiyāni v[a]sāni ya hakaṁ . . . . sake [5]
no tu kho bāḍhaṁ prakaṁte husaṁ
ekaṁ savachharaṁ [6] sātireke tu kho saṁvachhareṁ [7]

3 Yaṁ mayā saṁghe upayīte [8] bāḍhaṁ cha me pakaṁte
iminā chu kālena amisā samānā
munisā Jaṁbudīpasi

[1] Line 1 up to this word does not occur in the north Indian versions of this Edict; the words "hevaṁ cha vataviyā" do not occur in the Siddapur version.

[2] The Maski version reads here: "Dev[ā]na[ṁ]piyasa Asok[a]sa."

[3] *Āha* or *āhā* in other versions.

[4] *Sāti[ra] kekāni* [Rup.].

[5] Rūp. Ya sumi prakāsa [Sa]k[e].
Bair. Ya hakaṁ upāsake
Sah. [A]ṁ upāsake sumi.
Mas. Aṁ sum[i] Bu[dha]-Śake.

[6] The chronologically important expression "ekaṁ savachharaṁ" does not occur in the north Indian versions.

[7] A mistake for *saṁvachhare*.

[8] *Upagate* (Mas.); *upayāte* (Bair.); *upete* (Rūp.).

LINE

4 mi[s]ā devehi [1]
pakamasa hi iyaṁ phale
no hīyaṁ sakye mahātpeneva pāpotave [2]
kāmaṁ tu kho khudakena pi
5 paka[m]i . . ṇeṇa [3] vipule svage [4] sakye ārādhetave [5]
e[t]āyaṭhāya iyaṁ sāvaṇe sāvāpite [6]
6 . . . . mahāt[p]ā [7] cha imaṁ pakame[yu t]i aṁtā [8]
cha mai [9] jāneyu [10] chiraṭhitīke cha iyaṁ
7 [paka [11]]. . . . .
Iyaṁ cha aṭhe vaḍhisiti vipulaṁ cha vaḍhisiti avaradhiyā
diyaḍhiyaṁ
8 [vadh]isiti [12]
iyaṁ cha sāvaṇ[e] sāv[ā]p[i]te vyūthena 200 50 6 [13]

[1] Rūp. Yā [i]māya kālāya Jaṁbudipasi.
Sah. [Etena cha aṁta] lena Jaṁbudīpasi.
Mas. pure Jaṁbu . . . . s[i].
Rūp. amisā devā husu te dāni m[i]s[ā] kaṭā.
Sah. aṁmisaṁ-[de]vā saṁta munisā [m]isaṁ-deva [kaṭā]
Mas. [ye amisā devā husu] te [dā]n[i] misibhūtā.

[2] Bair. [no] hi e[s]e ma[ha]taneva chakiye.
Mas. Na hevaṁ dakhitaviye [uḍā]lake va ima adhigachh[e]yā.

[3] Mas. uses the significant word "*dhama-yute[na]*" instead of this word. The word as written here is a mistake for *pakamamīṇeṇa*.

[4] Mas. uses here the word *aṭhe*.

[5] *Adhigatave* (Mas.)

[6] Rūp. Etiya aṭhāya cha sāvane kaṭe.

[7] Rūp. Kh[u]dakā cha uḍālā.

[8] Rūp. and Sidd. use the form "*atā*."

[9] A mistake for *me*.

[10] *Jānaṁtu* (R., S., and B.).
Mas. gives here a different reading : [khudak]e [cha] [uḍ]ālake cha vataviyā hevaṁ ve kalaṁtaṁ bha[dak]e [se aṭhe ti se aṭhe chirathi]t[i]k[e] cha va[ḍhi]siti chā diya[ḍhi]yaṁ he[vaṁ] ti ; " both the lowly and the exalted must be told : 'If you act thus, this matter (will be) prosperous and of long duration, and will thus progress to one and a half' " [Hultzsch].

[11] *Pakame* (S.) ; *palākame* (Sa.) ; *pakarā* (R.).

[12] Here Rūpnath and Sah. interpose some new matter :
Rūp. Iya cha aṭhe pavatis[u] lekhāpeta vālata
Sah. Ima cha aṭham pavatesu [likhāpa]yāthā
Rūp. Hadha cha athi sālā-ṭh[abh]e silāṭha[ṁ]bhasi lākhāpetavaya ta
Sah. Ya . . [vā] ath[i] hetā silā-thaṁ[bh]ā tata pi [likhāpayatha t]i.

II

[Brahmagiri]

(*Continued from previous Edict*)

LINE

8 Se hevaṁ Devāṇaṁpiye

9 āha

mātā-pitisu susūs[i]taviye hemeva garu[su] prāṇesu drahyitavyaṁ sachaṁ

10 vataviyaṁ se ime dhaṁma-guṇā pavatitaviyā hemeva aṁtevāsinā

11 āchariye apachāyitaviye ñātikesu cha [ka]ṁ ya . . rahaṁ [1] pavatitaviye

12 esā porā[ṇ]ā pa[k]itī d[īgh]āvuse cha esa hevaṁ esa kaṭiviye

13 Chapaḍena likhite li[pi]kareṇa [2]

B. The Bhabru or Bairat No. 2 Rock Edict

1 Pr[i]yadas[i] l[ā]jā Māgadhe saṁghaṁ abhivāde[tū]naṁ āhā ap[ā]bādhataṁ cha phāsu-vihālataṁ chā

2 vidite v[e] bhaṁte āvatake h[a]mā Budhasi Dhaṁmasi Saṁghasī ti gālave chaṁ prasāde cha e kechi bhaṁte

3 bhagavatā Budhe[na] bhāsite sarve se subhāsite vā e chu kho bhaṁte hamiyāye diseyā [3] hevaṁ sadhaṁme

4 chil[a-ṭhi]tīke hosatī ti alahāmi hakaṁ taṁ v[ā]tave [4] imāni bhaṁt[e dha]ṁmapaliyāyāni Vinaya-samukase

---

After this, R. has the following sentence, which may be compared wit⸱ a similar sentence occurring in Sarnath M.P.E :

Rūp. Etinā cha vayajanenā yāvataka tupaka ahāle
Sar. Āvate cha tuphākaṁ āhale

Rūp. savara vivasetavā[ya] ti
Sar. savata vivāsayātha tuphe etena viyaṁjanena

13 Rūp. Vy[ū]ṭhenā sāvane kaṭe 200 50 6 sata vivāsā ta.
Sah. Iyaṁ [cha savane v]ivuthena duve sapaṁnā lāti-satā vivuthā ti 200 50 6.

---

1 *Yathārahaṁ* in Jat. Ram. version.

2 This word is written in Kharoṣṭhī characters.

3 The word appears from the plate of the inscription to be *diseyo*, as pointed out by Dr. B. M. Barua [*Ind. Hist. Quarterly*, II. 88].

4 It should be read as *vitave*, as shown by Barua [*Ib.*].

LINE

5 Aliya-vasāṇi Anāgata-bhayāni Muni-gāthā Moneya-sūte Upatisa-pasine e chā Lāghulo—

6 vāde musā-vādaṁ adhigichya bhagavatā Budhena bhāsite etāni bhaṁte dhaṁma-paliyāyāni ichhāmi

7 kiṁti bahuke bhikhu-[p]āye chā[1] bhikhuniye ch[ā] abhikhinaṁ sun[e]yu chā upadhāl[a]yeyū chā

8 hevaṁmevā upāsakā chā upāsikā chā
eteni[2] bhaṁte imaṁ likhā[pa]yāmi abhipretaṁ me janaṁtū ti

C. The Kalinga Rock Edicts

I

[Dhauli]

1 [Devāna]ṁ[pi]y[asa vacha]nena Tosaliyaṁ· ma[hā]māta [naga]la[v]i[yo]hālak[ā]

2 [va]taviya[3]
[aṁ kichhi dakhā]mi hakaṁ taṁ ichhāmi k[i]ṁ[t]i kaṁ[manapa]ṭi[pāday]ehaṁ

3 duvālate cha ālabhehaṁ
esa cha me mokhya-mata duvā[la etasi aṭha]si aṁ tuph[esu]

4 anusathi
tuphe hi bahūsu pāna-sahasesuṁ ā[yata] p[a]na[yaṁ] [ga]chh[e]ma su munisānaṁ
save

5 munise pajā mamā
ath[ā] pajāye ichhāmi h[a]ka[ṁ kimti sa]ve[na hi]tasukhena hidalo[kika]-

6 pālalokike[na] y[ūjev]ū [t]i [tathā . . . . muni]sesu[4] pi [i]chhāmi [ha]ka[ṁ]
no cha pāpunātha āv[a]-ga-

[1] The expression in the plate of the inscription as reproduced in Hultzsch's work reads like "bhikhupo ye chā bhikhuni ye chā," "many who are monks and who are nuns." This is pointed out by Barua [*Ib.*].

[2] A mistake for *etenā*.

[3] J. reads: "Devānaṁpiye hevaṁ āhā: Samāpāyaṁ mahāmātā nagalaviyohālaka hevaṁ vataviyā."

[4] Restore *sava-munisesu*.

LINE
7 [m]u[k]e [iyaṁ aṭhe]
[k]e[chha] v[a] eka-puli [se] . . . . nāti [1] e[ta]ṁ se pi desaṁ no savaṁ
de[kha]t[a hi t]u[phe] etaṁ
8 suvi[hi]tā pi
[n]itiyaṁ [2] eka-pulise [pi athi] y[e] baṁdhanaṁ vā [p]ali-kilesaṁ vā pāpunāti
tata hoti
9 akasmā tena badhana[ṁ]tik[a] aṁne cha . . . . . hu jane [3]
da[v]iye dukhīyati [4]
tata ichhitaviye
10 tuphehi kiṁti m[a]jhaṁ paṭipādayemā ti
imeh[i] chu [jāteh]i
no saṁpaṭipajati isāya āsulopena
11 ni[ṭhū]liyena tūlanā[ya] anāvūtiya ālasiyena k[i]lamathena
se ichhitaviye kitiṁ [5] ete
12 [jātā no] huvevu ma[m]ā ti
etasa cha sava[sa] mūle anāsulope a[tū]l[a]nā cha
niti[ya]ṁ e kilaṁte siyā
13 [na] te uga[chha] [6] saṁchalitaviy[e] tu
va[ṭ]ita[v]iy[e] etaviye vā [7]
hevaṁmeva e da[kheya] t[u]phāk[a] tena vataviye
14 ānaṁne dekhata [8] hevaṁ cha hev[a]ṁ cha [D]evānaṁpiyasa anusathi
se [9] mah[ā-pha]le [e] t[a]sa [saṁpa]ṭipāda
15 mahā-apāye asaṁpaṭipati
[vi]paṭ[i]pādayamīne hi etaṁ nathi svagasa [ā]l[a]dhi no lāj[ā]la[dh]i
16 duā[ha]le hi i[ma]sa kaṁm[asa] m[e] kute man[o]-atileke
sa[ṁ]paṭipajam[ī]n[e] chu [etaṁ] svaga[ṁ]
17 ālādha[yi]sa[tha mama cha ā]naniyam ehatha
iyaṁ cha l[i]p[i] t[i]sana[kha]tena [10] so[ta]viy[ā]

[1] Read *pāpunāti* as at Jaugaḍa.

[2] J. reads *bahuka*, i.e., "frequently."

[3] J. reads *anye cha* [*va*]*ge bahuke*.

[4] *Vedayati* (J.).

[5] A mistake for *kiṁti*.

[6] *Uthāy*[*ā*] (J.); *ugachha* is a mistake for *ugachhe*.

[7] *Etaviye pi nīt*[*i*]*yaṁ* (J.).

[8] *Nijhap*[*e*]*ta*[*vi*]*ye* (J.)

[9] *Etaṁ* in J.

[10] *Anutisaṁ* in J.

LINE

18 aṁta[l]ā [p]i cha [t]i[s]e[na kha]nasi kha[nas]i ekena pi sotaviya
hevaṁ cha kalaṁtaṁ tuphe

19 chaghatha saṁpa[ṭi]pād[a]y[i]tave
[e]t[ā]ye aṭhāye iya[ṁ] [l]i[p]i likhit[a] [h]ida ena

20 nagala-vi[y]o[hā]lakā [1] sas[v]ataṁ samayaṁ yūjevū t[i] . . . . .
[na]sa [2] akasmā [pa]libodhe va

21 [a]k[a]smā paliki[l]e[s]e va no siyā ti
etāye cha aṭhāye haka[ṁ] . . . . mate [3] p[a]ṁchasu paṁchasu [va]se-

22 su [4] [n]i[khā]may[i]sāmi e [5] akhakhase a[chaṁ]d[e] s[a]khinā-laṁbhe hosati etaṁ aṭhaṁ jānitu . . . . . . [ta]thā

23 kala[ṁ]ti atha mama anusathī it
Ujenite pi chu kumāle etāye v[a] aṭhāye [ni]khāma[yisa]
. . . .

24 hedisameva vagaṁ no cha atikāmayisati tiṁni vasāni
hemeva T[a]kha[s]ilāte pi
[a]dā a . . . . .

25 te mahāmātā [6] nikhamisaṁti anusayānaṁ tadā ahāpayitu
atane kaṁmaṁ etaṁ pi jānisaṁti

26 taṁ pi ta[thā] kalaṁti a[tha] lājine anusathī ti

II

[Jaugada]

1 Devānaṁpiye hevaṁ ā[ha]
Samāpāyaṁ mahamatā l[ā]ja-vachanik[a] vataviyā [7]
aṁ kichhi dakh[ā]mi hakaṁ taṁ i[chh]āmi hakaṁ k[im]ti kaṁ kamana

2 paṭipātayehaṁ duvā[la]te cha ālabhehaṁ
esa cha me mokhiya-mat[a] duvāl[a] etasa a[tha]sa a[ṁ] t[uph]esu anusa[thi]

[1] J. has "mahāmātā nagalaviyohālaka."

[2] Restore *ena janasa*; J. has "ena [muni]s[ānaṁ."

[3] Read *mahāmātaṁ*.

[4] J. here adds the word "anu[sa]yānaṁ."

[5] J. here has the words "mahāmāta[ṁ] achaṁḍa[ṁ] aphal[usa]ṁ ta."

[6] J. has here the word ". . . vachanik[a]" = probably *lājavachanika* as used in the second K.R.E., Jaugaḍa.

[7] D. reads: "Devānaṁpiyasa vachanena Tosaliyaṁ kumāle mahāmātā cha vataviya."

LINE

3 sava-muni-sā me pajā
atha pajāy[e] ichhāmi kiṁti me saveṇā hita-su[kh]ena
yu[je]yū [a]tha pajāye ichhāmi kiṁ[ti] m[e] savena hita-su-
4 kh[e]na yujeyū [1] ti hidalogika-pālaloki[k]e[ṇa] hevaṁmeva
me ichha savamunisesu
siyā aṁtānaṁ [a]vijitā
5 -naṁ kiṁ-chhāṁde su lājā aphesū ti
etākā [2] [vā] me ichha [a]ṁtesu pāpuneyu lājā hevaṁ
ichh[a]ti anu[v]i[g]ina hve[yū]
6 mamiyāye [a]svaseyu cha me sukhaṁ[m]ev[a] cha lahey[ū]
mamate [n]o kha[ṁ] [3] hevaṁ cha pāpuneyu kha[m]i[sa]ti
ne lājā [4]
7 e s[a]kiye khamitave mamaṁ nimitaṁ cha dhaṁma[ṁ]
chaley[ū]ti hidalog[aṁ] cha palalogaṁ cha ālādhayey[ū]
etāye
8 cha aṭhāye hakaṁ tupheni anusāsāmi ana[ne eta]kena
[ha]kaṁ tupheni a[nu]sāsitu chhaṁda[ṁ cha] vedi-
9 [t]u ā mama dhiti patiṁnā cha achala
sa hevaṁ [ka]ṭū k[aṁ]me [cha]litaviye asvāsa[n]iyā ch [a]
te en[a] te pāpune-
10 yu a[th]ā pita [h]evaṁ [n]e lājā ti atha [a]tānaṁ anukaṁpat[i
he]vaṁ a[ph]eni anuka[ṁpa]ti athā pajā he-
11 vaṁ [may]e lā[j]ine
tupheni hakaṁ anusāsita [5] [chh]āṁdaṁ [cha v]e[di]ta [6]
[ā] [ma]ma dhiti paṭi[ṁ]nā chā achala [7] [saka]la-
12 desā-āy[ut]ike [8] hosāmī et[a]si [a]thas[i]
[a]laṁ [9] [h]i tuphe asvāsa[nā]ye hi[ta]-sukhāye [cha
te]sa[ṁ] hida-
13 logi[ka]-p[ā]lal[o]ki[k]ā[y]e
hevaṁ cha kalaṁtaṁ svaga[ṁ cha ā]lādhayisa[tha] mama
cha ā'a[n]eyaṁ es[a]tha [10] e-

[1] The last eight words are repeated by a mistake, one of the few mistakes of the scribe (cf. *lipikarāparādhena*, R.E. XIV).

[2] Probably a mistake for *etakā*.

[3] For *dukhaṁ*, as in D.

[4] In place of this word, D. has " Devānaṁpiye aphākā ti."

[5] A mistake for *anusāsitu*.

[6] A mistake for *veditu*.

[7] The last six words do not appear in the D. text.

[8] D. reads " desāvutike." The word is a mistake for *desāyutike*.

[9] *Paṭibalā* in D.

[10] *Ehatha* in D.

LINE

14 tāye cha a[th]āye i[ya]ṁ lipī li[kh]i[ta hi]da e[na ma]h[ā]-
mātā sāsvataṁ samaṁ [1] yujeyū asvāsanāye cha

15 dhaṁma-chala[nā]ye [cha] aṁtā[na]ṁ
iyaṁ cha lipī a[nu]ch[ā]tuṁ[m]āsaṁ [2] s[ota]viyā tisena
aṁta[lā] [3] pi cha sotaviyā

16 khane saṁtaṁ eke[na] pi [sota]v[i]yā
heva[ṁ] cha [ka]laṁ[ta]ṁ chaghatha saṁpaṭipātayit[ave]

D. The Fourteen Rock Edicts

I

[Shabazgarhi]

1 [aya] dhrama-dipi [4] Devanapriasa raño likhapitu
hida no kich[i] jive ara[bhitu p]rayuhotave
no pi ch[a] sama[ja] kaṭava
ba[hu]ka [hi] doṣa sa[maya]spi
Devaṇapriy[e] Priadraśi ray[a da]khati

2 [a]sti pi chu ekatia samaye sasu-mate [5]
Devanapiasa Priadraśisa raño
pura [6] mahana[sas]i [Devana]pr[i]asa
Priadraśisa raño anudivaso bahuni pra[ṇa]-śata-sahasani
[arabhi]yis[u] supaṭhaye
s[o i]daṇi [7] yada aya

3 dhrama-dipi likhita tada trayo [8] vo praṇa haṁñaṁt[i] [9]
majura [10] duv[i] 2 mrugo 1 so pi mrugo no dhruva[ṁ]
eta pi praṇa trayo pacha no arabhiśaṁti

[1] A mistake for *samayaṁ*.

[2] After this word D. adds the words "tisena nakhatena."

[3] D. has a variant here: "kamaṁ chu khaṇasi khanasi aṁtalā pi tisena."

[4] This word is followed in J. by the words "Khepiṁgalasi pavatasi" and in D. by "... [si pava]tasi."

[5] *Sādhu-matā* (G.).

[6] *Puluvaṁ* (J.).

[7] *Aja* (G., D. and J.).

[8] *Tī* (G.), *tiṁni* (K.).

[9] *Ārabhare* (G.).

[10] *Morā* (G.), *majūlā* (J.).

II

[GIRNAR]

LINE

1 sarvata vijitamhi [1] Devānaṁpriyasa Piyadasino rāño

2 evamapi prachaṁtesu [2] yathā Chodā Pādā [3] Satiyaputo [4] Ketalaputo [5] ā Taṁba-

3 paṁṇī Aṁtiyako Yona-rājā ye vā pi tasa Aṁtiy[a]kas[a] sāmīp[aṁ] [6]

4 rājāno sarvatra Devānaṁpriyasa Priyadasino rāño dve chikīchha katā

5 manusa-chikīchhā cha pasu-chikīchhā cha osuḍhāni cha yāni m[a]nusopagān[i] cha

6 paso[pa]gāni cha yata yata nāsti sarvatrā hārāpitāni cha rop[ā]pitāni [7] cha [8]

7 mūlāni cha phalāni cha yata yatra nāsti sarvata hārāpitāni cha rop[ā]pitāni cha

8 paṁthesū [9] kūpā [10] cha khānāpitā vrachhā [11] cha ropāpit[ā] paribhogāya [12] pasumanusānaṁ

III

[GIRNAR]

1 Devānaṁpiyo Piyadasi r[ā]jā evaṁ āha dbādasa-vāsā-bhisitena mayā idaṁ āñ[a]pitaṁ

2 sarvata vijite mama yutā cha rājūke cha prādesike cha paṁchasu paṁchasu vāsesu anusaṁ-

[1] *Vijitasi* (K.), *vijite* (S.).

[2] *Aṁtā* (K), *ata* (M.).

[3] *Paṁdiyā* in other texts.

[4] *Sātiyaputo* (K.), *Satiyaputro* (S.).

[5] A mistake for *Keralaputra* (M.) ; *Kelalaputo* (K.), *Keraḍaputro* (S.).

[6] *Sāmaṁtā* in other texts.

[7] *Vuta* in S.

[8] The words from this up to the word *paṁthesū* in l. 8 are omitted in the S. text.

[9] *Magesu* in other texts.

[10] *Udupānāni* in other texts.

[11] *Lukhāni* (K., D. and J.), *ruchhani* (M.). The three words from this are omitted in the S. text.

[12] *Paṭibhogāye* (K., D. and J.).

LINE

3 y[ā]na[ṁ n]iyātu[1] etāyeva athāya imāya dhaṁmānusasṭiya yatha añā-

4 ya pi kaṁmāy[a]
[s]ādhu mātari cha pitari cha susrūsā mitra-saṁstuta-ñātīnaṁ bāmhaṇa-

5 samaṇānaṁ sādh[u d]ānaṁ prāṇānaṁ[2] sādhu anāraṁbho apa-vyayatā apa-bhāḍatā[3] sādhu

6 parisā pi yute āñapayisati gaṇanāyam hetuto cha vyaṁjanato cha

IV

[Girnar]

1 atikātaṁ aṁt[a]raṁ bahūni vāsa-satāni vadhito eva prāṇāraṁbho vihiṁsā cha bhūtānaṁ ñātīsu

2 a[s]aṁpratipatī brā[m]haṇa-sramaṇānaṁ[4] asaṁpratīpatī ta aja Devānaṁpriyasa Priyadasino rāño

3 dhaṁma-charaṇena [bhe]rī-ghoso aho dhaṁma-ghoso vimānadarsaṇā cha hasti-da[sa]ṇā cha

4 agi-kh[a]ṁdhāni[5] cha [a]ññāni cha divyāni rūpāni dasayitpā janaṁ
yārise bahūhi v[āsa]-satehi

5 na bhūta-puve tārise aja vadhite Devānaṁpriyasa Priyadasino rāño dhaṁmānusasṭiyā anāraṁ-

6 [bh]o prāṇānaṁ avihīsā bhūtānaṁ ñātīnaṁ saṁpaṭipatī bramhaṇa-samaṇānaṁ[6] saṁpaṭipatī mātari pitari

7 [s]usrusā thaira[7]-susrusā
esa añe cha bahuvidhe [dha]ṁma-charaṇe va[dhi]te vaḍhayisati cheva Devānaṁpriyo

8 [Pri]ya[da]si rājā dhaṁma-[cha]raṇaṁ idaṁ
putrā cha [p]otrā cha prapotrā[8] cha Devānaṁpriyasa Priyadasino rāño

[1] *Nikramatu* (S. and M.), *nikhamaṁtu* (K.), *nikhamāvū* (D. and J.).

[2] *Jīvesu* in D. and J.

[3] *Apabhaṁḍatā* in other texts.

[4] The two words of the compound are reversed in other versions.

[5] *Joti-kaṁdhani* in S.

[6] *Samana-bābhanesu* in D.

[7] *Vuḍha-susūsā* (D.), *vuḍhanaṁ suśruṣa* (S.).

[8] *Natāle chā panātikyā chā* (K.).

LINE

9 [pra]vadhayisaṁti idaṁ [dha]ṁma-charaṇaṁ āva savaṭakapā [1] dhaṁmamhi sīlamhi tisṭamto [dha]ṁmaṁ anusā-
sisaṁti

10 [e]sa hi sesṭe [2] kaṁme ya dhaṁmānusāsanaṁ
dhaṁma-charaṇe pi na [bha]vati asīlasa
[ta]imamhi athamhi

11 [va]ḍhī cha ahīnī cha sādhu
e[t]āya athāya ida[ṁ] lekhāpitaṁ [3] imasa atha[sa] v[a]dhi
yujaṁtu hīni ch[a]

12 [no] lochetavyā [4]
dbādasa-vāsābhisitena Devān[a]ṁpriyena Priyadasinā
rāñ[a] idaṁ lekhāpitaṁ [5]

V

[Mansehra]

1 De[vanaṁ]priyena Priyadraśi raja eva[ṁ] aha
kalaṇa[ṁ] dukara[ṁ]
ye adikare kayaṇasa se dukaraṁ karoti
taṁ maya bahu
[ka]ayaṇe [ka]ṭe
[ta]ṁ ma[a] putra [cha]

2 natar[e] cha para cha t[e]na ye apatiye [6] me [a]va-[ka]paṁ
tatha anuvaṭīśati se sukata ka[ṣa]ti
ye [chu] atra deśa pi hapeśati [7] se dukaṭa kaṣati [8]

3 pape hi nama supadarave [9]
s[e] atikrata[ṁ] a[ṁ]tara[ṁ] na bhuta-pruva dhrama-
[ma]hamatra nama
se 'reḍaśa-va[ṣa]bhisitena maya dhrama-mahamatra
kaṭa
te savra-pa[ṣa]deśa

[1] *Ā-kapaṁ*(D.), *āva-kapaṁ* (K.).

[2] *Sreṭhaṁ* in S.

[3] *Nipistaṁ* in S.

[4] *Alochayisu* (K., M., D. and J.).

[5] *Nipesitaṁ* in S.

[6] S. has " me apacha vrakṣaṁti."

[7] *Hāpayisati* in K. and D.

[8] *Kachhaṁti* in K. and D.

[9] G. here reads " *sukaraṁ hi pāpaṁ.*"

LINE

4 vapuṭa dhramadhitha[na]ye cha dhrama-vadhriya hida-
sukhaye cha dh[r]ama-yutasa Yona-Kaṁboja-Gadharana [1]
Raṭhika-Pitinikana [2] ye va pi añe aparata [3]
bhaṭamaye-

5 ṣu bramaṇibhyeṣu anatheṣu vudhresu [4] hida-su[khaye]
dhrama-yuta-apalibodhaye [5] viya[p]uṭa te
badhana-badha[sa] paṭivi[dhanay]e apalibodhaye mok-
ṣay[e] [cha iyaṁ]

6 anubadha p[r]aja [6] t[i] va kaṭrabhikara ti va mahalake [7]
ti va viyapraṭa te
hida [8] bahireṣu cha nagareṣu savreṣu [9] [o]rodhaneṣu [10]
bhatana [11] cha spas[u]na [12] [cha]

7 ye va pi añe ñatike savratra viyapaṭa
[e] iyaṁ dhrama-niśito [13] to va dhramadhithane ti va
dana-saṁyute ti va savratra vijitasi [14] maa dhrama-yutasi
vapuṭa [te]

8 dhrama-mahamatra
etaye athraye ayi dhrama-dipi [15] likhita [16] chira-ṭhitika hotu
tatha cha me
praja anuvaṭatu

[1] *Gaṁdhārānaṁ* (G.).

[2] *Risṭika-Peteṇikānaṁ* (G.); *Raṭhikanaṁ Pitinikanaṁ* (S.); *Laṭhika-Pitenikesu* (D.).

[3] *Aparaṁta* (S.), *Āpalaṁtā* (D.).

[4] *Mahālakesu* (D.).

[5] *Aparigodhāya* (G.), *apaligodha* (S.).

[6] *Pajāva* (K.).

[7] *Thairesu* (G.).

[8] *Pāṭaliputе cha* (G.).

[9] D. has "*savesu savesu.*"

[10] Between this word and the next, D. adds "*me e vā pi.*"

[11] *Bhātīnaṁ* (D.); *bhatana* is a mistake for *bhatuna.*

[12] *Bhaginīnaṁ* (D.).

[13] *Dhaṁma-nisrito* (G.).

[14] D. has "*sava-puṭhaviyaṁ.*"

[15] *Lipi* in other texts.

[16] *Nipista* in S.

VI

[GIRNAR]

LINE

1 [Devā] . . . . [1] [s]i rājā evaṁ āha
atikrāt[a]ṁ aṁtara[ṁ]

2 na bhūta-pru[v] [2]. [s] . [v] . . . [l] . [3] atha-kaṁme va paṭivedanā vā
ta mayā evaṁ kataṁ

3 s[a]ve kāle bhuṁj[a]mānasa [4] me [5] orodhanamhi gabhāgāramhi vachamhi va

4 vinītamhi cha uyānesu cha savatra paṭivedakā sṭitā athe me [ja]nasa

5 paṭivedetha [6] iti
sarvatra cha janasa athe karomi
ya cha kiṁchi mukhato

6 āñapayāmi svayaṁ [7] dāpakaṁ vā srāvāpakaṁ [8] vā ya vā puna mahāmātresu

7 āchāyi[ke] [9] aropitaṁ bhavati [10] tāya athāya vivādo nijhatī v[a s]aṁto parisāyaṁ

8 ānaṁtaraṁ [11] paṭ[i]vedeta[v]yaṁ me [12] sa[r]vatra sarve kāle
evaṁ mayā āñapitaṁ [13]
nāsti hi me to[s]o

9 usṭānamhi atha-saṁtīraṇāya va
katavya-mate hi me sa[rva]-loka-hitaṁ

10 tasa cha puna esa mūle usṭānaṁ cha athasaṁtīraṇā cha
nāsti hi kaṁmataraṁ

[1] Restore " Devānaṁpriyo Piyadasi."

[2] Read " *purva*."

[3] Restore *save kāle*.

[4] *Adamānasā* (K.), *aśamanasa* (S.), *aśatasa* (M.).

[5] D. and J. read " *me aṁte olodhanasi*."

[6] " *Praṭivedayaṁtu me ti* " in J.

[7] *Ahaṁ* in S. and M.

[8] *Sāvakaṁ* in K., D. and J.

[9] *Atiyāyike* in K., D., and J.

[10] *Hoti* in K., M., D. and J.

[11] *Anaṁtariyena* in S.

[12] The words from *sarvatra* in l. 5 up to this word have been repeated by mistake in S.

[13] D. and J. read " *hevaṁ me anusathe*."

LINE
11 sarva-loka-hitatpā [1]
ya cha kiṁchi parākramāmi ahaṁ kiṁti bhūtānaṁ ānaṁṇaṁ gachheyaṁ [2]
12 idha cha nāni [3] sukhāpayāmi paratrā cha svagaṁ [4] ārādhayaṁtu ta [5]
etāya athāya
13 ayaṁ dha[ṁ]ma-lipī lekhapitā [6] kiṁti chiraṁ tis̤eya iti [7]
tathā cha me putrā potā cha prapotrā cha
14 anuvataraṁ sava-loka-hitāya
dukaraṁ [t]u idaṁ añatra agena parākramena

VII

[SHAHBAZGARHI]

1 Devanaṁpriyo Priyaśi [8] raja savatra ichhati savra-
2 [p]raṣaṁda vaseyu
save hi te sayame bhava-śudhi cha ichhaṁti
3 jano chu uchavucha-chhaṁdo uchavucha-rago
te savraṁ va eka-deśaṁ va
4 pi kaṣaṁti
vipule pi chu dane yasa nasti sayama bhava-
5 śudhi kiṭrañata driḍha-bhatita niche paḍham [9]

VIII

[SHAHBAZGARHI]

1 Atikrataṁ ataraṁ Devanaṁpriya vihara-yatra nama nikramiṣu [10]
atra mrugaya añani cha ediśani abhiramani abhuvasu [11]
so Devanaṁpriyo Priyadraśi raja daśavaṣabhisito sataṁ

[1] Other texts have "*sava-loka-hitena.*"

[2] *Yehaṁ* in other texts and *vracheyaṁ* in S.

[3] *Kāni* in K., D. and J. ; *ṣa* in S. and *ṣe* in M.

[4] *Spagraṁ* in S.

[5] *Se* in K. and M. ; =" now."

[6] "*Dhrama nipista*" in S.

[7] "*Chirathitika bhotu*" (S.), "*chila-ṭhitikyā hotu*" (K.).

[8] Read *Priyadraśi*.

[9] *Bāḍhaṁ* in other texts.

[10] *N̄ayāsu* G(.).

[11] *Ahuṁsu* (G.), *husu* (K.), *huvaṁti naṁ* (D., J.).

LINE

nikrami [1] Sabodhi [2]
tenada dhraṁma-yatra
atra iyaṁ hoti śramaṇa-bramaṇanaṁ [3] draśane danaṁ vuḍhana[ṁ] [4] daśana hirañа-p[r]aṭividhane cha [jana]-padasa janasa draśana dhramanuśasti dhrama-pa[ri]p[ru]-chha cha tatopayaṁ
ese bhuy[e ra]ti [5] bhoti Devanaṁpriyasa Priyadraśisa raño bhago aṁñi

IX

[Kalsi]

1 Devānaṁpiye Piy[a]da[s]i lā[jā] āhā
jan[e] uch[āv]uchaṁ maṁgalaṁ ka[l]eti ābādhasi av[āha]si vivāhasi pajopadāne [6] pavāsasi e[tā]ye aṁnāye chā edisāye jane bahu magala[ṁ] k[a]leti
heta [ch]u abaka-jani[yo] [7] bahu chā bahuvidhaṁ chā khudā [8] [ch]ā nilathiyā chā magalaṁ ka[la]ṁti
2 se kaṭavi [9] cheva kho maṁgale
apa-phale [ch]u kho [e]s[e]
[i]yaṁ chu kho mah[ā]-ph[a]le ye dhaṁma-magale
he[tā] [10] iyaṁ dāsa-bhaṭakasi s[a]myāpaṭip[a]ti gulunā apachiti [p]ā[n]ān[aṁ] saṁyame s[a]man[a]-baṁbhanā-naṁ [11] dāne ese aṁne chā heḍise | [12] dhaṁma-magale nāmā se vata[v]iye pitinā pi putena pi bh[ā]tinā pi suvāmiken[a] [13] pi mita-saṁthuten[ā] ava paṭivesiyenā [p]i

[1] *Ayāya* (G.).

[2] *Saṁbodhiṁ* (G.).

[3] *Bāmhaṇa-samaṇānaṁ* (G.)

[4] *Thairānaṁ* (G.).

[5] *Abhilāme* (D. and J.).

[6] According to Kalsi grammar, the locative of *upadāna* should end in *-asi*; hence it should be *pajopadāye* as in D. and J. G. has "*putra-lābhesu*."

[7] *Mahiḍāyo* (G.), *striyaka* (S)., *ithī* (D.).

[8] *Chhudaṁ* (G.), *putika* (S.).

[9] A mistake for *kaṭaviye*.

[10] *Tateta* (G.), *atra* (M.), *tatesa* (D.).

[11] G. has the usual " *bamhaṇa-samaṇānaṁ*.

[12] This mark of punctuation is read as the word *taṁ* by Senart and Bühler.

[13] *Spaṁikena* (S. and M.).

LINE

3 iyaṁ sādhu iyaṁ kaṭaviye [ma]g[a]le āva [ta]sā athasā
ni[v]utiyā [1] imaṁ kachhāmi ti
e hi i[ta]le magale sa[ṁ]sayikye se
siyā va taṁ aṭhaṁ nivaṭey[ā] siyā punā no
hi[da]lokike chev[a] se
iyaṁ punā dhaṁma-magale akāliky[e]
haṁche pi taṁ aṭhaṁ no niṭeti [2] hida aṭham [3] palata
anaṁtaṁ punā pavasati [4]
haṁche puna taṁ aṭhaṁ nivateti hidā tato ubhaye[sa]ṁ
4 ladhe hoti hida chā se aṭhe palata chā anaṁtaṁ punā [5]
pasavati tenā dhaṁma-magalen[ā]

IX

[Girnar Variant [6]]

6 asti cha pi vutaṁ
7 sādhu dana [7] iti
na tu etārisaṁ astā [8] dānaṁ va ana[ga]ho [9] va yārisaṁ
dhaṁma-dānaṁ va dhamanugaho va
ta tu kho mitrena va suhadayena [v]ā
8 ñatikena [10] va sahāyana [11] va ovāditavyaṁ tamhi tamhi
pakaraṇe [i]daṁ kachaṁ idaṁ sādha [12] iti iminā sak[a]
9 svagaṁ ārādhetu iti
ki cha iminā katavyataraṁ yathā svagāradhi

[1] *Nistānāya* (G.), *niphatiyā* (D.).

[2] A mistake for *nivaṭeti* (M.).

[3] A mistake for *atha*, as in S.

[4] A mistake for *puṁnaṁ pasavati*.

[5] Read *puṁnam*.

[6] The variant starts from the word *nivutiyā* of l. 3 in Kalsi text. The Girnar reading is also followed in the Dhauli and Jaugaḍa versions.

[7] A mistake for *dānaṁ*.

[8] A mistake for *asti*.

[9] A mistake for *anugaho*.

[10] A mistake for *ñātikena*.

[11] A mistake for *sahāyena*.

[12] A mistake for *sādhu*.

X

[Kalsi]

LINE

1 Devā[naṁ]piye Piy[a]dasā [1] lajā y[a]ṣo vā kiti vā no [ma]hathāvā [2] manati an[a]tā [ya]ṁ pi yaso vā ki[t]i vā ichh[at]i
tadatvāye ayatiye [3] chā jane dhaṁma-susuṣā susuṣātu me ti
dhaṁma-vataṁ vā anuvi[dh]iya[ṁ]tu ti
dhata[k]āye [4] Devāna[ṁ]piye Piyadasi

2 lājā yaṣo vā kiti vā ichha [5]
aṁ ch[ā] kichhi lakamati [6] Devanaṁpiye Piyadaṣi lajā ta [ṣa]va pālaṁtikyāye [7] vā kiti sakale apa-p[a]lāṣave [8] ṣiyāti ti
[e]ṣe chu palisave e apune
dukale chu kho eṣe khudakena vā vagenā [9] uṣuṭena vā ana[ta] agen[ā pa]lakamenā ṣava[ṁ] palitiditu
[h]e[ta chu] kho

3 [u]ṣaṭe[na] vā dukale

XI

[Shahbazgarhi]

1 Devana[ṁ]priyo Priyadraśi raya evaṁ hahati
nasti ed[i]śaṁ danaṁ yadiśaṁ dhrama-dana dhrama-saṁstav[e] dh[r]ama-saṁvihago dh[r]ama-saṁba[ṁ]dha
tatra etaṁ [10] dasa-bhaṭakanaṁ saṁmma-paṭipati mata-pitusu suśruṣa mi[t]ra-saṁstuta-ñatikanaṁ śramaṇa-bramaṇana

2 dana praṇana anara[ṁ]bho
etaṁ vatavo pituna pi putrena pi bhratuna pi [spa]mikena pi mitra-saṁstutana [11] ava prativeśiyena [i]ma[ṁ] sadhu ima ṅ kaṭavo

[1] A mistake for *Piyadaṣi*.

[2] *Mahāthāvahā* in G.

[3] *Tadātpano dighāya* in G.

[4] A mistake for *etakāye*.

[5] A mistake for *ichhati*.

[6] A mistake for *palakamati*.

[7] *Pāratrikāya* in G.

[8] A mistake for *-paliṣave*.

[9] *Janena* in G.

[10] G. has *tata idaṁ bhavati*.

[11] A mistake for *-saṁstutena*.

LINE

so tatha karata[ṁ] ialoka cha a[ra]dheti paratra cha anataṁ puña prasavati [1]

3 [te]na dhrama-danena

XII

[GIRNAR]

1 Devānaṁpiye Piyad[a]si rājā sava-pāsaṁḍāni cha [pa]vajitāni cha gharastāni cha pūjayati d[ā]nena cha vivādhāya [2] [cha] pūjāya pūjayati ne

2 na tu tathā dānaṁ va pū[jā] va D[e]vānaṁpiyo maṁñate yathā kiti sāra-vadhī asa sa[va-pā]saṁḍānaṁ sār[a]-vadhī tu bahuvidhā

3 tasa tu idaṁ mūlaṁ ya vachi-gutī kiṁti ātpa-pāsaṁḍapūjā va para-pāsaṁḍa-garahā va no bhave aprakaraṇaṁhi lahukā va asa

4 tamhi tamhi prakaraṇe pūjetayā tu eva para-pāsaṁḍā tena tana [3] prakareṇa [4] evaṁ karuṁ ātpa-pāsaṁḍaṁ cha [5] vaḍhayati para-pāsaṁḍasa cha upakaroti

5 tad-aṁñathā karoto ātpa-pāsaḍaṁ cha chhaṇati [6] parapāsaṁḍasa cha pi apakaroti yo hi kochi ātpa-pāsaṁḍaṁ pūjayati para-pāsaṁdaṁ v[a] garahati

6 savaṁ ātpa-pāsaṁḍa-bhatiyā kiṁti ātpa-pāsaṁḍaṁ dīpayema iti so cha puna tatha karāto [7] ātpa-pāsaṁda[ṁ] bādhataraṁ upahanāti ta samavāyo [8] eva sādhu

7 kiṁti [a]ñamaṁñasa dhaṁmaṁ sruṇāru cha susuṁsera cha evaṁ hi D[e]vānaṁpiyasa ichhā kiṁti sava-pāsaṁḍā bahu-srutā cha asu kal[ā]ṇāgamā cha [a]su

8 ye cha tatra tata prasaṁnā tehi vatavyaṁ Devānaṁpiyo no tathā dānaṁ va pūjāṁ va maṁñate

[1] Sans. *prasavyate* ; G. has *bhavati*.

[2] A mistake for *vividhāya*.

[3] A mistake for *tena*.

[4] *Akarena* in S. and M.

[5] *Baḍhaṁ* in K. and M.

[6] *Kṣaṇati* in S.

[7] A mistake for *karoto*. The five words from this are repeated by mistake in S.

[8] *Sayamo* in S.

LINE

yathā kiṁti sāra-vaḍhī asa sarva-pāsadānaṁ
bahakā [1] cha etāya
9 athā [2] vyāpatā dhaṁma-mahāmātā cha ithījhakha [3]-mahāmātā cha vachabhūmikā [4] cha añe cha nikāyā
ayaṁ cha etasa phala ya ātpa-pāsaṁda-vaḍhī cha hoti
dhaṁmasa cha dīp[a]nā

XIII

[SHAHBAZGARHI]

1 [aṭha]-vaṣa-a[bhis]ita[sa Devana]pri[a]sa Pri[a]draśisa ra[ño]
Ka[liga] vi[j]ita [5]
diaḍha-mat[r]e praṇa-śata-[saha]sre y[e] tato apavuḍhe
śata-sahasra-matre [6] tatra hate [7] bahu-tavata[ke va] m[uṭe]
2 tato [pa]cha a[dhu]na ladh[e]ṣu [Kaligeṣu tivre dhramaśilana] [8] dhra[ma-ka]mata dhramanuśasti cha Devanapriyasa
so [a]sti anusochana Devanap[ria]sa vijiniti Kaliga[ni]
3 avijitaṁ [hi vi]jinamano yo tat[r]a vadha va maraṇaṁ va
apavaho va janasa taṁ baḍhaṁ v[e]dani[ya]-ma[taṁ]
guru-mata[ṁ] cha Devanaṁpriyasa
idaṁ pi chu [tato] guru-matataraṁ [Devanaṁ]priyasa ye
tatra
4 vasati bramaṇa va śrama[ṇa] [9] va a[ṁ]ñe va praṣaṁda
gra[ha]tha [10] va yesu vihita eṣa agrabhuṭi-suśruṣa matapituṣu suśruṣa guruna suśruṣa mitra-saṁstuta-sahaya-
5 ñatikeṣu dasa-bhaṭakanaṁ samma-pratipa[ti] driḍha-bhatita
teṣa tatra bhoti [a]pag[r]atho [11] va vadho va abhiratana va
nikramaṇaṁ [12]

[1] A mistake for *bahukā*.

[2] *Etāyāṭhāve* (K.).

[3] *Ithidhiyakha-* (K.) ; *istridhiyakṣa-* (S.) ; *istrijakṣa-* (M.).

[4] *Vracha-* (M.).

[5] *Kaligyā vijitā* in K.

[6] *Sata-sahasra-mātram* (G.).

[7] *Tatrā hataṁ* (G.).

[8] *Dhaṁmavāyo* (G.).

[9] *Brāhmaṇa* precedes the *śramaṇa* here in every version.

[10] *Gihithā* (K.).

[11] *Upaghāte* in K.

[12] *Vinikhamaṇa* in G.

LINE

yeṣa va pi suvihitanaṁ [si]ho [1] aviprahino [e te]ṣa mitra-saṁstuta-sahaya-ñatika vasana

6 prapuṇati [ta]tra taṁ pi teṣa vo apaghratho bhoti
pratibhagaṁ cha [e]taṁ savra-manuśanaṁ guru-mataṁ cha Devanaṁpriya[sa]
nasti [2] cha ekatare pi praṣaḍaspi na nama prasado
so yamatro [3] [ja]no tada Kalige [ha]to cha muṭ[o] cha apav[uḍha] cha tato

7 śata-bhage va sahasra-bhagaṁ va [a]ja guru-mataṁ v[o] Devanaṁpriyasa
yo pi cha apakareyati kṣamitaviya-mate va Devanaṁp[r]iyasa yaṁ śako kṣamanaye
ya pi cha aṭavi Devanaṁpriyasa vijite bhoti ta pi anuneti anunijapeti [4]
anutape pi cha prabhave

8 Devanaṁpriyasa vuchati teṣa kiti avatrapeyu na cha [ha]ṁñeyasu
ichhati hi D[e]vanaṁpriyo savra-bhutana akṣati sa[ṁ]yamaṁ sama[cha]riyaṁ rabhasiye [5]
ayi cha mukha-mut[a] vijaye Devanaṁpriya[sa] yo dhrama-vijayo
so cha puna ladho Devanaṁpriyasa iha cha saveṣu cha aṁteṣu

9 [a] ṣaṣu pi yojana-śa[t]eṣu yatra Aṁtiyoko nama Y[o]na-raja paraṁ cha tena Atiyok[e]na [6] chature 4 rajani Turamaye nama Aṁtikini nama Maka [7] nama Alikasudaro nama nicha Choḍa-Paṁḍa ava Ta[ṁ]bapaṁ[ṇi]ya
[e]vameva [hi]da raja-viṣavaspi [8] Yona-Ka[ṁ]boyeṣu Nabhaka-Nabhitina [9]

[1] A mistake for *sineho*.

[2] Here Kalsi (as well as Mansehra) offers the following variant:
Nathi chā ṣe jan[a]pade yatā nathi ime nikāyā ānatā Y[o]neṣ[u].
baṁhmane ch[ā] ṣamane chā nathi chā kuvāpi jan[a]padaṣi
[ya]tā n[a]thi m[a]nuṣān[a] ekatalaṣ[i] pi pāṣaḍaṣi

[3] *Yāvatako* (G.).

[4] A mistake for *anunijhapeti*; M. has *anunijhapayati*.

[5] *Mādava* (G.).

[6] *Aṁtiyogenā* (K.).

[7] *Magā* (G.).

[8] *Rāja-visayamhi* (G.).

[9] *Nābhaka-Nābhapaṁtiṣu* (K. and M.).

LINE
10 Bhoja-Pitinikeṣu Aṁdhra-Palideṣu [1] savatra Devanaṁpriyasa dhramanuśasti anuvaṭaṁti
yatra pi Devanaṁpriyasa duta no vrachaṁti [2] te pi
śrutu Devanaṁpriyasa dhrama-vuṭaṁ vidh[a]naṁ
dhramanuśasti dhramaṁ [a]nuvidhiyiśaṁ[ti] cha
yo [sa] ladhe etakena bho[ti] savatra vijayo sava[tra] pu[na]
11 vijayo priti-raso so
ladha bh[oti] priti dhrama-vijayaspi
lahuka tu kho so priti
paratri[ka]meva maha-phala meñati Devana[ṁ]priyo
etaye cha aṭhaye ayi dhrama-dipi nipi[sta] kiti putra
papotra me asu navaṁ vijayaṁ ma vijetav[i]a [3] mañiṣu
spa[kaspi] [4] yo vijay[e kṣaṁ]ti [5] cha lahu-da[ṁ]ḍata cha
rochetu taṁ cha yo vija [6] maña[tu]
12 yo dhrama-vijayo
so hidalokiko paralokiko
sava-chati-rati bhotu ya [dh]raṁma-rati
sa hi hidalokika paralokika [7]

XIV

[GIRNAR]

1 ayaṁ dhaṁma-lipī [8] Devānaṁpriyena Priyadasinā [9] r[ā]ñā
l[e]khāpitā [10] asti eva

[1] *Pāriṁdesu* (G.), *Pāladeṣu* (K.).

[2] *Yaṁti* (K. and M.).

[3] *Vijetavyaṁ* (G.), *vijayataviya* (K.).

[4] *Sarasake* (G.), *ṣayakaṣi* (K.).

[5] *Chhāti* (G.).

[6] A mistake for *vijayaṁ*.

[7] Below the Girnar text on the *left* side occur two mutilated lines. In the first line Hultzsch recovers the word *t[eṣa]*, which he takes to be a part of the well-known Buddhist formula—"*hetuṁ teṣāṁ Tathāgato hyavadat* | *teṣāṁ cha*," etc. In the second line he recovers the letters *[p]i[p]ā*, and supposes it to have been followed by the word *lipikareṇa*.

On the *right* side of the same text occur the following words: "*[Sa]rva-sveto hasti sarva-loka-sukhāharo nāma*," "the altogether white elephant, the bringer of bliss for the whole world."

[8] *Dhrama-dipi* (S. and M.).

[9] *Priśi[na]* in S., a mistake for *Priyadraśina*.

[10] *Nipesapita* in S.

LINE

2 saṁkhit[e]na asti maȷhamena asti vistatana [1]
na cha [2] sarvaṁ [ṣa]rvata ghaṭitaṁ [3]

3 mahālake hi vijitaṁ bahu cha likhitaṁ likhāpayisaṁ cheva [4]
asti cha eta kaṁ [5]

4 puna puna vutaṁ [6] tasa tasa athasa mādhuratāya kiṁti [7]
jano tathā paṭipajetha

5 tatra ekadā [8] asamāt[a]ṁ likhitaṁ asa desaṁ [9] va sachhāya [10] [kā]ranaṁ va

6 [a]lochetpā lipikarāparadhena va [11]

E. The Seven Pillar Edicts

I

1 Devānaṁpiye Piyadasi lāja hevaṁ āhā
saḍuvīsati-

2 vasa-abhisitena me iyaṁ dhaṁma-lipi likhāpitā

3 hidata-pālate dusaṁpaṭipādaye aṁnata agāyā dhaṁma-kāmatāyā

4 agāya palīkhāyā agāya su[sū]yāyā agena bhayenā

5 agena usāhena
esa chu kho mama anusathiyā

6 dhaṁmāpekhā dhaṁma-kāmatā chā suve suve vaḍhitā
vaḍhīsati chevā

7 pulisā pi cha me ukasā chā gevayā chā majhimā chā anuvidhīyaṁtī

8 saṁpaṭipādayaṁti chā alaṁ chapalaṁ samādapayitave
hemevā aṁta-

[1] A mistake for *vistatena* ; *vithaṭenā* (K. and J.) ; *vistriṭena* (S.).

[2] *Hi* =for, in other versions.

[3] *Gaṭite* in S., a mistake for *ghatite*.

[4] K. adds after this the word *nikyaṁ* =*nityaṁ*, constantly.

[5] Instead of *eta kaṁ*, K. has *hetā*, S. and M. have *atra*.

[6] *Lapitaṁ* (S.).

[7] *Yena* in K., S., and M.

[8] There are the following variants for *tatra ekadā* :

K. *ṣe ṣāyā ata k[i]chhi*

S. *so siyā va atra kiche*

D. and J. } *e pi chu heta asamati*

[9] *Diṣā* (K.), *deśaṁ* (S.).

[10] *Saṁkhaya* (S. and M.), *ṣaṁkheye* (K.).

[11] *Dipikarasa va aparadhena* (S.).

LINE

9 mahāmātā pi
esa hi vidhi yā iyaṁ dhaṁmena pālanā dhaṁmena vidhāne
10 dhaṁmena sukhiyanā dhaṁmena gotī ti

II

1 Devānaṁpiye Piyadasi lāja
2 hevaṁ āhā
dhaṁme sādhū kiyaṁ chu dhaṁme ti
apāsinave bahu kayāne
3 dayā dāne sache sochaye
chakhu-dāne pi me bahuvidhe diṁne dupada-
4 chatupadesu pakhi-vālichalesu vividhe me anugahe kaṭe ā pāna-
5 dākhināye
aṁnāni pi cha me bahūni kayānāni kaṭāni
etāye me
6 aṭhāye iyaṁ dhaṁma-lipi likhāpitā hevaṁ anupaṭipajaṁtu chilaṁ-
7 thitikā cha hotū tī ti
ye cha hevaṁ saṁpaṭipajīsati se sukaṭaṁ kachhatī ti

III

1 Devānaṁpiye Piyadasi lāja hevaṁ ahā
kayānaṁmeva dekhati iyaṁ me
2 kayāne l-aṭe ti
no mina pāpaṁ d[e]khati iyaṁ me pāpe kaṭe ti iyaṁ vā āsinave
3 nāmā ti
dupaṭivekhe chu kho esā
hevaṁ chu kho esa dekhiye
imānī
4 āsinava-gāmīni nāma atha chaḍṁiye niṭhūliye kodhe māne isyā
5 kālanena va hakaṁ mā palibhasayisaṁ
esa bādha dekhiye
iyaṁ me
6 hidatikāye iyaṁmana me pālatikāye

IV

LINE

1 Devānaṁpiye Piyadasi l[ā]ja hevaṁ āhā
saḍuvīsati-vasa-
2 abhisitena me iyaṁ dhaṁma-lipi likhāpitā
lajūkā me
3 bahūsu pāna-sata-sahasesu janasi āyatā
tesaṁ ye abhihāle vā
4 daṁḍe vā ata-patiye me kaṭe kiṁti lajūkā asvatha abhītā
5 kaṁmāni pavatayevū janasa jānapadasā hita-sukhaṁ upadahevū
6 anugahinevu chā
sukhīyana-dukhīyanaṁ jānisaṁti dhaṁma-yutena cha
7 viyovadisaṁti janaṁ jānapadaṁ kiṁti hidataṁ cha pālataṁ cha
8 ālādhayevū ti
lajūkā pi laghaṁti paṭichalitave maṁ
pulisāni pi me
9 chhaṁdaṁnāni paṭichalisaṁti
te pi cha kāni viyovadisaṁti yena maṁ lajūkā
10 chaghaṁti ālādhayitave
athā hi pajaṁ viyatāye dhātiye nisijitu
11 asvathe hoti viyata dhāti chaghati me pajaṁ sukhaṁ palihaṭave
12 hevaṁ mamā lajūkā kaṭā jānapadasa hita-sukhāye
yena ete abhītā
13 asvatha saṁtaṁ avimanā kaṁmāni pavatayevū ti etena me lajūkānaṁ
14 abh[i]hāle va daṁḍe vā ata-patiye kaṭe
ichhitaviye [h]i esā kiṁti
15 viyohāla-samatā cha siya daṁḍa-samatā chā
ava ite pi cha me āvuti
16 baṁdhana-badhānaṁ munisānaṁ tīl[i]ta-daṁḍānaṁ patavadhānaṁ tiṁni divasā[n]i me
17 yote diṁne
nātikā va kāni nijhapayisaṁti jīvitāye tānaṁ
18 nāsaṁtaṁ vā nijhapayitā[1] dānaṁ dāhaṁti pālatikaṁ
upavāsaṁ va kachhaṁti
19 ichhā hi me hevaṁ niludhasi pi kālasi pālataṁ ālādhayevū ti
janasa cha
20 vaḍhati vividhe dhaṁma-chalane saṁyame dāna-savibhāge ti

[1] *Nijhapayitave* in the three Bihar P.E.

V

LINE
1 Devānaṁpiye Piyadasi lāja hevaṁ ahā
saḍuvīsati-vasa-
2 abhisitena me imāni jātāni avadhiyāni kaṭāni seyathā
3 suke sālikā alune chakavāke haṁse naṁdīmukhe gelāṭe
4 jatūkā aṁbā-kapīlikā daḷī anaṭhika-machhe vedaveyake
5 Gaṁgā-pupuṭake saṁkuja-machhe kaphaṭ[a]-sayake paṁnasase simale
6 saṁḍake okapiṁḍe palasate seta-kapote gāma-kapote
7 save chatupade ye paṭibhogaṁ no eti na cha khādiyatī
. . . . i [1]
8 [e]ḷakā chā sūkalī chā gabhinī va pāyamīnā va avadhi[y.
p.ta]ke [2]
9 pi cha kāni āsaṁmāsike
vadhi-kukuṭe no kaṭaviye
tuse sajīve
10 no jhāpetaviye
dāve anaṭhāye vā vihisāye vā no jhāpetaviye
11 jīvena jīve no pusitaviye
tīsu chātuṁmāsīsu tisāyaṁ [3] puṁnamāsiyaṁ
12 tiṁni divasāni chāvudasaṁ paṁnadasaṁ paṭipadāy[e]
dhuvāye chā
13 anuposathaṁ machhe avadhiye no pi viketaviye
etāni yevā divasāni
14 nāga-vanasi kevaṭa-bhogasi yāni aṁnāni pi jīva-nikāyāni
15 no haṁtaviyāni
aṭhamī-pakhāye chāvudasāye paṁnadasāye tisāye
16 punāvasune tīsu chātuṁmāsīsu sudivasāye gone no nīlakhitaviye
17 ajake edake sūkale e vā pi aṁne nīlakhiyati no nīlakhitaviye
18 tisāye punāvasune chātuṁmāsiye chātuṁmāsi-pakhāye
asvasā gonasā
19 lakhane no kaṭaviye
yāva-saḍuvīsati-vasa-abhisitena me etāye
20 aṁtalikāye paṁnavīsati baṁdhana-mokhāni kaṭāni

[1] *Ajakā nāni* in three other versions.

[2] Restore *avadhiyā potake*.

[3] From *tisā* = *tiṣyā* ; other versions use the form *tisiyaṁ* from *tisi*.

VI

LINE
1 Devānaṁpiye Piyadasi lāja hevaṁ ahā
  duvādasa-
2 vasa-abhisitena me dhaṁma-lipi likhāpitā lokasā
3 hita-sukhāye se taṁ apahaṭā taṁ taṁ dhaṁma-vaḍhi
  pāpovā
4 hevaṁ lokasā hita-[sukhe] ti paṭivekhāmi atha iyaṁ
5 nātisu hevaṁ patiyāsaṁnesu hevaṁ apakaṭhesu
6 kimaṁ [1] kāni sukhaṁ avahāmī ti tat.ia cha vidahāmi
  hemevā
7 sava-nikāyesu paṭivekhāmi
  sava-pāsaṁdā pi me pūjitā
8 vividhāya pūjāyā
  e chu iyaṁ at[a] nā pachūpagamane
9 se me mokhya-mate
  saḍuvīsati-vasa-abhisitena me
10 iyaṁ dhaṁma-lipi likhāpitā

VII

LINE
1 Devānaṁpiye Piyadasi lājā hevaṁ āhā
  ye atikaṁtaṁ
2 aṁtalaṁ lājāne husu hevaṁ ichhisu kathaṁ jane
3 dhaṁma-vaḍhiyā vaḍheyā no chu jane anulupāyā dhaṁma-
  vaḍhiyā
4 vaḍhithā
  etaṁ Devānaṁpiye Piyadasi lājā hevaṁ āhā
  esa me
5 huthā
  atikaṁtaṁ cha aṁtaṁl[a]ṁ [2] hevaṁ ichhisu lājāne kathaṁ
  jane
6 anulupāyā dhaṁma-vaḍhiyā vaḍheyā ti no cha jane anulupāyā
7 dhaṁma-vaḍhiyā vaḍhithā
  se kinasu jane anu[pa]ṭipajeyā
8 kinasu jane anulupāyā dhaṁma-vaḍhiyā vaḍheyā ti
  k[i]nasu kāni
9 abhyuṁnāmayehaṁ dhaṁma-vaḍhiyā ti
  etaṁ Devānaṁpiye Piyadasi lājā hevaṁ

---

[1] *Kiṁmaṁ* in the Bihar versions.

[2] A mistake for *aṁtalaṁ*.

LINE
10 āhā
esa me huthā
dhaṁma-sāvanāni sāvāpayāmi dhaṁmānusathini
11 anus[ā]sāmi
etaṁ jane sutu anupaṭīpajīsati abhyuṁnamisati
12 dhaṁma-vaḍhiyā cha bāḍhaṁ vaḍhisat[i]
etāye me aṭhāye dhaṁma-sāvanāni sāvāpitāni dhaṁmānusathini vividhānī ānapitāni [ya] . . . . . [is]ā [1] pi bahune janasi āyatā e te paliyovadisaṁti pi pavithalisaṁti pi lajūkā pi bahukesu pāna-sata-sahasesu āyatā te pi me ānapitā hevaṁ cha hevaṁ cha paliyovadātha
13 janaṁ dhaṁma-yu[ta]ṁ
[Dev]ānaṁpiye Piyadasi hevaṁ āhā
etameva me anuve-khamāne dhaṁma-thaṁbhāni kaṭāni dhaṁma-mahāmātā kaṭā dhaṁ[ma] . ā . . . e [2] kaṭe
Devānaṁpiye Piyadasi lājā hevaṁ āhā
magesu pi me nigohāni lopāpitāni chhāyopagāni hosaṁti pasu-munisānaṁ aṁbā-vaḍikyā lopāpitā
aḍha-[kos]ikyāni pi me udupānāni
14 khānāpāpitāni niṁsi[dha]yā cha kālāpitā
āpānāni me ba[h]ukāni tata tata k[ā]lāpitāni paṭībho-gāye p[a]su-munisānaṁ
[la] . . . . . [3] esa paṭībhoge nāma
vividhāyā hi sukhāyanāyā pulimehi pi lājīhi mamayā cha sukhayite loke
imaṁ chu dhaṁmānupaṭīpatī anupaṭīpajaṁtu ti etadathā me
15 esa kaṭe
Devānaṁpiye Piyadasi hevaṁ āhā
dhaṁma-mahāmātā pi me te bahuvidhesu aṭhesu ānugahikesu viyāpaṭāse pavajītānaṁ cheva gihithānaṁ cha sava . . . . [d]esu [4] pi cha viyāpaṭāse
saṁghaṭhasi pi me kaṭe ime viyāpaṭā hohaṁti ti hemeva bābhanesu Ā[j]īvikesu pi me kaṭe
16 ime viyāpaṭā hohaṁti ti Nigaṁṭhesu pi me kaṭe ime viyāpaṭā hohaṁti nānā-pāsaṁdesu pi me [ka]ṭe ime viyāpaṭā hohaṁti ti paṭivisiṭhaṁ paṭīvisiṭhaṁ tesu tesu [te] . . . . . mātā [5]
dhaṁma-mahāmātā chu me etesu cheva viyā[pa]ṭā savesu

[1] Restore *yathā pulisā.*

[2] I.e., *dhaṁma-sāvane.*

[3] Restore *lahuke chu.*

[4] Restore *sava-pāsaṁḍesu.*

[5] Restore *te te mahāmātā.*

LINE

cha aṁnesu pāsaṁḍesu
Devānaṁpiye Piyadasi lājā hevaṁ āhā
17 ete cha aṁne cha bahukā mukhā dāna-visagasi viyāpaṭāse
mama cheva devinaṁ cha savasi cha me olodhanasi te
bahuvidhena ā[kā]lena tāni tāni tuṭhāyatan[ā]ni paṭī
. . . . . . [1] hida cheva disāsu cha
dālakānaṁ pi cha me kaṭe aṁnānaṁ cha devi-kumālānaṁ
ime dāna-visagesu viyāpaṭā hohaṁti ti
18 dhaṁmāpadānaṭhāye dhaṁmānupaṭipatiye
esa hi dhaṁmāpadāne dhaṁmapaṭīpati cha yā iyaṁ dayā
dāne sache sochave madave sādha[v]e cha lokasa hevaṁ
vaḍhisati ti Devānaṁpiye [P. . . . . s . [2] l]ājā hevaṁ āhā
yāni hi [k]ānichi mamiyā sādhavāni kaṭāni taṁ loke
anūp[a]ṭīpaṁne taṁ cha anuvidhiyaṁti
tena vaḍhitā cha
19 vaḍhisaṁti cha mātā-pit[i]su sususāyā gulusu sususāyā vayo-
mahālakānaṁ anupaṭīpatiyā bābhana-samanesu kapana-
valākesu āva dāsa-bhaṭakesu saṁpaṭīpatiyā
Devānaṁp[iy . . . ya]dasi [3] lājā hevaṁ āhā
munisānaṁ chu yā iyaṁ dhaṁma-vaḍhi vaḍhitā duvehi
yeva ākālehi dhaṁma-niyamena cha nijhatiyā [cha]
20 tata chu lahu se dhaṁma-niyame nijhatiyā va bhuye
dhaṁma-niyame chu kho esa ye me iyaṁ kaṭe imāni cha
imāni jātāni avadhiyāni
aṁnāni pi chu bahu[k] . . . [4] dhaṁma-niyamāni yāni me
kaṭāni
nijhatiyā va chu bhuye munisānaṁ dhaṁma-vaḍhi vaḍhitā
avihiṁsāye bhutānaṁ
21 anālaṁbhāye pānānaṁ
se etāye a[th]āye iyaṁ kaṭe putāpapotike chaṁdamasu-
liyike hotu ti tathā cha anupaṭīpajaṁtu ti
hevaṁ hi anupaṭīpajaṁtaṁ hi[da]ta-[pāla]te āladhe hoti
satavisati-vasābhis[i]tena me iyaṁ dhaṁma-libi likhā-
pāpitā ti
etaṁ Devānaṁpiye āhā
iyaṁ
22 dhaṁma-libi ata athi silā-thaṁbhāni vā silā-phalakāni vā
tata kaṭaviyā ena esa chila-ṭhitike siyā

[1] *Paṭīpādayaṁti* according to Bühler ; *paṭīvedayaṁtu*.

[2] Restore *Piyadasi*.

[3] Restore *-piye Piyadasi*.

[4] Restore *bahukāni*.

F. The Four Minor Pillar Edicts

I

LINE [Sarnath]

1 Devā [1] . . . .

2 el . . . .

3 Pāṭa [2] . . . . ye [3] kenapi saṁghe bhetave
e chuṁ kho

4 [bhikh]ū [vā bhikh]uni vā saṁghaṁ bh[ākha]t[i] [4] s[e]
odātāni dus[ān]i [sa]ṁnaṁdhāpayiyā ānāvāsasi

5 āvāsayiye
hevaṁ iyaṁ sāsane bhikhu-saṁghasi cha bhikhuni-saṁghasi cha viṁnapayitave

6 hevaṁ Devānaṁpiye āhā
hedisā cha ikā lipī tuphākaṁtikaṁ huvāti saṁsalanasi nikhitā

7 ikaṁ cha lipiṁ hedisameva upāsakānaṁtikaṁ nikhipātha
te pi cha upāsakā anuposathaṁ yāvu

8 etameva sāsanaṁ visvaṁsayitave anuposathaṁ cha dhuvāye
ikike mahāmāte posathāye

9 yāti etameva sāsanaṁ visvaṁsayitave ājānitave cha
āvate cha tuphākaṁ āhāle

10 savata vivāsayātha tuphe etena viyaṁjanena
hemeva savesu koṭa-viṣavesu etena

11 viyaṁjanena vivāsāpayāthā

II

[Kauśāmbī]

1 [Devānaṁ][p]iye ānapayati
Kosaṁbiyaṁ mahām[ā]ta

2 . . . . [sa]ma[ge ka]ṭe
sa[ṁ]gh[a]si no l[a]hiye

3 . . . . [saṁghaṁ bhā]khati bhikh[u] v[ā] bhikh[u]ni vā [se pi] chā

4 [o]dāt[ā]ni dusāni [sa]naṁdhāpayitu a[nāvā]sas[i ā]v[ā]-sayiy[e]

[1] Restore *Devānaṁpiya.*

[2] I.e., Pāṭaliputra.

[3] Restored by Boyer as "*na sakiye.*"

[4] Read by Venis.

III

[Sāñchī]

LINE

1 . . . .

2 . . [y]ā bhe[ta] . . [1]

. . [gh]e [2] . . . . mage [3] kaṭe

3 [bhi]khūna[ṁ] cha bhi[khun]īnaṁ ch[ā] ti [p]uta-pa-

4 [po]tike chaṁ[da]m[a-sū]ri]yi]ke

ye saṁghaṁ

5 bh[ā]khati bhikhu vā bhikhuni vā odātā-

6 ni dus[ān]i sanaṁ[dhāpay]itu aṅā[vā]-

7 sasi vā[sā]petaviy[e]

ichhā hi me kiṁ-

8 ti saṁghe samage chila-thitīke siyā ti

IV

[Queen's Edict]

1 Devānaṁpiyaṣā v[a]chanenā savata mahamatā

2 vataviyā.

e hetā dutiyāye devīye dāne

3 aṁbā-vaḍikā vā ālame va dāna-[gah]e [va e vā pi a]ṁne

4 kīchhi ganīyati tāye deviye ṣe nāni

[he]vaṁ . .[na] . . [4]

5 dutīyāye deviye ti Tīvala-mātu Kāluvākiye

G. The Commemorative Pillar Inscriptions

I

[Rummindei]

1 Devāna[pi]yena Piyadasina lājina vīsati-vasābhisitena

2 atana āgācha mahīyite hida Budhe jāte Sakyamunī ti

3 silā vigaḍabhī chā kālāpita silā-thabhe cha usapāpite

4 hida Bhagavaṁ jāte ti

Luṁmini-gāme ubalike kaṭe

5 aṭha-bhāgiye cha

[1] Restore *bhetave*, as in Sar. M.P.E, l. 3.

[2] Restore *saṁghe*.

[3] Restore *samage*, as in l. 8.

[4] Hultzsch restores *vinati* = Sans. *vijñapti*.

II

[NIGLIVA]

LINE
1 Devānaṁpiyena Piyadasina lājina chodasavasā[bh]i[si]-t[e]n[a]
2 Budhasa Konākamanasa thube dutiyaṁ vaḍhite
3 . . . . sābhisitena [1] cha atana āgācha mahīyite
4 . . . . pāpite [2]

H. THE CAVE INSCRIPTIONS

I

[NIGRODHA]

1 lājinā Piyadasinā duvādasa-[vasābhisitenā]
2. [iyaṁ Nigoha-]kubhā di[nā Ājīvikehi]

II

[KHALATIKA HILL]

1 lājinā Piyadasinā duvā-
2 dasa-vasābhisitenā iyaṁ
3 kubhā Khalatika-pavatasi
4 dinā [Ājīvi]kehi

III

[KHALATIKA HILL, NO. 2]

1 lāja Piyadasī ekunavī-
2 sati-vasā[bh]isi[t]e ja[lagh]o-
3 [sāgama]thāta [me] i[yaṁ kubhā]
4 su[p]i[y]e Kha . . . . [3] [di]-
5 nā [4]

[1] Bühler restored *vīsati-vasābhisitena*, as in l. 1 of Rummindei P.I.

[2] Bühler restored *silā-thabhe cha usapāpite* after l. 3 of Rum. P.I.

[3] Restore *Khalatikapavatasi*.

[4] At the end of the inscription are figured a *svastika* and a dagger with a fish below them. V. H. Jackson reads the fourth line as " *supiye kha Ājīvikehi di-* " [*JBORS*, xii. 52], on the ground that there is room in the vacant space of the inscription for only *five* and not *ten* letters as supposed by Hultzsch.

APPENDIX C

ON THE SCRIPT, DIALECT, AND GRAMMAR OF THE INSCRIPTIONS

THE Asokan Inscriptions are written in two scripts known as Kharoṣṭhi and Brāhmī. The former is a cursive script written from right to left, and is traced to a Semitic origin, the Aramaic script, in which wrote the clerks of the Achaemenian Emperor, Darius, of Persia, as distinguished from the monumental cuneiform in which are written that great emperor's inscriptions at Persepolis, Nakshi-rustam, or Behistun. Sylvain Levi calls the script Kharoṣṭrī after the name of the country of Kharoṣṭra just outside India, where it was first traced. One peculiarity of this script is that it does not mark *long* vowels. Of the Asokan inscriptions, only those at Shahbazgarhi and Mansehra, and the short note of the scribe, Chapaḍa, at the end of the Mysore versions of the Minor Rock Edict II, are written in this script.

The other inscriptions of Asoka are all written in the popular Brāhmī script running from left to right, the parent of all Indian scripts, including Burmese, Tibetan, and even Sinhalese. But even this script Bühler has sought to trace to a Semitic source, and its introduction in India to her trade with Mesopotamia dating from about 800 B.C. The connection of Brāhmī with a Semitic prototype is, however, far less obvious than that of Kharoṣṭhī with Aramaic, and is now being widely disputed. Cunningham first disputed it on the ground that Brāhmī, unlike the Semitic scripts, was always written from left to right. But Bühler has shown how Brāhmī, too, was originally written from right to left, of which relics are traced in even the Asokan inscriptions in the reversed forms of certain single letters like *dh*, *t*, and *o*, and of certain conjunct consonants like *tpa*, *sta*, and *vya*, which are written as if they were *pta*, *tsa*, and *yva*, or in such words as *dhrama*, *krama*, and *mrugo* for *dharma*, *karma*, and *murgo*. The theory of the indigenous origin of the Brāhmī has, nevertheless, been stoutly maintained by some scholars on the strength of certain prehistoric writings traced on primitive pottery recently

PLATE XV.

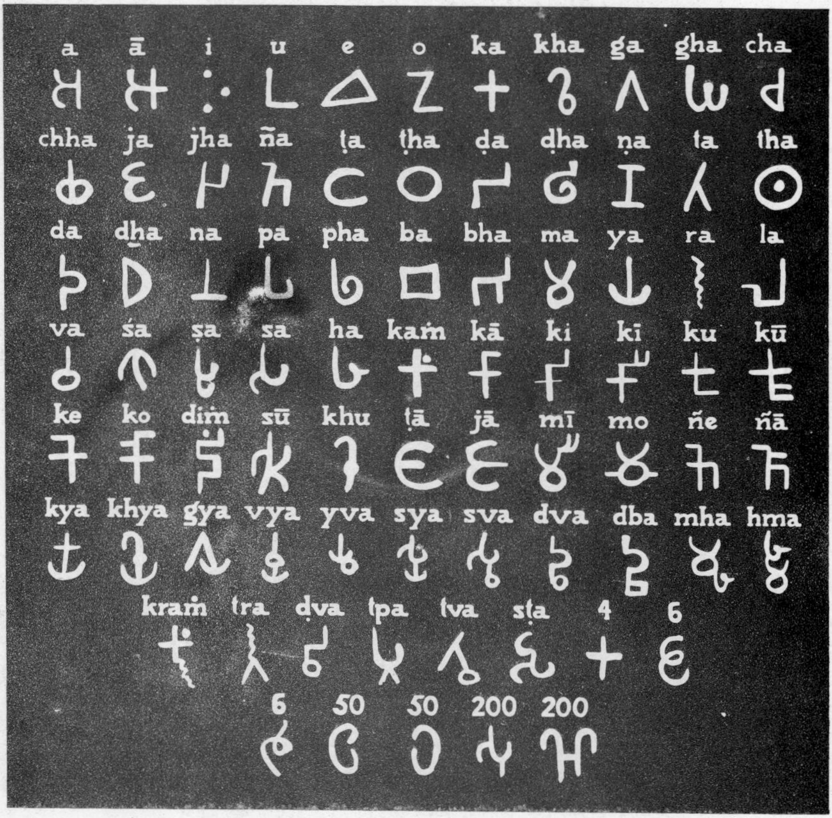

ASOKAN ALPHABET.

discovered in some cairns in the Nizam's dominion, which very closely resemble the Asokan characters.

It is, however, quite clear that for both the scripts and the alphabets in the developed forms in which they are found and used in the inscriptions of Asoka, we must allow for the time taken in such development. They must have been developing for centuries before we come to their finished forms in the time of Asoka. And this fact should be taken into account in its bearings on the origin of the Brāhmī script, on which there is besides a large body of very old evidence from a Vedic work like the *Satapatha Brāhmaṇa* which knows of distinctions of number and gender, from Pāṇini, and from the *Vinaya Piṭaka*, all pointing to the antiquity of writing in India.

The differences of form and grammar exhibited in the Edicts show that they were composed in two broadly distinguished dialects. One of these may be called the *Eastern*, represented in the Dhauli and Jaugada Rock Edicts, as also in most of the Pillar Edicts. It may be recognised by its chief peculiarities of having nom. sing. in *e*, *l* for *r*, loc. s. in *-asi*, and conjuncts assimilated. The other dialect may be called *Western*, and is represented in the Girnar version of the Edicts, with its special features, among them, of having nom. s. in *o*, the use of *r*, *pr*, *tr*, and loc. s. in *-amhi*.

The Eastern dialect was the standard and official language of Asoka's court, and served as a sort of *lingua franca* for his whole empire, admitting only of minor variations introduced by local speech, such as may be noticed in the language of the Kālsī Edicts in the north, and of Mysore in the south. Kālsī shows a tendency to lengthen the final *a*, and a peculiarity in its treatment of sibilants. The Mysore inscriptions do not substitute *l* for *r*, and use the palatal and cerebral nasals (as in *ñātika*, *prāṇesu*).

Of the Western language, the local variations are noticed in the Shahbazgarhi and Mansehra versions of the Edicts, where we find illustrated what was probably the official court language of the Viceroyalty of Taxila. One striking feature in the language of Girnar, Shahbazgarhi and Mansehra is its Sanskritisms such as *priya*, *putra*. This was due, however, not to the scribe's knowledge of Sanskrit, as is readily supposed, but because the local language of those places was in some respects more archaic, and, therefore, nearer to Sanskrit than Pāli or the Māgadhī of the Eastern inscriptions.

The Eastern, or the standard, language of the Asokan inscriptions may be described in a general way as Māgadhī, provided it is understood that it is not exactly the orthodox Māgadhī Prakrit of the grammar, or of the dramas. For instance, while Asoka's Māgadhī knows only of the dental sibilant as in *susūsā* (Kālsī, only, using *ṣuṣusā*), the Māgadhī Prakrit proper has only the palatal sibilant (*sussusā*).

It is evident that the dialect of the Shahbazgarhi and Mansehra redactions is much nearer to Sanskrit than the dialects of the other versions of the fourteen edicts. At the same time, as Michelson has pointed out, this dialect cannot be regarded as a mere lineal descendant of Sanskrit. It presents certain forms which establish its affinity to *Avestan* rather than Sanskrit; e.g. *atikrātam* (G.); *susrusā, susrusatām* (G.) corresponding to Avestan *susrusemno;* G. *sruṇāru,* Shb. *śruṇeyu,* and M. *śruṇeyu,* which agree with Avestan *surunaoiti* in structure as opposed to Sans. *śriṇoti.* Side by side with these archaic forms, this dialect also presents many recent ones, *Māgadhisms,* ear-marks of the *Middle-Indic* (Prakrit) stage of development, such as the assimilation of stops of one order to those of another order. These Māgadhisms occurring in the G., Shb., and M. recensions give the impression that they were simply taken over bodily from the original MS. and were really foreign to the spoken vernaculars of those localities. The original MS. of the edicts was composed in a dialect which was essentially the same as that represented in the Dhauli, Jaugada, and Kalsi recensions of the fourteen R.E., and in the six versions of the P.E. The Shb., Man., and Girnar redactions are translations, incorporating elements borrowed from this original, the Māgadhan dialect, the official imperial language, which must have been understood even where it was not spoken as a vernacular. It may be noted that there are traces of *Middle-Indic* even in the *Ṛigveda* so far as phonetics are concerned, while Epic Sanskrit teems with *Middle-Indicisms* morphologically. Thus the fact of the matter is that the dialect of Shb. and M. hardly belongs to the *Middle-Indic* (Prakrit) stage of development, and geographically this is just what may be expected.

Incidentally it may be noted that the theory generally held that during the period of the composition of the Vedic hymns two distinct groups of Indic dialects were developed and separated by an uncrossable gulf does not thus seem to be probable by this analogy of the Asokan dialects. If it is not possible to draw hard and fast lines in the time of Asoka, why should we assume such lines for earlier times? The conclusion of the matter, as put by Michelson, is that Sanskrit, though not in the very form in which it occurs in literature, was a truly *spoken* vernacular. Even the late classical Sanskrit cannot have been wholly artificial: the existence of such an enormous literature necessarily presupposes a large audience who normally spoke a language that did not differ from the written one too violently. That the audience belonged to cultivated circles of society goes without saying.

Thus the Asokan dialects throw interesting light on the obscure and difficult questions of the genetic relationship of the Middle-Indic (Ṗrakrit) dialects [see Michelson's writings, specially in *JAOS*, 30 and 33, on which this note is based].

The dialectical peculiarities and variations of the inscriptions may be illustrated by the following typical examples :

Sanskrit	*West Asokan*	*East Asokan*
Mṛigaḥ	Mago (G.), mrugo (S.)	Mige
Mayūrāḥ	Morā (G.), majura (S.)	Majulā
Vṛikṣāḥ	Vrachhā (G.) ruchhani (M.)	Lukhāni
Sthitvā	Tiṭhiti (S.)	Chiṭhitu
Chikitsā	Chikīchha	Chikisa
Atra	Eta	Heta
Tādriśam	Tārise	Tādise
Pulindeṣu	Pārimdesu (G.)	Pāladṣeu (K.)
Ātyayikam	Āchāyike	Atiyāyike
Gṛihastha	Grahatha, gharasta	Gahatha
Mṛitam	Muṭe, matam	Maṭe
Vyuṣṭena		Vyuṭhenā, vivuthena
Vistṛitena	Vistatana (G.) vistriṭena (S.)	Vithaṭenā
Pṛithivyām		Puṭhaviyam
Adhikṛiyta		Adhigichya
Parityajya	Parichajitpā (G.) paritijitu (S.)	Palitiditu, palitijitu
Toṣaḥ	Toso	Dose (K.)
Duṣprativ̇ekṣyam		Dupaṭivekhe
Nityam	Niche (?)	Nikyaṁ (K.) Nichaṁ
Satyam		Sache
Duṣkara	Dukare dukaraṁ	Dukale, dukalaṁ
Avarodhane	Orodhanamhi (G.), orodhanaspi (S.)	Olodhanasi
Kṣudraka	Chhudaka (G.), Khudraka (S.)	Khudaka
Iha	Idha, ia, hida	Ida, hida
Kṣamitum	Chhamitave, Kṣamanaye	Khamitave

It is to be noted that these dialectical differences are merely phonetic differences, and not any fundamental differences of grammar. Both the Western and Eastern dialects come under a common grammar, the grammar of the Magadhan court language of Pāṭaliputra. This grammar may be outlined as follows with reference to the declension of (*a*) Nouns and Adjectives, (*b*) Pronouns, (*c*) Numerals, and (*d*) Verbs, as illustrated in the inscriptions. From this outline are omitted those forms which do not show any departure from Sanskrit.

(*a*) NOUNS AND ADJECTIVES

1. MASCULINE AND NEUTER

		Nom.	*Acc.*	*Ins.*	*Dat.*	*Abl.*	*Gen.*	*Loc.*
(i.) In *-a* :								
	Sing.	Samāje[1] phale (n.)	Janaṁ pāpam (n.)	Dhaṁmena	Athāye[2]	Viyaṁ-janate[3]	Janasa	Vijitasi[4]
	Plur.	Aṁtā lukhāni[5] (n)	Pulisāni yutāni[6] (n.)	Devehi	—	—	Devānaṁ	Aṭhesu
(ii.) In *-i* :								
	Sing.	Piyadasi, asamati (n.)	—	Piyadasinā	Piyadasine	Suvaṁna-girīte	—	—
	Plur.	Āsinava-gāmīni (n.)	Hathīni	Lājīhi	—	—	N̄ātīnaṁ	N̄ātīsu
(iii.) In *-u* :								
	Sing.	Sādhu, bahu (n.)	—	—	—	Hetute[7]	—	Punāvasune, bahune (n.)
	Plur.	Bahūni (n.)	—	Bahūhi	—	—	Gulūnaṁ	Gulusu, bahūsu (n.)
(iv.) In *-an* :								
	Sing.	Lājā, kaṁme (n.)	Atānam, nāma (n.)	Lājinā[8] atanā, kaṁmana (n.)	Lājine, atane, kaṁmane (n.)	— —	Lājine,[9] atane, kammasa (n.)	—
	Plur.	Lājāne	kaṁmāni (n.)	Lājīhi	—	—	—	—
v.) In *-r* :								
	Sing.	Pitā, *but* nati, panati	—	Pitinā bhātinā	—	—	Mātu	Matari, pitari
	Plur.	Natāle	—	—	—	—	Nātinaṁ, bhātinam	Pitisu, nātisu
(vi.) In *-s* :								
	Sing.	Yaṣo (n.) *but* bhūye	—	—	Dighāvuse	—	—	—

[1] M. has *-a* in *Kartabhikara*. S. and G. have usually *-o* : *e.g. samājo, jano*. K. also has *Satiyaputo, Ketalaputo*.
As regards neut., we have such forms as *sachaṁ* (Br.), *anusāsanaṁ* (K.), *danā* (Mas.), *sasana* (M.). S. and G. have usually *-aṁ*.

[2] G. has *-āya* as in *athāya*.

[3] S., M., G. have *-to* as in *mukhato* ; G. has *vyaṁjanato*.

[4] Also *vijite* (S.), *vijitamhi* (G.) and *vijayaspi, vinitaspi* (M. and G.). G. has also *Pātalipute*.

[5] We have also such forms as *jātā, hālāpitā, lopāpitā* as nom. pl., neut

[6] G. has *yute*.

[7] S., G. have *hetuto*.

[8] *Rāña* (G.).

[9] *Rāño* (G.).

2. FEMININE

	Nom.	*Acc.*	*Ins.*	*Dat.*	*Abl.*	*Gen.*	*Loc.*
(i.) In *-ā :*							
Sing.	Susūsā	Susūsaṁ	Susūsāyā	Vāṣaniṣidi- yāye	Takhasilāte	Dutīyāye	Samāpāya tisāyaṁ, tisāye, palisāye, parisaye, parisāyaṁ
Plur.	Aṁbā- vaḍikā, upāsikā, chikisā palisā, mahiḍāyo (G.)	—	—	—	—	—	—
(ii.) In *-ī :*							
Sing.	Ithī, piti, vaḍhī	Saṁbodhi, *but* chhātiṁ	Nijhatiyā, bhatiyā	Vaḍhiye, vaḍhiyā (K.)	Ujenite	Devīye	Kosaṁbiyaṁ Tosaliyaṁ Tisāyam
Plur.	Niṁsidhiyā	Dhaṁma- nusathini	—	—	—	Devinaṁ, bhāginīnaṁ bhagininā	Chatuṁ- māsīsu,

(*b*) PRONOUNS

	Nom.	*Acc.*	*Ins.*	*Dat.*	*Abl.*	*Gen.*	*Loc.*
(i.) *1st Person :*							
Sing.	Hakaṁ, ahaṁ (S., M., G.)	Maṁ	Me, mayā, maya, mamayā	—	Mamate	Me, mama	—
Plur.	Maye	Aphe, apheni, ne (G.)	—	—	—	Aphākam,	Aphesu ne (=no)
(ii.) *2nd Person :*							
Plur.	Tuphe	Tuphe, tupheni, ve	—	Ve	—	Tuphākaṁ tupaka (Ru.)	Tuphesu
(iii.) *Demonstrative Pronoun, ta-, eta- :*							
Sing.							
Masc.	Se, So (S., G.), ese	Etaṁ, taṁ	Etena, etinā (Ru.), tena	Etāye, etiya (Ru.), taye, etāya (G.)	—	Etasa, etisa (S.), tasa, (taśa, taṣā, K.)	Tasi, etamhi, tamhi (G.), taśi (K.)
Fem.	Esā sā	Taṁ	—	Tāye	—	—	—
Neut.	Se, ese, esa, etaṁ (S.)	Etaṁ, taṁ, se	—	—	—	—	—
Plur.							
Masc.	Se, te, ete	—	Tehi	—	—	Etānaṁ, tesaṁ, teṣaṁ (S.) tānaṁ	Etesu, tesu
Fem.	Esā, tā (eṣa)						
Neut.	Etāni tāni						

(iv.) *Demonstrative Pronoun, ayam, ima*, etc. :

		Nom.	*Acc.*	*Ins.*	*Dat.*	*Gen.*	*Loc.*
Sing.	Masc.	Iyaṁ ayo (S.) ayaṁ (G.)	Imaṁ	Imena, iminā (G., Br., Sd.)	Imāye, imāya	Imasa imisa (S.)	Imamhi (G.)
	Fem.	Iyaṁ ayaṁ (S., G.) ayi (S., M.)	Imaṁ	—	Imāye, imāya	—	—
	Neut.	Iyaṁ iya (S., M.), iyo (S.), imaṁ, idaṁ (S., G.)	Imaṁ, iyaṁ, idaṁ	—	—	—	Imasi
Plur.	Masc.	Ime	—	Imehi	—		—
	Neut.	Imāni	—	—	—	—	—

(v.) *Relative Pronoun* :

		Nom.	*Acc.*	*Ins.*	*Dat.*	*Gen.*	*Loc.*
Sing.	Masc.	ye, e, yo (S., G.)	yaṁ	yena ena	—	yasa, asa, asā (K.)	—
	Fem.	yā, ā	yaṁ	—	—	—	—
	Neut.	Ye, e, yaṁ (ya) aṁ	ye, e yaṁ (ya), aṁ	—	—	—	—
Plur.	Masc.	Ye, e	—	—	—	Yesaṁ	Yesu
	Fem.	Yā (G.)	—	—	—	—	—
	Neut.	Yāni, āni	—	—	—	—	—

(c) NUMERALS

½, aḍha.
1, eke,
ikaṁ (Sn.).
1½, diyaḍha-
2, duve,
duvi (S.),
dvo, dve (G.).
2½, aḍhātiyāni.
3, tiṁni,
trayo (S.),
tri (G.).
4, chatu,
chatāli,
chature (S.),
chatpāro (G.).
5, paṁchasu
(loc.).
6, ṣaṣu (S., M., K., loc.).
8, aṭha, asta (S.).

10, dasa,
daśa (S., M.).
12, duvāḍasa,
dbādasa (G.),
badaya (S.)
=badaśa (Hlz.).
13, tedasa, tredaśa (M.).
13, chāvudasaṁ, chodasa (Nig.).
15, paṁnaḍasa, paṁchadasaṁ.
19, ekunavīsati.
20, vīsati.
25, paṁnavīsati.
26, saḍuvīsati.
27, satavisati.
56, sapaṁṅā- (?).
100, sata-, śata (S., M.).
1000, sahasāni, ṣahaṣa (K.),
sahasra (S., M., G.).

(*d*) VERBS

	1st Person.	2nd Person.	3rd Person.
1. *Present Indicative :*			
Sing.	Ichhāmi	—	Ichhati, maṁnate (*ātmanepadam*) dukhīyati (*passive*)
Plur.	—	Pāpunātha	Ichhaṁti, ālabhiyaṁti ārabhare (G.), (*passive*).
2. *Imperative :*			
Sing.	—		Susūsatu, susrusatāṁ (*ātm.*).
Plur.	—	Lekhāpayāthā	Anupatīpajaṁtu, *also* paṭivedetu
3. *Optative :*			
Sing.	Ālabhehaṁ, vracheyam	—	Paṭipajeya, paṭipajetha (*ātm.*).
Plur.	Paṭipādayema	—	Pāpunevu, pāpuneyu (J.), sususera (*ātm.*), haṁñeyasu (*passive*).
4. *Aorist :*			
Sing.	Husaṁ	—	Nikhami, nikhamithā, vaḍhithā, huthā (*ātm.*).
Plur.	—	—	Nikhamisu, niyāsu, locheṣu, husu, ālabhiyisu (*passive*).
5. *Future :*			
Sing.	Nikhāmayisāmi, likhāpayisaṁ (G.)	—	Vaḍhisati.
Plur.	—	—	Vaḍhisaṁti, ārabhisare (*passive*).

6. *Perfect*, of which the only examples are "*āhā*" and "*ayāya*."

7. *Causative :* vaḍhayati, vaḍheti ; ānapayāmi ; anapemi ; vivāsāpayāthā (*imperative pl.*).

8. *Participle.* (i) *Present Active : Sing. Nom.* anupaṭīpajaṁtaṁ, saṁtaṁ (saṁto, G., sato, S.) ; G. *has* karoto, karāto (*from* "karanto") *and* karu = karuṁ (tathā karu, *acting thus, from* "kurvan") ; *Gen.*, aśatasa ; *Plur.*, tiṣtaṁto.

(ii) *Ātmanepadam :* bhuṁjamānasa (*gen.*), samānā (*nom. pl.*)—"amisā samānā munisā" ; *also in* "-mina," *like* pakamaminenā, sampaṭipajamīne, vipaṭipādayamīnehi.

Present Passive : vijinamane, anuvekhamāne.

(iii) *Past Participles :* (*a*) tīlita, (*b*) upagate, vistrita (S.), (*c*) āyatā, nikhitā, yutaṁ, āladhe, (*d*) diṁne, dinā.

(iv) *Past Participles Causative :* (*a*) sāvite, sukhayite, (*b*) likhāpitā, nijhapayitā, (*c*) sāvāpite (*double caus.*).

(v) *Future Participles Passive :* (*a*) *from* "tavyam": kaṭaviye, sotaviyā (*fem.*), haṁtaviyāni (*neut. pl.*) ; *causative*—nijhapetaviye, vāsāpetaviye ; G. *has* "-tavyaṁ," *as in* prajūhitavyaṁ, lochetavyā (*fem.*), katavyo (*mas.*) ; S. *has* kaṭava, prayuhotave. (*b*) *From* "-anīya" : asvāsaniyā. (*c*) *From* "ya" : kachaṁ, dekhiye, chakiye, pūjetayā (G.) =pūjayitavya.

9. *Infinitive :* (*a*) nijhapayitave, ālādhayitave, pāpotave ; (*b*) ārādhetu (G.) *from acc.* "-tum."

10. *Gerund :* paritijitu, kaṭu, sutu, saṁnaṁdhāpayitu (*from* "-tvā"), *but* G. *has* "-tpa" *as in* parichajitpā, dasayitpā, alochetpā, ārabhitpā ; S. *has an additional form in* "-ti," *as in* tīstiti, alocheti, draśeti (M.). We have also a few forms from "*-ya, -tya,*" as in āgacha, adhigichya, apahaṭa.[1]

[1] This note is based on the masterly and comprehensive study of the subject contained in Hultzsch's *Corpus I. I.* vol. i. chh. vi-xi, and is also indebted to the outline of Asokan Grammar forming pp. xxv-xxxvii of Woolner's *Asoka Text and Glossary*.

INDEX

Accession and coronation dates, 11, 37, 39-41, 44
Administration, Asoka on, 121-2
Administrative orders, 55
Aged and infirm (*see* Old)
Agnibrahmā, nephew of Asoka, 8, 9, 10, 45, 110 *n.*
Ajantā, fresco at, 36
Ājīvikas, 3, 31, 65, 101, 190, 210; caves granted to, 37, 64, 81, 89, 205, 206
Akbar, emperor, 1, 14, 86, 199 *n.*
Alakadeva, 33
Alexander of Epirus, 29, 40, 166
Alfred, of England, 2
Aliya-vasāṇi, 67, 118
Allahabad, Asokan pillar at, inscribed by Gupta emperor, 88 *n.*
Allahabad-Kosam Pillar, viii, 15, 86, 199 *n.*
Almshouses, 200
Ambassadors or envoys (*dūtas*) to foreign states, 29, 30, 34 *n.*, 36, 38, 56, 78 *n.*, 165-9; first political, then religious, 169 *n.*
Anāgata-bhayāni, 67, 118
Ānanda, 27
Anantavarman, king, 89
Andhras, 21, 29, 168
Animal fights, 129 *n.*, 130 *n.*
Animal branding and castration restricted, 21-2, 184; — life, sacred, 72, 175; — slaughter prohibited, 20, 21-2, 39, 43, 62, 66, 69, 180-4, 192, 193, 211
Animals, kindness to, 22, 70, 72, 103, 175
Anta-Mahāmātras, 42, 56, 173, 211
Antas, 14 *n.*, 140 *n.*, 166-7 *n.*, 211 (*see* Borderers)
Antelopes or deer, 20, 38, 62, 130, 182 *n.*, 211
Antigonos Gonatas of Macedonia, 29, 56, 166
Antiochos Soter, 78 *n.*
Antiochos Theos of Syria, 15, 29, 38, 56, 166
Āpagīva, 35
Aparānta or Aparāntaka, Western India, 33, 34, 104, 140, 167 *n.*, 168 *n.*
Arachosia, 12, 15
Aramaic script, 246
Aria, 12, 15
Arthur of Britain, 1
Asandhimitrā, chief Queen of Asoka, 8, 9, 45, 46
Asceticism in Asoka's time, 103-4
Ascetics (Brāhmaṇas and Śramaṇas), Asoka and, 20, 39, 65, 77, 152, 190, 210; behaviour to, 69, 70, 103, 135, 141, 155, 158, 163, 192; classes of, 141-2 *n.*; five ways of serving, 135 *n.*, 141-2; none among Yonas, 164
Asoka, the Righteous King (105): not fully interpreted, vii; place in history, 1, 104-5; in legend, 1-2, 104-5; inscriptions as autobiography, 2; parentage, 2-3; Ājīvika influence on parents, 3; Viceroy at Ujjain or Taxila, 3, 4, 51, 125; seizes and holds throne at Pāṭaliputra, 3, 44; disputed succession, 3, 4, 44; legends of criminality and their motive, 4-5, 62; love for relatives shown in legends and Edicts, 5-7, 71-2, 116, 135, 136, 137, 143-4, 158, 163, 190-1, 200-1; brothers as Viceroys, 6, 51, 123, 125 *n.*; relations with younger brother, 6-7; brother as Vicegerent and monk, 7, 44, 45, 51-2, 63; family and connections, 7-9; domestic and public events dated, 9-10, 37, 39-41,

44-6, 214; age at accession and coronation, 11; royal titles and their origin, 11-12, 105, 108; empire, extent of, 13-16, 50, 144, 171; tours of inspection, 16, 20, 50, 55, 152; war with Kalinga—Asoka on war's cruelties, 16-17, 37, 162-5; embraces *Dharma* and non-violence, 17-18, 20-1, 22-3, 76 *n.*, 108-9, 162-3, 165-6, 213-14; conversion to Buddhism, 17-18, 23, 37, 41, 45, 62-4, 108-9, 214; propagandist activities, 18, 108-9, 162-3; conception of the Edicts, 18-19, 25-6, 185, 186-8; changes in life and habits, 19-20, 61, 130, 150-1, 185; cruel amusements (merry-makings) prohibited, 20, 38, 62, 129-30; eschews politics for religion—bases empire on Right, not Might, 20-1, 22-3, 167-9; prohibits animal slaughter, 20, 21, 38, 39, 61, 66, 128-30, 135, 137, 158, 175, 180-2; restricts branding, castration, fish-killing, etc., 21-2, 39, 61, 183-4; humanitarian measures—public works, 22, 38, 39, 131-2, 188-9; not a monk, but server and temporal ruler of the Saṁgha, 23-4, 45, 46, 63-4, 109, 110 *n.*, 117-19, 190, 193, 194, 199-200; Buddhist propaganda — processions and shows, 24-5, 39, 136-7; "pious tours" instituted, 26-8, 39, 46, 61, 63, 150-3; periodical tours by officials, 28-9, 38, 123-6, 133-4; Welfare Officials, *Dharma-Mahāmātras*, an Asokan conception, 29-31, 37, 38-9, 40, 42, 43, 54, 56, 61, 74, 139-44, 188, 194-6; supervisors of women, 31, 39, 43, 56, 143-4, 160, 190-1; missions of peace, goodwill and social service to foreign countries, 29, 31-2, 35-6, 38, 56, 77-8, 139-41, 165-6; missions—details from the legends, 32-4; missions—evidence of relics and inscriptions, 34-5; sea-going fleet, 36; publication of Edicts dated, 36, 37, 214; measures passed before the Edicts, 38-9; chronology from Edicts, 36-7, 39-43, 214, and from legends, 44-6; death of Asoka, 37, 46; tradition of his last days, 37 *n.*; his Civil Service, 42, 56-7, 58, 127, 146, 160, 173, 177, 187; builder of *vihāras* and *chaityas*, 45, 79, 80-1, 82-3, 152 *n.*; a self-limited autocrat, paternal monarch and hard-working king, 48-9, 50, 144-8, 151-2; government, imperial and local—his personal share, 54-5; King's council or cabinet, 55, 135, 147-8; fear of schism, 55, 64, 68; orders against schism, 193-8, 199, 200; King's orders—how issued, 55; frontier policy and administration, 57-8, 123-6, 126-8; imperial policy, 58-9, 127, 136, 165-6; personal religion—Buddhism, 60-4, 68-9, 108-9, 170 *n.*, 183-4, 190; public religion—Toleration, 64-6, 68, 72-3, 101, 111-12 *n.*, 135, 136, 149, 152, 155, 160, 185, 190, 192; *Dharma* of the Edicts—moral law—essence of all religions, 68-78, 101; originality of Asoka's message and terminology, 72-5, 113, 138, 154-5, 156, 157, 157-8, 159-60, 173-4, 175-6, 192; his belief in the other world, 75, 121, 149, 156, 169, 170, 172, 180, 193; his *Dharma* the basis of a universal religion, 75-7, 159-61; as builder and improver of cities, 79-80, 94-6; *stūpas* or topes, 80-3, 88, 105-6; pillars and their transport, 83-8, 89-92, 92-3; cave dwellings, 89, 205, 206; irrigation works, 93-4; capital, palace and park at Pāṭaliputra, 94-7; Asokan art, essentially Indian, 98-100; social conditions of his time, 101-6

Aśoka-avadāna, 4, 179 *n.*

Asokan scholarship, growth of. x, xi

Asokan script, lost knowledge of, vii ; romance of its rediscovery, viii-xi ; two kinds of, 102 (*see* Brāhmī, Kharoṣṭhi)
Ātman, in Brahmanism, 66 *n.*
Autocracy, limited, in Hindu polity, 47-9
Avestan affinities to Western dialect of the Edicts, 248
Ayupālā, 45

Bairat M.R.E., x, 13-14, 117 *n.*
Bakhra, pillar near, 86
Bālapaṇḍita, or Samudra, 110 *n.*
Banerji-Sastri, Dr. A. P., on damaged cave inscriptions, 206 *n.*
Banyan shade trees, 22, 39, 188
Barabar hill caves described, 89 ; first visited, viii ; granted to Ājīvikas, 37, 81, 205, 206 (*see* Cave Inscriptions I, II, III)
Barua, Dr. B. M., xi ; new view of Edict chronology, 43 *n.* ; on position of M.R.E. I., 213 ; other citations, 110 *n.*, 118 *n.*, 147 *n.*, 179 *n.*, 181 *n.*, 188 *n.*, 202 *n.*
Beadon, C., xi
Behaviour, 65, 69, 70-1, 116, 157-8, 163, 192
Benares, 85, 95 *n.*
Besnagar, 97, 98.
Bhabru or Bairat No. 2 Rock Edict : Annotated translation, 117-19 ; Asoka's address to the Saṁgha, 37, 43, 67, 117, 210 ; Asoka's authority implied, 54, 60, 119 ; canonical texts prescribed by Asoka, 67, 118-19 ; declares faith in Buddhist Trinity, 117 ; discovery of Edict, ix ; location, 14, 117 *n.* ; text, 217-18
Bhadrasāra, 33
Bhandarkar, Dr. D. R., xi ; (on) Asoka's borrowing from Jainism, 71 *n.* ; Buddhist influence on Western thought, 77 *n.* ; chronology, 41 *n.* ; Minor Rock Edicts, 14 *n.* ; peoples named in Edicts, 140 *n.*, 168 *n.* ; *Sambodhi*, 26 *n.* ; white elephant, 136 *n.*, 137 *n.*
Bhandarkar, Sir R. G., cited, 29 *n.*, 202 *n.*
Bharhut, *stūpas* at, 81-2, 88, 152 *n.*
Bhattiprolu *stūpa*, 98
Bhikkhu, Buddhist monk, qualifications of, 23
Bhikkhugatika, Asoka a, 23
Bhitā, 88
Bhitargaon temple, 88-9
Bhojakagiri, rock, 7
Bhojas, 21, 29, 168 *n.*
Bindusāra, father of Asoka, 2, 3, 9, 13, 44, 64-5 *n.*, 78 *n.* ; Brahmans fed by, 130 *n.* ; length of reign, 41 ; ministry, 3 *n.* ; Prime Minister, 3 *n.*, 52 ; Privy Council, 55
Birds protected, 20, 39, 72, 130, 175, 180, 181, 182
Bloch, Dr., on the Bharhut relievo, 152 *n.* ; Bodhi-Tree, 154 *n.*
Bodh-Gayā, 15 ; Asokan *chaitya* (shrine) at, 152 *n.* ; Asoka's pilgrimage to, 18, 26, 27, 37, 46, 151, 214 ; Burmese inscription at, 105
Bodhi or Bo-Tree at Gayā, 4-5 ; Asoka visits, 26, 27, 46, 105 ; branch sent to Ceylon, 35-6 ; Tiṣyarakṣitā's jealousy of, 4-5, 46, 105
Bodhisattva, 25, 61 *n.* ; in sculpture, 203, 204 *n.*
Borderers, unsubdued (frontagers, *Antas*), 15, 21, 29, 42, 57, 58, 59, 76, 113, 126-7, 131, 140, 166, 167 *n.*
Botanical (physic) gardens, 22, 38, 58, 132
Brahmani geese, 90
Brahmanical law, Asoka and, 66
Brahmāvarta, 112 *n.*
Brāhmī script, 34 ; original direction reversed, 246 ; parent of Indian scripts, 246 ; source disputed, 146-7
Brahmins, Brahmans, Brāhmaṇas, 17, 20, 30, 31, 39, 65, 101, 103, 190, 210 ; fed by Asoka, 20, 130 *n.* ; not the caste, but ascetics, 141 *n.* ; punishment of schism by, 199 *n.*
Brotherhood, Asoka's faith in, 21, 59
Brothers of Asoka, 3, 4, 5, 6, 7, 9, 44, 45, 51, 123, 125 *n.*, 150 *n.* (*see* Susīma, Tiṣya, Vītāsoka)

Buddha Gautama (Śākyamuni): animal symbols of, 61-2; *Dharma* of 84,000 sections, 80; memorials to, 79, 80, 83, 100, 201-4; on the next world, 75; pillar inscription to, 201-4; predicts Asoka's rule, 4 *n.*; relics of, 60-1 *n.*, 80-1 *n.*; six quarters of, 116-7 *n.*

Buddha Koṇākamana (Kanakamuni), 27, 37, 65, 81, 84, 88, 103, 205

Buddha Krakuchhanda, 84

Buddhaghosa on Asoka's medical aid, 152 *n.*; Asoka's way with schismatics, 64; *Bhikkhugatika*, 23; ideal monk, 119 *n.*; pea-fowl, 62, 131 *n.*; shows, 129 *n.*

Buddhism: Asoka's spiritual view of, 66-7; Asoka's status in, 23-4; based on analysis of, causes, 177 *n.*; date of Asoka's conversion important, 45; effects of Asoka's patronage, 1; evangelists (*theras*), 32-5; fundamental tenets, 68; holy places, 27, 100; image-worship a post-Asokan development, 25; influenced Western thought, 77-8; popular doctrine, 103; proofs of Asoka's faith in, 60-2, 68-9; texts used by the *theras*, 33-4

Buddhist Church: Asoka temporal head of, 54; Asoka's reputed gifts to, 64, 79; career for young aristocrats, 104; divisions in, 68

Buddhist canon as selected by Asoka, 67, 118-9

Buddhist Council, second, 68; third, 32, 34, 35, 46, 60-1, 63, 68

Buddhist monasteries ascribed to Asoka, 79

Buddhist Trinity, 117

Buddhists, 31, 65, 101; slander on, refuted by Asoka, 6-7

Bühler: editions of the Edicts by, xi; on origin of Brāhmī script, 246

Bull or ox symbol, 62, 90, 91

Burma, high literacy in, 102

Burmese inscription on Asoka, 105

Burnouf, x

Burt, Captain T. S., viii, ix

Cambridge History of India cited, 24 *n.*, 40, 45, 56 *n.*, 80, 166 *n.*, 214; quoted, 31, 47, 68, 97-8

Capital punishment, 66, 179

Caponing prohibited, 182

Carlleyle, x

Caste subordinate to religion, 104

Cave dwellings, 89

Cave Inscription I. (Nigrodha):
- Annotated trans., 205; grant to Ājīvikas, 205; text, 245

— — II. (Khalatika Hill):
- Annotated trans., 206; grant to Ājīvikas, 206; text, 245

— — III. (Khalatika Hill No. 2):
- Annotated trans., 207; grant as rain shelter, 207; text, 245

Ceremonial, True, 73, 153-6

Ceremonies, 103; useful and useless, 153-6

Ceylon (Tāmraparṇī, Laṅkā): ambassadors to, 56, 166; Asokan traditions, 2, 20; medical missions to, 132; mission of Mahendra to, 33, 35-6; missions to Asoka from, 35, 36.

Chaṇḍāsoka and Dharmāsoka, 4, 5, 17 *n.*, 166 *n.*

Chandragupta Maurya, 10, 12; annual sports, 130 *n.*; at work, 144-5 *n.*; capital city, 94-5; defeats Selukos, 13, 15; empire, 12-13; foreign relations, 96 *n.*, 100; legendary abdication and sainthood, 13; length of reign, 41; love for the chase, 150-1 *n.*; milestones, 188 *n.*

Chapaḍa, scribe, 117, 246

Chariot races, 130 *n.*

Chariots and horses, 145-6 *n.*

Charity, 31, 190, 191, 200-1, 210

Charlemagne, 1

Chārumatī, daughter of Asoka, 9, 79

Chatterji, C. D., cited, 3 *n.*, 7 *n.*, 23 *n.*, 35 *n.*, 62 *n.*, 115 *n.*, 119 *n.*, 125 *n.*, 131 *n.*, 164 *n.*, 181 *n.*

Childers on sin in Buddhism, 71 *n.*

Children, Asoka's love for his, 6, 121; service of parents by, 69, 116, 135; subjects regarded as, 48, 121, 127

Chitaldroog, Mysore, Minor Rock Edicts at, 13

Cholas or Choḍas, 15, 21, 29, 56, 131, 166

Chronology of Asoka, xi ; from the Edicts, 36-7, 39-41, 214 ; from legends, 9-10, 44-6
— of the Edicts, 41-3, 208-14
Chunar quarries, 93
City Magistrates, 28, 56, 123
Civil Servants : *Prativedakas*, 146 ; *Puruṣas*, 42, 56-7, 173, 177, 187, 211 ; *Yuktas*, 57, 127-8 *n.*, 133, 135, 209
Classes and castes in Asokan society, 103
Cloister of the *vihāra*, 194
Code of Duties (*Dharma*), 69-71
Codrington on Indian and Persian bell-capitals, 99
Coins, 97, 98
Commemorative Pillar Inscription I. (Rummindei) :
Annotated trans., 201-4 ; discovery, x ; history, 27, 46 ; locality, 14, 27 ; text, 244
— — — II. (Niglīva) :
Annotated trans., 205 ; locality, 14, 27, 28 ; text, 245
Conquest, military, abrogated, 38, 58, 163, 169-70 ; True or Moral (see *Dharma-Vijaya*)
Constantine and Christianity, 1
Contemporaries of Asoka, 29, 32, 40, 41, 56, 104, 166
Coomaraswamy, Dr. A. K., on Indian " folk art," 97
Coronation year, Asoka's epochal date, 11, 37, 39-41, 44, 214
Coryate, Tom, on the Delhi pillar, 92
Council of Ministers, Privy Council, *pariṣat*, 55, 56, 57, 135, 147-8
Court, M. A., viii
Cow, protected, 21, 182 *n.*, 184
Cromwell, Oliver, 1, 73
Cunningham : *Corpus Inscriptionum Indicarum*, x ; discovery at Sankisa, 84 *n.* ; imitation Asokan pillars, 90 *n.* ; pre-Asokan pillars, 87 *n.* ; source of Brāhmī script, 246 ; *Stūpa of Bharhut*, 61 *n.* ; Vaiśālī pillar, 86 ; weight of Asokan pillars, 92-3
Curries, slaughter for, 20, 130

Darius, cursive script of, 246 ; " thus saith " formula, 108 *n.*
Daśaratha, grandson of Asoka, 8, 9, 12, 89
Dates (*see* Chronology)
David of Israel, 1
Davids, Rhys (quoted), 1, 77 ; on Asoka's treatment of relics, 81 *n.* ; on " obedience," 137 *n.*
Death sentences, days of grace granted, 39, 66, 179
Deb, H. K., on chronology, 41 *n.* ; *Svastika* symbol, 126 *n.*
Debts of men and kings, 50
Deer Park of Buddha, Asoka's visit to, 106
Deimachos, Greek envoy, 78 *n.*
Delhi, pillars removed to, viii, 14, 86, 92, 93
Delhi-Mirath pillar, first discovered, viii, ix
Delhi-Topra pillar, viii ; first to be read, ix ; text used for translation, 172 *n.*
Democracy, never perfectly realised, 49
Deo-Patan, reputed Asokan city, 80
Dependents, support of, 155 *n.*
Destitute, 30, 142
Devānaṁpiya and *Piyadasi*, royal titles, 11-12, 105 ; supposed degradation of meaning, 105, 108-9
Devapāla Kṣatriya, a son-in-law of Asoka, 9, 79
Devī, Asoka's first wife, 8, 9, 44, 46
Devotion, firm or constant, *dṛidhabhaktitā*, 70, 150, 162-3
Dhammacheti inscription, 105
Dhammapālā, *upādhyāyā*, 45
Dharmā (*see* Subhadrāṅgī)
Dharma, Aryan religious law : accepted by Asoka, 17 ; Asoka's five applications of, 157-8 *n.* ; common to all religions, 75-6 ; conquest of, 17, 21, 36, 38, 59, 74, 165-6, 169-70 ; defined, 70, 76 *n.*, 174-5 ; index to, as expounded in the Edicts, 69-70 ; instruction in, 20, 42 ; originality of Asoka's propaganda, 76 *n.* ; pre-Asokan, 75 *n.* ; regulation by, 74-5, 172-4, 192, 212 ; summarised, 42, 70-1, 186-93, 212 ; terminology of, 74, 157-8 *n.*

Dharma-lipis, religious Edicts, 40, 74, 185
Dharma-Mahāmātras foreshadowed, 43, 127; instituted, 29, 37, 38-9, 40, 56, 74, 139, 188; many functions of, 29-31, 42, 43, 139-44, 190, 194-6, 200 *n.*, 212; of imperial scope, 54; transfer of judicial functions to *Rājūkas*, 178-9 *n.*
Dharmaraksita, or Dhammarakkhita, 33, 34, 104
Dharma-Vjaya, moral conquest, 17, 36, 38, 74, 165-6, 169-70
Dhauli elephant, 61
Dhauli R.E. (*see* Kalinga Rock Edict I)
Dialects of the Edicts, 247-50; grammar in common, 250-5
Didarganj, 97
Diodotus of Bactria, 40; coin of, 98
Dionysios, Greek envoy, 78 *n.*
Dīpavaṁsa cited, 2, 12, 33
District Officers or divisional commissioners, *Prādeśikas*, 28, 53, 56, 57, 134
Divyāvadāna cited, 3, 6, 8, 9, 51, 64 *n.*, 65 *n.*; Asoka as builder, 79; Asoka's Buddhism, 110 *n.*; Asoka's last days, 37 *n.*; chronology, 44-6; illustrated in stone at Sānchī, 105-6
Domestic measures, P.E. VII as a résumé of, 41, 186-93, 212
Domestic or family life, 70, 103
Dundubhissara (Dadabhisāra), 33, 35
Dutt, Sukumar, cited, 199 *n.*

Edicts, Asoka's: a unique personal record, 2; chronology of, 208-14; date events from coronation, 11; dates of publication, 36, 37, 214; epilogue to, R.E. XIV, 171-2; exaggerations in, 20, 130, 162; express the King's orders, 55; few imperfections in, 50-1; genesis and purpose, 18-19, 144, 149, 187-8; geographical distribution, 13-14, 51; grammar outlined, 250-5; home life in, 103; imperfections apologised for, 16, 50, 171-2; indicate policy, principles and laws, 54, 186-7; Moral Law (*Dharma*) of, 69-71; peoples and places named in, 15-16; permanency assured, 19, 55, 87, 113 *n.*, 193; recitation of, 54, 128; refer to Asoka by title, 12; relatives mentioned in, 5-6; scripts of, 246-7; style of, 1; *Upaniṣads* echoed in, 66 *n.*, 116 *n.*; written in vernacular dialects, 102, 247-50
Edmunds, A. J., 118 *n.*
Ekbatana, 95
Elders, seniors, behaviour to, 20, 69, 137, 152, 163
Elephant forest, 58, 184
Elephant symbol, 61-2, 90, 91, 99, 106, 170 *n.*, 204 *n.*
Elliot, Sir Walter, ix
Ellis, Colonel, x
Emperor's mission, 22
Empire of Asoka, extent of, 13-16, 50, 144, 171; pacifist after Kalinga war, 20-1, 22, 126-7, 163, 164-6
Equality of States, modern doctrine anticipated by Asoka, 21, 126-7, 165
Essenes, 77 *n.*
European Great War, 20
Evil, *apuṇya*, 71, 103

Fa-hien cited: Asoka and his brother, 6; Asoka's gift to the Church, 64; Asoka's "hell," 4 *n.*; Bo-Tree legend, 5; Buddhist car procession, 25; Dharmavivardhana, 8, 51; inscriptions misread, vii-viii; legend of the 84,000 topes, 80-1; six pillars of Asoka, 83
Fang-chih, 85, 204 *n.*
Feminine morals, 31, 39
Firoz Shah removes pillars to Delhi, 14, 86, 93, 199 *n.*
Fish, protected, 21-2, 72, 175, 181, 183
Fleet, xi, 33 *n.*, 81 *n.*, 94 *n.*
Follet, M. P., on group life, 49
Foreign missions, Asoka's, 29, 31-2, 35-6, 38, 56, 59, 165-9; messengers of peace, goodwill and social service, 77; names and destinations of missionaries, 32-4; relics and inscriptions at Sānchī, 34-5

Foreign Office, 77, 100
Forest folks, 57, 58, 59, 76; civilisation enjoined on, 165
Forgiveness of enemies, 20-1, 165
Forrest, x
Foucher: *Beginnings of Buddhist Art*, 61 *n.*, 91 *n.*; on sculpture at Sānchī, 26, 105
Franke, O., xi
Freedom of unsubdued peoples conditioral on morality, 21, 58, 59, 127, 165
Friends, behaviour to, 69, 135, 158; five ways of serving, 135 *n.*
Frontier administration, 57-8, 126-8, 173-4 *n.*
Fuhrer, x

Game forest, 146 *n.*
Gandhāra, 8, 32, 34, 51
Gandhāras, 15, 29, 30, 140
Ganges, 95 *n.*, 105
Garuḍa symbol, 90, 91 *n.*
Gedrosia, 12, 15
Gentleness, mildness, *mārdavam*, 70, 165 *n.*, 170, 191
Gift, the True, 72, 73, 156 *n.*, 157-8
Giridatta Thera, 7
Girnar, capital of Surāṣṭra, 14 *n.*, 51
Girnar Rock Edict, viii, ix, 13, 14 *n.*, 61; defaced lines under, 170 *n.*; dialect, 247
Glory, True, 74, 156
Gnostic sects and Buddhism, 77
Gods, "popularising" the, 24, 37, 110-12
Gold workings, ancient, 107-8 *n.*
Goltz on fighting strength of a nation, 162 *n.*
Good deeds, 71, 139, 175, 191
Gotiputa, 35
Government by *Dharma*, 74-5, 172-4
Governors compared to nurses, 48-9, 53, 178; independent jurisdiction of, 39, 176-7; neglectful, admonished, 53-4, 121-2
Grammar of the Edicts, 250-5
Gratitude, *kṛitajñatā*, 70, 150
Great Ministers, *Mahāmātras*, 28
Greater India, spiritual foundation of, 104
Greek elements, supposed, in Indian art, 98
Greeks, Asoka's relations with, 77, 78 *n.*, 100, 169 *n.* (*and see* Yavanas)
Group life increasing, 49; under ancient Hindu monarchy, 49-50
Gupta of Benares, 27

Happiness, Asoka's formula for, 70-1; of a King, 148-9 *n.*
Hāritīputa, 35
Harmony of religions, 111 *n.*
Harington, J. H., viii
Havell on Persian and Mauryan palace design, 96; on the lotus, 90, 99
Heads of Departments, *Mukhas*, 56, 190
Heaven, *svarga*, objective of Asoka's life, 75, 103, 156, 158, 169; popular presentment of, 137 *n.* (*see* Other world)
Heber, Bishop, on the Delhi pillar, 92
Heliodorus, 104
"Hell," Asoka's, 4, 86
Hellenistic contemporaries, five, 29, 32, 40, 41, 56, 104, 166
Heretics or dissenters, *pāsaṇḍas*, 101, 163
Hill caves, viii (*see* Barabar, Nagarjuni, Cave dwellings)
Himalaya country, 33, 93
Hindu Greeks, 104
Hoare, Captain James, viii
Hodges, viii
Home or family life, 70, 103
Horse symbol, 62, 85, 90, 91, 202 *n.*
Horticulturists, 58
Hospitals and medical treatment, 22, 38
Householders, *gṛihasthas*, 103, 141, 190, 210; virtues of, 103, 163-4
Hultzch, xi, 60; authority on Asokan grammar, 254 *n.*; on priority of Minor Edict I, 212, 213; on the defacer of the word "*Ājīvikehi*," 206 *n.*; other citations, 111 *n.*, 114, 116 *n.*, 118 *n.*, 126 *n.*, 128 *n.*, 140 *n.*, 142 *n.*, 143 *n.*, 144 *n.*, 150 *n.*, 153 *n.*, 155 *n.*, 157 *n.*, 160 *n.*, 163 *n.*, 165 *n.*, 168 *n.*, 171 *n.*, 172 *n.*, 173 *n.*, 174 *n.*, 175 *n.*, 176 *n.*, 178 *n.*, 179 *n.*,

180 *n.*, 181 *n.*, 185 *n.*, 186 *n.*, 187 *n.*, 188 *n.*, 189 *n.*, 191 *n.*, 193 *n.*, 195 *n.*, 196 *n.*, 199 *n.*, 201 *n.*, 205 *n.*, 218 *n.*, 235 *n.*, 245 *n.*
Hunting abolished, 20, 26, 38, 150-2

Images carried in procession, 25; Mauryan trade in, 25
Imitation Asokan pillars, 90 *n.*
Immortality, Asoka's belief in, 75, 158
Imperial government, 50-3, 54-5
India, divisions of, 140-1 *n.*
Indian Museum, 81-2
Indo-Aryan traditions common to India and Persia, 96 *n.*, 100
Indraji, Dr. B. L., x
Injustice, remedying, 30 *n.*, 43, 121-2, 142-3, 209
Inscriptions, Asokan, romance of, vii-xi; well-cut letters of, 98 (*see* Edicts, etc.)
Inscriptions commemorating Asoka, 105
Inscriptions, undiscovered, 14 *n.*
Inspection, tours of, 16, 20, 50, 55, 152
Intelligence Officers, *Prativedakas*, 146
Internationalism, advanced, of Asoka, 58-9
Isila, 13, 16, 52, 108
Isipatana (Sarnath), 27
I-tsing cited: image of Asoka as monk, 64 *n.*; monastery guests, 23 *n.*; prophecy of Buddha, 4 *n.*

Jackson, V.H., inscriptions found by, 205-6 *n.*
Jail deliveries on coronation day, 39, 66, 184-5
Jainism, Asoka and, 60, 71 *n.*; Chandragupta and, 13; founder of, 86; works on, 71 *n.*
Jains (*see* Nirgranthas)
Jalauka, a son of Asoka, 8, 9
Jambudvīpa, Asoka's country, 4 *n.*, 105; legendary gift of, 64; propaganda in, 24, 110; spirituality of, 112 *n.*
Janasāna, Ājīvika saint, 3, 64-5 *n.*
Jaugada R.E. (*see* Kalinga Rock Edict II)
Jayaswal, K. P., cited xi, 135 *n.*, 138 *n.*, 147 *n.*, 153 *n.*, 167 *n.*, 168 *n.*, 176 *n.*, 177 *n.*; compares Edicts with *Smṛitis*, 143 *n.*; estimates population of Kalinga, 162 *n.*
Jeweller's art, 97-8
Job quoted, 2
Jones, Sir William, viii
Judicial reforms, 39

Kabiruddin, Shah, ix
Kalhaṇa on Asoka's building, 79
Kalinga: Asoka's only conquest, 16; date, 37, 214; Edicts special to the locality, 13, 126 *n.*, 210, 214; estimate of war losses, 16-17, 162-5; fighting strength, 162 *n.*; pre-conquest followers of *Dharma*, 75 *n.*, 163; primitive condition, 28-9, 104-5; reactions of conquest, 17, 18, 19-20, 76 *n.*, 162-5, 213, 214; reassurances, 48, 165
Kalinga Rock Edict I (Dhauli):
Annotated trans., 120-6; children, 6, 121; City Magistrates, 56, 123; dialect, 247; discovery, ix; Governors exhorted, 53-4, 122-3; judicial inspectors foreshadowed, 123-4, 208-9; King's orders, 55, 122; locality, 13, 14 *n.*; next world, 75, 121; official tours, 28, 57, 123-6; outlying towns, 15, 16, 123, 125; Princely Viceroys, 6, 51, 123; rectifying injustice, 30 *n.*, 43, 121-2; text, 218-20; Viceroy's Ministers, 52, 124, 125-6
Kalinga Rock Edict II (Jaugaḍa):
Annotated trans., 126-8; *Dharma-Mahāmātras* foreshadowed, 28, 43, 127, 208; dialect, 247; equality of states, 21, 126-7; first copied, ix-x; locality, 13, 14 *n.*; paternal government, 48, 127; Provincial Governors, 52, 126; recitation of Edict, 54, 128; text, 220-2; Tiṣya day, 54, 128; unsubdued borderers, 58, 126-7, 211; Viceroy's officers, 52, 127

Kalsi Rock Inscription: dialect, 247; discovered, x; locality, 13; elephant symbol, 61, 170 *n.* (*see* Rock Edicts IX and X)
Kambojas, 15, 20, 29, 30, 140, 168
Kāñchipura (? Satiyaputra), 15
Kānta, Pandit Kamalā, ix
Kapilavastu, 27; pillars near, 84
Kapis (Kafiristan), 15
Karma, 103
Kāruvākī, second Queen of Asoka, 8, 9, 144 *n.*; Edict of, 200-1
Kashmir, 15, 32, 34; traditionally given to the Church, 79; *vihāras* in, 79, 82
Kashmir Chronicle cited, 8, 9
Kassapagotta (Kotiputta), 33, 34, 35
Kathāvatthu treatise, 61
Katra, 88
Kauśāmbī (Kosam), 52, 86; pillar at, 93 (*see* Minor Pillar Edict II)
Keralaputra (Malabar), 15, 21, 132
Kauṭilīya references: *Arthaśāstra* compared with Edicts, xi, 107 *n.*, 108 *n.*; cattle enclosure, 145 *n.*; conqueror's duty, 161 *n.*; conquerors, three classes of, 165-6 *n.*; drinking bouts, 130 *n.*; elephant officer, 58; free imports, 132 *n.*; frontagers, 131 *n.*; frontier offlcers, 57; game forest, 146 *n.*; government servants, 124 *n.*, 125 *n.*, 127 *n.*, 133 *n.*, 134 *n.*; guardian of trade routes and live stock, 160-1 *n.*; hunting, 151 *n.*; jail deliveries, 185 *n.*; king and his council, 148 *n.*; — as father, 121 *n*; king's activity, 148-9; — cabinet, 55; — duties, 146 *n.*, 148; — orders, 55, 108 *n.*; *Mahāmātras*, 107 *n.*, 120 *n.*, 127 *n.*, 143 *n.*, 173 *n.*; overseers or inspectors, 146-7 *n.*; protected creatures, 182 *n.*; public finance, 136 *n.*; public works, 189 *n.*; ransom, 180 *n.*; royal formulæ, 108 *n.*; royal harems, 191 *n.*; secret agents, 57; secretariats, 56 *n.*; segregation of sects, 149 *n.*; slaves and hirelings, 154-5 *n.*; State's duty to poor and afflicted, 121 *n.*, 142 *n.*; Tāmraparṇī, 132 *n.*; tax-gatherer, 147 *n.*; treatment of prisoners, 121 *n.*; 123 *n.*, 143 *n.*; Western India (Aparānta), 141 *n.*
Kern's *Manual of Indian Buddhism*, 68
Kesariya, *stūpa* at, 83
Khalatika Hill (Barabar Hill), 205 *n.* (*see* Cave Inscriptions II, III)
Khallāṭaka, Prime Minister, 3 *n.*, 52
Khāravela of Kalinga, 11, 206 *n.*
Kharoṣṭhī or Kharoṣṭrī script, ix, 117 *n.*; Semitic in origin, 246
Kindness, *dayā*, 70, 72, 175, 191
King's care for all, 72, 185-6
King's duties, 16, 50, 144-9; relative urgency of, 148 *n.*
King's highest work, preaching *Dharma*, 72, 73, 137-8, 148, 152, 163; — orders, generally in writing, 55, 147 *n.*, 148 *n.*; — sons, status of, 9, 191
Kingship, Indian conception of, 47, 48; of Asoka, democratic, 49
Kittoe, Captain, at Dhauli, ix
Kodiniputa, 35
Kosāmbī, 15 (*see* Kauśāmbī)
Kosikiputa, 35
Kumarādevī's tribute to Asoka, 105
Kumāras and *dālakas*, 9
Kuṇāla (Dharmavivardhana), son of Padmāvatī, 8, 9, 45; Viceroy at Taxila, 46, 51, 52, 125 *n.*
Kuśinagara or Kusinārā, 27; pillars at, 85; relics at, 60 *n.*

Lāghulovāda, 67, 119
Land revenue, 204
Lang, Captain, ix
Language of the Edicts: Eastern and Western dialects compared, 247-50; grammar in common, 250-5; original and translation, 248
Lapidary art, 97, 98
Lassen, identifies Greek kings, 166 *n.*
Lauriya Ararāj pillar and Edict, ix, 14, 27, 86

Lauriya Nandangarh pillar and Edict, ix, 14, 27-8, 86
Law, a natural growth from group life, 48 ; sources of, 47-8
Law, N., cited, 184 *n*.
Laws, Asoka's, indicated by the Edicts, 54
Lay-worshippers, *upāsakas*, 194, 196 *n*.
Leigh, Captain, x
Levi, Sylvain, on Deo-Patan, 80 ; on Kharoṣṭrī script, 246
Liberality, 65, 69, 70, 135 ; the highest, 156 *n*.
Life, as valued by Asoka, 66, 116, 211 ; boon or gift of, 39, 72, 175
Lion symbol, 62, 83, 84, 90, 91
Literacy, high in Asoka's time, 102-3
Lotus and honeysuckle abacus, 91 ; capital, 90, 99 ; symbol, 204 *n*.
Louis, king and saint, 2
Love through moral conquest, 169
Lüders, xi ; cited, 122 *n*., 165 *n*., 176 *n*., 178 *n*., 179 *n*. 189 *n*.
Lumbini Garden or Grove (Rummindei), 27, 37, 46, 85, 203 *n*.
Lummini village (*see* Rummindei)

Magadha, Bihar, Asoka as king of, 117 ; intercourse with Ceylon, 36
Māgadhī, Asokan court language, 247-8 ; grammar of, 250-5
Magas of Cyrene, 29, 40, 56, 166
Mahābhārata cited : fire of destruction, 138 *n*. ; king as mother, 121 *n*. ; *samāja* as Śaiva festival, 129 *n*.
Mahābodhivaṁsa cited, 3, 8
Mahādeva, 33, 34, 45
Mahādharmaraksita, Yonaka preacher, 7, 33, 34, 45
Mahāmātra, status of, in the Edicts and *Kauṭilīya*, 107
Mahāmātras, ministers, classes of, 52-3, 56, 120 ; duties of, 123-6, 127, 147 ; Edict references to, as guide to chronology, 208-10
Mahāmāyā, Buddhist Madonna, 202 *n*., 203, 204 *n*.
Mahārakṣita or Mahārakkhita, 32, 34
Mahārāṣṭra, 33
Mahāvaṁsa : Asokan legends, 3, 4, 7, 41, 110 *n*., 130 *n*. ; chronology of, 9-10, 40-1, 44-6 ; credits Asoka's missions to Buddhist Church, 32, 34 *n*. ; legend of the 84,000 *vihāras*, 80
Mahāvaṁsaṭīkā cited, 3, 64 *n*.
Mahavānaya, 35
Mahāyāna Buddhism, 25
Mahendra, son of Devī, 8, 9, 10, 44 ; appointed Viceregent, 45, 51 ; head of *Saṁgha*, 45 ; mission to Ceylon, 33, 35-6 ; ordained, 45, 104, 110 *n*. ; sails from Pāṭaliputra, 95 *n*. ; visits mother, 46
Mahiṁsakamaṇḍala, 34
Mahisamaṇḍala, 33
Majjhantika, 32, 34, 54
Majjhima, missionary, 33, 35
Mango gardens or groves, 22, 39, 58, 188, 200
Mansehra Rock Edicts, x, 13, 14 *n*. ; dialect, 247 (*see* Rock Edict V)
Manu, defines Brahmāvarta, 112 *n*. ; on sacred law, 47-8 ; on *Yuktas*, 127 *n*.
Marcus Aurelius, 1
Marshall, Sir John : *Guide to Sanchi*, 35 *n*., 106 ; on Asokan sculptures, 91
Maski Minor Rock Edict, xi, 14, 60 ; only one to name Asoka, 12, 108 *n*.
Masson, C., ix
Mathurā, 88 ; statues near, 97, 98
Maudgalāyana, 27
Mauneya-sūte, 67, 118
Mauryan bricks, 88-9
Mauryan engineering : irrigation, 93-4 ; town-planning, 94-5 ; transport of Asokan pillars, 92-3
Mauryan minor arts, 97-8 ; polished stone, 89, 91-2, 96, 97 ; woodwork, 97
Mauryas or Moriyas, clan of, 3 ; *Mayūra* ensign of, 92
Measures of distance, 83 *n*., 188 *n*.
Meat diet, Asoka and, 20, 38, 62
Medical aid, 32, 38, 58, 131-2
Medicinal plants, 22, 30, 38, 58, 132
Meerut pillar and Edict, 14, 86
Meditation (*see* Reflection)

Megasthenes, ambassador at Pāṭaliputra, 78 *n.*, 100 ; (on) ascetics, 142 *n.* ; Chandragupta's park, 146 *n.* ; describes the capital, 94-5 ; (on) Indian Foreign Office, 77, 100 ; irrigation officers, 94, 133 *n.* ; Kalinga, 16 ; King at the chase, 150-1 *n.* ; overseers and inspectors, 146 *n.* ; royal elephants, 58 ; waterside wooden cities, 95

Merry-makings, *samājas*, Asoka and, 20, 38, 62, 129-30

Michelson, xi ; cited, 119 *n.*, 145 *n.*, 173 *n.*, 174 *n.*, 175 *n.*, 178 *n.*, 189 *n.* ; on Sanskrit, 248, 249

Middle-Indic (Prakrit) dialects, 248, 249

Milinda Pañha on Asoka, 105

Minor Pillar Edict I (Sarnath) :
- Addressed to *Mahāmātras*, 210-11 ; annotated trans., 193-8 ; date, 43 ; discovery, x ; King's order against schism, 54, 60, 64, 68 *n.*, 193-4 ; locality, 14, 87, 93 ; publishing the King's order, 194-6 ; text, 243

— — — II Kauśāmbī :
- Addressed to *Mahāmātras*, 52, 210-11 ; annotated trans., 199 ; in Cunningham's *Corpus* x ; King's order against schism, 54-5, 60, 64, 199 ; locality, 14, 86, 93 ; text, 243

— — — III (Sānchī) :
- Addressed to *Mahāmātras*, 210-11 ; annotated trans., 200 ; date, 43 ; in Cunningham's *Corpus*, x ; King's order against schism, 55, 60, 64, 200 ; locality, 14, 86-7, 93 ; text, 244

— — — IV. (Queen's Edict) :
- Annotated trans., 200-1 ; locality, 144 *n.*, 199 *n.* ; relatives, 5, 200-1 ; royal charities, 31, 200-1 ; text, 244

Minor Rock Edict I (Brahmagiri) :
- Annotated trans., 107-15 ; *Antas*, frontagers, 42, 113, 211 ; Asoka's Buddhism, 18, 60, 108-9, 213, 214 ; date, 214 ; first of the Edicts, 18, 19, 212-3 ; Isila, 52, 108 ; locality, 13 ; Ministers of the Viceroy, *Mahāmātras*, 52, 56-7, 107 ; permanency of the message, 19, 87, 113 *n.* ; popularising the gods, 24, 37, 110-12 ; preamble to King's orders, 55, 108 ; Prince (Viceroy, Asoka's brother) at Suvarṇagiri, 6, 51, 107 ; self-exertion, 73, 109, 113 ; text, 215-6

— — — II (Mysore) :
- Annotated trans., 116-7 ; King's orders, 55, 116 ; relatives, 5, 116 ; respect for life, 116, 211 ; scribe, 57, 117 ; text, 217

Minor Rock Edicts : earlier than Rock Edicts, 43 ; localities of, 13-14, 113 *n.*

Mitra, S. N., 118 *n.*

Moderation, or Middle Path, 70, 122, 135

Moggaliputta Tissa (*see* Upagupta)

Monasteries and education, 101-2

Monasteries (*vihāras*) attributed to Asoka, 80, 81 ; noted by Yuan Chwang, 79, 82

Monk, was Asoka a ? 23-4, 45, 63-4, 109

Monks and nuns, heretical, how punished, 193-4, 197, 198 *n.*, 199, 200

Mookerji, R. K., cited, 48, 112 *n.*, 138 *n.*, 196 *n.*, 199 *n.*

Moral Law (*Dharma*) of the Edicts, 68-71, 72-7 ; personally lived by Asoka, 71-2

Moral Welfare Department, 29-31

Morality, the condition of freedom, 58-9

Moriyas (*see* Mauryas)

Morris, 181 *n.*

Mudrā-rākṣasa, 12

Mukharji, P. C., on excavations at Pāṭaliputra, 96 ; Nativity sculpture at Rummindei, 202-3 *n.* ; Rummindei Pillar, 85

Mūlakadeva, 33

Munigāthā, 67, 118

Mysore, Minor Rock Edicts at, x ; peculiarities of dialect, 247 ; scribe's signature, 117, 246

Nābhapantis, or Nabhakas, 21, 29, 168

Nabhitis, 168

Nagar (Jalalabad), 15

Nagarjuni hill caves described, 89, 205 *n.*; first visited, viii; granted to Ājīvikas, 89, 206 *n.*; inscriptions of Daśaratha, 12, 89, 206 *n.*, 207 *n.*
Nāgas, Nāgīs, symbolic figures, 106
Nandas, empire of the, 13
Nativity sculpture at Rummindei, 202-4 *n.*; other examples, 204 *n.*
Nepal, 15, 27, 28, 80, 93
Nigali Sagar Pillar Edict, x
Niglīva, pillar at, 14, 27, 28, 84, 87 (*see* Commemorative Pillar Inscription II)
Nigrodha, nephew of Asoka, 18 *n.*, 41, 44, 62-3, 110 *n.*
Nigrodha Cave, 205, 245
Nirgranthas (Jains), 7, 31, 65, 190, 210
Nirvāṇa, not taught by Asoka, 68
Non-Violence, *ahiṁsā*, 17, 20, 69-70, 137, 155, 158, 211; implied, 43, 128-9, 135
Numerals, 252

Obedience, 69, 71, 137 *n.*
Objectionable shows (*samāja*), 20, 38
Oertel, x
Official tours of *Yuktas*, *Rājūkas* and *Prādeśikas*, 28, 38, 57, 123-6, 133-5
Ojha's Hindi edition of the Edicts, 138-9 *n.*
Old and infirm, 30, 39, 69, 142, 143, 192
Omar, Khalif, 1
Other world, happiness in, through *Dharma*, 75, 121, 149, 156, 169, 170, 172, 180, 193
Outlawry of war first proclaimed by Asoka, 21, 58
Ox symbol, 83, 84, 90

Padmāvatī, third or fourth wife of Asoka, 8, 9, 45
Palidas, 169
Pāṇḍyas, 15, 21, 29, 56, 131, 166
Parents, service to, 69, 116, 135
Parks, 58, 146
Parvan days, Brahmanical Sabbaths, 183 *n.*
Pastures or ranch, *vraja*, 58, 145, 160; officer in charge of, 58, 160

Pāṭaliputra, Asoka's capital, 15, 28, 29, 89, 90, 105, 193, 210; Buddhist Council at, 32, 68; contested throne of, 3-4; described by Megasthenes, 94-5; family associations of, 5; founded by Udaya, 94; improved by Asoka, 95-6; missions to, from Ceylon, 35, 36; monastery at, 80; palace and grounds, 95, 146 *n.*; pilgrims' road, 27-8, 83 *n.*, 93, 100; processions, 25; prohibitions at, 20, 38; prophecies on, 94, 97 *n.*; site excavated—marks of flood and fire, 96-7; Tiṣya at, 6, 7; tope and pillar at, 64, 86
Patañjali on Mauryan trade in images of gods, 25
Patna, 97, 98
Peace basis of Asoka's empire—21, 22, 58-9
Peacock as food of kings, 62, 130-1 *n.*; restricted slaughter of, 20, 38, 62, 130, 182 *n.*, 211
Peacock device of the Mauryas, 92, 106
Persian and Indian art: palaces of like design, 96; pillar details, 98, 99; suggested common origin, 96 *n.*, 100
Persian and Indian inscription formulæ, 108 *n.*
Pew, Major P. L., ix
Pilgrimage, an institution in India, 22; Asoka's, with Upagupta, 27, 46, 61, 63, 151-2 *n.*, 201 *n.*, 203 *n.*
Pillar Edict I:
Annotated trans., 172-4; *Anta-Mahāmātras*, 42, 56, 173, 211; date, 36, 172; next world, 75, 172; *Puruṣas*, Civil Servants, 42, 56, 173, 211; regulation by *Dharma*, 74-5, 172-4; self-examination, 73-4, 173; text, 236-7
— — II:
Annotated trans., 174-5; boon or gift of life, 39, 72, 175; good deeds, 72, 175; spiritual insight, 72, 175; text, 237
— — III:
Annotated trans., 175-6; self-examination, 73-4, 175-6; sin, 175; text, 237

Pillar Edict IV :
Annotated trans., 176-80 ; date, 36, 176 ; Governors likened to nurses, 48-9, 53, 178 ; independence of Governors, 39, 176-7 ; other world, 75, 180 ; *Puruṣas*, 42, 56-7, 177, 211 ; *Rājūkas*, 42, 53, 176-80, 211 ; respite to death-sentenced persons, 39, 66, 179 ; text, 238
—— V :
Annotated trans., 180-5 ; date, 36, 180, 184-5 ; elephant forests, 58, 184 ; fish preserves, 21-2, 184 ; jail deliveries, 39, 66, 184-5 ; protection of animals, 39, 43, 62, 180-4, 211 ; *Punarvasu* day, 184 ; text, 239 ; *Uposatha* days, 61, 183-4
—— VI :
Annotated trans., 185-6 ; changed life through *Dharma* ordained, 20, 185 ; date, 36, 40, 186 ; King honours all sects, 65, 185 ; not relatives only, but all others cared for, 72, 185 ; purpose of Rock Edicts, 18, 19, 185 ; text, 240
—— VII :
Annotated trans., 186-93; ascetics, 103, 190, 192 ; chronological position, 211-12 ; date, 36, 41, 193 ; *Dharma-Mahāmātras*, 188, 190, 210, 212 ; *Dharma* propaganda summarised, 42, 186-93 ; harems, 6, 190-1 ; householders, 103, 190 ; indulgences and charity, 31, 190, 191 ; *Mahāmātras*, 190, 212 ; *Mukkas*, Departmental Heads, 56, 190 ; other world, 75, 193 ; permanency of the message, 87, 193, 213 ; proper behaviour, 192 ; publishing pious precepts, 186-7 ; *Puruṣas*, 42, 56, 187, 211 ; *Rājūkas*, 187, 212 ; reflection, 74, 192-3, 212 ; relatives, 5, 190, 193 ; résumé of domestic measures, 41, 186-93, 212 ; *Saṁgha*, 61, 67, 190 ; servants and hirelings, 103, 192 ; sons, status of, 9, 191 ; text, 240-2 ; works of public utility, 22, 30, 39, 42, 58, 188-91, 212
Pillar Edicts : Asoka's account of, 18-19 ; date of issue, 36, 37, 172 *n.* ; dialects, 247, 248 ; earlier measures, 39 ; later than Rock Edicts, 41-3, 211-12 ; " Pillars of piety," 187-8 ; symbolic animal capitals, 61-2, 90-1
Pillars ascribed to Asoka : Allahabad, 86 ; Delhi-Topra, 86, 92 ; Kapilavastu, 84, 90 ; Koluha, 86, 90, 92 ; Kusinārā (two), 85 ; Lauriya-Ararāj, 86, 90 ; Lauriya-Nandangarh, 86, 90, 92 ; Mahāsāla, 85-6, 90 ; Meerut, 86 ; Niglīva, 84, 87, 100 ; Pāṭaliputra (two), 83, 86, 90 ; Rājagriha, 86, 90 ; Rampurwa, 86, 88, 90, 92 ; Rummindei (Lumbini), 85, 87, 90, 100 ; Sānchī, 86-7, 90, 106 ; Saṅkāśya (Sankassa), 83-4, 90 ; Sankisa, 84 *n.* ; Sarnath road (two), 85, 87, 90, 99, 100 ; Śrāvastī (two), 83, 84, 90 ; Vaiśālī-Kuśinagara road, 83
Pillars, Asokan : design, dimensions, quality and symbolism, 89-92, 96, 98 ; foreign inspiration supposed, 96 *n.*, 98 ; Indian originality vindicated, 99-100 ; later imitations, 90-1 *n.* ; uninscribed, 86 *n.* ; utilised by Guptas, 87-8 *n.*
Pillars, pre-Asokan, 86 *n.*, 87-8, 95, 96
Piṅgalavatsa, 3 *n.*, 65 *n.*
Pioneers in Asokan research, vii-xi
" Pious tours " of the King, 18, 20, 26-8, 39, 46, 61, 63, 151 ; of Viceroys and Governors, 28-9, 123-6, 133-6
Piprahwa *stūpa*, 98
Piṭakas, 7, 107 *n.*
Pitinikas, 21, 29, 30, 140, 168
Pleasure in morality, *Dharma-rati*, 70, 170
Police, under the *Prādeśika*, 134 *n.*
Polier, Captain, viii
Polygamy and early marriage, 104
Poor and miserable, 69, 192
Poverty, absolute, not advocated by Asoka, 157 *n.*
Praśnavyākaraṇa Sūtra, cited, 71 *n.*, 181 *n.*

Preamble to King's orders, 55, 108, 116, 122, 133
Prinsep, James, first reader of Asokan script, viii, ix, x
Private secretaries, 55
Processions and shows, 24-5
Proper treatment, 69, 157-8, 163, 192
Provincial government, 51-4, 55-8
Provincial Governors, *Rājūkas, Prādeśikas*, 42-3, 52, 53, 57, 126, 133, 134, 176-8, 179, 187, 209 ; admonishment of, 53-4, 122-3 ; independent jurisdiction of, 39, 176-7
Ptolemy, geographer, cited, 131 *n.*
Ptolemy Philadelphos of Egypt, 29, 56, 78 *n.*, 166
Public amusements, *samāja*, interdicted, 20, 38, 129-30
Public religion of Asoka, 68 ; Moral Law, practical and doctrinal, 69-71, 72-7 ; not Buddhism, 68
Public works : an imperial concern, 54 ; care of, 58 ; described 22, 30, 42 ; pre-Edict, 38, 39 ; résumé of, 188-9
Pulindas, 21, 29, 169 *n.*
Punarvasu day, 184
Puṇyavardhana, 15
Purāṇas cited, 41, 140 *n.*
Purity, *śaucham*, 70, 175, 191 ; of heart, *bhāva-śuddhi*, 70, 150
Puṣyagupta, 51, 94

Queen's Edict (*see* Minor Pillar Edict IV)
Quinquennial tours, 28, 38, 53, 57, 123, 133-5

Rādhagupta, Asoka's Minister, 3, 52
Rain shelters, caves granted for, 207
Rājagṛiha, pillar at, 86 ; *samāja* at, 129 *n.*
Rājūkas, Provincial Governors, Asoka's appeal to, 53-4, 122-3 ; status and powers of, 53, 56, 57, 176-80, 209
Rakṣita or Rakkhita, 33, 34
Rāmagrāma, *stūpa* at, 82 *n.* ; visited by Asoka, 106
Rampurwa Pillar Edict, x, 14, 28 ; pillars at, 86, 88
Rāṣṭrikas, 29, 30, 140
Ravenshaw, E. L., ix
Reflection, 74, 179, 192-3
Relatives, Asoka's affection for, indicated in Edicts, 5, 6, 116, 135, 136, 137, 143-4, 158, 163, 190-1, 200-1 ; proper treatment of, 69, 116, 137, 163
Relic caskets, 98
Relics of Buddha, 60-1 *n.*, 80-1 *n.* ; of missionaries, 34-5, 36
Religions, *Dharma* the essence of all, 75-6, 159-61
Religious catholicity of Hindus, 104
Religious change of life ordained, 20, 185
Religious conferences, 39, 65, 101-2
Religious publicity, 18-19, 25-6, 185, 186-7, 212
Religious shows and processions, 24-5, 39, 136-7
Religious symbols, 99
Respect, 69, 116
Rest-houses, 22, 39, 58, 188
Restraint of passions, 150, 165 ; of speech, 73 ; of violence, 70, 155
Rhinoceroses, 181
Rice, Lewis, x, 33 *n.*
Riṣṭriya, 33
Rock Edict I (Shāhbāzgarhi) :
Annotated trans., 128-30 ; blood sacrifices abolished, 20, 61, 128-9, 130, 211 ; dialect, 247, 248 ; merry-makings, *samāja*, forbidden, 20, 38, 62, 129-30 ; non-violence implied, 43, 128-9 ; royal table, 20, 130 ; text, 222
— — II (Girnar) :
Annotated trans., 131-2 ; *Antas*, frontagers, 29, 42, 131, 211 ; dialect, 247, 248 ; medicinal plants, herbs, roots and fruits imported and planted, 22, 30, 132 ; medical aid for man and beast at home and abroad, 32, 38, 58, 131-2 ; roadside wells and trees, 30, 38, 42, 58, 132 ; Tāmraparṇī or Ceylon, 36, 132 ; text, 223 ; welfare work, 41, 131-2, 211
— — III (Girnar) :
Annotated trans., 133-6 ; dialect, 247, 248 ; liberality, 65, 135 ; moderation, 135 ; non-violence implied, 43, 135, 211 ; official tours, 28, 38, 57, 133-5, 208,

209; *Prādeśika*, 53, 134; preamble, 55, 133; *Rājūka*, 43, 57, 133, 211; relatives, 5, 135; text, 223-4; *Yuktas*, 57, 133, 135

Rock Edict IV (Girnar):
Annotated trans., 136-8; dialect, 247, 248; King's highest work—preaching *Dharma*, 72, 73, 137-8; non-violence, 43, 137, 211; obedience, 69, 137; relatives, 5, 136, 137; religious shows and processions, 39, 136-7; text, 224-5; unseemly behaviour to ascetics condemned, 65, 136; war-drum silenced, 21, 38, 58, 136

— — V (Mānsehrā):
Annotated trans., 139-44; ascetics, Brahmanical, 103, 141; borderers, western, 15, 41, 140, 211; destitute and infirm, 142; *Dharma-Mahāmātras*, 29, 30, 38-9, 42, 43, 56, 139-44, 209, 211; dialect, 247, 248; "here," meaning Pāṭaliputra, 15, 143; householders, 103, 141; purpose of Edicts, 19, 144; rectifying injustice, 30 *n.*, 43, 142-3, 209; relatives, 5, 6, 143-4; soldiers, 103, 141; supervision of women, 43, 143-4, 210; text, 225-6

— — VI (Girnar):
Annotated trans., 144-9; dialect, 247, 248; kingly duties, 16, 50, 144-8; King's highest duty, 72, 148; *Mahāmātras*, 56, 147; parks, 58, 146; pastures or ranch, 58, 145; purpose of Edict, 149; text, 227-8

— — VII (Shāhbāzgarhi):
Annotated trans., 149-50; dialect, 247, 248; sects not to be segregated, 65, 149; text, 228

— — VIII (Shāhbāzgarhi):
Annotated trans., 150-3; Bodh-Gayā, 15, 37, 151, 214; dialect, 247, 248; inspection, visits of, 16, 20, 50, 152; King's moral teaching, 72, 152; King's title, 12, 151, 153; "pious tours," 18, 20, 151; pleasure trips and hunting, past, 20, 26, 38, 150-1; text, 228-9; visits and gifts to ascetics and elders, 20, 65, 152

Rock Edict IX (Kalsi):
Annotated trans., 153-6; ascetics, liberality to, 65, 155; ceremonies—true ceremonial, 66, 73, 103, 153-6; dialect, 247, 248; next world, 75, 156; non-violence, 43, 155, 211; slaves and employees, 103, 154; text and variant, 229-30

— — X (Kalsi):
Annotated trans., 156-7; dialect, 247, 248; glory, 74, 156; King's effort for the hereafter, 75, 156; self-exertion, 73, 156-7; text, 231

— — XI (Shāhbāzgarhi):
Annotated trans., 157-8; ascetics, 103, 158; *Dharma*, the supreme gift, 72, 73, 157-8; dialect, 247, 248; non-violence, 43, 158, 211; relatives and friends, 5, 158; slaves and servants, 103, 158; text, 231-2

— — XI (Girnar):
Annotated trans., 158-61; dialect, 247, 248; essence of religions, 76, 159-61; honour to all sects, 65, 72-3, 158-60; *Strī-adhyakṣa-mahāmātras*, 31, 39, 43, 160, 210; text, 232-3; *Vrajabhūmika* or *Vachabhūmika*, 58, 160

— — XIII (Shāhbāzgarhi):
Annotated trans., 162-70; *Antas*, 42, 166, 167 *n.*, 211; ascetics, 103, 163, 164; Asoka's Buddhism, 18, 162-3, 213, 214; Ceylon, Tāmraparṇī, 36, 166; conquest abrogated, 38, 58, 163, 164-5; Conquest, True, 74, 165-6; date, 40, 166; dialect, 247, 248; *Dūtas*, and their moral conquests, 29, 30, 38, 56, 165-9, 211-12; forgiveness of enemies, 20-1, 165; Hellenistic contemporaries, 32, 40, 41, 166; householders, virtues of, 107, 163-4; Kalinga conquest, King's remorse for, 16-17, 162-5; King's preaching of *Dharma*, 72, 163; next world, 75, 169, 170; not published in Kalinga, 13, 162 *n.*;

outside peoples reassured, but admonished, 21, 58, 59, 165; primitive condition of Kalinga, 28-9, 164-5; relatives, 6, 163; servants and dependents, 103, 163; text, 233-5
Rock Edict XIV (Girnar):
Annotated trans., 171-2; dialect, 247, 248; dominion, vastness of, 14, 171; epilogue, Edict as, 19, 171; imperfections, 16, 50, 171-2; King's orders, written down, 55, 172; text, 235-6
Rock Edicts: date of issue, 37, 43, 138 *n.*, 214; dialects, 247-8; earlier than Pillar Edicts, 41-3; issued in two stages or chronological orders, 43; purpose of, 18-19, 185-6
Royal harems, 6, 30, 31, 48, 143-4, 145, 190-1, 210; pleasure trips, abolished, 20, 26, 38, 150-2; table, 20, 62, 130; titles, 11-12, 105, 108, 150 *n.*
Rudradāman's inscription cited, 51, 93-4, 105
Rummindei (Lummini), author's visit to, 202 *n.*; pillar at, 85, 87, 202 *n.*, 203-4 *n.*; temple and sculpture at, 202-4 *n.* (*see* Commemorative Pillar Inscription I)
Rupnath Minor Pillar Edict, x, 13, 43, 60

Sacrifice with bloodshed abolished, 20, 61, 66, 128-9, 130
Sahadeva, 33
Sahasram Minor Rock Edict, ix, 13, 43
Saintliness, *sādhutā*, 70, 191 ?
Śākyasiṁha, a name of Buddha, 62
Śākyas, Buddhists, 8, 60, 62, 109 *n.*
Samantapāsādikā, 33, 110 *n.*
Samāpā (Jagauda), 16, 52, 126
Samataṭa, 15
Sambala, 33
Saṁbodhi, enlightenment, Tree of Knowledge, 26, 46, 106
Saṁbuddha doctrine, 46
Saṁgha or *Saṅgha*: as the entire Buddhist Order, 67; Asoka and, 37, 46, 54-5, 60, 63, 64, 67, 68-9, 109, 119 *n.*; Asoka dictates the true *Dharma*, 43, 117-19; Asoka's orders against schism, 54-5, 64, 68, 193-8, 199, 200; *Dharma-Mahāmātras* and, 31, 61, 190, 194-6, 210; divisions in, 68; headship of, 45-6; laws of concerning schism, 196-9 *n.*
Samprati, grandson of Asoka, 8, 9; disloyalty of, 37 *n.*
Sānchī, pillar at, 86-7, 93 (*see* Minor Pillar Edict III); relics found at, 34-5; sculpture at, 26; *stūpa* at, 81, 105-6; why favoured by Asoka, 8
Saṅghamitrā, daughter of Devī, 8, 9, 10, 35, 44, 45, 104, 110 *n.*
Sankāśya or Sankassa, pillar at, 83, 83-4
Sankisa, pillar at, 84 *n.*
Sanskrit and Asokan dialects, 247, 248, 249
Sāriputta, 27
Sarnath M.P.E. (*see* Minor Pillar Edict I); pillars at, 14, 87, 93
Śāstri, Vidhuśekhara, 145 *n.*
Śatapatha Brāhmaṇa, 247
Satiyaputra, 15, 21, 131
Schism among Buddhists, 54-5, 60, 64, 68, 193-4, 199, 200
Scribe, *lipikara*, 55, 57, 117, 172
Seal, Sir B. N., on representative government, 49
Sects, impartially treated by Asoka, 64-5, 72-3, 77, 101, 158-60, 185; not to be segregated, 65, 149; supervision of, 31, 101, 210; treatment of popular Brahmanism exceptional, 66
Self-control, *saṁyama*, 72, 150
Self-examination, 67, 71, 73-4, 173, 175-6
Self-exertion, 73, 109, 113, 156-7
Self-indulgence, 174, 175
Selukos or Seleukos, defeated by Chandragupta, 13, 15
Senart, authority on inscriptions, xi; (on) *Aparāntas* and *Antas*, 140 *n.*; Asoka's selection of Buddhist texts, 119-20 *n.*; legendary cruelty of Asoka, 4, 17 *n.*; Rock Edicts, 128 *n.*
Servants and hirelings or dependents, Śūdras, 103; five duties to, 154 *n.*; proper treatment of, 154, 158, 163, 192

Shāhbāzgarhi Rock Edict, viii, 13, 14 *n.*, 39 (*see* Rock Edicts I, VII, VIII, XI, XIII)
Shakespeare quoted, 17
Shipping, 36
Sin, *pāpa*, *āsinava*: as bondage, 157; blindness to, 175; fear of, 71, 173; forgiveness of, 75, 179-80; meaning of, 174 *n.*; to be trodden down, 139
Singh, Chyt, viii
Singh, Maharaja Ranjit, viii
Slaughter, abstention from, 69 (*see* animal slaughter)
Slaves, proper treatment of, 154, 158
Small nations, rights of, respected by Asoka, 21, 58, 126-7
Smith, V. A., xi; (cited on) Asokan stone-cutting, 91-2, 93; Asoka's fleet, 36; Buddhist influence on Western thought, 77; chronological method, 45; high literacy in Asoka's time, 102-3; Indian originality in art, 99; King's birthday and jail deliveries, 185 *n.*; language of the Edicts, 102; lion or garuḍa? 90; Lat Bhairo pillar, 85; proof of Asoka's zeal for Buddhism, 68-9; Sankisa, 84 *n.*; Satiyaputra, 131 *n.*; sculpture at Rummindei, 203; transport of pillars, 92, 93
Smṛitis, 47, 143 *n.*
Society based on the joint family, 17; classes and castes, 17, 101, 103
Soldiers, Ksatriyas, 103, 141; of Kalinga, 162 *n.*, 164 *n.*
Solomon, 1
Soṇa, 33, 34
Sonari, 35
Sopārā Rock Edict, x, 13, 14 *n.*, 141 *n.*, 171 *n.*
Speech, restraint of, 73
Spiritual insight, 67, 72, 175
Spooner, Dr. D. B., excavations of at Pāṭaliputra, 96, 97
Śramaṇas, ascetics, 17, 65, 101, 103, 141 *n.*
Śrāvastī, 27; Jetavana Vihāra and pillars at, 83, 84
Śrīnagara, supposed Asokan city, 79
States, equality of, 21, 126-7
Statuary, 97
Stevenson, Mrs., *Heart of Jainism*, 71 *n.*
"Stone bearing a figure," 201
Stone-cutter's art, 98
Strabo on sailing the Ganges, 95 *n.*
Stūpas, topes, attributed to Asoka, 79, 80-1; Bharhut, 81, 88, 152 *n.*; Kesariya, 83; Mahāśāla, 86; Niglīva, 81, 84; noted by Fa-hien, 80; noted by Yuan Chwang, 80 *n.*, 82, 83, 84-5; Sānchī, 81, 88, 105-6; wide distribution of, 14-15
Stūpas, pre-Asokan, 88
Subhadrāṅgī, or Dharmā, mother of Asoka, 2-3, 9; a Brahman, 2; a Ksatriya, 3
Sudarśana artificial lake, 13, 94
Sudatta and Sugātra, names of Tiṣya, 6, 9
Śukranīti on trees and water supply, 189 *n.*
Sumana, grandson of Asoka, 8, 9, 35, 36, 45
Sumitta or Sumitra, 45, 63
Superiors, "men of high caste or pay," obedience to, 69, 163 *n.*
Susa, 95
Susīma or Sumana, brother of Asoka, 2, 9; death in war of succession, 3, 5 *n.*; son of, 18 *n.*, 41, 62-3; Viceroy at Taxila, 3, 125 *n.*
Suvarṇabhūmi, 33, 34
Suvarṇagiri, 6, 16, 107; princely Viceroys of, 51, 123-4 *n.*; supposed site in gold region, 107-8 *n.*
Svastika symbol or sacred monogram, 126 *n.*, 245 *n.*

Tāmralipti, 15, 35, 36
Tārānath on Asoka, 4
Taxila or Takkhasilā, 15; Asoka supersedes Susīma as Viceroy, 3, 51; Asoka's brothers as Viceroys, 6, 124 *n.*; Asoka's sons as Viceroys, 51, 124 *n.*, 125; coins and jewels found at, 98; court language of 247; Kuṇāla as Viceroy, 46, 51; official tours, 28, 57, 125-6, 208-9; revolts at, 3, 46, 52, 125 *n.*

Teachers, five modes of service to, 155 *n.*
Terminology, Asoka's original, 74-5
Terra-cottas, 97
Theocracy, Asoka and, 1
Thera-gāthā Commentary, 7, 9
Therapentæ, 77 *n.*
Thomas, Dr. F. W., xi; cited, 150 *n.*, 156 *n.*, 180 *n.*, 194 *n.*, 195 *n.*, 204 *n.*; (on) officials, 56 *n.*, 107 *n.*, 133 *n.*, 134 *n.*, 190 *n.*; *paligodka* and *palibodha*, 142 *n.*; sects, 31 (and see *Cambridge History of India*)
Tieffenthaler, Padre, viii
Tīrthikas, 6, 141 *n.*
Tissa, King of Ceylon, 12, 35
Tiṣya or Tissa, Asoka's uterine brother, 2, 3, 4, 45, 63; legendary conversion by Asoka, 6-7, 45; ordination of, 45, 110 *n.*; other names of, 6, 7, 9; Viceregent of Asoka, 7, 44, 51
Tiṣya days, 54, 123, 128, 183, 184
Tiṣyarakṣitā, last Chief Queen of Asoka, 8, 9, 46; legendary jealousy of Bodhi-Tree, 4-5, 46
Tīvara, son of Kāruvākī, 8, 9, 201
Tod, Major James, viii
Toleration, Asoka's conception of, 65, 72-3, 158-60; limitations of, 66, 68
Tolls superintendent, 57
Topes (see *Stūpas*)
Topra Pillar Edict, 14, 86; removal of pillar to Delhi, 93; text of, used for translation, 172 *n.* (*see* Pillar Edicts)
Torture, 30 *n.*, 121 *n.*, 123, 143 *n.*, 209
Tosalī (Dhaulī), 6, 16; princely Viceroys, 51, 120, 124 *n.*
Transit dues on imported goods, 57
Transport problem of Asokan pillars, 92-3
Trees planted along roads, 38, 42, 58, 132
Trident symbol, 99
Triennial tours, 28, 57
Truthfulness, *satyam*, 70, 116, 175, 191
Tusāspha, Raja, Viceroy at Girnar, 51, 94, 167 *n.*

Udyāna, 15
Ujjain or Ujjenī, 15; Asoka at, 3, 4, 8, 44, 124 *n.*; official tours, 28, 57, 124, 208-9; princely Viceroys, 51, 123, 124 *n.*
United Provinces, literacy in, 102
Universal religion, Asoka's basis for, 76
Upagupta of Mathurā (Moggaliputta Tissa), Asoka's preceptor, 27, 110 *n.*, 203 *n.*; fifth *Vinaya* teacher, 63; given cave-dwellings, 89; informed of Asoka's building aspirations, 79; legend of the 84,000 *vihāras*, 80-1; ordains Mahendra, 45; presides at Third Buddhist Council, 32, 60-1, 63; relics of, 35; retires and is recalled, 45, 46; sends out missionaries (*theras*), 32, 46 (*see* Pilgrimage)
Upaniṣads echoed in Edicts, 66 *n.*, 116 *n.*
Upatisa-pasine, 118
Uposatha days, 61, 183-4, 195 *n.*
Utriya, 33
Uttara, 33, 34

Vāchhi Suvijayata, 34, 35
Vaiśālī (modern Basarh), Buddhist Council at, 68; pillar near, 86
Vaiśyas, 103
Vanavāsi, 33, 34
Vardhamāna Mahāvīra, founder of Jainism, 86
Vāsudeva, column to, 104
Vedas, 47
Vedic origins of Asokan pillars, 99
Vedisa, 8, 44, 46
Vedisagiri, Great Vihāra of, 8
Viceregent, 52
Viceroys, brothers or sons of Asoka, 123; princely, in Edicts and legends, 6, 51, 52, 143 *n.*; subordinate officials of, 52, 56-7, 107, 125-6, 127
Viḍūdabha, 8
Vimānavatthu account of heaven, 75
Vinaya Piṭaka, 107 *n.*, 247
Vinaya-samukasa, 23, 118
Vinaya teachers, 63
Vītāśoka, brother of Asoka, 3, 4, 7, 9; name sometimes applied to Tiṣya, 6, 9; studies—becomes a monk, 7

Vrajabhūmika, guardian of routes and pastures, 58, 160
Vrijian monks, 68

Waddell cited, 63
Wages, law of, 154-5 *n.*
War-drums become call to *Dharma,* 20-1, 38, 58, 136
War losses of the Kalingas, 16-17, 162
"War of the Relics", 60-1 *n.*
Watters (on) Bo-Tree legend, 5 ; Nativity sculpture at Rummindei, 203 ; tope seen by Wukung, 204 *n.*
Wells and watering places, 22, 30, 38, 39, 58, 132, 188, 189
Wheel symbol or *dharma-chakra,* 83, 84, 90, 91, 99
White Elephant symbol, 61, 75, 136 *n.*, 137 *n.*, 170 *n.*
Wilson, Rev. Dr. J., ix, x
Women, supervision of, 30, 31, 39, 43, 143-4, 160, 190-1, 210
Woolner, A. C., xi, 143 *n.*, 172 *n.*, 173 *n.*, 254 ; on rest-houses, 189 *n.*
Writing, antiquity of, in India, 246-7

Yavana or Yona country of the Greeks, 104
Yavanas (Yonas, Ionians, Greeks), 15, 21, 29, 30, 77, 78 *n.*, 140, 168
Yona province, a Greek colony, 32, 168 ; not Hinduised, 103 ; without ascetics, 64
Yonaraṭṭham, 34
Yuan Chwang cited : Asoka and Tisya, 6 ; Asoka's Buddhist preceptor, 27, 63 ; — building activities, 79 ; — gift of Kashmir, 79 ; — "hell", 4 *n.*, --- last days, 37 *n.* ; --- *stūpas,* 80 *n.*, 82, 83 , --- *vihāras,* 79, 82 , Bodhi-Tree legend, 4-5, 154 *n.* ; cave dwellings, 89 , Indian measures of distance, 188 *n.* ; inscriptions misread, vii : inscriptions not identified, 14 *n.*; Kāñchīpura, 131 *n.* ; pillars not ascribed to Asoka, 86 *n.*, 87 ; Rummindei pillar, 85, 202 *n.*, 204 *n.* ; topes mentioned indicate vastness of empire, 15

ADDENDA

I

A supposed Asokan inscription in Aramaic script found at Taxila.

A new Asokan inscription of twelve lines written in the Aramaic language and script of the 3rd century B. C. was discovered at Taxila by Sir John Marshall in 1914-15. A facsimile of it was published in the Annual Archaeological Survey Report for the year. Later, Dr. E. Herzfeld deciphered the inscription written from right to left, but was unable to explain the text. In lines 9 and 12 Herzfeld reads the words '*mran Prydr*' and '*imran Prydrsh*' which are taken to mean 'Our Lord Priyadarśī'. In line 10 Herzfeld reads the word '*hḷkvth*' which he renders as '*Vmlkvth*' meaning 'And his queens' or perhaps 'His kingdoms'. In line 11 he reads the words '*Vap bnvhy*' which he takes to signify 'And his sons.'

The Aramaic script like Kharoshṭhī was written from right to left and was used in their inscriptions by Achaemenian Kings. The Aramaic language was once extensively used throughout Western Asia as the language of commerce.

It may be noted that the term *Piyadasi* or *Priyadarśi* is not the name of a king but his title, a title which was used both by Asoka and his grandfather Chandragupta. It may, however, be taken for certain that this particular Aramaic Inscription of Taxila was issued by *Piyadasi* Asoka rather than his grandfather who is not credited with the issue of any such inscriptions. Asoka was the first king in India to have issued inscriptions in the manner of the old Achaemenian kings. The contents of this inscription also are supposed to be Buddhist and therefore more Asokan. For instance, line 5 (?) contains the word 'Huh' = Good, i. e., morally good like the good thoughts, good deeds and good words of Zoroastrianism comparable to '*Airo Aṭṭhaṅgiko Maggo*' of Budhism (D. C. Sircar's *Select inscriptions* p. 81).

Further, the reference in this inscription to the queens and princes may be compared with the references in Asokan inscriptions to his queens and princes and their charities.

It may be further noted that the Achaemenian conquest of some parts of North Western India described in the Achaemenian inscription as *Gadāra* (Gandhāra) and *Hidush* (=Hindu=Sindhu=land of the Indus) by Emperor Darius I (c. 516 B.C.) brought into these regions the Aramaic language and script which became thus known in India in those days. Accordingly, Pāṇini with his mastery of linguistic facts and formations could not fail to have within his purview the existence of this foreign language and script in his own native land, Gandhāra. This foreign script he describes as *'Yavanānī'* (=*Yavanānāṁ lipiḥ* =script of the Yavanas). Pāṇnini's time is taken by Sir R. G. Bhandarkar to be 750 B. C. It should be at least as early as the time of the Achaemenian Empire.

These foreign settlements which thus date from the Persian conquest of India extended farther into the interior of India in the time of Chandragupta Maurya as a result of his counter-conquest of the Syrian Empire of which the eastern parts known as Gedrosia (Baluchistan), Aria (Herat), Arachoṣia (Kandahar) and Paropamsidai (Hindukush) were ceded to him by Emperor Seleukos in *c.* 304 B.C.

The existence of this foreign population at the remote metropolis of the Mauryan Empire at Pāṭaliputra called for appropriate administrative arrangements to look after their special interests. The Greek ambassador Magasthenes wrote from his first-hand knowledge that the municipal administration of Pāṭaliputra included a Foreign Committee in charge of the interests of the city's foreign population.

At the time of Asoka we find that these foreign peoples won their status as autonomous communities within his empire. Their political and cultural interests were duly recognized by Asoka. They are specifically mentioned in Rock Edicts V and XIII as Yonas and Kāmbojas. Their special cultural needs were thus recognized by Asoka by issuing an inscription in the Aramaic language and script at

Taxila, the then most important centre of foreign population in India. It was Asoka's zeal for his new faith that led him to preach it in a foreign colony in its own occidental language and script.

Their cultural autonomy is further recognized by Asoka by his statement that in the Yona country Society, unlike that of India, was casteless. It knew only of two *varṇas* or classes, Employers (*Ārya*) and Employed (*Dāsa*), and therefore his regular Dharma was not preached among them.

The existence of a strong Yona colony in Asoka's empire is further proved by the interesting fact that a Yona chief was recruited by Asoka as his provincial Governor of Aparānta-Surāshṭra. He is named Yavanarāja Tushāspha Rāshṭriya who succeeded Vaiśya Pushyagupta as Governor under his grandfather Chandragupta (Junāgaḍh Inscription of Rudradāman, *c.* 150A. D.).

To sum up, originally the term Yavana denoted the Ionian Greeks as subjects of the Persian Empire. But the language and script of the Empire were Aramaic. This Aramaic was first introduced into India by the Achaemenian conquest of Gandhāra and the land of the Sindhu. Thus when Pāṇini uses the term '*Yavanāni*', he had before him this concrete example of a foreign script which must have been Aramaic.

Later, the term *Yavana* came to imply any *Mlechchha* or a foreigner such as Iranian or Ionian. By the time Asoka, the Yonas and Kāmbojas formed important foreign settlements in his empire. These Yonas were not to be confused with the Ionian Greeks. They were Iranians for whom Asoka issued his inscription in their local Aramaic script. Later, Sanskrit texts, like *Vishṇu Purāṇa,* describe these *Yavanas* and Kāmbojas by their repugnant customs, such as keeping beard, shaving the head and beef-eating.

We may, lastly, note how Rudradāmana I describes the Iranian chief Rājā Tusāspha as Yavanarāja, showing that the term *Yavana* was a term for a foreigner without reference to the particular people or community to which he belonged.

II

Yerraguḍi Inscriptions.

Discovery : Yerraguḍi is situated some eighty miles north-east of Śiddāpur on the southern border of the Kurnool District and at a distance of some eight miles from Gooty, a Railway Station on the Raichur-Madras Section of the Southern Rly. In the vicinity of this village, the late Mr. Anu Ghose, F.C.S., F.G.S., a Geologist, discovered many years ago, engraved on six boulders of a hill called Yenakoṇḍā (Elephant Hill), another version of the Fourteen Rock Edicts of Asoka, together with a Minor Rock Edict. He kept this discovery to himself for a long time, and confided it to me as his classmate. Finally, he announced it to the Archaeological Department. Then these inscriptions were published by late Daya Ram Sahni in the Annual Progress Report of the Archaeological Survey for 1928-29, pp. 161-67.

Script : The script is Brāhmī and does not call for any remarks except that in the Minor Edict as many as eight of the twenty-three lines (Viz. 2, 4, 6, 9, 11, 13, 14, and 23) are inscribed from right to left and the rest as usual. If we eliminate from consideration lines 8 and 14, the first fifteen lines are at once found to be in boustrophedom style, *i.e.*, written alternately from left to right and from right to left. No other Brāhmī or Kharoshṭhī inscription is written in this manner. The dialect of the Rock Edicts is Magadhan, as pointed out by Dr. D. C. Sircar.

Text : The text of the Fourteen Rock Edicts comes nearest to that of the Kālsī version.

In the Minor Rock inscription the first portion up to the middle of line 12 closely follows the corresponding portion of the Brahmagiri, and other versions. The second section from middle of line 12 up to the end contains much new matter and its Text and Translation are given below, together with some comments.

Yerraguḍi Minor Rock Edict

TEXT

12. ......hevaṁ Devānaṁpiye āha yathā Devānaṁ-
13. piye āhā tathā kaṭaviya yepi rājūke ānapitaviye
14. te dānī jānapadaṁ āna-
15. payisati rāṭhikāni cha mātāpitūsu
16. susūsitaviye hemeva garūsu susūsitaviye pānesu dayitaviye sacha vataviya
17. susuma dhaṁmagunā pavatitaviyā hevaṁ tuphe ānapayātha Devānaṁ-piyasa vachanena hemeva ānapa-
18. yatha hathiyārohāni kāranakāni yūgyachariyāni baṁbhanāni cha tuphe hevaṁ nivesayā-
19. tha atevāsīni yārisā porānā pakiti iyaṁ susūsitaviye apachāyanā ya vā sava me āchariyasa
20. yathāchārina āchariyasa nātikāni yathāraha nātikesu pavatitaviye hesāpi
21. aṁtevāsīsu yathāraha pavatitaviye yārisā porānā pakiti yathāraha yathā iyaṁ
22. āroke siyā hevaṁ tuphe ānapayātha nivesayātha cha aṁtevāsīni hevaṁ De-
23. vānaṁpiye ānapayati.

TRANSLATION

Thus declares (king) Devānāṁpriya (literally, Beloved of the Gods) : Whatever Devānāṁpriya ordains, that must be carried out. The Rājūkas (Provincial Governors) are to be thus instructed (by the *Mahāmātras* concerned) : That they should forthwith (*idānīm*) instruct the people of the countryside (*Jānapadam*) and also the *Rāshṭrikas* (in-charge) to the following effect : that Mother and Father are to be obeyed ; so should be obeyed the Preceptor ; All creatures are to be treated with compassion; Truth is to be spoken. These glorious (*śushma*) moral virtues (*dharma-guṇāḥ*) are to be cultivated.

Likewise, Ye (*Mahāmātras*) are also being thus instructed in terms of the king's order : De ye thus instruct (*āñyāpayata*) the different classes of people such as (I) the Elephant Corps (*Hastyārohaṇa*); (2) *Kāraṇakas* [Kāyasthas=Scribes or Judges (*Prāḍavivāka*)]; (3) Charioteers (*Yugyacharyān =Rathārohān*); (4) *Brāhmaṇas, i.e.* Teachers.

Thus, further, should ye instruct (*niveśayata*) the *Brāhmaṇas* (teachers) that they should on their part admonish (*niveśayata*) their pupils (*aṅtevāsīnaḥ*) that they should, in accordance with the traditional rule of conduct (*purāṇī prakṛiti*) observe the following (*idaṁ*) duties : (I) that the teacher (*āchārya*) be obeyed (*śuśrūshitavya*) (by them) ; (2) Full (*sarva*) service (*apachāyanā =pujā*) of the teacher (*āchāryasya*) by puplis (*aṅtevāsinaḥ*) as his worthy devotees (*yathāchariṇaḥ āchāryasya*) ; (3) that they (the pupils) should similarly behave towards their kinsmen.

Likewise should these their kinsmen be instructed.

Similarly, this time-honoured principle of dedication of pupils to the service (*apachāyanā*) of their teachers should be duly (*yathārhaṁ*) established (*pravartayitavya*) among them, in accordance with the traditional rules of *Brahmacharya*.

Likewise should ye (teachers) admonish (*āñyāpayata*) and instruct (*niveśayata*) the student population that they be steadfast (*arokā=dṛiḍhā*)[1] in their pursuit of these traditional rules of studentship.

Thus ordains (king) Devānāṁpriya.

This Minor Rock Edict is unique in its new matter which is not found in any other of its versions. Its meaning, however, is not quite clear. Asoka seems to be extending here the scope of his preaching of Dharma. He appears to enjoin its preaching among both the civil and militar classes, and especially among the youth, the student population of the country as its future citizens who should be trained in disciplined life. The teachers are also enlisted by him, along with the administrative officers, the Mahāmātras, in the

1. Some scholars read *tiroka* and take it in the sense of "possessed of th ee-fold comfort of attainment of bliss in three *lokas*" (*oka*=refuge).

work of carrying his Dharma or message to the student population as the appropriate sphere of their work, while the rural welfare officers, the *Rāshṭrikas*, are to work for the same mission in the country-side in their charge.

III

Gavīmaṭh and Pālkīguṇḍu Minor Rock Edicts

Two new versions of the Minor Rock Edict of Asoka were found near Kopbāḷ (old name Kopananagara), which is about 60 miles from Śiddāpura and a Railway Station on the Southern Railway situated between Hospet and Gadag junctions. In the vicinity of the Kopbāḷ town two Brāhmī inscriptions were discovered in 1931 by Sri N. B. Śāstri of Kopbāl, one engraved on the Gavīmaṭh rock and another on the Pālkīguṇḍu hill.

The two inscriptions are almost identical and represent another version of the Minor Rock Edict of Asoka already known in slightly different forms at Rūpanāth, Ṣahasram, Bairāṭ (which version agrees very closely with that of Gavīmaṭh), Brahmagiri, Śiddāpura, Jatiṅga-Rāmeśvara Māski and Yerraguḍi. These two new versions add nothing to the general contents of the Edict, but with the exception of Rūpanāth, the Gavīmaṭh version is the only one completely legible.[1]

IV

Rajula Mandagiri Rock-Edict.

Recently, another Asokan Minor Rock Edict has been discovered at a hamlet called Rajula Mandagiri in Village Chinnatulti in Pattikouda Taluq of Kurnool District in Andhra State. The place is about 20 miles from Yerragu*ḍ*i.

1. These two versions were edited by Dr. R. L. Turner and published in the Hyderabad Arch. Series, No. 10, '*The Gavīmaṭh and Pālkīguṇḍu Inscriptions of Asoka*', (1932).

V

A Minor Rock Edict discovered at Gujarra in Vindhya Pradeśa.

A Minor Rock Edict of Asoka has been recently discovered by the Deputy Director-General of Archaeology, Dr. B. Ch. Chhabra, at a village called Gujarra which is about 11 miles from Datia and also from Jhansi. The hillock behind the rock bearing the Inscription is known as *Siddhan-Kī-toriyā*, 'the rock of the *Siddhas* or the Emancipated Ones.'

This Inscription is the *tenth* version of Asoka's Minor Rock Edict.

The importance of this Inscription lies in the fact that, out of a total of over 200 Inscriptions of Asoka, this is the only one which mentions his full designation and name in the passage : *Devānaṁpiyasa Piyadasino Asokarājasa.* The Minor Rock Edict found at Maski also mentions the name *Asoka* but not his full appellation or titles by which he is described in most other Edicts, such as (I) *Devānaṁpiya Piyadasi Rājā* (2) *Devānaṁpiya Piyadasi* (3) *Devānaṁpiya* or (4) *Priyadasi lājā Māgadhe* Bairat). Maski uses the form *Devānaṁpiyasa Asokasa* (Adapted from a Note kindly supplied by Dr. B. Ch. Chhabra).

In conclusion, it may be noted that these Minor Rock Edicts were practically as widely distributed by Asoka through his dominion (*Vijita*) as his other Rock or Pillar Edicts. They are found in most of the Provinces of his far-flung Empire, from Rajasthan in the North through Hyderabad and Andhra up to Mysore. This publicity was due to Asoka's decision to lay emphasis on the special feature embodied in his Minor Rock Edicts which put in a nutshell, and present pithily his main religious injunction as the substance of all his teachings repeated and dispersed through all his other Inscriptions. That central injunction, which may be taken as the basis of his religious system or *Dharma*, as distinguished from the details of its doctrines and practices as enumerated in his other Edicts, is the supreme need of uttermost self - exertion (*parākrama*) as the primary requisite of spiritual life and progress for all persons of all ranks, high or low, and especially for those of high rank with its many distractions. Asoka gives eloquent expression in this Edict to his deep feeling and conviction that a steady and strenuous practice of morals and cultivation of proper and correct conduct in all relations of life by the people will help to make them godly and establish on earth the Kingdom, the Heaven, of Righteousness (*ammisaṁ devā saṁta munisā misaṁ devā kaṭā*).

This thought is expressed in another sentence : *Khudāke chā udāre chā dhaṁmam charaṁtā yogaṁ yuṁjāṁtā* 'Let small and great (equally) devote themselves to the practice of morality so that they may be united with the Divine'.

VI

The Kandahar (Shar-i-Kuna) Inscription of Asoka

This rock inscription has been recently discovered near Kandahar in Afghanistan and is unique as a bilingual record written in both Greek and Aramaic. The Greek version was meant for the Greek (Yona—Yavana) subjects of Asoka's empire, and the Aramaic for the non-Greek foreigners like the Kāmbojas, of Asoka's Rock Edicts V and XIII.

Texts : The two texts have been rendered into Asokan Prākṛit by Dr. D. C. Sircar (*E I*: XXXIII) as follows :

Greek : (A) Daśa-vash-abhisitena rañа Priyadraśina janaspi dhramanuśasti pravaṭita.

Aramaic : (A) Daśa-vash-abhisitena raña Priyadyaśina pamikena no (=naḥ) tada dhramanuśasti pravaṭita.

G. (B) Tata chu tena manuśa baḍhataram dhramayuta kaṭa praṇa cha vaḍhita hita-sukhena savraputha-viyaṁ.

A : (B) Tata apayasa hiṁ jata savraspi cha janaspi tena dupaṭi-bhaga nivaṭita ! Asti pi saṁ ti cha priti cha savraputhaviyaṁ.

G : (C) Raña chu praṇ-araṁbho paritijita savrehi cha manuśchi ludakehi cha savrehi kevaṭehi cha raño paritijita vihiṁsa bhutanaṁ.

A : (C) Eta cha pi bhutaṁ. Sup-aṭhaya chu raño no spamikasa lanukaṁ arabhiyati. Tasa cha draśana savra manuśa na arabhaṁti Evaṁ pi ye cha Kevaṭa te pi cha niyaṃena saṁyata.

G : (D) Yesaṁ chun=asi saṁyamo te pi cha saṁyata bhuta yatha tena tena śakam.

A : (D) Evaṁ pi yesaṁ cha n=asi saṁyamo te picha saṁyata bhuta.

G. (E) Te pi cha mata-pitushu buḍheshu cha suśrūshaṁti : Vadiśaṁ no bhuta-pruvaṁ.

A. (E) Savre cha mata pitushu suśrūshanti vuḍheṣhu cha suśrūshanti yatharahaṁ yadiśam tasa tasa Kaṭavaṁ aropitaṁ.

G : (F) Evaṁ cha karamina te pacha hita-sukhena vaḍhisaṁti bādhaṁ cha c vaḍhisaṁti.

A : (F) Dhrama-yutanaṁ chu kho paratra n=asti vicharaṇa.

A : (G) Savre cha manuśa dhrama-charaṇena abhuṁnata abhuṁnamiśaṁti cha=eva.

Translation :

Greek Text. After the 10th year of his coronation was inaugurated (pravartita) by King Priyadarśī ('Our Lord' *Spamikena no* in Aramaic text) his preaching of *Dharma* (Morality) among the people (*Janaspi*).

And, since then (*tata chu*), the people have been rendered more moral (*dharmayuta*) by him (by his moral propagandism, *dharmānuśasti*), and all living beings (*prāṇāḥ*) all over the world (*sarvapṛithivyāṁ*—India) have had their welfare (*hita*) and happiness (*sukha*) increased (*vardhitāḥ*).

Aramaic Text : Since then there has been (*jata*) decrease (*hāni*) of suffering (*apāya*), and for all people misfortunes have been averted (*dushpratibhāgāḥ nivartitāḥ*) through his instrumentality. And there has been (*asti*) all over the world peace (*śānti*) as well as fellow-feeling (*prīti*),

Greek Text : And by the King also has been renounced (*parityakta*) slaughter of living beings, and also by all people, the King's own hunters (*lubdhakaiḥ*) as well as fishing folks

(*Kaivartaiḥ*). By them all has been renounced violence towards life.

Aramaic Text : And , besides, this has happened in regard to food (*sūpārthāya*) also : there has been reduction (*laghukaṁ*) of slaughter (of animals and birds) by our Lord (*svāmī*) the King, and, after seeing that (*tasya cha darśanāt*), all people have abstained from slaughter (*na ālabhante*), and this also (that) those who are fishermen by occupation, even they are restrained (*saṁyata*) by moral rules (*niyamena*).

Greek Text : And thus (*cha tu*), of those who were not used to restraint (*saṁyamo*), even they have become restrained (*saṁyataḥ bhūtaḥ*), as far as they are capable of it respectively (*yathā tena śakyam*).

And, further (*api cha*), they are also ready to listen to (the behests of) (*śusrūshanti*) of their mother and father, and their elders (*vṛiddheshu*), as was not the case before (*na bhūtapūrvam*).

And, thus doing, they will henceforth (*paśchāt*) progress in prosperity (*hita*) and happiness (*sukha*) aud such progress will be steadily on the increase (*bāḍham*).

Aramaic version : And obedience to mother and father and obedience to elders (are now forthcoming) in accordance with the obligations (*kartavyam*) resting on the different parties concerned (*āropitam*).

And of people who are devoted to duty (*dharmayuta*), there is certainly no judgement (*vichāraṇa*) (awaiting them) in the other world (*paratra*).

By the practice of morality (*dharmā-charaṇena*), all men are already uplifted (*abhyunnata*) and will also be so uplifted in future.

This Edict has been rightly ranked by Dr. D. C. Sircar a minor Rock Edict of Asoka, Minor Rock Edict IV. This is indicated by the fact that its subject-matter is of a limited scope, and is not general, like that of his main Rock Edicts or Pillar Edicts. It, however, brings to light some new facts in Asoka's life and reign. Its provenance is important as confirming the literary evidence as to the extent of Asoka's Empire which was a Greater India extending towards the north-west beyond the natural boundaries of India (Undivided) up to the borders of Persia. Thus the location of this Edict in Arachosia or Kandahar furnishes the only epigraphic evidence so far known to corroborate the literary evidence of Greek historical works as to India's North-Western frontiers. These works record the fact that, as a result of the defeat inflicted in c. 304 B.C. by the Indian King, Chandragupta Maurya, Asoka's grandfather, upon the Syrian Emperor Seleukos who invaded India, the entire Eastern portion of his Empire comprising the regions then known as Gedrosia (Baluchistan), Arachosia (Kandahar), Aria (Herat) and Paropamisadae (Hindukush) was annexed by the victor to his empire. Accordingly, Asoka who came into the possession of this extensive empire by inheritance was able to call as his immediate neighbour (*anta*) in his rock Edict II (and also in Rock Edict XIII), the Syrian King Antiochus (Aṁtiyoko). He also counts in his R. E. V and XIII the Yonas (or Greeks) and the Kāmbojas as his own subjects inhabiting those parts of Afghanistan.

This Edict also definitely dates Asoka's religious propagandism from the 10th year after his coronation i.e. after 260 B. C. His other Edicts indicate only the stages in his religious history. The turning-point of that history is the 8th regnal year of Asoka, the year 262 B. C., the date of Asoka's conquest of Kalinga mentioned in Rock Edict XIII. It resulted in colossal casualties and suffering inflicted upon the brave Kalingas who fought for their freedom. The horrors of this bloody conquest made the conqueror a changed man. Asoka now changed from the creed of violence to the opposite creed of non-voilence. Hitherto, (before 262 B. C.) as stated in his minor Rock-Edict I, he had been only an indifferent Buddhist, a mere *upāsaka*, and continued as such for "more than 2½ years," and was thus up to the cruelties of a conquest in violation of the Buddhist creed, the principle of sanctity of life. Asoka's moral change of 262 B.C. was thus preceded by this period of indifference, 265-262 B.C. After 262 B. C. his interest in Buddhism became intense (*tivra*) and expressed itself in his practice of the Dharma of Non-violence in his own life (*Dharmaśīlana*), his devotion to Dharma (*Dharmakāmatā*), and its public preaching (*Dharmānuśasti*). The process of this inner change or moral revolution in Asoka, according to MRE I, took "more than a year", i.e. up to 260 B.C. After 260 B.C., the 10th year of his reign, according to this new Edict, Asoka officially organised (*pravartana*) his work of moral propagandism (*Dharmānuśasti*) with utmost (*tīvra*) exertion (*Parākrama*) [MRE I]. His work soon yielded results. These are described with new and concrete details in this Edict, supplementing those so far known from the other Edicts. These are only generally indicated in MRE I which states that "The people of Jambudvīpa were gradually becoming more godly, or religious-minded (*Amisā samānā munisā Jambudīpasi misā devehi*).

It was about this time, after his 10th regnal year, that Asoka set out on his first pilgrimage to the holiest place of Buddhism, viz., Bodhgaya, as stated in his R.E. VIII. The present Edict throws some new light on the beginnings and results of Asoka's moral propagandism (*Dharmānuśasti*, a term also used in R. E. XIII). According to Aramaic Text, Asoka made the beginning by himself setting the example of Non-Violence in giving up (*parityakta*) slaughter of living creatures for purposes of his own food (*sūpārthāya*) and turning a vegetarian. 'Seeing the royal example' (*tasya cha darśanāt*), the people at large also abstained from violence towards life (*vihiṁsā bhūtānām*), even the royal hunters (*lubdhakas*) and fishing folks (*kaivartas*) who derived their living from these violent pursuits.

The general result following Asoka's inaugaration (*pravartana*) of this new religion (*Dharma*) has also been described in this Edict in new terms. The people have been rendered more moral (*dharmayuta*), and all living beings have had now their good and happiness (*hita-sukha*) increased through spread of Non-Violence. There has been a decrease of suffering (*apāya*) and misfortunes (*dushpratibhāga*) for the people, while all the world over there is a reign of Peace (*Śānti*) and fellow-feeling (*Prīti*), and abstention from violence (*Saṁyama*). The prevailing spirit of Non-Violence in the country also raised the level of moral life in the home and family through the cultivation by its youths of proper relataions with their father and mother, as well as Elders, to whose behests they were now ready to listen. This practice of Morality or Non-Violence was the most potent factor of social uplift (*abhyunmata*) for all time.

Asoka thus stands out as the Pioneer of Peace. He rightly recognised its foundation in the spirit and religion of universal non-violence (*vihiṁsā bhūtanām*) which alone could usher in the era of "Peace on Earth (*Śānti*) and Goodwill (*Prīti*) among men". He felt that War begins in the minds of men, in hate (as distinguished from *prīti-rasa*) and hostility of which their minds must be purified by the upsurge of a universal amity. Asoka established peace within his own dominion (*vijita*) which was planned as a *Dharma-chakra*, a Kingdom of Righteousness, on the basis of ideals which humanity is still struggling to achieve.

It will thus be evident that the cult of physical non-violence had its inevitable moral effects and reactions in a wider sphere. It influenced domestic life, the home and family, which were purified by the cultivation of proper relations (*sampratipatti*), beginning with those between the youth and their parents and elders. Society felt more secure, as it was free of the fear of violence (*apāya*). Thus Peace (*Śānti*) settled on earth with abundance of goodwill (*prīti*) among men. Asoka took non-violence, physical and moral, as the root of human happiness and prosperity (*hita-sukha*).

VII

Ahraurā

A version of the Minor Rock Edict has been discovered on a hill at Ahraurā near Chunār (U. P.). It has not yet been published.

VIII

Amrāvatī

At Amrāvatī has been discovered a small fragment of an inscription engraved on what looks like a section of an Asokan pillar according to Dr. D. C. Sircar. *Epigraphia Indica*, Vol. XXXV on the ground of both palaeography and language. Its contents also "look more like those of the Asokan Edicts". In that case, as Dr. Sircar points out, the Buddhist Stupa at Amrāvatī was originally built by Asoka.

IX

A revised Text of the Queen's Edict with its Translation (by Sri C. D. Chatterjee, M.A., of Lucknow University).

TEXT[1]

(1) Devānaṁpiyaṣā vachanenā savata mahamatā

(2) vataviyā (//) E heta dutiyāye deviye dāne (/)

(3) aṁbāvaḍikā vā ālame va dāna (ga)he va (/)
[e vā pi a] ṁne

(4) kichi ganīyati tāye deviye (/) ṣe nāni
he vaṁga na ye (/)

(5) dutīyāye deviye ti (/) Tivalamātu Kāluvākiye (//)[2]

TRANSLATION

By the injunction of His Gracious Majesty ('Beloved of the Gods'), the *Mahāmātras* ('Officers of the highest rank') in all stations (i.e., departments), are to be instructed thus :

"Whatever be the gift of the Second Queen that is (instituted) here, whether a mango-orchard, a monastic building, or an alms-house, and whatever else is being counted as (a gift) of that queen, all those (now) should be (officially) reckoned (in full) in the manner following :

'Gift of the Second Queen Chāruvāki ('Sweet of Speech') mother of Trivara ('Triple Blessing' : Buddha, Dharma, and Saṅgha)'."

1. *Reading as restored.* cf. *Annals, Bhan. Ori. Res. Ins.* xxxlv. pp. 43-47.

2. *The punctuation marks* (*within brackets*) *in the text have been interted for the convenience of the readers.*